# Studying Asia Pacific Security

## The Future of Research Training and Dialogue Activities

he Future of Asia Pacific Security Studies and Exchange Activities
Conference Proceedings
Bali, Idonesia, December 12-15, 1993

### Paul M. Evans
Editor

University of Toronto
York University
Joint Centre for
Asia Pacific Studies, Canada

Centre for
Strategic and
International
Studies, Indonesia

University of Toronto – York University
Joint Centre for Asia Pacific Studies
York Lanes, Suite 270
York University
4700 Keele Street
North York, Ontario
CANADA M3J 1P3

Printed and typeset by Becker Associates, Concord, Ontario

**Canadian Cataloguing in Publication Data**

Main entry under title:
Studying Asia Pacific security : the future of
research, training and dialogue activities : the
future of Asia Pacific security studies and
exchange activities : conference proceedings,
Bali, Indonesia, December 12–15, 1993

ISBN 1–895296–15–3

1. National security – East Asia – Research –
Congresses. 2. National security – Pacific Area –
Research – Congresses. I. Evans, Paul M.
II. Joint Centre for Asia Pacific Studies.

UA832.5.S78 1994        355'.033        C94–931467–6

# Table of Contents

# Preface

PAUL EVANS
and
JUSUF WANANDI

The 1990s have witnessed remarkable ferment in regional security relations and security studies around the world. In the context of Asia Pacific, the reaction of governments and researchers to a post–Cold War situation has set the stage for a new phase in regional security relations and regional security studies. In addition to adjustments to existing bilateral security arrangements, new processes and institutions have been created at the governmental and nongovernmental levels for multilateral dialogue and consultation on Asia Pacific security matters. Research and publication on Asia Pacific security issues has also expanded in both quality and quantity.

It has been our view that these developments provided an imperative and an opportunity for a systematic review of the current state and future directions of Asia Pacific security studies and exchange activities of which the dialogues are an increasingly important part. Based on the initial encouragement of the Ford Foundation and the Rockefeller Brothers Fund, we created an international steering committee to lay the foundations for such a review through the mechanism of a series of commissioned papers and a conference. Jusuf Wanadi chaired the committee and Paul Evans served as secretary and took responsibility for overseeing the research and writing. The other members of the planning committee included Peter Geithner of the Ford Foundation in New York, Stuart Harris of the Australian National University, Kim Kyung-Won of the Institute of Social Sciences in Seoul, Charles Morrison of the East-West Institute, Noordin Sopiee of ISIS Malaysia, and Yuan Ming from Peking University. A planning meeting took place in Hong Kong in March to identify participants, authors and conference themes.

From the outset the objective of the project was to gain an understanding of the "state of the field" in Asia Pacific security studies. The purpose was to define the field in a way which is intellectually challenging, provides benchmarks for future studies, and identifies possible lines of future cooperation. The participants in the project were asked to consider the following: current trends in Asia Pacific security and their implications for research; the nature of security expertise at national levels; the roles of multilateral security dialogues; the question of human resources; and the problem of establishing priorities for both study and action by the Asia Pacific security studies community.

The conference was held at the Hotel Sanur Beach in Bali from December 12 to 15, 1993, and involved fifty-eight participants and observers drawn from universities, research institutes, foundations, and government agencies in seventeen countries. The Centre for Strategic and International Studies managed conference logistics and the Joint Centre for Asia Pacific Studies administered the commissioning and editing of the papers. We wish in particular to thank Clara Joewono and Shirley Yue for their energetic contribution to the project at every stage. Financial support for the planning committee, the conference and this publication was provided by the Ford Foundation, the Rockefeller Brothers Fund, the Asia Foundation, the MacArthur Foundation, the Center for Global Partnership, the Sasakawa Peace Foundation, and the Chaiyong Foundation (Bangkok).

This volume includes revised drafts of the sixteen papers presented at the conference plus a summary of the discussion. Recognizing our desire to publish the volume as quickly as possible after the conference, we appreciate the speed and care with which the authors responded to requests for specific changes and additions to their initial essays. Though they vary considerably in length and focus, in combination they provide a very valuable comparative perspective on the nature and direction of security studies and dialogue activities on a regionwide basis. Among other things, they constitute a fascinating sociology of knowledge of ideas and institutions focusing on regional security issues.

The conference and volume were not intended to produce specific recommendations for future projects. Rather they aimed to raise a series of questions about the current state of the field and some of the ways it might develop in the future. As indicated in the final section of the book, the most obvious point is the diversity of the region as measured in the scope and level of security studies, the intellectual and political circumstances in which research and exchange take place, and the range of interpretations about what should be studied.

Considering this diversity, it is not surprising that the papers and discussion were wide ranging and rarely conclusive. But consensus was evident on four main points.

First, while acknowledging that the analytical and geopolitical boundaries of the region are indeed soft, almost all of the participants agreed that "Asia Pacific" (defined to include Northeast and Southeast Asia, North America and Australasia) was useful in providing a creative and forward-looking forum for discussion of both economic and security issues. Further, there was considerable agreement that the focus of most of the research and concern was a narrower area conceived of as "Asia-Pacific" (or Pacific Asia) including Northeast and Southeast Asia.

Second, the level of theoretical sophistication and basic research is lower than desired. There was some disagreement about whether social science can best be viewed from a universal perspective or in light of differing regional and national conditions and traditions. But it is widely felt that a major challenge in the coming months will be to develop projects that are more collaborative, more interdisciplinary and better rooted in social science theory. A related task will be to pay particular attention to the dynamics of the region itself in creating a theoretical understanding rather than simply applying frameworks that have been developed in other historical and geopolitical settings.

Third, the requirements and opportunities for training future generations of security specialists vary substantially in different national contexts. It was universally accepted, however, that more opportunities for exchange for advanced students and researchers is essential for developing better analytical skills and improving international communication.

Fourth, the dialogue activities that have proliferated in recent years need sustained support. Similar dialogue and community-building exercises in Europe have been occurring for a very long time and have been well funded. Though some feel there might now be too much emphasis on dialogues as compared to research and training in Asia Pacific, no one argued that the number of dialogues should be decreased. Rather they need to be supplemented by more original and collaborative research, and more theorization and basic social science. They also need to be better coordinated. Here a special case was made for the Council for Security Cooperation in Asia Pacific.

The conference discussion and the papers reflect some of the tensions and differences in the Asia Pacific research community. At the same time, they provide evidence of some creative and original thinking on how best collectively to define and approach the range of contemporary security challenges which need to be addressed.

Toronto and Jakarta, April 1994

# PART I

Asia Pacific Security Studies

# Security Studies in ASEAN: Trends in the Post–Cold War Era

HERMAN JOSEPH S. KRAFT

The momentous events and rapid changes of the past three years have paved the way for the redrawing of the global landscape. The end of the Cold War and the subsequent collapse of the Soviet Union are but the most significant of developments responsible for the transformation of the international system. This transformation, however, also brought with it new theoretical challenges which have significant policy repercussions. Within this context, conceptualizing security has become one of the most important concerns of the post–Cold War era.

From the onset of the bipolar rivalry between the United States and the Soviet Union, security studies had largely been unidimensional, focusing primarily on military power and its utilization in gaining political ends. This can be attributed mainly to the nature of strategic studies, the principal area engaged in the study of security.[1] Strategic studies has generally been concerned with the relationship between force and its use in foreign policy. More specifically, it has dealt primarily with warfare in its varying forms, American and Soviet defense policy, and nuclear deterrence. With the rapid pace of change in the international system, this narrow orientation has only served to limit the ability of strategic studies to cope with the changing dimensions of security problems. Economic and fiscal concerns—such as trade competitiveness (or the lack thereof) and protectionism, budget deficits, and national indebtedness—are already at the forefront of policy debates on emerging threats to the well-being of nations and the stability of states. New issues such as the environment, immigration, drugs and AIDS have also begun to infringe on an area that was formerly the preserve of strategic studies. Confronted by these developments, both experts and students of security are pressed to reassess the conceptualization of their field.[2]

The changes wrought by the end of the Cold War have also served to highlight new issues and developments in Southeast Asia. While the effect of these changes on the security perspectives of states in the region vary according to the degree of a state's involvement in the rivalry between the two superpowers, generally the need to "rethink" the concept of security in Southeast Asia has not yet reached the same level of urgency as in Europe and North America. This is particularly evident in the case of the member states of ASEAN.[3]

Stephen Walt once wrote that "any effort to delineate the precise scope of security studies is somewhat arbitrary."[4] It is tied in with a state's view of the "core values" it has to protect. In common with other developing states, security as perceived by the ASEAN states is a multifaceted phenomenon marked by a complex relationship between internal and external concerns. As one scholar pointed out, this is "reflected in the vulnerability and 'penetrability' of most developing societies and economies, which are suffering from crises of self-definition and from problems of political and historical legitimacy."[5] It is clear that this situation only tended to further complicate the tasks facing "ruling elites seeking to manage security (at all levels) while striving simultaneously to achieve the goals of development and state-building."[6]

It is precisely this complication, however, which defines the intellectual bounds of security studies in ASEAN. The post-colonial imperatives of nation building and state formation were molded by historical nuances which were also responsible for making threat definition and security policy-making the preserve of those in power. This made "security" subjectively based on the perceptions of the authoritative decision makers of the state. Any challenge to the political authority of the ruling elite and to policies directed towards the goals of nation building and state formation were (and are still) stigmatized as a threat to the security of the state. The relative nature of security among developing states often provoked challenges from those outside the circles of power which were usually rooted in ethnic and/or ideological differences, and regime legitimacy.[7] These domestic challenges explain the relatively greater significance of internal threats to national security among developing states, more so as these factors make the state more vulnerable to external intervention and more susceptible to overt external threats.

Within this context, the ASEAN states have defined security as encompassing more than purely military or defense issues. Using the concept of comprehensive security, they consider the political, economic, and social well-being of society and the state as equally significant aspects of security.[8] However, subsequent changes in the regional order caused by the end of the Cold War have had an important impact on the security perspectives of individual states and the overall stability of the Southeast Asian region. This paper seeks to present how security studies in the ASEAN states have adjusted to these developments. It examines the state of the field following the collapse of the bipolar structure that dominated the international system for most of the post–World War II era.

## The Post–Cold War Security Environment and the ASEAN States

The end of the Cold War marked the restructuring of the security environment of Southeast Asia. Though its impact upon this region is less dramatic than the changes it wrought in superpower relations and in Europe, the collapse of the Cold War structure established new problems and highlighted previously unheeded issues which directly impinge upon the security interests of the ASEAN states. Inevitably, most of these new problems relate to their external security environment. While their postcolonial concerns with nation building and state formation had led them to emphasize the domestic dimensions of political stability, more and more attention is now being given by the ASEAN states to regional stability.

Perspectives on regional stability and security among the ASEAN states are built around concentric layers of concern. The first layer involves intra-ASEAN relations. This perspective was particularly dominant at the inception of ASEAN, when Indonesia, Malaysia, and Singapore were just emerging from the period of *konfrontasi*, and Philippine-Malaysian relations were dangerously strained over the Sabah issue. The need for a framework for the prevention of interstate conflict and the maintenance of intraregional stability was in fact the understated raison d'etre of ASEAN.[9] The second layer covers the rest of Southeast Asia, and became of paramount concern in the aftermath of the Vietnam War in 1975, and during the Cambodian conflict. Initiatives and current discussions within ASEAN about the feasibility of expanding ASEAN to include Vietnam, and possibly Cambodia, Laos and even Myanmar in the short and medium term also reflect this level of security concerns.[10] The third layer extends to Northeast Asia but also includes major players in the region who are not geographically part of the East Asia Pacific littoral, such as the United States and India. Despite their geographical proximity to Southeast Asia, Australia, New Zealand and the South Pacific states have not been given much prominence by most of the ASEAN states because of differences in cultural and strategic outlooks.[11] These layers are not mutually exclusive and merely indicate priorities of concern during specific time periods. With the end of the Cold War, the third layer of concern has become significant in the ASEAN states' strategic calculations.

The end of the bipolar superpower rivalry was initially thought to be the harbinger of a more benign security environment in the region. The global danger of a nuclear war diminished with the steady waning of the rivalry between the United States and the Soviet Union. In addition, the subsequent normalization of Sino-Soviet relations ushered in an era of great power cooperation which dramatically influenced the stability of the region. This was directly manifested in Southeast Asia in the endorsement by the permanent members of the UN Security Council in August 1990 of a comprehensive framework for the settlement of the Cambodian conflict.

Improvements in great power relations have also influenced relations between the ASEAN states and the Soviet Union and the People's Republic of China. The historic visits made by President Suharto of Indonesia and Prime Minister Lee Kuan Yew of Singapore to Moscow in 1989 and 1990 respectively were followed by an invitation extended to the Soviet Union by ASEAN to attend the opening of the ASEAN Ministerial Meeting in July 1991. Diplomatic relations were reestablished by Jakarta with Beijing after a twenty-three year hiatus in August 1990. The formalization of ties between Singapore and Beijing followed in October of the same year.

This era of goodwill, however, proved to be short-lived as the bipolar global order gave way to a complex, multipolar structure filled with uncertainties. For the ASEAN states, these uncertainties revolved around four important and related concerns: (1) the reduction of the US military presence in the region; (2) the emerging role of regional powers; (3) unresolved territorial disputes in Southeast Asia; and (4) trade-related tensions.

The withdrawal of US forces from their facilities in the Philippines and the deep cuts in the US defense budget has raised questions about the ability of the United States to perform the role it set for itself of regional balancer, honest broker, and, eventually, the guarantor of stability in the Asia-Pacific region.[12] The rules which defined the conditions under which US military forces will be used have become unclear. For the ASEAN states, the main issue is the willingness of US political leaders to commit military forces in the event of a regional conflict involving one or more of its allies in the region.[13] The degree of uncertainty varies among the different ASEAN states with the Philippines clearly the most affected by the issue. Decades of reliance on US military support has left the Philippine military in a poor position to take over the external defense missions that US forces performed in the past. Furthermore, guarantees of military support given in the Mutual Defense Treaty (MDT) now begin to sound hollow with the US disengagement from the Philippines.[14]

On the other hand, the other ASEAN states are more concerned about the effects on the overall stability of the Western Pacific rim of a complete US disengagement from the region. This is further reinforced by anxieties about the ambitions of rapidly rising Asian powers. Individual country perspectives differ, but in general China, India and Japan are considered to be potential threats to the future stability of the region.[15]

Apprehensions over the unclear US role in the security of the region, and the rise of China, India, and Japan as possible hegemonistic powers in the region have pushed the ASEAN states to take steps to improve their military preparedness, a course that could lead to the outbreak of an arms race in the region. Current arms acquisition and military modernization policies among the ASEAN states are already being presented as indicative of a nascent arms race in Southeast Asia.[16] Whether military procurements and arms upgrading in ASEAN foreshadow a nascent arms race or should be seen as merely the response to a long overdue need, it has nonetheless raised the question of what they are intended for. This has become more important as intraregional disputes have once again come into the fore.

The strengthening of intra-ASEAN relations resulting from the Bali Summit of 1976 and the unity brought about by the common ASEAN stand on the Cambodian conflict also led to the relegation of conflicting and overlapping territorial claims involving the ASEAN states to the background. Inevitably, however, these issues reemerged as the geostrategic issues of the Cold War era diminished in significance and as the threat posed by the Cambodian conflict receded in the consciousness of ASEAN policymakers. Foremost among these territorial issues is the competing claims for ownership of the islands in and the continental shelf of the South China Sea. This involves Brunei, China, Malaysia, the Philippines, Taiwan and Vietnam. The militarization of the area and China's intransigence over the issue of sovereignty has created a situation fraught with the potential for armed conflict. The disputes over Sabah between Malaysia and the Philippines; over Pedra Branca (*Pulau Batu Puti*) between Malaysia and Singapore; over Sipadan/Ligitan between Malaysia and Indonesia; over Limbang between Malaysia and Brunei; and the numerous overlapping claims over continental shelves and exclusive economic zones in Southeast Asia also contribute to intraregional tensions.

Even as the global military confrontation between the superpowers gave way before regional controversies, the emergence of contentious trade issues in the late 1980s has conferred greater saliency to economics in international affairs. It is again the United States which is at the center of these issues. The diminished significance of the Soviet threat shifted the focus of US foreign policy towards the domestic effects of its abridged position in the international economic system. The current emphasis of the United States government on domestic social and economic problems brought it into conflict with its Asian allies. While US policies are primarily geared towards the reduction of its trade deficits with Japan, these have also overspilled into its relations with other East Asian countries including the ASEAN states. Consequently, differences over perceptions of acceptable trade practices and concerns over protectionism have now replaced fears of conflict between the great powers as the foremost threat to regional stability.

This new mix of international security concerns creates a new security environment which the member states of ASEAN will have to address.

## Security Studies in the ASEAN States

Defining security comprehensively in response to the requirements of nation building and state formation significantly affected the development of security studies in the ASEAN states. One of its major consequences is the emergence of a field which has generally been policy-oriented. There has been very little demand for and consequently very little work done on theoretical and conceptual studies on security within ASEAN.[17] This is in spite of the fact that the field of security studies in ASEAN has significantly expanded beyond the institutions of the military to include members of academia as important contributors to its discourse. As one scholar who had been extensively involved in security studies in the region noted:

> Southeast Asian strategic studies...have not been, to any significant degree, philosophical, methodological, disciplinary, or missionary constructs. Rather they primarily involve recognition of prevailing reality not in terms of what a particular situation should be but instead what it actually is.[18]

The existence of clear threats, such as a Communist insurgency seeking to overthrow the state, demand immediate and clear-cut policy recommendations. This is unlike, for instance, the case of the nuclear threat posed by the Soviet Union to the United States and vice versa. Though no less real a threat as a rebellion, the threat of a nuclear exchange is not immediate and therefore allows for some theoretical and conceptual reflection.

A second major consequence is the focus on domestic threats to the well-being of the state. This orientation made the evolution of a common regional security perspective in ASEAN merely a function of the internal security interests of the respective ASEAN states. As a consequence, it was not until the late 1980s (with the waning of the Cold War era) that Asia-Pacific regional security became part of their agenda. This is the opposite of the trend in security studies in the United States and Europe which had always emphasized *international security*.[19] That Southeast Asia has been a "region of revolt" in the last forty years must be taken into consideration, with "nearly fifty rebellions or sets of rebellions, both communist and separatist,. . . [having] taken place or [still] taking place due to a variety of different causes and circumstances and for a variety of goals and objectives."[20] There have, however, been changes as the threat of Communist insurgency has almost completely disappeared in ASEAN. Even in the Philippines, which is the only ASEAN country which continues to face an active Communist insurgency, the movement suffers from ideological factional differences.[21] Security analysts have in fact already begun to look at security concerns beyond this.[22] The domestic challenges to the security of the ASEAN states, however, remain.

Nation building in the ASEAN countries continues to face obstacles rooted in sectoral and ethnic differences. Impressive economic growth rates (with the Philippines as a notable exception) have not resolved, and in most cases have worsened, the inequitable distribution of wealth in ASEAN societies. Disparities remain between rural and urban areas, agricultural and industrial sectors, and among ethnic groups.[23] Rapid economic growth and the consequent modernism accompanying it also set the stage for possible political backlash from embedded traditionalism in the guise of protecting religious and ethnic values and rights.[24] On the other hand, greater economic pluralism, a by-product of government policies of economic deregulation, pose a potential challenge to the authority of what have traditionally been states with "developmental" tendencies. Though the end of the Cold War may now force the ASEAN states to more seriously consider the implications of an uncertain international security environment, internal security will continue to play an important role in their strategic considerations.

## Indonesia

Security studies in Indonesia developed along very broad lines of national concern defined by the principle of *ketahanan nasional* (national resilience). Officially recognized in 1973 as the central concept of Indonesia's security doctrine, national resilience brings together economic, ideological, political, and sociocultural, as well as defense concerns, under the rubric of national security; but its focus has primarily been on economic development. As the former Indonesian Foreign Affairs Minister Mochtar Kusuma-atmadja pointed out, it emphasizes that societal development and self-reliance are the principal means for enhancing national security.[25] This belief is borne out of the acknowledged vulnerability of Indonesia as a unitary state due to its physical size, archipelagic configuration and, most specially, its multiethnic societal makeup. The emphasis on internal security and national unity is also reflected in the geopolitical concept of *Wawasan Nusantara*, which emphasizes (together with the idea of Indonesia as a unitary state) one nation (emphasizing strength in diversity of language, religion and culture); one system of laws and administration; one common political destiny; and *Pancasila* as the state ideology.[26] The thrust of national resilience towards national development indelibly linked Indonesian security policies with its strategies for economic growth.

Due to the inward-looking nature of *ketahanan nasional*, Indonesia's external security concerns were primarily focused on the implications of international developments on internal security, particularly external intervention in internal or even regional affairs. This concern is reflected in the concept of regional resilience, the extension of national resilience over a regional context which has become the guiding framework for stability in ASEAN. It stressed that all the ASEAN states must seek to strengthen their national resilience which in turn would collectively have a positive influence on the national stability of the respective ASEAN countries. As described by Jusuf Wanandi, this framework assumes that "if each of the member nations [of ASEAN] can accomplish an overall national development and overcome internal threats, regional resilience will automatically result much in the same way as a chain derives its overall strength from that of the individual links."[27] Internal stability in individual countries will likewise reduce the possibilities of external interference in national and regional affairs. At the same time, Indonesia's adherence to such an introverted security posture reassured its ASEAN neighbors who continue to hold reservations about Indonesia's regional ambitions.[28]

This framework is still closely adhered to by a number of analysts and research institutions involved in security studies in Indonesia, particularly those with close relations to the military. The important role of the military in a doctrine which treats defense-security matters as integral to national development, and the dual function (*dwifungsi*) of the military embodied in the constitution is principally responsible for this. The Indonesian Institute for National Defense (LEMHANAS) has organized its curriculum and study groups along lines defined by *ketahanan nasional*. The studies conducted by its student body, however, is classified and is not normally open to scholars. On the other hand, the Institute for Strategic Studies of Indonesia (ISSI) publishes a regular bilingual magazine (*Telstra*) which features articles on issues of national development and security, as well as working papers on important security issues. The ISSI was established in 1987 by alumni of the LEMHANAS to provide a forum for discussing strategic issues in terms of national resilience. It is currently headed by former Minister of Home Affairs General Rudini (Ret). Despite its close ties with both the LEMHANAS and the military (the ABRI), the ISSI is a private institution maintained by support from private contributors in Indonesia.

Government institutions involved in foreign policy-making and analysis, however, have begun to put more emphasis on regional issues that go beyond traditional perspectives of security in Indonesia. The Indonesian Institute of the Sciences' (LIPI) Center for Political and Regional Studies and the Department of Foreign Affairs' Agency for Research and Development, in particular, are looking at what an active and independent foreign policy means in a changing strategic environment. Ms. Dewi Fortuna Anwar, head of the LIPI Center for Political and Regional Studies' Regional and International Affairs Division, pointed out that the end of the Cold War has given governments more room to maneuver in the international arena.[29] At the same time, however, it is forcing Indonesia to review fundamental concepts which had been central to its foreign policy. The concepts of a Zone of Peace, Freedom and Neutrality (ZOPFAN), and nonalignment need to be redefined and reworked for them to be relevant within the context of new international realities.[30] How the four major powers in the region, namely China, Japan, the Russian Federation and the United States, can be accommodated constructively by the Southeast Asian states is another area which needs to be explored.

The Center for Strategic and International Studies (CSIS) is also a proponent of a broader regional security perspective. A privately endowed research institution established in 1971 in Jakarta, the CSIS has generally been a strong advocate of greater regional security cooperation among the ASEAN countries. Though this advocacy had generally centered on the promotion of economic and social cooperation, the CSIS has recently become more active in pushing greater military cooperation (but definitely not in terms of the formalization of an ASEAN military alliance) among the ASEAN states.[31]

That there are no clear immediate external military threats to Indonesia tends to preserve the inward-looking perspective which has characterized Indonesian security concerns. Yet, the significance of regional security issues, particularly the need to create a favorable regional condition given the uncertainties of the post–Cold War environment, is receiving greater attention and recognition by analysts and scholars involved in security studies in Indonesia.

## Malaysia

Unlike Indonesia, Malaysia has not developed a formal security doctrine. Yet, just like Indonesia, its security perspective is based on the notion that military and defense concerns are inseparable from political stability, economic development, and social harmony and well-being. Malaysia's concept of comprehensive security gives greater priority to internal security concerns over external security issues, a condition which derived from the experience of the Emergency of 1948–60.[32] Former Prime Minister Tun Hussein Onn identified in 1986 the problems of economic slowdown, religious extremism, racial strife, drug addiction, illegal immigration, and Communist insurgency and subversion as the most important threats which have a direct or indirect bearing on Malaysia's national security.[33] The significance of this comprehensive perspective of security to regional stability was promoted by Defense Minister Najib Tun Razak when he declared in 1992 that making each country in the region politically stable, economically strong and resilient, with a united and strong-willed population, and militarily sufficient would inevitably strengthen regional security.[34]

While domestic threats remain more critical in the security calculus of Malaysia, regional developments have pushed external security issues to the fore. Former Chief of the Defense Forces General Tan Sri Hashim Mohamed Ali said in 1989 that the security situation in Southeast Asia has become increasingly complex and uncertain due to the expanding Chinese influence over the region and the withdrawal of the United States from the Philippines.[35] The need to protect vital interests in the South China Sea has now led Malaysia to put more emphasis on the development of the external defense capabilities of the Malaysian Defense Forces.

Malaysia has also become more concerned over what it perceives to be Western challenges to its sovereign jurisdiction. This is reflected in acts of intervention by Western governments and private organizations in issues where they believe intervention to be morally required and politically laudable. This includes issues over trade and intellectual property rights, human rights, the environment, and even over arms acquisition. Director Noordin Sopiee of the Institute of Strategic and International Studies (ISIS), has described this as "threatening to the interests of the weaker nations since double standards will abound and it will be the strong who will determine its very selective application."[36]

These concerns have become even more significant within the context of Malaysia's Vision 2020, the plan initiated by Prime Minister Datuk Seri Dr. Mahathir Mohamad directed towards turning Malaysia into a fully developed nation by the year 2020. As a consequence of these new threats and their implications for Vision 2020, security studies in Malaysia has begun to move along new directions. Intraregional cooperation and reconciliation are being given more prominence by analysts and institutions involved in security studies. ISIS, in particular, has been involved in the search for a wider framework for both Southeast Asia and Asia.[37] More importantly, the relationship between the emerging strategic environment in the region and Vision 2020 led to the establishment of a variety of think tanks all over the country.

Strategic and security studies in Malaysia had been largely the preserve of the military and the police prior to 1983. The Defense Staff College, the Police College and the Special Branch School were the institutions most involved in the initial development of security studies in the country. Academic institutions, particularly the Departments of Political Science and History in the *Universiti Kebangsaan Malaysia* have also made some contributions to security studies. A Strategic Studies Unit is also currently based in this university under the direction of Dr. Zakaria Haji Ahmad. The Malaysian International Affairs Forum (MIAF), which started out as the International Affairs Forum of the Malaysian Economic Association in September 1978, also started out with the support of the academic community around Kuala Lumpur.[38] It has been involved in organizing seminars and discussions on issues of international affairs. None of these academic institutions, however, exercised a major influence in the security discourse in Malaysia. It was only in 1983, with the establishment of ISIS, that a major think tank outside of the military became involved in security studies in an attempt to influence the directions of Malaysian security policy.

ISIS has since then become a key institution in the development of security studies in Malaysia. It has contributed policy inputs on defense and security issues, and foreign affairs, and has particularly made a name for itself in organizing international conferences and dialogue activities. The Asia-Pacific Roundtable on Security Cooperation, the largest annual informal dialogue mechanism on security in the Asia-Pacific region (with more than 200 delegates in 1993), was initiated by ISIS in 1987. Though it was eventually taken over by the ASEAN Institutes of Strategic and International Studies in 1993, it remains the annual showcase of ISIS. At present, ISIS is one of the largest think tanks in ASEAN having nearly 100 full-time research and support staff.

The year 1993 saw the flowering of think tanks in Malaysia. It was estimated that more than twenty institutions were established in response to the demand for new ideas for Vision 2020.[39] The Malaysian Strategic Research Center (MSRC) was established in September 1993 and was immediately involved in bringing together Malaysian and foreign residents of Malaysia in taking a hard look at the implications of Vision 2020 for Malaysian foreign and defense policies. The MSRC is committed to work in the fields of defense and foreign affairs, economics, resource management and science. The Malaysian Institute of Islamic Understanding (IKIM) is a government-funded institution launched in July 1992 by no less than Prime Minister Mahathir himself. According to its current director-general, Ismail Ibrahim, it addresses the same national and international issues as ISIS "but from an Islamic point of view."[40] The Malaysian Institute of Maritime Affairs (MIMA) was registered in July 1993 and looks into the significance of maritime affairs in Malaysia's thrust towards full industrial status. Other institutes are less focused on the area of security studies but are involved in research work in areas that fall within the rubric of Malaysia's comprehensive security perspective. The Institute of Strategic Analysis and Planning (INSAP) seeks to help Malaysians think "Malaysian" rather than along communal lines.

Evidently, security studies in Malaysia is growing well especially with the challenges provided by Vision 2020 and the new strategic environment in Southeast Asia.

## *Philippines*

The Philippines has not articulated a national security doctrine, but there is a clear enunciation of the idea that the security of the country could best be ensured by "maintaining a desirable level and pace of economic development on the one hand, and the public order at the national and local levels on the other."[41] Economic development and public order, however, are seen only to be the by-products of national unity and consensus. It is through the establishment of a cohesive national community that Philippine security can be ascertained. Based on this framework of security, national unity should be established around a moral/spiritual consensus (positive Filipino values based on ecumenism), cultural cohesiveness (the idea of a synergy between indigenous cultural values of community, and wide democratic space), economic solidarity (widening of the base of entrepreneurship and economic participation), sociopolitical stability, ecological balance, territorial integrity, and external peace and harmony. This framework has been articulated only during the administration of President Fidel Ramos by his National Security Adviser Jose T. Almonte. Similar to the more formal security doctrine of Indonesia, it stresses a more inward-looking security orientation. At the same time, however, it recognizes the need to push self-sufficiency in relation to external security.[42]

The formalization of this security framework, however, has only proceeded in the past two years. Prior to May 1992, the mainstream of the security discourse in the Philippines did not have any guiding framework (except perhaps anti-Communism) and was largely focused on two issues, the Communist insurgency and the US facilities in the Philippines. With the weakening of the Communist movement and the withdrawal of the United States from its facilities in the Philippines, there is a clear need to review Philippine security priorities.

The national unity/cohesiveness framework briefly described above was conceptualized by the National Security Council of the Philippines. Its operationalization, however, requires the participation of the other agencies in government. The most developed aspect of the framework is its economic component which is presented as the Medium-Term Development Plan (1993–98) put together by the National Economic Development Administration (NEDA). This is primarily the strategy for economic growth of the Ramos administration. Its other components, however, have not yet been completely worked out. Within the context of this process, however, the security discourse has largely been dominated by the state. A major reason for this is the relatively weak security studies community outside of the institutions of government.

Aside from the National Security Council, the security discourse in the Philippines is also influenced by the Department of National Defense and the Armed Forces of the Philippines (AFP). It is through their offices that the military component of the security framework is being worked out. The AFP is undertaking a ten-year modernization program to upgrade its external defense capability. The program is directed towards modern arms acquisition particularly for the navy and the air force. This program is significant because of the implied shift in focus from an antiinsurgency-oriented defense posture to a more externally oriented one. The National Defense College of the Philippines (NDCP) is involved more in training than in research, offering a Masters Degree in National Security Administration (MNSA). But it has sponsored seminars and conferences on significant security issues involving the Philippines. The Command and General Staff College is likewise a training institute though its clientele is more strictly military than the NDCP. It is also involved in studies on the more technical aspects of the defense posture of the Philippines and on military administration.

Outside of the military, the Foreign Service Institute of the Department of Foreign Affairs is also involved in research in the area of security. Its focus, however, is in the more general prospects for security in the region. Among its concerns at the moment is exploring mechanisms for security cooperation in ASEAN, and the wider Asia-Pacific region.

Though belated, academia also sought to become involved institutionally in security studies. The University of the Philippines' Center for Integrative Studies (CIDS) was established in August 1985 to develop, organize and manage research on critical national issues using a multidisciplinary approach. Between 1992 and 1993, it initiated studies on the peace process in the Philippines involving the Communist insurgency, the Muslim separatist movement in Mindanao, and the military uprising that threatened the state between 1986 and 1990. Its contribution to security policy, however, has not been very extensive.

There are very few nongovernment institutes which specifically deal with security in the Philippines. The Center for Research and Communications Institute for International and Strategic Studies (CRC-IISS) was established in 1988 to explore international relations and security issues. Its work is policy-oriented and deals with national and foreign policy matters, as well as developments in the Western Pacific region. The CRC-IISS also serves as a forum for discussion and debate among members of the academic political, military and business communities interested in security and international affairs.

The Institute for Strategic and Development Studies (ISDS) is the newest nongovernment institute which is specifically oriented towards security studies. It was established in April 1991 by a group of academics based in the University of the Philippines in response to the need for a continuing evaluation and interpretation of changes in national and global affairs. It has been active in organizing international conferences relating to critical issues on regional security.

Security studies in the Philippines remains dominated by the perspectives of the state due to the sparse number of nongovernment institutes involved in it.

The greater involvement and participation of nonstate institutions in the security discourse will definitely enliven and strengthen security studies in this country.

## *Singapore*

Singapore's concept of total defense originates from the postindependence philosophy which emphasized national identity, internal unity, and economic development. While it is directed towards the general well-being of Singaporean society, this doctrine is more externally oriented than the comprehensive security doctrines of either Indonesia, Malaysia, or even the Philippines. This has been principally due to perceptions of the strategic vulnerabilities of Singapore because of its small physical size (which makes for a lack of strategic depth), geostrategic position in relation to the Malacca Strait, and its short time of existence as a country (which is thought to be insufficient for the establishment of a common bond for its multiethnic population).

The core of total defense is the strengthening of Singaporean national resilience to minimize domestic sources of conflict, and to deny opportunities for the involvement of external forces. This has justified the tight control the state has consistently exercised over Singaporean society. Beyond the domestic sphere, however, there is a strong emphasis on the development of military defense capabilities to protect the state against external threats.[43] Singapore's external defense program stresses national service and, more recently, the development of a significant retaliatory capability.[44] It recognizes, however, that military capability alone will not ensure the external security of Singapore. Singapore relies equally on a policy of nonalignment and on active diplomacy to maintain peace and security in the region. At present there is also a growing emphasis on regional cooperative mechanisms which also includes military cooperation.[45] While it remains a member of the Five-Power Defense Arrangement (FPDA), it has also built up bilateral security cooperation with Brunei, Indonesia, Thailand, and, since 1993, with the Philippines.

The strong impact of regional developments on perceptions of security trends has had an equally strong impact on security studies in Singapore. More than in any other ASEAN state, security studies in Singapore has been very much influenced by the Cold War rivalry between the United States and the Soviet Union as well as the general stability of the region. Since the early 1980s, Singapore's external threat perception had focused on the Soviet Union and its support for Vietnam, and Vietnam's policies in Indo-China.[46] Despite the collapse of the Soviet Union, there has been a continuum in the threat perception of Singapore of "*certain* external powers making unwelcome moves into Southeast Asia."[47] This time, however, the focus of Singapore's concern is India and Japan. This continued focus on external forces and the threat they pose to the security of Singapore is strongly reflected in the work of research institutions which have been important contributors to the development of security studies in Singapore.

In contrast with Indonesia, Malaysia and the Philippines, most of the research institutes associated with security studies have close ties with the National University of Singapore (NUS). The Center for Advanced Studies (CAS) is a unit of the NUS involved in research on both economic and political issues.

While much of the working papers it has published have principally economic themes, the CAS has also been active in organizing study groups and research programs which focus on security concerns. Among its largest projects at present is organizing an international conference on international boundaries and how they affect security affairs and the environment.

The Institute of Policy Studies (IPS) is another institute based in the NUS, but it operates independently of the university. Its work focuses on three broad areas of research: Singapore's economic relations and financial developments; entrepreneurship development in Singapore and the internationalization of Singapore business; and selected social issues such as ethnic relations, migration trends and quality of life. While it does not do research directly on security matters, the work of IPS involves areas that have security implications.[48]

The Singapore Institute of International Affairs (SIIA) is an institute which likewise has close ties with the university. It was founded by a group of academics as a society in 1961 as a forum for promoting greater knowledge about strategic and international issues. The SIIA's membership is principally constituted by faculty members of the Department of Political Science in the NUS. Recently, however, it has linked up with the Information Resource Center (IRC) and transferred its physical base out of the university.

The IRC is a private, nongovernmental and independent research institution committed to, among other things, the study of strategic, topical, and prospective issues relating to peace and stability in the region. It specializes in research on Indo-China, the Philippines, the Southeast Asian sea lanes, the South Pacific, radical ideologies and Islam. The IRC at present is active in trying to bring Vietnam into the ASEAN and has organized three major conferences on the issue. Since 1992, it has linked up with the SIIA, a partnership designed to build on each other's strength and at the same time allow both to maximize their resources by identifying the areas of concern for each institute.

The Institute of Southeast Asian Studies (ISEAS) is easily the most well known among the think tanks and research institutes involved in security studies in Singapore, and perhaps even in Southeast Asia. Established through an act of parliament as an autonomous organization in 1968, it has become the regional research center for scholars and other specialists studying stability and security, economic development, and political and social change in contemporary Southeast Asia. ISEAS instituted a Regional Strategic Studies Program (RSSP) in 1981 "in response to the need to supplement global concepts and methods of analysis with a close understanding of the realities in the region and with as much input as possible by Southeast Asians themselves."[49] The RSSP's principal objective is to foster study of security issues and developments affecting the region.

From the brief survey of these research institutions, it is evident that regional stability and security concerns have become the main focus of security studies in Singapore. While it is not likely that this trend will lead to a major review of the locus of the security doctrine of Singapore, it will certainly put more emphasis on external security concerns in the perspective of Singapore's policy-makers.

## Thailand

Thailand's security perspective varies on specific items of concern with each regime. However, there are areas of commonality which show preference for a multidimensional perspective of security (emphasizing political economic, psychosocial, and military concerns) rather than its narrow military definition.[50] Unlike the other ASEAN states, however, internal strife is not a major threat to the domestic stability of Thailand. Thailand has a largely homogeneous population which makes it unique among the ASEAN states. The domestic challenges to the state were posed primarily by ideological and secessionist movements, and these threats have largely been mitigated by economic development. The only real threat to domestic harmony, regime stability and state security in Thailand is the threat of military intervention.[51] The main concern of the democratically elected government of Prime Minister Chuan Leekpai is how to ensure its survival given the overhanging threat of military intervention. Whether the democratic gains of the "people power" revolt in Bangkok in May 1992 can be sustained remains uncertain.

Despite the persistent threat of military intervention, however, historical and geographical conditions have forced Thai security perspectives to be outward-looking with a focus on military exigencies. This may simply indicate the influence of the military in the security discourse in Thailand; but the concern is undeniably real. Thailand shares a long border with Kampuchea, Laos, Malaysia, and Myanmar, a fact that has been central to their involvement in a number of dangerous confrontations in continental Southeast Asia. The need to maintain the stability of these borders has pushed Thailand to seek security relations with the major powers even as it maintains its commitment to ASEAN aspirations towards a Zone of Peace, Freedom and Neutrality (ZOPFAN). There is the US-Thai defense arrangement based on the now defunct Southeast Asia Treaty Organization. More recently, and to the consternation of its partners in ASEAN, Thailand sought closer military ties with China in an effort to counterbalance the significant Vietnamese military presence in Kampuchea between 1978–89. This episode demonstrated how Thai foreign and security policy is shaped more by "pragmatic flexibility" rather than an uncompromising adherence to the ideals it supposedly shares with the rest of ASEAN. This is a realist model based on the definition of the particular interests involved at a particular moment in time regarding a particular issue. The overarching interest, however, is always the maintenance of the stability of Thailand's borders and of the region as a whole to create the environment needed for sustained economic growth (and consequently, to maintain domestic harmony and peace). These factors have shaped security studies in Thailand.

Military institutions have been a major influence in the development of the security discourse in Thailand. The National Defense College and the Strategic Research Institute (SRI) have been involved in the evolution of security studies. Much of the work which influenced the development of doctrines and policies have come from the military. But while the work of the National Defense College has been principally for internal (military) consumption, the SRI has been organizing workshops and seminars involving nonmilitary participants. In 1993, for instance, it organized a series of seminars directed towards the drafting of a Defense White Paper for Thailand wherein academics and businesspeople were invited to contribute their ideas. The SRI was only established in 1991 but it is becoming a major conduit between military and civilian security specialists.

Institutions outside of the military both within and outside of government have also made their contributions to the security discourse in Thailand. The International Studies Center of the Institute of Foreign Affairs has been active in promoting regional stability. It has been the principal organizer of the series of international meetings on "ASEAN-UN Cooperation in Peace and Preventive Diplomacy." These meetings have been directed towards discussing models, issues and mechanisms whereby preventive diplomacy can strengthen regional security.

Academia has also been active in security studies. The Institute of International and Security Studies (ISIS) of Chulalongkorn University was formally established as an institution in February 1982. Its mandate is the conduct of independent, academic research on and disseminating knowledge of international and strategic issues. It has been involved in studies of Thailand's defense and foreign policies, the insurgency problem and the Cambodian conflict. Its principal activities include the organization of international conferences and seminars, research, public lectures and panel discussions. The Institute of Asian Studies at Chulalongkorn University and the Institute of East Asian Studies at Thammasat University have also been involved in studies which have implications for regional security. Neither, however, is concerned specifically with security issues.

While the security discourse in Thailand has been largely the preserve of the military, it has begun to broaden in participation as more government and non-government institutions become more involved in discussions of the security issues which concern the country. The emerging synergy will definitely help in furthering the development of the field in Thailand.

# Current Developments in Security Studies in ASEAN

The end of the Cold War has coincided with a number of new developments which have taken place within the field of security studies in the ASEAN region.

## *Institutional Developments*[52]

A number of important developments have colored security studies among the ASEAN states in the last few years. First is the greater contribution of nongovernmental institutes in the security discourse in the region. Special study groups and regular classes within the different defense and military staff colleges and institutions in each individual country had been important resource centers for security studies. Furthermore, the emphasis on a comprehensive view of security, with its development orientation, was perpetuated in the curriculum of military training institutions in the ASEAN states. This contributed immensely to the inception of the idea that the military had to play a major role in national development.[53] In addition, the Foreign Affairs Ministries of the individual ASEAN states, particularly their in-house think tanks, have also made and continue to make important contributions to the development of security studies. The Agency for Research and Development of Indonesia, the Institute of Diplomacy and Foreign Relations in Malaysia, the Foreign Service Institute of the Philippines, and the Institute for Foreign Affairs in Thailand have been very active in the analyzing and examining international security issues. Much, however, of the work done in these offices is for the consumption of government only and contributes little to the general discourse on security. Even theses written by students of defense and military staff colleges are generally classified. It is only among nongovernmental institutes that a free flow of information on what might be considered sensitive topics actually exist.

In general, the strategic studies institutes that have gained prominence in each ASEAN state are involved in research programs on different areas of security concerns. But even as security was defined in a broad sense, emphasis was given to political and military issues. With the emergence of contentious international trade issues, political economy has become an important aspect of the security agenda in the region. The CRC-IISS in the Philippines, for instance, made a policy shift in their focus from politicomilitary issues of the international system to the politics of international trade and economic relations. At the same time, institutions which do not claim to be interested in security issues per se have been involved in research on regional stability and the economic tensions that have emerged from trade and economic issues in the Asia-Pacific region. Among the most important of these are the Institute of East Asian Political Economy of the National University of Singapore, the Institute of Policy Studies of Singapore, and the Institute of Political Economy of Thammasat University in Thailand.

While political economy issues have led to greater prominence for traditionally nonsecurity-oriented institutions, the linkages and shared experiences of those institutions which have been prominently involved in security studies have led to the establishment of an ASEAN Institutes for Strategic and International Studies (ASEAN-ISIS) network in June 1988. It is a nongovernmental organization involving five institutes from the different ASEAN countries (except Brunei). The founding members were CSIS-Jakarta, ISIS-Kuala Lumpur, the CIDS of the University of the Philippines, the SIIA, and ISIS-Chulalongkorn University in Bangkok. CIDS, SIIA, and ISIS-Bangkok are staffed professionally by university academics though only CIDS and ISIS are part of their respective universities. As mentioned earlier, CSIS and ISIS-Kuala Lumpur are both staffed by full-time professional and support staff. ISEAS, the third largest research organization in the region is precluded by its rule from representing any one country and thus not formally a part of ASEAN-ISIS. It, however, cooperates with the ASEAN-ISIS in whichever way it can.

The linkages have much to do with the interpersonal ties that have been built since the early 1980s between the heads of the different institutions. That these interpersonal ties are actually the basis for the linkage much more than the institutional linkages was shown when Dr. Carolina Hernandez was replaced as the director of CIDS. CIDS became inactive in the network and was eventually replaced by the ISDS in 1992, which is directed by Dr. Hernandez.

ASEAN-ISIS is recognized by the ASEAN and its contributions to the work of the organization was specifically cited in the communique of the ASEAN Minister's Meeting in 1993. The ASEAN-ISIS has been playing a role designed to extend the limits of cooperation beyond what is acceptable in normal diplomatic arrangements. Through the distillation of the ideas of scholars, scientists and opinion leaders unconstrained by their official capacities, the ASEAN-ISIS seeks to discuss issues and find a way by which differences can be resolved without resort to violence.[54] For this purpose, ASEAN-ISIS hosts, through its component institutions, several conferences and meetings each year. It is involved in meetings with like-minded institutions in Australia, Canada, China, Japan, South Korea, and even Taiwan.

## *Multilateral Dialogues and Research*

Within the last five years, multilateral security dialogues have become a growing industry among strategic and security studies institutions in ASEAN. This has occurred even more so as the ASEAN states begin to focus on external security issues even as domestic concerns continue to maintain their prominence in the consciousness of opinion leaders and policy-makers. These dialogues perform an important function within the region as they parallel official dialogues and meetings without the stiffness and limit of officialdom constraining the free exchange of ideas. Largely referred to as "track two" diplomacy, it enables scholars, military officers, foreign relations officials and other opinion leaders to discuss issues without having to be constrained by the official positions of their respective countries. Officials participate in their unofficial capacity—a myth that enables the countries concerned to air their ideas before they have to officially discuss them.

Multilateral security dialogues in ASEAN have been taking place at three levels: subregional (involving only the ASEAN member states); regional (with Southeast Asian countries other than those in ASEAN); and Asia-Pacific wide. Subregional meetings have taken place in different forums. Among the most important series currently going on is the ASEAN-ISIS "Workshops on Enhancing Security Cooperation in ASEAN." The first of these workshops took place in Jakarta on June 4–5, 1993. The discussions were summarized in a memorandum which was submitted to the senior officials of ASEAN. A second meeting was convened in October 1993 in Kuala Lumpur. This meeting sought to discuss in greater detail the areas where ASEAN can actualize security cooperation. These two meetings revealed that there is a need to clarify the concepts that would be the basis for further discussions on security cooperation. The fact that these meetings were held at all, however, indicates that serious work is being done to advance security cooperation among the ASEAN states. In January 1994, two meetings were held in the Philippines to discuss intra-ASEAN concerns. The first was on unresolved issues among the ASEAN states, and the second was on human rights in ASEAN, its meaning and interpretations across the region.

At the regional level, ISIS Kuala Lumpur has been hosting a series of meetings entitled the Southeast Asia Forum. The fifth meting was held in Kuala Lumpur in October 1993. The forum seeks to engage participants in a dialogue on issues of common and critical concern and to promote better understanding of these issues and national policies through informal exchange of views among policymakers, scholars, and the private sector. The last meeting discussed two items: the aspirations of individual Southeast Asian countries towards the coming century; and modalities for cooperation and tension reduction in Southeast Asia. Aside from the forum, the ASEAN-ISIS institutions are also involved in an ongoing series of dialogue meetings with South Korea, Vietnam, Cambodia and China.

ISEAS has also been busy on multilateral research and workshops on issues concerning the region. The Regional Strategic Studies Program (RSSP) of ISEAS, which was established in July 1981, has organized four different research programs which have focused on sources of instability in Southeast Asia. These programs are "Sources of Armed Instability (in Southeast Asia), "Leadership and Security in Southeast Asia," "Defense and Development in Southeast Asia," and "Democratic Practices and the Conceptualization of Power in Southeast Asia." The last is ongoing, and is one of the few major multilateral mechanisms which addresses the domestic political front at present. These programs were launched with the following objectives: (1) to supplement global concepts and methods of analysis with the closer understanding of the actual realities in the region; (2) to ensure as much involvement as possible by Southeast Asians in this endeavor; and (3) to take into account the different strands of Southeast Asian professional opinion expertise, including not only government and military personnel, but also the academic community, mass media and business. An important aspect of all these programs is the development of a body of expertise on security studies.

Special mention must be made of the Indonesian initiative on the Spratlys issue. The Indonesian Foreign Ministry, representing a nonclaimant in the Spratlys dispute, has hosted four workshops on "Managing Potential Conflict in the South China Sea." These workshops were intended to seek peaceful means of resolving the South China Sea issue. The last workshop was held in August 1993 in Surabaya. Due, however, to China's steadfast position on the question of sovereignty, the effectiveness of the workshops in building confidence and reducing tension among the disputants is reaching its limits without any major breakthrough being achieved. The meetings by themselves are significant (going by the Churchillian adage that it is always better "to jaw-jaw than to war-war"), but moving towards a resolution to the issue is still uncertain after four meetings.

At the level of the Asia-Pacific region, an ongoing dialogue program has successfully become a major affair in track two diplomacy. The Asia-Pacific Roundtable (APR) was first held in January 1987. It was the first informal process involving the Asia-Pacific region on strategic and security issues. Over the seven years that it has been regularly held, the APR has become a machinery for confidence building through constructive consultations and exchange of ideas. The APR was hosted by ISIS-Kuala Lumpur during the first six years that it was held. The Seventh Roundtable was also held in Kuala Lumpur but was hosted by the ASEAN-ISIS. As mentioned earlier, the APR is now the largest informal dialogue mechanism in the Asia-Pacific region.

The Philippines and Thailand worked together on a two-leg conference on "ASEAN and the Asia-Pacific Region: Prospects for Security Cooperation in the 1990s." The first leg of the conference was held in Manila in June 1991 and the second leg was held in Bangkok a year later. The conference was directly a response to the rapid changes occurring in the East Asian region caused by the reduction of US forces in the region, the eventual collapse of the Soviet Union, and the prospective rise of China, Japan and India as major powers in the region.

## Training

Who are the scholars currently involved in security studies? What are their professional backgrounds? One of the interesting facts about the current state of security studies in ASEAN is the extremely limited pool of scholars who have been working in the field. This pool at present is dominated by senior scholars who have been in security studies for most of their professional lives. Most of these scholars possess postgraduate degrees in political science or in international relations received from universities in the United States or in Europe, and have been associated with academia for most of their professional lives. Their interest in security studies is for the most part a by-product of their professional training. There are important exceptions to this general rule, namely Jusuf Wanandi (who for a long time was head of CSIS), who received his Master of Laws from the University of Indonesia; Dr. Noordin Sopiee who received his PhD from the London School of Economics, but began his career as a journalist with the *New Straits Times*, rising to the position of group editor-in-chief before he became director-general of ISIS-Kuala Lumpur; and Dr. Hadi Soesastro, currently the executive director of the CSIS, who received his PhD from the Rand Graduate School, but had previously received a Masters in Engineering from West Germany. Regardless of their backgrounds, however, these scholars have successfully established a consensus on the parameters of security studies in the ASEAN. Those parameters are defined by realism and pragmatism. They have been responsible for much of the research on security in the region and, eventually, for the current state of security studies in the region. To a significant extent, however, the development of security studies in the ASEAN has largely been made possible by the personal ties which underlie the professional relationship established over years of interaction by these senior scholars in the region.

There are also a small number of younger scholars currently involved in the field. Similar to the senior scholars, many of them received their formal training in the United States and Europe. A few have received their training in Australia, particularly at the Strategic and Defence Studies Centre of the Australian National University. Unlike the trend among the senior counterparts, however, most of these young scholars are more specialized in their capabilities—the product of a more methodologically oriented training. While continuing to adhere to the pragmatism which has characterized security studies in ASEAN, they utilize approaches other than the usual content analysis of policy pronouncements.

## Publications

The different institutions in the region have their respective publications. These come in the form of single-author books, edited volumes, occasional papers, quarterly journals and annuals. Among the different institutions, ISEAS has the most extensive collection of publications, including the prominent journal currently being published in the ASEAN, *Contemporary Southeast Asia*. The articles featured in *Contemporary Southeast Asia* are a mix of submissions from within and outside the ASEAN region. This journal has been since 1987 focused on the concerns of the RSSP. The findings of the RSSP programs discussed above are published in the institute's publication series entitled *Issues in Southeast Asian Security*. ISEAS also publishes an annual (*Southeast Asian Affairs*) which presents the most salient issues of the past year in the respective Southeast Asian countries. The RSSP has also published several edited volumes based on conferences and workshops it had organized. It has also a *Pacific Strategic Papers* series which focuses on political-military issues in the Asia-Pacific region.

The CSIS and ISIS-Kuala Lumpur are the other two institutions with an extensive collection of publications. Aside from single- and multiple-authored books, both publish occasional papers. ISIS-Kuala Lumpur has a series on strategic and international relations issues entitled the *ISIS Pacific Papers*. The CSIS has a well-established English-language quarterly journal (*The Indonesian Quarterly*) which primarily features Indonesian scholars but, on occasion, includes guest articles from outside Indonesia. In the Philippines, CRC-IISS publishes its own occasional papers and a quarterly journal entitled *Strategic Papers*. Since its shift into international political economy, the future of *Strategic Papers* is uncertain.

### Financial Support

The achievements of the different strategic and security studies institutes were largely facilitated by funding provided by either government or foreign funding institutions. The American foundations, particularly the Ford Foundation, Asia Foundation, and Rockefeller Foundation have been very generous in providing support for institutional development, programs, or projects. The RSSP, for instance, was given a founding grant by the Ford and Rockefeller Foundations. ISIS-Bangkok, likewise, has benefited from their financial assistance. Aside from these American foundations, the Friedrich Ebert Stiftung, Konrad Adenauer, and Hanns Seidel Foundation have been very active in supporting workshops and conferences organized by the ASEAN institutes. Likewise with the Canada ASEAN Fund and CIDA, Japan's Sasakawa Peace Foundation has been active in Singapore and Malaysia while the Japan Foundation has been instrumental in the development of a Japan Studies Center in Thammasat University in Bangkok.

Aside from the activities of research institutes, philantrophic agencies have also been instrumental in the development of the community of scholars in security studies in ASEAN. The MacArthur Foundation provided scholarships for the MA in Strategic Studies program of the Strategic and Defense Studies Center of the Australian National University until 1991 for students from the ASEAN countries. Fullbright Scholarships have also enabled scholars to conduct research or complete their studies. The Japan Institute for International Affairs (JIIA) also provides generous fellowships to ASEAN scholars.

## Gaps and Problems

For all that has been achieved in security studies in ASEAN, there are issues that need to be addressed.

## Research Topics

Based on current trends in research studies, the following areas need to be explored further:

1. Refining the theoretical/conceptual base of security studies in ASEAN. This is important in relation to being precise about what constitutes good work in security studies. The use of comprehensive security as a concept is only useful insofar as it is possible to clearly identify the specific parts of the comprehensive security structure and how these relate to each other.

2. The determinants of regional stability in the absence of a hegemonic power. What are the factors that should be considered a *sine qua non* to regional stability without a hegemonic power as the final guarantor of stability? How are they to be secured in a regional environment that is filled with uncertainties and suspicions?

3. Exploring specific mechanisms for enhancing ASEAN security cooperation. The ASEAN-ISIS workshops have dealt with the general concepts of cooperation in ASEAN. It had bogged down on conceptual uncertainties about comprehensive security before it could discuss specific areas of cooperation which the ASEAN states could explore. It is perhaps time now to look at how security cooperation could be operationalized and in what areas it can be operationalized.

4. Confidence building in ASEAN. The continued existence of mutual suspicions among the ASEAN states is a threat to ASEAN itself. What specific policies should be implemented to reduce the effects of those mutual suspicions between ASEAN partners?

5. Confidence building in Southeast Asia. The need for transparency in areas were suspicions exist and conflict may arise is a must for the establishment of a Southeast Asian economy.

6. ASEAN perspectives on economic relations and regional security.

7. The environment and the security of Southeast Asia. The emerging concern over environmental issues should be explored in terms of a clarification of the different ASEAN perspectives on the issue.

8. Human rights. Is there an ASEAN perspective on human rights? How should ASEAN respond to the "doctrine of interventionism" now emerging in the United States in relation to the issue of human rights?

## Training

There are no statistics available to indicate how many young scholars in ASEAN are involved in security studies or consider themselves to be involved in security studies. What is evident, however, is that there are not many who remain involved in security studies. There are a number of reasons for this. First, the field has become more complex even as the comprehensive nature of security is taken into consideration. This has become more evident as the saliency of economic issues become more evident in the current security environment. A formal training in political science or international relations may not be enough to cover the requirements of security studies unless more specialized subfields of security studies are defined.

Second, even as such subfields are defined, the formal training needed to address the skills requirement of these subfields may not be present within the region. In the same way that the previous generation of scholars had received most of its training in the United States or Europe, the new generation must do the same thing. There is little in the way of research technology that can be transferred to aspiring security scholars. Japan and Australia are currently among the preferred countries in which to study, primarily due to existence of generous study grants.

Third, in the same way that regular meetings held among the senior scholars contributed to their training on security issues in the region, more young scholars should be invited to attend workshops or to do research in other ASEAN countries in order to provide them with the opportunity to interact with other scholars in the region, specially their peers. The ASEAN Young Leaders Conference that was held annually for five years up to 1992 was important in the sense that it contributed to the education and training of young scholars in the region. The opportunity to exchange ideas with peers formed part of their informal training.

# Conclusion

That security studies has been able to carve a niche for itself in ASEAN is evident. What the future brings, however, is not. Changes in the international security environment have impinged on the security perspective of the ASEAN states so much so that more attention is being given to external threat concerns. This, however, has not completely replaced the course of nation building and state formation in ASEAN. The principal threat is still domestic stability. And the only way to deal with this is through national development.

Security studies in ASEAN is now largely dominated by the various strategic and security institutes. There are few if any problems regarding their role in their respective societies that need to be addressed by these institutes as it moves into the new era. At the same time there are clear opportunities for further growth. How the ASEAN institutes respond to the emerging challenges will determine the future directions of security studies in ASEAN.

## Notes

1.  An excellent discussion of this point can be found in Barry Buzan, *People, States and Fear: The National Security Problem in International Relations* (Hertfordshire: Harvester Wheatsheaf, 1990), pp. 3–12. See also Joseph S. Nye, Jr., "The Contribution of Strategic Studies: Future Challenges," *Adelphi Paper 235* (Spring 1989), pp. 22–23.

2.  There is now a growing literature on this issue. See Mark M. Lowenthal, "National Security as a Concept: Does it need to be redefined?" *CRS Report for Congress* (January 7, 1993); James R. Golden, "Economics and National Strategy: Convergence, Global Networks, and Cooperative Competition," *The Washington Quarterly* (Summer 1993), pp. 91–113; Alpo M. Rusi, *After the Cold War: Europe's New Politi-*

*cal Architecture* (Hampshire, U.K.: MacMillan Press, 1993); Graham Allison and Gregory Treverton, eds., *Rethinking America's Security: Beyond Cold War to New World Order* (New York and London: W.W. Norton and Co., 1992); and Theodore C. Sorensen, "Rethinking National Security," *Foreign Affairs* (Summer 1990), pp. 1–18. There are also, however, those who have warned that expanding the scope of security studies to accommodate these new concerns "would destroy its intellectual coherence, and make it more difficult to devise solutions to any of these important problems." See Stephen Walt, "The Renaissance of Security Studies," *International Studies Quarterly*, vol. 35, no. 2 (June 1991), p. 213.

3. The ASEAN states referred to in this paper are Indonesia, Malaysia, the Philippines, Singapore, and Thailand. The Sultanate of Brunei Darussalam is not covered by this research. Security studies in Brunei remains at the preliminary stage of development. Though efforts to establish an Institute of Policy and Strategic Studies have been underway since 1989, nothing concrete has been accomplished to date. It has been the Ministry of Foreign Affairs which has been participating in the extensive exchanges on security among the ASEAN countries, regardless of whether these exchanges are official or not. As a result, there has been very little in the way of published research that would indicate developments in security studies in Brunei.

4. Walt, "The Renaissance of Security Studies," p. 212.

5. Yezid Sayigh, "Confronting the 1990s: Security in the Developing Countries," *Adelphi Paper 251* (Summer 1990), p. 3.

6. Ibid.

7. The following discussion is adapted from sections of Muthiah Alagappa. *The National Security of Developing States: Lessons from Thailand* (Dover, Massachusetts: Auburn House Publishing Co., 1987), pp. 5–14.

8. The concept of comprehensive security is more popularly associated with Japan. The Japanese concept, however, largely focuses on external threats to Japanese security whereas the concept shared by most of the ASEAN states is more inward-looking to the point of negating the need for alliances with regional and extraregional states in the case of Indonesia. For a general comparison of the different conception of comprehensive security, see David B. Dewitt, "Concepts of Security for the Asia-Pacific Region in the Post–Cold War Era: Common Security, Cooperative Security, Comprehensive Security." Paper presented at the Seventh Asia-Pacific Roundtable, 6–9 June 1993, pp. 5–10.

9. See Chan Heng Chee, "ASEAN: Sub-regional Resilience," in James W. Morley, ed., *Security Interdependence in the Asia-Pacific Region* (New York: Columbia University Press, 1986), pp. 112–15.

10. See "Shared Destiny: Southeast Asia in the 21st Century," Report of the ASEAN-Vietnam Study Group, February 1993; and A.K.P. Mochtan, ed., *Cambodia: Toward Peace and Reconstruction* (Jakarta: Center for Strategic and International Studies, 1993).

11. There are tensions in the bilateral relations between Australia and Indonesia caused to some degree by Australian defense doctrines which stipulate that any threat to Australia will most likely come from the north (though not necessarily from the Indonesian state itself). See Kim Beazley, "The Defence of Australia 1987," (Canberra: The Australian Government Publishing Service, 1987); and Paul Dibb, *Review of Australia's Defence Capabilities: Report to the Minister for Defence* (Canberra: The Australian Government Publishing Service, 1986).

12. See US Department of Defense, *A Framework for the Asian Pacific Rim*. A Report to Congress prepared by the Office of the Assistant Secretary of Defense for International Security Affairs, 1992.

13. Zakaria Haji Ahmad, *Images of American Power: Perspectives from Southeast Asia,* (*UPSK* Occasional Paper, Strategic and Security Studies Program, *Universiti Kebangsaan Malaysia*, 1991), p. 23.

14. See "Facing the Future: A Philippine Agenda for Philippine-American Relations," *Solidarity* (Special Issue), nos. 137–38 (January-June 1993: pp. 19–46 and pp. 61–69; Carolina G. Hernandez, "The Philippines: Preparing for the Aftermath of the Phaseout," in Viberto Selochan, ed., *Security in the Asia-pacific Region: The Challenge of a Changing Environment* (Canberra: Australian Defence Studies Center, 1993), pp. 107–19; and Herman Kraft, "After the Bases are Gone: A Philippine Perspective on the Future of Philippine-U.S. Security Relations," *Pacific Forum/CSIS Policy Report Series* (May 1993).

15. See Chandran Jeshurun, ed., *China, India, Japan and the Security of Southeast Asia* (Singapore: Institute for Southeast Asian Studies, 1993); A. Hasnan Habib, "ASEAN and Regional Security," Ministry of Foreign Affairs, *Indonesia Dan Kerjasama Keamanan.* (Jakarta: 1993), pp. 28–29; Sukhumband Paribatra, "Asia-Pacific Regional Security Issues," in Rohanna Mahmood and Rustam A. Sani, eds., *Confidence Building and Conflict Reduction in the Pacific* (Kuala Lumpur: Institute of Strategic and International Studies, 1993), 366 and 40; Abdul Razak Abdullah Baginda, "The Changing Strategic Environment of the Asia-Pacific Region: A Malaysian Perspective," in Selochan, *Security in the Asia-Pacific Region*, pp. 78–86; and Julius C. Parrenas, "China and Japan in ASEAN's Strategic Perceptions," *Contemporary Southeast Asia*, vol. 12, no. 3 (December 1990), pp. 198–224.

16. Bilveer Singh, "ASEAN's Arms Procurements: Challenge of the Security Dilemma in the Post-Cold War Era," *Comparative Strategy*, vol. 12 (1993), pp. 199–223.

17. Muthiah Alagappa is perhaps noteworthy among the ASEAN security scholars for his contributions to theory and model building, and conceptualization in the field of security.

18. K.S. Sandhu, "Strategic Studies in the Region," in Desmond Ball and David Horner, eds., *Strategic Studies in a Changing World: Global, Regional and Australian Perspectives* (Canberra : Strategic and Defence Studies Centre, 1992), p. 299

19. Joseph S. Nye, Jr., "The Contributions of Strategic Studies: Future Challenges," *Adelphi Paper 235* (Spring 1989), pp. 22–23; and Neta C. Crawford, "Once and Future Security Studies," *Security Studies*, vol. 1, no. 2 (Winter 1991), p. 285.

20. Chai-Anan Samudavanija and Sukhumband Paribatra, "Development for Security, Security for Development: Prospects for Durable Stability in Southeast Asia," in Kusuma Snitwongse and Sukhumband Paribatra, eds., *Durable Stability in Southeast Asia* (Singapore: Institute for Southeast Asian Studies, 1987), p. 3.

21. For a discussion on these ideological differences, see the Special Issue on the Philippine Left of *Kasarinlan*, vol. 18, no. 1 (third quarter 1992).

22. An important illustration is Julius C. Parrenas, "Beyond the Insurgency: Prospects for Philippine Security in the Year 2000," *Strategic Papers*, vol. 1, no. 1 (1989).

23. Kusuma Snitwongse, "Strategic Developments in Southeast Asia," in Desmond Ball and David Horner, eds., *Strategic Studies in a Changing World: Global, Regional and Australian Perspectives (Canberra: Strategic and Defence Studies Centre, 1992) p. 281.*

24. Mohamad Abu Bakar, "External Influences on Contemporary Islamic Resurgence in Malaysia," *Contemporary Southeast Asia*, vol. 13, no. 2 (September 1991), p. 227.

25. Mochtar Kusuma-atmadja, "Some Thoughts on ASEAN Security Cooperation: An Indonesian's Perspective," Ministry of Foreign Affairs, *Indonesia dan Kerjasama Keamanan Regional* (Jakarta: 1993), p. 15.

26. *Pancasila* as a state ideology is embodied in the preamble of the 1945 constitution. It is based on the tenets of: belief in the One, Supreme God; a just and civilized society; democracy which is guided by the inner wisdom in the unanimity arising out of deliberations among representatives; creating a condition of social justice for the people of Indonesia; and the unity of Indonesia.

27. Jusuf Wanandi, "ASEAN Perspectives on International Security: an Indonesian View," in Donald Hugh McMillen, ed., *Asian Perspectives on International Security* (New York: St. Martin's Press, 1984), p.41. See also Dorodjatun Kuntjorojakti and T.A.M. Simatupang, "Indonesia: Defense Expenditures in the Period of the New Order, 1967–85," in Chin Kin Wah, ed., *Defense Spending in Southeast Asia* (Singapore: Institute of Southeast Asian Studies, 1987), p. 112.

28. See Dewitt, "Concepts of Security for the Asia-Pacific Region," (see note 8), p. 9. As recently as August 1990, for instance, in informal discussions involving a number of Philippine legislators and policymakers, then Secretary of Foreign Affairs Raul Manglapus mentioned Indonesia as a potential threat to the region because of its size and resources. See Belinda A. Aquino, ed., "Reflections on the U.S. Bases in the Philippines," *Pansol Reflection Series* (Quezon City: University of the Philippines, 1990), pp. 11–15.

29. Interview with Dr. Dewi Fortuna Anwar on October 12, 1993.

30. Jakarta has in fact proposed that ZOPFAN be discussed as part of the agenda in the next ASEAN Senior Officials Meeting (SOM) in 1994. This was mentioned by Ambassador Singgih Hadipranowo, Head of the Agency for Research and Development, in an interview on October 13, 1993.

31. The First Workshop on Enhancing Security Cooperation in ASEAN was organized by the CSIS and held in Jakarta on June 4–5, 1993. Though this meeting and the subsequent follow-up meeting held in Kuala Lumpur in October 1993 were held under the auspices of the ASEAN Institutes for Strategic and International Studies (ASEAN-ISIS), the CSIS had a leading role in pushing security cooperation in intra-ASEAN military relations.

32. Muthiah Alagappa, "Comprehensive Security: Interpretations in ASEAN Countries," in Robert A. Scalapino et al., eds., *Asian Security Issues: Regional and Global* (Berkeley: Institute of East Asian Studies, 1988), p. 50.

33. The full quote may be found in *ISIS Focus* 17 (August 1986), p. 22.

34. Quoted in Dewitt, "Concepts of Security for the Asia-Pacific Region." p. 10.

35. See interview with Tan Sri Hashim Mohamed Ali in *Jane's Defense Weekly*, July 29, 1989, p. 159.

36. Noordin Sopiee, "New World Order: Implications for the Asia-Pacific," in Rohanna Mahmood and Rustam A. Sani, eds., *Confidence Building and Conflict Reduction in the Pacific* (Kuala Lumpur: Institute of Strategic and International Studies, 1993), p. 10.

37. ISIS has been organizing a series of meetings entitled the Southeast Asia Forum which engages participants in a dialogue on issues of common and critical concern and works to promote better understanding of these issues and national policies through informal exchange of views among policymakers, scholars, and the private sector. In the last meeting held in October 1993, the forum discussed mechanisms for cooperation and tension reduction in Southeast Asia. Within the

broader context of Asia, ISIS is involved in the establishment of a "Commission for a New Asia."

38. Sandhu, "Strategic Studies in the Region," (see note 18), p. 253.

39. See "Making the Vision Work," *Asiaweek*, September 15, 1993, p. 31.

40. Quoted in "Making the Vision Work," *Asiaweek*, September 15, 1993, p. 31.

41. Fidel V. Ramos, "Nation Building and National Security." Speech given on the eighty-first Foundation Day of the Philippine Columbian Association, Plaza Dilao, Paco, Manila, on December 11, 1988.

42. It is interesting to note that the framework articulated by General Almonte has important similarities with the ideas advocated in a volume written by an informal working group on Philippine national security. See Clarita Carlos et al., "Toward a National Security Strategy for the Philippines" (Manila: n.p., 1988).

43. See Chin Kin Wah, "Singapore: Threat Perception and Defense-Spending in a City-State," in Chin Kin Wah, ed., *Defense Spending in Southeast Asia* (Singapore: Institute of Southeast Asian Studies, 1987), pp. 194–223.

44. The development of Singapore's deterrent capability is now based on the acquisition of modern weapons systems which gives it preemptive strike capability. This is a policy which deviates from the former doctrine of Singapore as a "poisonous shrimp," which presupposes that the defensive capabilities of Singapore will make any act of aggression against it costly to the aggressor.

45. Alagappa, "Comprehensive Security" *Asian Security Issues* (see note 32), p. 75.

46. Quite a number of publications have come out of Singapore on the Soviet Union and its relations with the Asia-Pacific region. See Lau Teik Soon and Bilveer Singh, eds., *The Soviet Union in the Asia-Pacific Region* (Singapore: Heinemann Asia for the Singapore Institute of International Affairs, 1989); Derek da Cunha. *Soviet Naval Power in the Pacific* (Singapore: Lynne Reider for Institute of Southeast Asian Studies, 1990); and Derek da Cunha, "Major Asian Powers and the Development of the Singaporean and Malaysian Armed Forces," *Contemporary Southeast Asia*, vol. 13, no. 1 (June 1991), p. 57–71.

47. Da Cunha, "Major Asian Powers," p. 60.

48. See Institute of Policy Studies, *The IPS Report: The First Five Years (1987–1992)*.

49. Sandhu, "Strategic Studies in the Region," (see note 18), p. 255.

50. Alagappa, *The National Security of Developing States,* (see note 7), pp. 38–39.

51. See Suchit Bunbongkarn, *Military in Thai Politics 1981–1986* (Singapore: Institute of Southeast Asian Studies, 1987).

52. The discussion in this section draws much from K.S. Sandhu, "Strategic Studies in the Region," (see note 18), pp. 224–55.

53. J. Soedjati Djiwandono and Yong Mun Cheong, "The Military and Development in Southeast Asia: Perspectives from Observers and Practitioners," in J. Soedjati and Yun Mun Cheong, eds., *Soldiers and Stability in Southeast Asia* (Singapore: Institute for Southeast Asian Studies, 1988), p. 9.

54. For greater elaboration in the role of the ASEAN-ISIS, see Carolina G. Hernandez, "The Role of the ASEAN-ISIS," *ASEAN-ISIS Monitor*, issue no. 6 (April 1993), pp. 1–3.

# The Future of Asia-Pacific Security Studies in Australia

PAULINE KERR
and
ANDREW MACK[1]

## Introduction

The end of the Cold War prompted vigorous discussions within academic and policy circles around the world about the nature of security. In Australia, significant revisions in security policy, under way since the mid-1980s, were both validated and accelerated by the removal of the ideological divisions of the Cold War. Today that process continues with few signs of agreement on the directions security policies and concepts should take. One of the few issues which has been resolved is that Australia's security interests are increasingly located within Asia-Pacific. But how these interests will evolve and what the impact of them will be on Australia's own security is a subject which policymakers and academics will be debating for some time.

The direction of this debate, both at the policy and intellectual level, will depend to a large extent on the intellectual and material resources of the Australian security community. Indeed, the debate should focus in part on the competency of Australian security studies to address the complex new security issues which have replaced the certainties of the Cold War. This paper reviews the current status of security studies in Australia in the hope that it will contribute to a more informed security debate. We start by outlining Australia's security interests, from the perspectives of the Department of Defence, the Department of Foreign Affairs and Trade and the Australian public. Second, we review the status of security studies within Australia from a number of standpoints. Third, we look at factors influencing security studies, including funding and the relationships with government. Fourth, we discuss some criticisms of the mainstream discourse. Fifth, we review training of Asia-Pacific security specialists in Australia. And finally we make some suggestions for improving security studies within Australia and the region.

### Australian Conceptions of Security

"Security" is generally conceived in fairly narrow terms in Australia. In the mainstream security discourse, security relates to military threats to perceived national interests and military means to deal with those threats. As one of Australia's best known security analysts, Paul Dibb, put it in his official review of

Australia's defense capabilities, security policy should protect the nation "from armed attack and from constraints on independent national decisions imposed by the threat of such attack."[2]

The Australian Minister for Foreign Affairs and Trade, Senator Gareth Evans, in an important ministerial statement on *Australia's Regional Security*, also stressed that security policy should maintain the "physical integrity and sovereignty"[3] of the nation. With respect to means, as against ends, Evans argues increasingly that nonmilitary policy instruments for enhancing security are of critical importance. These include economic and trade policies, development assistance, traditional diplomacy and more recently, preventive diplomacy.[4]

For the purpose of this chapter, unless otherwise indicated, we see security issues as those which relate, directly or indirectly, to potential or actual threats of armed inter- and intrastate conflict. We are, of course, aware that there is a range of external and internal threat to the well-being of nations which do not fall into this category. Chernobyl, the AIDS epidemic and acid rain remind us that it is not only armies which can cross borders and threaten citizens. Declining economies can cause increased poverty, undermine health services and cause considerable social harm. But to include all such incidences of harm in this review would not only have been impossible, but also outside our sphere of expertise. Moreover, we believe that there are no good analytic, policy or moral reasons for conflating such widely disparate phenomena as environmental degradation, AIDS, poverty and war under the common rubric of "insecurity."[5] Attempting to do so will simply lead to confusion. Environmental degradation and underdevelopment are vitally important issues. They may also be *causes* of insecurity conventionally defined—but cause is not usefully conflated with consequence which is why we prefer the relatively traditional usage of the terms "security" and "insecurity."

## Australian Conceptions of Region

In the Australian security community the term "region" usually means Northeast and Southeast Asia and the Southwest Pacific. Australians are somewhat ambivalent about whether or not *they* are part of the region; indeed some opinion poll data suggest that a majority *do not* see Australia as an Asian country. Gareth Evans argues that Australia is the "odd man in" the Asia-Pacific, not the "odd man out." It is not always clear that this is a view shared by Australia's neighbors, as our exclusion from the East Asian Economic Caucus suggests.

In the Australian security community, "region" almost never includes Latin or Central American and rarely includes the Indian Ocean and South Asia. The United States is generally considered in the region because of its critical alliance role, because it is forward-deployed in the region, and because of Hawaii, Guam and American Samoa. Canada is not generally considered to be part of the region because of Canada's traditional security orientation towards Europe and because it does not have forward-deployed military forces in the region. This view of Canada is changing, however, as Canadian policy becomes increasingly oriented towards the Pacific.

Definitions of region can vary with context and issue. Australia's foreign ministry proposals for regional security dialogue forums, for example, conceived region in broad and fairly inclusive terms, including states in Northeast Asia (except North Korea and Taiwan) as well as Southeast Asia and New Zealand. For Australian defense planners the focus is very different. The 1987 White Paper, for example, refers to an "area of direct military interest," which includes Australia, its territories and proximate ocean areas, Indonesia, Papua New Guinea, New Zealand and other nearby countries of Southwest Pacific.[6] This definition includes all of the Southwest Pacific, but only one Southeast Asian state. A second area of "broad strategic concern" extends "beyond the area of direct military interest to include Southeast Asia, Indochina, the eastern Indian Ocean and the Southwest Pacific."[7] This latter definition excludes China, Japan and Korea.

Australian security analysts generally believe that subregions—Southeast Asia, Northeast Asia and Southwest Pacific—form natural "security complexes" and that it is more appropriate to analyze particular subregions than the region as a whole. China, which is of critical security importance in Northeast Asia and for Southeast Asia, is a slightly anomalous case.

There are also some issues which are better analyzed and dealt with on a global basis, the proliferation regimes (MTCR, NPT, CWC) being the most obvious example. But it may make sense even in these cases to pursue *regional initiatives* to support *global* regimes—Australia's Chemical Weapons Regional Initiative (CWRI) for Southeast Asia is a case in point.

In the 1990s, as concern about America's continued commitment to the region grows, Australia is paying increased attention to Northeast Asia, where its first and second most important trading partners are located. The major regional military buildup is taking place in Northeast Asia, the combined Northeast Asian defense budgets are some eight times greater than ASEAN's, and there are real worries about nuclear proliferation. The concern with Northeast Asia relates to these factors, to China's military buildup, and in part to fears that Northeast Asian conflicts could spill over and impact on Australia's area of broad strategic concern. Thus Paul Dibb argues that, not only should Australia develop a "community of strategic interests" with ASEAN states,[8] but that it should "consult more closely with Japan."[9]

## Australia's Security Interests

### Background

Australia is a thinly populated, affluent, resource-rich, mostly European country with a defense force of less than 100,000. To the north, its Asian neighbors—and potential adversaries—are densely populated, generally less affluent, resource-poor, and have many times more men under arms. These facts help explain why Australians have traditionally perceived themselves to be vulnerable. Reliance on allies has been a central feature of Australian defense policy for most of the nation's history. Prior to World War II, Britain was Australia's "great and powerful friend"; subsequently the United States has played this role, most prominently through the Australia, New Zealand, United States (ANZUS) alliance.

Initially perceived by Canberra as an insurance policy against a resurgence of Japanese militarism, the ANZUS alliance quickly came to be seen by all parties as part of the network of US alliances designed to contain Communism. Under a series of conservative governments, Australia was an enthusiastic proponent of "forward defense," which meant, in practice, that the Australian Defence Force (ADF) was configured primarily to fight overseas in conjunction with US and other allied forces. Defense planners assumed that, if forward defense failed, the United States could be relied on to come to Australia's aid.

Forward defense began to be questioned after the Nixon/Guam Doctrine in 1969 signaled to US allies in the Pacific that they should take greater responsibility for their own defense in regional conflicts. Australian defense planners began to think increasingly about a more self-reliant security posture where the primary focus would be the defense of continental Australia—a theme that was spelled out in the 1976 Defence White Paper of Malcolm Fraser's Conservative government. But it was not until the publication of the so-called Dibb Review of 1986,[10] and the subsequent 1987 Defence White Paper[11] of the Hawke Labor government, that the new self-reliant defense policy was given a coherent rationale.

## *The Perspective of the Defence Department*

The 1987 Defence White Paper, which is still the basis of defense planning, argued for a strategy of defense in depth. It was predicated on the following assumptions. First, that there was no current high level (e.g., invasion) threat to Australia. Second, that while the *intentions* of regional states might conceivably change from benign to hostile quite rapidly, regional powers could only acquire the sort of offensive *capabilities* needed to pose a high level threat to Australia relatively slowly. Third, any attempt to acquire such capabilities would not go undetected. Fourth, Australia's extant force structure could be expanded as, or more, rapidly than potential adversaries could expand their offensive capabilities. Australia was thus capable of countering emergent threats.

Whether dealing with high- or low-level military threats to Australia, the primary military goal of the ADF in the event of hostilities would be essentially the same—to use maritime strike forces to stop an attacking force in the sea-air gap which separates Australia from likely attack/invasion embarkation points in the archipelagoes to its north.

Whereas the central focus of the 1986 Dibb Review and the 1987 White Paper was the defense of continental Australia, in the 1990s the Defence Department is devoting attention to increasing and enhancing defense relationships with the region, in particular Southeast Asia. This is evident in increased interaction between Australian and regional defense forces—including exchange visits, exercises and discussion of a range of other cooperative activities. Regional security cooperation will be a major theme of the upcoming 1994 Defence White Paper.

Neither the Defence Department nor the Department of Foreign Affairs and Trade have explained publicly *why* they believe that building linkages with Southeast Asia will *necessarily* make Australia more secure. After all, the complex "networks of connective tissue," to use a favorite phrase of Foreign Minister Gareth Evans, and high levels of interdependence which bound what was Yugoslavia together were clearly unable to prevent the savage civil violence which has accompanied the breakup of that country.

Even though there has been no public explanation of the rationale for Australia's security engagement in the region, it would seem to be based on the following assumptions:

1. Closer professional contacts between military personnel in the region will reduce possibilities for misperception and misunderstanding, and are thus a form of confidence building.

2. Defense cooperation will help ensure Australian participation if a more structured regional defense community were to be created in future.

3. Intelligence exchanges, joint exercises, ship visits, exchanges of personnel and enhanced transparency will *in themselves* help create a regional security community.

4. Defense cooperation is an element in a broader process of growing interdependence which is assumed by its very nature to be security enhancing.

5. Australian participation in the Five Power Defence Arrangements (the five powers are Australia, the United Kingdom, New Zealand, Malaysia and Singapore), whatever its original rationale may have been, is now important because it provides a *formal* security linkage with at least part of the region.

While the above rationale of cooperation is clear enough, there is a certain tension underlying current defense policy. Australia is spending $25 billion to arm itself against potential threat from the same Southeast Asian nations with which it is seeking to cooperate more intensively. The tension exists because the logic of cooperation is frequently antithetical to the "realist" logic of deterrence which provides most of the rationale for the $25 billion force modernization program.

## The Perspective of the Department of Foreign Affairs and Trade

Under its current minister, Senator Gareth Evans, the Department of Foreign Affairs and Trade has sought, through a variety of policy initiatives, to enhance global as well as regional security. The pursuit of the former is seen as assisting the achievement of the latter.

Lacking the military power to use coercion,[12] or the economic power to use bribery in pursuit of its foreign policy goals, Australia has pursued what Gareth Evans calls "niche diplomacy," i.e., the concentration of diplomatic resources on a limited number of specific issue areas. "Niche diplomacy" involves innovative, timely and doable policy initiatives, backed by the intellectual and institutional resources of the Department of Foreign Affairs and Trade. In practice, niche diplomacy involves multilateral consultation and coalition building with like-minded states—including the creation of expert groups charged with creating detailed policy proposals. The initiatives to create the Cairns Group and APEC, and the critical contribution of the UN's Cambodia peace plan, are examples of Australian niche diplomacy in practice.

There has been a considerable evolution in Evans' thinking on security since the 1989 policy document, *Australia's Regional Security*. Here Evans had stressed military approaches to security and the diplomatic utility of military power, but he was criticized for saying nothing about the security enhancing role of multilateral security dialogue and confidence and security building regimes. Evans conceded that these criticisms had some validity and, some six months after *Australia's Regional Security* was launched, he presented his proposal for a Conference for Security and Cooperation in Asia (CSCA).[13] CSCA was clearly too radical for the times, but many of the ideas that Evans had canvassed in 1990 have subsequently moved onto the regional security agenda.

In September 1993, Evans gave a major speech a the UN which introduced the concept of cooperative security. The concept, developed in a study by Evans entitled *Cooperating for Peace*,[14] is much broader in scope than conventional military concepts. Evans described it as:

> ... a broad approach to security which is multi-dimensional in scope and gradualist in temperament; emphasizes reassurance rather than deterrence; is inclusive rather than exclusive; is not restrictive in membership; favours multilateralism over bilateralism; does not privilege military solutions over non-military ones; assumes that states are the principal actors in the security system, but accepts that non-state actors may have an important role to play; does not require the creation of formal institutions, but does not reject them either; and which, above all, stresses the value of creating "habits of dialogue" on a multilateral basis.[15]

In practice the central thrust of Evans' approach is towards preventive diplomacy and what, in UN-speak, is called "peace building."

In the Australian context, *Cooperating for Peace* should be seen as a contribution to an evolving security dialogue, rather than as a set of concrete proposals for a new national security policy. The elements of cooperative security which are most relevant at the national level are common security and preventive diplomacy, neither of which has thus far received more than rhetorical attention.

## The Public and Security

In sharp contrast to the official and academic security community, a majority of Australians continue to perceive their country as threatened, unable to defend itself and thus in need of a great and powerful friend as an ally. Within the security community there is a broad consensus that the country confronts no immediate threat, that it *is* capable of defending itself, and that there is no need to rely on the United States for direct protection.

A major public opinion survey on popular attitudes towards security taken in 1993[16] showed that 76 percent of those polled believe that the ANZUS alliance is important for protecting Australia's security. High levels of popular support for the alliance have been one of the constants of Australian political life since the 1950s.

But the most interesting results of the 1993 poll are those which relate to threat perceptions.[17] According to the polls, Australians feel more threatened in 1993 than they did in the Cold War era.[18] Within the security community (official as well as academic) such threat perceptions would be seen as absurdly alarmist. For example, Indonesia, the country most feared by Australians, has no major strike capability and is one of the few countries in the region whose defense spending had been declining.

# Australian Security Studies

## *The Security Community*

### The Academic Security Research Community

The Australian academic security studies community is relatively small. There are no institutes comparable in size to the major US think tanks, or European institutions like IISS and SIPRI, or even such Asian institutes as the Korean Institute of Defense Analyses. There are no major foundation-funded private research institutions, since Australian tax laws have not encouraged the emergence of charitable educational foundations.

The greatest concentration of academics working in security studies is found at the Australian National University (ANU), primarily in the Research School of Pacific and Asian Studies (RSPAS). The Division of Politics and International Relations in RSPAS encompasses the Strategic and Defence Studies Centre (SDCS), the Peace Research Centre (PRC), and the Departments of International Relations (IR) and Political and Social Change (P&SC). The division houses some fourteen full-time academics whose research focuses either wholly or in large part on security issues. At any one time, a further eight to twelve Visiting Fellows, some from the armed services, many be working within the division on security or security-related topics. The ANU centers undertake and publish considerably more security-related research than all academics in the rest of Australia combined. Indeed, of the seventy publications on regional security listed in a forthcoming bibliography on Australian foreign policy, 81 percent were by ANU authors.[19] Five academics in the Political Science Department in the Faculties[20] at the ANU undertake research which encompasses some security issues; three have written on regional security issues in the Asia-Pacific.

Griffith and Deakin Universities and the Australian Defence Force Academy have the only other centers in Australia which have regional security research interests. Apart from these centers individual academics with Asia-Pacific security interests are located in various universities around the country. During the mid-1980s a number of peace research/studies centers were established in Australian universities—at Sydney, Monash and La Trobe. All have suffered from inadequate funding. There are also a number of small privately funded, nonacademic and generally conservative think tanks, some of whose work is security-related. But apart from seminars and conferences, the product of these institutions tends towards essay-style commentary rather than extensive empirical research or theoretical reflection. (See Appendix 1 for a list of the principal institutions engaged in security research in Australia.)

### Security Studies Within the Military

Some of the most detailed work on practical aspects of rational security cooperation and confidence building is produced by analysts in the military.

The Royal Australian Navy (RAN) and Royal Australian Air Force (RAAF) have established in-house think tanks which undertake research on a range of security issues, particularly those concerned with regional security.

The RAN's Maritime Studies Program (MSP) and the RAAF's Air Power Studies Centre (APSC) have in-house researchers, run conferences and publish books and working papers in the public domain. This latter fact has meant that the military, especially the MSP, has made a considerable input into the public debate on regional security. The army has no specific in-house center, but has various sections, such as the Directorate of Army Studies and Public Affairs (DAAPA), and the Doctrine Branch, Headquarters Training Branch, which contribute to security studies.

The approaches adopted by the three services vary and continue to evolve. Material published in the public domain by the Maritime Studies program initially focused on RAN naval strategy, but more recently it has focused on issues of maritime cooperation, nonmilitary as well as military, with regional states. In November 1993, the MSP held a major international conference on Australia's Maritime Bridge into Asia.

The Air Power Studies Centre's publications in the public domain have focuses on a range of air power issues.[21] The APSC recently published an edited volume, *the Qualitative Edge*, which discussed, "air power from the perspective of cooperation ... and security for the Asia-Pacific region."[22] In August 1993, the RAAF sponsored a regional or a power workshop to "further [strengthen] regional ties."[23]

There has been considerable in-house research in the army on a range of doctrinal and other issues; however, until 1993 research publications were not available in the public domain.[24] Prior to this, in 1991, the Directorate of Army Studies had commissioned a series of papers by academics and other outsiders which was published under the title *Reshaping the Australian Army: Challenges for the 1990s.*[25]

In 1993, the army published the proceedings of two conferences which dealt with Australian and regional security issues. The first was from the Chief of General Staff's (CGS) Australian Army's Land Warfare Conference, which was held as an open conference for the first time in 1992.[26] The second, was from the 1993, CGS's Land Warfare Centre Conference on the military aspects of peacekeeping.[27]

The increased commitment to openness in the armed services is of equal value to the military and to the academic communities. Each may learn from the other—even when they disagree. Interestingly the Department of Foreign Affairs and Trade does not have a studies center which openly publishes work on regional security issues. A number of centers within DFAT do produce position papers on a variety of regional security issues but they are not available in the public domain (see Appendix 1).

## NGOs with an Interest in Security Issues

Peace movement, military and a number of other NGOs have an interest in security issues but none undertake research on them. The Australian Institute of International Affairs, which has branches in all states, runs conferences, holds meetings and seminars and publishes the country's major IR journal, *The Australian Journal of International Affairs*. But the Institute has no independent research capacity. (See Appendix 1 for a list of the NGOs with a major or occasional interest in security.)

## The Security Research Agenda in Australia

In preparing this chapter we have sought to rely as far as possible on objective data rather than our own impressions. To do this, we interviewed academic security analysts from all over Australia and have also produced a crude content analysis of a number of publications and conference papers. Each of these offers different insights; the whole provides a reasonably accurate picture of the field at the current time.

Is should be said at the outset that security studies in Australia have long been concerned with Asia. During the early Cold War years scholars were divided over whether Australia should seek security *from* Asia or *with* it—a tension which persists in contemporary security discussions.[28] We should also reiterate that we have interpreted the term "security" in fairly conventional terms for this exercise.

The categories which are used in the tables in Appendix 3 are as follows:

1. security/peace research theory
2. global security (including new world order)
3. regional security (Europe, Middle East, South Asia)
4. defense of Australia
5. Australia and security: global and United States
6. Australian and Asia-Pacific security
7. military security in the Asia-Pacific
8. Asia-Pacific arms control / CSBMs / cooperative security
9. Asia-Pacific security broadly defined includes security and economics / environment / human rights / culture / ethnicity / refugees / piracy, etc.

Note should be taken that the categories indicate the different geographic areas on which security studies focus. With respect to regional security a distinction is made between studies of regional military issues, which have long been central to the Australian security studies agenda, and what might be called the "new" regional security agenda—that which emphasizes reassurance, transparency, confidence and security building measures (CSBMs), cooperative security, etc. Finally there is a catch-all category entitled "security broadly defined." This encompasses research which examines a range of relations—security and economics; security and environment; security and gender, culture, religion, ethnonationalism, human rights, etc. It also includes such issues as piracy, drug running, poaching, and refugees—issues which are creating growing problems for regional security forces, though not security issues in the traditional sense. In collating these data only the *titles* of papers and publications were used—creating obvious possibilities for errors in categorization. However, there is little reason to assume that the errors which have inevitably occurred are biased in any particular direction.

The indicators we selected to demonstrate the focus of security research in Australia were as follows: the annual Australian Political Science Association (APSA) conference papers; papers in two of the main Australian scholarly journals, and the publications produced by the ANU's three security research centers. In summary a number of points can be made. First, data on the APSA conferences showed no radical shift in the focus of security research in the papers presented, however relatively few members of the ANU security community attend APSA conferences. Second, data on scholarly journals demonstrate the major journal, the *Australian Journal of International Affairs* (AJIA) has a very strong global and Australia, Australia/US focus when it comes to security issues. There are few articles on security issues in the region or "new" security agenda issues—CSBMs/cooperative security. So-called broad security issues also receive relatively little coverage. The only other relevant scholarly journal is *Interdisciplinary Peace Research* (IPR), which was started in 1989. IPR has a far more theoretical orientation than AJIA. It is also concerned to a much greater degree with what we have called the broad security agenda. Since the period covered by the AJIA is ten years and that by IPR only four years, the IPR figures should be more than doubled to provide a real comparison. Third, data from the ANU's three research centers showed that: the Peace Research Centre publications had a very strong emphasis on the new security agenda issues in the Asia-Pacific (CSBMs/cooperative security, etc.) and an equally strong emphasis on security issues broadly defined. Research in the latter category is likely to expand in the future. SDSC's publications reflect the center's leading role in the study of military security in Australia and the region. The Asia-Pacific CSBM/cooperative security agenda is a *relatively* new research focus for SDSC, but is now being pursued energetically. So-called broad conceptions of security receive relatively little attention in SDSC. The IR Department, in contrast to SDSC and the PRC where research focuses almost exclusively on security issues, treats security as only one element of a much broader research agenda.

## Changes in the Security Research Agenda in the Past Decade

### The 1980s

During the 1980s concern with the East-West confrontation, the global nuclear balance and its implications for Australia via the ANZUS alliance, was central to the security research agenda. The most sensitive and controversial element of the alliance relationship was the hosting by Australia of US satellite ground stations (Pine Gap and Nurrungar) which played a critical role in America's nuclear war-fighting strategy.

Concern about the risks of nuclear war drew large numbers of academics from disciplines outside IR, peace research and strategic studies into the contemporary security debate. Organizations of concerned academics and professionals, such as Scientists Against Nuclear Arms, Lawyers Against Nuclear Arms, and the Medical Association for the Prevention of War sprang up, their members using their disciplinary/professional knowledge to address issues related to the nuclear confrontation. A climatological modeller addressed the question of the southern hemispheric implications of "nuclear winter," for example, while lawyers examined the legitimacy of nuclear war in international law and a medical researcher reported on the relationship between ciguatera poisoning in fish and French nuclear tests in Polynesia.

With the end of the Cold War, interest in global nuclear issues and their implications for Australia has almost completely vanished.

The mid-1980s also saw the emergence of peace studies[29] in schools and tertiary institutions. Much of the work in this area focused on the peaceful settlement of disputes. Some peace studies programs continue, but the focus, as with the Conflict Resolution Network, tends increasingly to be on interpersonal and intergroup conflict.

## The End of the Cold War

The end of the Cold War saw growing academic interest in the new global order—and the region's place within it. The post–Cold War order constituted a key theme in conferences at the ANU in 1989 (New Directions in International Relations), 1991 (Strategic Studies in a Changing World), and 1992 (The Post-Cold War International Order).

However, even before the official end of the Cold War, the new security agenda which examined the relevance of arms control, confidence building and reassurance strategies for the Asia-Pacific, had begun to emerge in Australia. The key event in this context was the Peace Research Centre's August 1987 conference, Security and Arms Control in the North Pacific. This was the first major international conference to have had Asia-Pacific arms control/confidence building as its major theme. In 1987, the Cold War was still a major issue and the risks attendant in superpower confrontation in the North Pacific was the focus for much of the early work in this area.

The years 1987 and 1988 were also those in which the new agenda began to emerge elsewhere in the region. The first of the Asia-Pacific Roundtables in Kuala Lumpur was held in 1987; the first of the UN's regional CSBM workshops in Kathmandu was held in 1989. Subsequently conferences and workshops focusing on new agenda security issues began to grow with extraordinary rapidity.

In 1990, Australia's defense policy was critically reviewed in the first of two books published by the Secure Australia Project, a diverse group of academics, politicians and activists. *The New Australian Militarism*[30] offered a radical critique of Australia's regional security policy which it described as increasingly militarist and a return to the discredited policy of forward defense. The then Defence Minister, Kim Beazley, in the concluding chapter to the book, argued that the evolving regional security cooperation was predicated on very different assumptions to forward defense and, that since Australia was spending less on defense as a percentage of GNP than at any time in its postwar history, it made little sense to describe the nation's defense policy as militarist. In 1992, the Secure Australia Project published *Threats Without Enemies*[31] which sought to broaden the concept of security and which dealt with such issues as human rights and security, the environment and security, and national identity and security. The Secure Australia Project advocates common security as the most appropriate security policy for Australia. The most comprehensive radical critique of extant official security policies is found in Australian Defence Force Academy academic, Graeme Cheeseman's 1993 study *The Search For Self-Reliance*, which also spells out some ideas for an alternative defense policy.[32]

By the early-1990s an increasing number of Australian academics were talking about nonmilitary determinants of security—and insecurity. But while the possible relationships between insecurity and uneven economic change, environmental degradation, refugee flows, human rights and a range of other issues are increasingly recognized, relatively little has been published on these issues thus far, nor has much research been undertaken. The work of the Peace Research Centre, particularly in the area of ethnonationalist conflict, peacekeeping and peace building, is a notable exception, as is the work of Professor Stuart Harris of the Northeast Asia Program at the ANU.

In terms of *process*, the 1990s has seen increasing attention paid to so-called Second Track diplomacy, as most obviously evident in the Council for Security Cooperation in the Asia-Pacific (CSCAP) initiative.

In summary a number of observations can be made about the research questions which currently characterize security studies (see Appendix 4 for list). First, published work on regional (including Australian) security is generally defined in very conventional terms and military issues dominate. There is a very large amount of work on such questions as force structure, weapons acquisitions, emerging threats, national defense policies, nuclear, chemical and missile prolif- eration, etc. Second, as noted earlier, during the past four years a new regional military security agenda has emerged which stresses CSBM transparency, reas- surance and cooperative approaches. Third, a range of broad security issues is increasingly being discussed, including the relationships between environmental, demographic and economic issues and security. Fourth, still notable by its absence, is research on what might be called the "causes of peace"—although Evans' *Cooperating for Peace* is clearly a step in this direction. Fifth, also conspic- uous by its absence is theoretically based research on such issues as the security implications of multipolarity (the Mearsheimer debate); the problems which inhere in multilateral approaches to security (Robert Cox's work with the UN University and the University of California, San Diego project are both relevant here) and the relationship between cooperation and security.

## *The Principal Intellectual Traditions Shaping Asia-Pacific Security Studies*

The academic IR community in Australia is relatively small, probably little more than seventy all told. The academic strategic studies community, depending on how it is defined, is less than a third of this number. The sheer lack of numbers means that there has been little opportunity for a large number of competing schools of international relations, strategic studies or peace research to emerge as has been the case in the United States and Europe. The dominant intellectual tradition in Australian security studies has been that of realism,[33] although this has been implicit more than explicit. Relatively little security research in Aus- tralia has been self-consciously theoretical. Much of the research coming from the ANU security community has tended to be descriptive, eschewing theoretical reflection and frequently addressing itself to the current security agendas of government. This will be evident from a brief examination of the conference themes of the last decade (see Appendix 3). Out of some forty conferences run by the PRC, IR and SDSC between 1983 and 1993, only five dealt extensively with theoretical questions to any significant degree, although more than 80 percent dealt directly or indirectly with regional security issues.

## Strategic Studies

The research of SDSC, the main strategic studies center in Australia, has been very firmly grounded in the realist tradition. There has been little interest in theoretical elaboration and reflection. There are no Australian strategic theorists in the tradition of Ken Booth, Barry Buzan or Robert Jervis.[34] There has been a very strong emphasis on richly detailed empirical studies and on policy prescription.

In SDSC today, there is growing interest in the prospects for security cooperation in the region and ongoing research reviewing the evolution of economic cooperation in the region (PECC to APEC) and its possible relevance for institution building in the security realm. In addition to its continuing emphasis on Australian defense, the major focus of SDSC's future research is likely to be on the region and such issues as proliferation and regional force expansion. There will be increased attention to the *modalities* or regional security cooperation. Policy-relevant research will continue to be central to the center's work.

## Peace Research

The peace research field is far more heterogeneous and difficult to categorize than strategic studies. With respect to regional studies, peace researchers tend to be more optimistic about the prospects for cooperation, being closer to the position of liberal institutionalism than the more pessimistic variants of realism. It is interesting to note that the ANU Peace Research Centre's approach to regional security, which was seen as radical and alternative in the mid- and late-1980s is now very much part of the mainstream. There has been a somewhat greater interest in the peace research community in theoretical questions, than among the strategic studies community, but little interest in theoretical elaboration for its own sake. The Peace Research Centre will continue pursuing its traditional concerns of regional security, arms control disarmament and confidence building, but its agenda is likely to expand, with greater attention being paid to ethnonationalist conflict, peacekeeping, conflict analysis, peace building and preventive diplomacy.[35]

## International Relations

The contribution of IR to the study of regional security has been rather different. There has been less concern with policy-relevant research, rather more with theoretical issues. This is particularly true of IR scholars outside Canberra.[36] The ANU IR Department's growing concern with theoretical issues is evident in the 1989 New Directions conference and the 1993 conference which examined the utility of theories of cooperation which had emerged in the US and Europe for the Asia-Pacific. Potential incommensurabilities between security policies which stress cooperation/reassurance and those which stress deterrence has been another area of research in IR—and peace research. In recent years concepts of security have become the focus of increased attention at the ANU (Peace Research and IR), in the Secure Australia Project, and elsewhere. The future IR contribution to regional security studies is likely to include continuing research on theories of cooperation, analysis of the long-term security implications of demographic, environmental and economic change; the relationships between economic growth and the emergence of more pluralist political systems, and between the latter and the declining risk of war. In both IR and Peace Research there is considerable interest in elaborating Gareth Evans' concept of cooperative security.

## Asia-Pacific Regional Studies

Australia has over forty academic institutes and centers of Asian studies. Over the years many of these centers have developed international reputations in country studies. However with the exception of CSARR at Griffith University, very little work in these centers focuses on security issues in the traditional sense—which is not to say that the work which *is* done has no relevance for security studies more broadly defined. (See Appendix 1 for list of those which address security issues either narrowly or broadly.) There is unfortunately very little exchange between regional country scholars who study the internal security issues of Asian states and those international relations and strategic analysts who look at external factors.

## *Impact of Strategic Studies/Peace Research/International Relations on the Public Debate*

There is no doubt that the academic security studies community has made a considerable impact on the public debate. Academics are frequently called on to provide commentary on regional security issues of the electronic media—they write for national newspapers, they give evidence to government committees, they speak at public meetings. The ANU's IR Department has on two occasions recently brought together academics from around the country for a workshop evaluating a major government report.[37] The PRC's journal *Pacific Research* also makes a major contribution to public and academic debates. Two other publications which were produced as contributions to the public debate on Australian security were the Secure Australia Project's *New Australian Militarism* and *Threats Without Enemies*.

## *Influence on Government*

Not surprisingly the ANU research centers which have ready access to the security bureaucracy and government, which have no undergraduate teaching duties and which are relatively well funded, have made the greatest impact on national security policy.

SDSC in particular has had a remarkable influence on aspects of national security policy in the twenty-six years since it was created. It has been involved in an advisory capacity on a number of key policy decisions; it has provided serving officers with time to write on policy issues; its staff act as consultants to both Defence and Foreign Affairs; Paul Dibb, its current head, was until recently the no. 2 civilian in the Defence Department and was one of the main architects of Labor's defense self-reliance policy. SDSC is not unlike those US think tanks in that there is a considerable degree of interchange between its staff and the official security bureaucracy. SDSC publications are widely circulated and read in official circles.

The fact that relationships between Defence and SDSC have been close does not mean they have always been comfortable, however. Revelations by one senior

SDSC academic of sensitive aspects of Australia's regional defense policy and the US/Australian nuclear relationship caused considerable anger in government and military circles.

The influence of the Peace Research Centre on the evolving debate about regional security is difficult to establish, in part because the center has never had as close a relationship with Foreign Affairs as SDSC has had with Defence. There is, however, no doubt, that what we described earlier as the new regional security agenda, was pioneered by the center in the mid- and late-1980s. Nor is there any doubt that these issues are now central to the Foreign Affairs security agenda. The degree to which the former influenced the latter is impossible to say. More recently Peace Research and International Relations staff were involved as consultants in the preparation of Gareth Evans' *Cooperating for Peace* study. The PRC is also working actively with Foreign Affairs on a number of other issues including an NPT workshop, peacekeeping, and the Inhuman Weapons Convention. PRC publications, like those of SDSC, are also widely circulated within the bureaucracy and media.

The International Relations Department has, in general and with few exceptions, not sought any direct policy and advisory role. The department has an indirect role in that the Director of the Department of Foreign Affairs, Graduate Diploma course is based in the department. The diploma course is mandatory for all diplomatic trainees.

Professor Stuart Harris, convenor of the Northeast Asian Program (within IR) and former secretary of the Department of Foreign Affairs, is frequently consulted by government on a range of foreign policy issues.

It is difficult for us to ascertain the impact of other academic institutions outside Canberra on government policy. It seems clear however, that up to this point none have had the same impact in the security field as the ANU centers.

## Participation in Regional and Global Research Programs

One of the most significant developments over the last five years has been the extraordinary increase in the number of conferences on regional security, in Australia and in the region. A small core of ANU academics currently attend between four to eight overseas conference/workshops/dialogue meetings a year each and have done so for five years or more. Other academics with interests in regional security might travel overseas once or twice. Increasing numbers of Asian security specialists are visiting Australia as interest in regional cooperation grows.

The PRC and SDSC have both held conferences in the region in collaboration with regional institutes. IR held a joint conference with Hawaii's East-West Center in 1993 in Canberra.

Academics from outside the ANU participate less frequently in regional meetings because they are less well known than those from the ANU; but they are less well known because they do not attend meetings. A further reason is financial; many state universities simply do not provide enough funding for individuals to attend regional meetings.

Australian academics rarely consult intensively with regional colleagues or write joint papers. One recent exception was the Australian-Asian Perceptions

Project (organized by the Academy of the Social Sciences in Australia) which invited Asian and Australian scholars to Canberra for five days. The workshop led to a jointly produced paper on national security perceptions.[38]

Interchange between the academic security community and government has already been discussed. While still limited, it is increasing, not least because former Defence Minister and Education Minister Kim Beazley and Foreign Minister Gareth Evans are both former academics and believe that the academic community has something to offer the policy community—and vice versa. A wide range of officials from Foreign Affairs and Defence regularly attend academic conferences and seminars in Canberra and elsewhere, sometimes presenting papers.

# Factors Influencing the Development and Direction of Security Studies

## *Funding*

Without doubt the single most important nonsecurity factor affecting security studies has been funding. The major source of academic research funding in Australia is the Australian Research Council (ARC),[39] but extraordinarily little money has been given the ARC for regional security projects. Few academics in Australia seek funding outside the country although there are no barriers to so doing. Between 1988 and 1991 three major grants from US foundations supported research projects directed towards Asia-Pacific security issues at the ANU's Peace Research Centre and International Relations Department. The Canadian Institute for International Peace and Security also provided support to the Peace Research Centre for a project to produce a major bibliography on Asia-Pacific security. This was published in mid-1993.[40] The only other center we know of which has received foundation support is CSAAR at Griffith University which was awarded a grant by the US Institute for Peace to undertake a project on Peace, Cooperation and Strategic Culture in the Asia-Pacific. Note should also be made of the project on Australian-Asian Perceptions. This project, funded in part by the Defence Department, the Department of Foreign Affairs and Trade and the Australian Research Council, has held a series of workshops including one on security. A paper entitled "Perceiving National Security: a Report on East Asia and Australia" was published in 1993.[41]

In general the relatively low level of foundation funding received by the Australian security studies community suggests that academic security research agendas are not much influenced by the agendas of major foundations.

A decade or so ago the International Relations Department and the Strategic and Defence Studies Centre both received start-up funding from the Ford Foundation for their MA programs. These programs are now self-funding from student fees, which are becoming an increasingly important source of revenue in Australian universities. At the ANU, graduate student fee monies are used in part to bring scholars from overseas to lecture in the MA programs.

The most important sources of additional funding for security research have been the Departments of Defence, Foreign Affairs and Trade, and Employment,

Education and Training. All are interested in expanding Australia's knowledge of the Asia-Pacific region and security research has benefited from this interest, with the most obvious beneficiary being the Strategic and Defence Studies Centre at the ANU. Knowledge that money for research on Asia is available (the government does not provide comparable funding for African, European or American studies) has certainly inclined some scholars to focus their research in this direction.

However all the non-ANU academics interviewed for this chapter thought that, in general, the scarcity of research funding, for travel, research assistance and to buy time off from teaching, was a major barrier to productivity.

## The Nexus Between Academia and Government

A second source of influence on security studies has been the relationship between academic centers and individuals and government. The ANU's Peace Research and Strategic Studies Centres have perhaps the closest relationships—each receives around half a million dollars direct government funding annually. Government funding does *not* preclude criticism, indeed both centers have published material highly critical of government security policies. But while it is possible to bite the hand that feeds, most individuals working in these centers would be concerned not to bite it off. Speaking from direct knowledge we can say with confidence that during our tenure at the Peace Research Centre (nearly seven years) there was never a hint of pressure from the Department of Foreign Affairs and Trade with respect to the center's academic agenda. The constraints are more subtle and come as much from *within* as without. If a government-funded center were to devote most of its time to highly visible public critiques of the policies of the department which funded it, it would hardly be surprising if at some stage government decided to cut back or stop its support. Clearly centers and individual academics wishing to be influential in determining policy generally accept the agenda—the broad assumptions—on which policy is predicated. Policy advice is essentially about means rather than ends—governments would, for example, be unlikely to fund pacifists to advise on force structure decisions.

Those academic researchers who produce critiques of the core assumptions on which official security policy is based tend to be ignored by the policy community for precisely that reason. While academic critics frequently deplore the failure of an unreflective official security community to examine critically the core realist assumptions on which most policy is based, officials are often impatient with what they see as irrelevant theorizing. As Paul Dibb put it, policymakers "unlike commentators are charged with making decisions in the real world."[42]

Where scholarship uses language which officials simply don't understand, it is also likely to be ignored, no matter how important the message. This is true of much of the rational choice formal modeling research and is equally true of poststructuralist writing on security issues.

During the 1980s, academics critical of the security status quo could hope to influence the public debate on security issues even it they could not influence government directly. Critical academic analysis which raised questions about such issues as Australia's role in hosting US satellite ground stations had a major impact on the public debate of the time. Such debates may not have had any direct impact on government policy, but they helped the cause of the peace movement, and the peace movement did have some limited impact on government policy.

In the 1990s, the contentious political issues of the 1980s have largely disappeared and today most academics working in the field of security studies are not opposed to the broad thrust of the government's security proposals for the region. Gareth Evans' advocacy of cooperative security, for example, is precisely the sort of initiative which the Secure Australia Project might be expected to endorse. This is not to say that there are not disagreements (over arms sales to the region, over the need for all of the $25 billion buildup, etc.),but it *is* to say that the end of the Cold War removed a major source of disputation between sections of the academic security community and the government.

The most recent example of convergence between academic and official interests in the security area is the establishment of CSCAP. As Desmond Ball, one of the founding members of CSCAP points out, the organization:

> ... is designated not only to link and focus the research activities of non-governmental organisations devoted to work on security matters across the whole of the Asia/Pacific region, but also to provide a mechanism for linkage and mutual support between the second track and official regional security processes.[43]

## Critiques of the Mainstream

The work of the Secure Australia Project is part of a broader radical tradition in Australia which has been critical of mainstream security studies. There are a number of elements to the critique which has emerged from this tradition. First, mainstream security analysts are seen as having compromised academic integrity by becoming too close to the policy community. Second, the half million dollars per annum each, which the ANU's SDSC and Peace Research Centre receive from the Departments of Defence and Foreign Affairs and Trade respectively, is seen as constraining the ability of these centers to offer hard-hitting critiques of the assumptions of current security policy. Third, the field is accused of concentrating far too much on military as against nonmilitary approaches to enhancing security. Fourth, research is seen as insufficiently critical of core assumptions of realism and neorealism which recent history has shown to be wanting. Fifth, and relatedly, the field is seen as being insufficiently reflective with respect to theory and epistemology. Sixth, it is argued that too little attention is paid to the moral issue, which policy prescription in this field inevitably raises. Seventh, the question "whose security" is rarely asked and thus, issues of violence against indigenous peoples, migrants and women is ignored or marginalized.

A quite different critique has come from those scholars whose primary interests are in regional or country studies, but who have broad interests in security issues. Here the argument is that the leading Australian analysts of regional security lack the country and linguistic expertise to enable them to analyze security issues in the region adequately. It is quite true that there are very few scholars who can claim to combine both strategic and country (including linguistic) expertise. Lacking country expertise, Australian security specialists are, it is claimed, insensitive to the subtle relationships between politics, economics and culture on the one hand, and security on the other. A related criticism is that security studies analysts have tended to bring with them the intellectual baggage of Western strategic thinking, particularly the strong emphasis on military security, which may be inappropriate for the study of security in Asia.

At least some members of the Australian Security community recognize that these are important issues. But it is also important to note that much of the research on Asia-Pacific security issues in Australia take a regionwide or subregionwide perspective. Local language ability would be essential in studying the defense policy of a single country, but where *regional security* is concerned, English is the *lingua franca* of the security discourse. When Indonesian, Koreans and Thais talk security together they almost always speak in English.

A third area of concern is not with the subject matter, methodology or biases of security studies, but its concentration in Canberra.[44] Many scholars from outside Canberra who were interviewed felt somewhat marginalized by the domination of the ANU security community. Some felt that ANU academics should make a greater effort to involve the non-Canberra security community.[45] It was noted by a number or respondents that there had been no consultation at all on how the CSCAP national committee might be formed.

In terms of disciplinary focus there is widespread agreement, however, that greater interaction between security and country specialists in the disciplines of politics, economics and history is desirable.

On a personal note we would point to what we believe has been an area which has received insufficient attention on the regional security research agenda. It is now almost axiomatic in the Australian security community, official as well as academic, that confidence building measures, limited transparency and increased defense cooperation are security enhancing. We agree, yet there have been no arguments made, nor research undertaken, to demonstrate *how* CSBMs and defense cooperation are supposed to build confidence and enhance security. This is not a trivial issue since some military planners believe that some CSBMs can *undermine security*. Nor has much attention been paid to the obvious tensions which may exist between the realist logic of deterrence (which tends to exacerbate security dilemmas) and the logic of common and cooperative security which seeks to prevent security dilemmas from arising in the first place. Again this is not a trivial issue since Australian security policy seeks security both *against* its regional neighbors (deterrence) and security with them (reassurance and cooperation).[46]

# Training Asia-Pacific Experts in Australia

For individuals intending to work in the security area in defense and foreign ministries and the media, MA programs are probably more important than doctoral programs. The latter, of course, remain essential for those wishing to become academic security specialists.

Over the last three to four years there has been a marked increase in interest in Asia-Pacific security issues and this is reflected in an increase in undergraduate and MA programs which focus on these issues. Only the Australian National University and the Australian Defence Force Academy (which is linked to the

University of New South Wales), and Deakin University offer MA programs which focus *primarily* on security issues, although the University of New England will shortly be offering an MA program (by correspondence) in defense studies. (See Appendix 5 for list of universities which deal, in whole or in part, with Asia-Pacific security issues.)

The ANU's MA/Graduate Diploma program in International Relations has doubled in size in the past three years and today has about thirty students, half of whom are from overseas. The SDSC MA program has around fifteen students.

Among individuals interviewed for this chapter one observed that while more academics are researching regional security, there were few MA and PhD theses being undertaken in this area. The exceptions were at Deakin, where 90 percent of the defense studies MA students are military officers. However the Division of Politics and International Relations at the ANU has a dozen students working on security and security-related PhD thesis topics and the number of students seeking to work on regional security issues is high. A considerable number of the ANU graduate students (including MA students) working on regional security issues are from overseas.

Very few Australian students interested in Asia-Pacific security issues train overseas, the major constraint being cost.

Training of specialists (and generalists) in the Australian military staff colleges has moved away from the rather narrow military focus which characterized the past and now embraces nonmilitary determinants of security (and insecurity). The level of training of military officers at the various staff colleges is often comparable in standard to master's level courses in universities. The Department of Foreign Affairs and Trade has expanded the training of its foreign service officers by introducing a new graduate diploma for trainees and short in-house training courses for more senior officers.

# Recommendations

Our recommendations fall into two categories: first those directed towards Australia and second, one for the region.

## *Australia*

### Training of Security Specialists

Whether or not one believes that there are enough security specialists being trained depends on what one thinks the future security agenda should be. There probably *are* enough MA and PhD students being trained in the realist tradition— certainly there are fewer security-related jobs than there are trained graduates and postgraduates to fill them. If, on the other hand, one believes that the security agenda should be broadened and that nonmilitary causes of insecurity and non-military means of enhancing security are of increasing importance, then there are not enough specialists with skills relevant to *this* agenda being trained in the academy.

The broader approach to security would benefit from interdisciplinary approaches, something which is all but absent across all levels of Australian security studies. Training in this area is required for graduates and established security scholars, if comprehensive security is to be more than a rhetorical flourish.

A further failure of the Australian security studies community, as with others in the region, has been to attract enough qualified women to security studies.

Another issue of importance is the total lack of training of most media commentators. Some are excellent, many are not; none are trained.

*Languages*
As noted earlier, few Australian regional security specialists have language skills. New generations of students working in regional security are, however, increasingly likely to have linguistic skills. This tendency should be encouraged.

*Conceptions of Security*
The critical question of what conception of security is most appropriate for the future remains, however. If the broader conception of security is seen as being of increasing importance, then more attention will need to be paid to the relationships between security, on the one hand, and economic, environmental and demographic change, on the other. It must be said, however, that this task will be difficult due to the relative lack of interdisciplinary collaboration and expertise in these areas.

*Opportunities for Training Overseas*
As regards opportunities for training and collaboration, ANU doctoral students working on regional security receive funds which permit them to spend three to six months in the region. This is not possible for doctoral students from many other universities unless they use their own funds. With respect to collaboration with overseas centers, there is a need for greater interaction, but here, the problem is resources and regional institutions willing to accommodate doctoral and established scholars.

## Contact and Influence with Policymakers
In general Canberra academic specialists have good access to the policy community if they choose to pursue it. The "tyranny of distance" makes access far more difficult for scholars who live outside Canberra.

Nonetheless, even in Canberra much more could be done to increase exchanges between the academic and official communities. One suggestion is to encourage more short-term visiting fellowships within university security centers for officials from the Department of Foreign Affairs and Trade and the intelligence organizations. The Department of Defence already funds visiting fellowships in SDSC for navy, army and air force officers but more could be done to encourage other security officials to contribute to academic security studies.

## The Principal Obstacles in Expanding Security Expertise

*Funding*
A major problem in Australia is that insufficient resources are allocated to studying security, especially in its broader dimensions. The level of funding which Sweden, with a population half that of Australia, provides for SIPRI is ten times the amount the Australian government provides for the ANU's Peace Research

Centre. The Korean Institute for Defense Analyses employs 150 full-time researchers; SDSC, the major Australian strategic studies center employs less than a tenth that number.

*Greater Communication*

In Australia the term "security community" hardly denotes a cohesive group of scholars. Indeed, the interviews conducted for this chapter revealed how divided the community is. Much more could be done to improve communication between scholars and provide some direction for security studies at all levels across Australia. This endeavour should include officials and military officers and be multidisciplinary. It should seek to engage the attention of regional scholars who work on issues relevant to security studies, and it should encourage the participation of younger scholars.

One way to develop scholarly collaboration and a stronger multidisciplinary approach to security might be to build on the experience of the Australian-Asian Perceptions Project (AAPP) referred to earlier. AAPP held a five-day workshop involving around fifteen participants from various disciplines and from a number of regional universities who were set the task of discussing and writing a comparative paper on national security from their national perspective. Scholars had to grapple with each others' arguments not just during the discussion and writing sessions but later, under the direction of some very demanding editors, through numerous faxes and e-mail. The benefits were twofold: an educational process for those involved and a paper for other scholars to read which, while not attempting to reconcile differences, at least acknowledges the tensions between approaches.

A less demanding approach is for scholars to circulate drafts of their papers to colleagues in other disciplines for comment. With e-mail this is an easy way to develop a network and add to the scholarly standard of papers.

## The Region

### An Asia-Pacific Research Institute

A major and recurring problem for security analysis in the Asia-Pacific is the relative lack of reliable data on a range of security issues, from arms transfers to the scope and intensity of ethnonationalist conflicts. In part, for this reason some analysts have proposed creating an Asia-Pacific SIPRI or IISS. This may be premature. What may be more practical and quite as useful would be an institution modeled more on the lines of the OECD, with its primary function being data collection and collation. The goal would be to increase transparency across a broad range of security questions. Analysis and policy prescription would not be part of the Asia-Pacific Security Institute's (APSI) brief, at least not initially. Security is, and is likely to remain, an extremely sensitive issue for many regional states, especially where such broad security issues as human rights and ethnonationalist conflict are concerned.

APSI would be more a major database than an institute as conventionally conceived. Data collected would be stored electronically with on-line access via e-mail to e-mail users worldwide.[47] Some general material of obvious relevance— e.g., BBC Summary of World Broadcasts and Reuters—is already available on-line. There are also specialist databases, on nuclear and missile proliferation, for example, with on-line access at a price. It might well be possible to arrange for data relevant to the Asia-Pacific to be downlinked automatically to APSI from such databases in exchange for APSI-provided data.

In addition to serving as an access point for data from extant databases, APSI would create its own. The work of the Monterey Institute for International Studies (MIS) provides a model here. MIIS collects information from the Russian vernacular press and academic journals on a range of nuclear and environmental issues. Russian-speakers produce detailed abstracts of the findings of key articles which are then translated into English and entered onto the database. Dozens of Russian-language academic journals are regularly searched and abstracted. The original (Russian) articles are kept on file and photocopies can in principle be obtained if the abstracted findings do not provide enough data. Such databases can be searched in a number of different ways—key words, etc. They are, as anyone who has used them knows, an extraordinary resource.

Conferences and workshop proceedings could be deposited at APSI giving all researchers access to papers that normally only a few would see. Greenwood Press has recently published a major bibliography on Asia-Pacific security. Australian National University researchers are completing a major bibliography of Australian foreign policy. No doubt other bibliographies are being prepared in other countries. All will have been produced electronically and each could, in principle, be transferred onto a searchable database. Once in place the databases could be constantly updated (unlike conventionally published works). Moreover, the updating could be done on-line by researchers in different regional states entering new references on the database remotely. Looking ahead the APSI network could be used for "prepcons" (preconference preparation) for electronic conferences and possibly even an interactive electronic journal. APSI would function as a giant electronic filing system for all analysts working on regional security issues.

APSI itself could be located physically anywhere in the region, its key research staff would be English-speaking graduate students who would be based in their home countries and be paid to review material, produce abstracts of it, categorize them under various headings, and translate them into English. This would be done directly onto APSI-provided computers. The abstracts would then be sent by e-mail (or APSI provided modems) to automatically load onto the APSI database.

Without having to buy large numbers of journals, or provide salaries and rooms for in-house researchers, the costs of APSI would be no greater and probably considerably less than a conventional security studies institute.

APSI would be an extraordinary research resource, not least because new software programs are making access to electronic databases far more user-friendly. Some training in using the system will still be necessary and intensive training of the researchers would also be necessary.

APSI could be "visited" and its resources used by scholars without the expense or delays of long-distance travel, without even leaving their home offices.

For APSI to work effectively, e-mail networks to connect all the key regional security institutes, university centers and, ideally, individuals, would be required. Since e-mail is spreading very rapidly throughout the region, creating such networks is not likely to be a problem for most regional states. PACNET already provides a fax network between regional institutes and is moving to create a regional e-mail link. Where it *is* a problem, modems would be used to provide direct access to the database via phone links.

APSI should be operated by young scholars and software specialists who have grown up with databases and are skilled in their management—again the Monterey institute provides a model. The APSI governing board would include more senior security specialists.

APSI could also serve as a networking center with different interactive electronic bulletin boards for different security issues. The Carnegie Endowment's nuclear nonproliferation database in Washington DC has one. A scholar in Korea can post an article on the latest development in the DPRK's nuclear program to the Washington bulletin board. Once sent, it is instantly accessible on the database by e-mail to other scholars who can read and comment on it either privately to the author or publicly via the bulletin board.

An electronic APSI would be a major research asset for the regional security community—particularly for the younger generation of scholars who have grown up with the computer revolution. It would be the first electronic security "institute" in the world—and it would be wholly appropriate that it should be located in Asia-Pacific.

## Notes

1. We would like to thank Helen Wilson, Michael Shaik, Lynne Payne, Mary-Lou Hickey and Barbara Owen-Jones for their help in publishing this paper.

2. Paul Dibb, *Review of Australia's Defence Capabilities* (Canberra: Australian Government Publishing Service 1986), p. 36.

3. Senator the Hon. Gareth Evans, *Australia's Regional Security*, Ministerial Statement, December 1989, reprinted in Greg Fry, ed., *Australia's Regional Security* (Sydney: Allen and Unwin 1991), pp. 165–216.

4. See Gareth Evans, *Cooperating for Peace: The Global Agenda for the 1990s and Beyond* (Sydney: Allen and Unwin, 1993).

5. It is possible to argue that there is a *political* advantage in such an exercise in relabelling. Security is a privileged concept. Redefining security to encompass issues like the environment and human rights may confer on them the privileged status and resources accorded to security as it is defined in the mainstream. This is a serious argument, but the political advantage may come at real analytic cost.

6. *The Defence of Australia 1987* (Canberra: Australian Government Publishing Service 1987), p. 2, footnote 1. According to the White Paper "[t]his area stretches over 7,000 kilometres from the Cocos Islands to New Zealand and the islands of the Southwest Pacific and over 5,000 kilometres from the archipelago and island chain in the north to the Southern Ocean. It constitutes about 10 per cent of the earth's surface," p. 2.

7. Ibid.

8. Paul Dibb, "The Future of Australia's Defence Relationship with the USA," *SDSC Newsletter*, September 1993, p. 1.

9. Paul Dibb, *The Future of Australia's Defence Relationship with the United States* (Sydney: The Australian Centre for American Studies, University of Sydney, 1993), p. 66.

10. Dibb, *Review of Australia's Defence Capabilities*.

11. *The Defence of Australia 1987*.

12. Except in the Southwest Pacific, the only area in which Australia contemplates the possibility of intervention.

13. The Hon. Senator Gareth Evans, "Australia's Asian Future", Speech at Monash University, Melbourne, July 19, 1990; *International Herald Tribune*, July 27, 1990.

14. Evans, *Cooperating for Peace*. "Cooperative security" was also a term used by Canada several years earlier. Evans' concept is not dissimilar to the Canadian, but places greater stress on collective security and preventive diplomacy.

15. Evans, *Cooperating for Peace*, p. 16. This description in fact came from a paraphrase by Andrew Mack of a section in a paper by Canadian security scholar David Dewitt, "Common, Comprehensive and Cooperative Security", *The Pacific Review*, vol. 7, no. 1, 1994, pp. 7–9

16. "Australians Remain Suspicious on Indonesia," *Canberra Times*, September 13, 1993, p. 11. Roger Jones et al., *Australian Election Study, 1993* (Canberra:Social Science Data Archives, The Australian National University, 1993, computer file). Those who carried out the original analysis and collection of the data bear no responsibility for the further analysis or interpretation of them.

17. Two points need to be made about these data. First, they represent the views of what might be called the "inattentive public" and not those of the security community. Other poll data suggest that, given greater information, Australians feel less threatened, less likely to automatically support ANZUS and more likely to believe that Australia can defend itself. Second, the fact that popular views are very different from those of officialdom means that public opinion can and does act as an indirect constraint on defense planning. The importance of this constraint should not be overemphasized, however. When members of the public are asked to rank foreign affairs or defense in terms of their relative importance they invariably place them last on their list.

18. In response to a question about threats to the "security of Australia" which could emerge in about five years time, Russia was perceived as a threat by 11 percent; China by 28 percent; Indonesia by an extraordinary 55 percent; Japan by 32 percent; Vietnam by 15 percent and India by 6 percent. Looking forward ten to fifteen years the public mood was even more pessimistic. China was perceived as a threat by 37 percent, while 57 percent feared a threat from Indonesia, and 37 percent a threat from Japan. In 1985, only 46 percent of the population thought that Australia would be subject to any threat from *any* source. Jones et al., *Australian Election Study, 1993*.

19. The bibliography, compiled by Pauline Kerr, David Sullivan and Robin Ward, will be published in 1994.

20. The Faculties is responsible for undergraduate teaching. The Institute of Advanced Studies, which includes the Research School of Pacific and Asian Studies, is a research only institution with the exception of some MA programs.

21. See Air Powers Studies Centre, *Cooperate Plan 1993–1995* (Canberra: Defence Publications, Defence Centre, 1993).

22. Gary Waters and John Mordike, "Regional Air Power Cooperation" (Air Power Studies Centre, unpublished paper, 1993).

23. Ibid.

24. In 1993 the Australian Army published *The Fundamentals of Land Warfare* (New South Wales: Doctrine Branch, Headquarters Training Command, 1993).

25. David Horner, ed., *Reshaping the Australian Army: Challenges for the 1990s* (Canberra: Strategic and Defence Studies Centre, Research School of Pacific and Asian Studies, Australian National University, 1991).

26. David Horner, ed., *The Army and the Future: Land Forces in Australia and Southeast Asia* (Canberra: Directorate of Departmental Publications, Defence Centre, 1993).

27. Hugh Smith, ed., *Peacekeeping: Challenges for the Future*, Australian Defence Studies Centre (Canberra: Australian Defence Force Academy, 1993).

28. For a discussion of the distinction see Martin Indyk, "The Australian Study of International Relations" in D. Aitkin, ed., *Surveys of Australian Political Science*, (Sydney: Allen and Unwin, 1985).

29. The term "peace studies" tends to be associated with teaching rather than research.

30. Graeme Cheeseman and St. John Kettle, eds., *The New Australian Militarism*, (Sydney: Pluto Press, 1990).

31. Gary Smith and St. John Kettle, eds., *Threats Without Enemies* (Sydney: Pluto Press, 1992).

32. Graeme Cheeseman, *The Search for Self-Reliance: Australian Defence Since Vietnam* (Melbourne: Longman Cheshire, 1993).

33. The very small number of poststructuralist and other scholars who dissent from the dominant realist tradition have not written on *regional* security issues.

34. Possible exceptions to this claim are found in earlier research by Coral Bell (on crises), Desmond Ball (on nuclear command and control), Andrew Mack and Brian Martin (strategies of nonmilitary defense) and most recently J.L. Richardson (on crises).

35. In the late 1980s the center's research agenda also included identity and nationalism, gender and ethnicity, and culture and militarism.

36. It is worth noting that while there are relatively few academics who would describe themselves as peace researchers or strategic analysts outside Canberra, there is a relatively large number of IR specialists.

37. The first such exercise debated economist Ross Garnaut's report, *The Northeast Asian Ascendancy*, which examined Australia's relationships (primarily economic, but including security) with Northeast Asia; the second discussed Gareth Evans' policy document *Australia's Regional Security*. (The concluding chapter was a rejoinder by Evans.) In both cases conference proceedings were published and each volume has subsequently been widely cited in the public domain. The IR Department and the Peace Research Centre are planning a similar exercise for 1994 in which Gareth Evans' new study, *Cooperating for Peace,* will be evaluated.

38. Anthony Milner, James Cotton, Pauline Kerr and Tsutomu Kikuchi, eds., "Perceiving National Security: A Report on East Asia and Australia," *Australian Journal of International Affairs*, vol. 47, no. 2 October 1993, pp. 221–38.

39. The Research Schools at the ANU are not eligible for ARC funding.

40. *Security, Arms Control, and Conflict Reduction in East Asia and the Pacific: A Bibliography, 1980-1991*, complied by Andrew McClean (Westport, Conneticut; and London: Greenwood Press, 1993).

41. Milner et al., eds., "Perceiving National Security".

42. Paul Dibb, "Whither Strategic and Defence Studies?" in Desmond Ball and David Horner, eds., (Canberra: *Strategic Studies in a Changing World*, Strategic and

Defence Studies Centre, Research School of Pacific and Asian Studies, Australian National University, 1992), p. 412. Many academics would dispute that the world of defense decision makers is any more real than that of academics!

43. Desmond Ball, "The Council for Security Cooperation in the Asia Pacific (CSCAP)" (Canberra: Strategic and Defence Studies Centre, Research School of Pacific and Asian Studies, the Australian National University, 1993, unpublished paper).

44. A somewhat contradictory complaint was that Canberra was failing to provide intellectual leadership in this field.

45. Efforts *are* being made in this direction. The Peace Research Centre held the first of what is intended to be an ongoing series of meetings of Australian peace researchers in early 1993. The International Relations Department plans a similar exercise for 1994.

46. Some of our own work has focused on these issues, as has that of Graeme Cheeseman at the Australian Defence Force Academy. The fact that "concepts of security" is on the CSCAP agenda is most welcome.

47. The PACNET network already exists, providing communication between major regional institutes by fax and, in most cases, by e-mail.

# APPENDIX 1
# Principal Institutions Engaged in Asia-Pacific Security Research

## Academic Centers

*Australian Capital Territory*

Australian National University:

> Research School of Pacific and Asian Studies: Department of International Relations
>> Strategic and Defence Studies Centre
>> Northeast Asia Program
>> Peace Research Centre

Some individuals in the following units have interests in security broadly defined:

| | |
|---|---|
| Australia-Japan Research Centre | Indonesia Project |
| Department of Economics | Pacific and Asian History |
| ASEAN-Australian Joint Research Project | Political and Social Change |
| Contemporary China Centre | National Defence for Development Studies |
| Japan Centre | Faculty of Asian Studies |
| East Asian History | Centre for Immigration and Multicultural Studies |
| Economic History of Southeast Asia Project | Asian-Australian Perceptions Project, ASSA |
| Pacific Islands Group | |
| Australian Defence Force Academy: | Politics Department |
| | Australian Defence Studies Centre |

*Queensland*

| | |
|---|---|
| Griffith University: | Centre for the Study of Australia Asia Relations (CSAAR) |
| University of Queensland: | Department of Japanese and Chinese Department of Government |

*Western Australia*

| | |
|---|---|
| University of Western Australia: | Centre for Asian Studies |
| Murdoch University: | Asia Research Centre |
| University of Western Australia: | Indian Ocean Centre for Peace Studies |
| Curtin University: | Indian OceanCentre for Peace Studies |

*Victoria*

| | |
|---|---|
| Monash University: | Asian Studies |
| Deakin University | |
| La Trobe University | |

*New South Wales*

| | |
|---|---|
| Sydney University: | Centre for Peace and Conflict Studies |
| University of New South Wales | |
| Macquarie University | |
| University of Wollongong | |

*Northern Territory*
  Northern Territory University

*South Australia*
  Flinders University

## Security Policy and Research Within Government

*Department of Foreign Affairs and Trade*

Policy Planning Unit

East Asia Analytical Unit

Regional Security Section

ASEAN and Regional Issues Section

Southeast Asia Division

Northeast Asia Division

Disarmament Branch

*Department of Prime Minister and Cabinet*

*Department of Parliamentary Library—Research Branch*

*Department of Defence*

International Policy Division

Defence Intelligence Organisation

Maritime Studies Program

Air Power Studies Centre

Various sections in army

*Intelligence Organizations*

Office of National Assessments

Defence Signals Directorate

Australian Secret Intelligence Service

## NGOs with an Interest in Security Issues

H.V Evatt Research Centre, Sydney

Australian Council for Overseas Aid

Australian Institute of International Affairs (states)

Institute for Public Affairs, Melbourne

Research Institute for Asia and Pacific, Sydney

Australia-Asia Institute, Sydney

Australia-China Council

Australian Defence Industries—Consulting Division

Pacific Research Institute, Sydney

Naval Institute

Royal United Service Institute

Greenpeace

# APPENDIX 2
## Australian Journals Which Contain Analyses of Security Studies

*Arena* (occasional articles)
*Australian Journal for International Affairs* (previously *Australian Outlook*)
*Australian Journal of Political Science* (occasional)
*Australian Defence*
*Australian Left Review* (occasional)
*Australian Quarterly* (occasional)
*Australian Society* (occasional)
*Asian Studies Association of Australia* (occasional)
*Asian Studies Review* (occasional)
*Current Affairs Bulletin* (occasional)
*Defender*
*Journal of the Australian Naval Institute* (occasional)
*Journal of Royal United Services Institutes of Australia*
*Labor Forum* (occasional)
*Maritime Studies*
*Pacific Review*
*Quadrant* (occasional)
*The Australian Journal of Politics and History* (occasional)

# APPENDIX 3
## Security Topics, Various Publications

Table A3-1 Security topics addressed in Australian Political Science Association (APSA) *Conference Papers* (1983–92); the *Australian Journal of International Affairs* (AJIA) (1983–92) and the *Journal of Interdisciplinary Peace Research* (IPR) (1989–92):[1]

| | APSA[2] conferences | AJIA[3] | IPR[4] |
|---|---|---|---|
| Security theory | 7 | 0 | 6 |
| Global security | 14 | 9 | 5 |
| Regional security (Europe, Middle East, South Asia) | 12 | 4 | 1 |
| Defense of Australia | 3 | 7 | 0 |
| Australia and security: global and US | 3 | 8 | 0 |
| Australian and Asia-Pacific security | 6 | 5 | 5 |
| Military security in the Asia-Pacific | 5 | 2 | 0 |
| Asia-Pacific arms control, CSBMs, cooperative security | 1 | 2 | 1 |
| Asia-Pacific security broadly defined (includes security and economics, environment, gender, human rights, culture, ethnicity, refugees, piracy, terrorism, etc.) | 11 | 3 | 6 |

1 Data on the table were compiled by Michael Shaik.

2 APSA is the professional association of Australian and New Zealand political scientists and international relations scholars.

3 AJIA is Australia's major international relations journal (previously *Australian Outlook*).

4 IPR started in 1989, is more theoretical in its orientation than AJIA and concerned to a much greater degree with what we have called the broad security agenda. (It should be noted that Australia has no scholarly defense journals. Two other important Australian journals are not covered here, *Pacific Research* published by the ANU's Peace Research Centre and the *Asia-Pacific Defence Reporter (APDR)*. Both cover issues under all the categories above and in some depth. But both tend to publish relatively short articles and neither are scholarly journals in the normal sense of that term, although the *Pacific Research* is produced entirely by academics and *APDR* has many academic contributors. The very large number of small articles would have made the task of categorization and collation impossible in the time available. A third journal which might have usefully been reviewed is *Current Affairs Bulletin* which contains occasional articles on security. But the purpose of those reviews is to detect changing trends and the publications/conference papers/conference themes reviewed here provide a good enough guide).

## The ANU's Security Research Centers

The three ANU centers which undertake research on security issues—the Strategic and Defence Studies Centre (SDSC), established in 1966; the Peace Research Centre (PRC), established in 1985; and the long-established Department of International Relations—undertake and publish considerably more security-related research than all academics in the rest of Australia combined. Indeed, of the seventy publications on regional security listed in a forthcoming bibliography on Australian foreign policy, 81 percent were by ANU authors. (The bibliography compiled by Pauline Kerr, David Sullivan and Robin Ward will be published in 1994.)

Outlined below are breakdowns of the research output of these centers as revealed by their in-house publication programs. Two caveats should be borne in mind when reviewing these data. First, the data only cover the in-house publications of center/department academics, not their output of commercially published books, chapters in books or papers in scholarly journals produced outside Canberra. Second, many of the in-house publications are written by outsiders. This is particularly true of SDSC where, for example, only one-third of the Working Papers and just over half the Canberra Papers in 1992 were written by SDSC academics or Visiting Fellows. In other words ANU in-house publications, particularly those of SDSC, are representative of a broader community of security researchers than just the ANU.

Table A3-2

Publications on security topics from PRC, SDSC and IR, 1983–92[1]

|  | PRC | SDSC | IR |
| --- | --- | --- | --- |
| Security theory | 11 | 4 | 5 |
| Global security | 20 | 8 | 8 |
| Regional security (Europe, Middle East, S. Asia) | 1 | 11 | 3 |
| Defense of Australia | 8 | 64 | 0 |
| Australia and security: global and US | 6 | 9 | 4 |
| Australian and Asia-Pacific security | 3 | 41 | 2 |
| Military security in the Asia-Pacific | 14 | 51 | 6 |
| Asia-Pacific arms control, CSBMs, cooperative security | 27 | 7 | 7 |
| Asia-Pacific security broadly defined (includes security and economics, environment, human rights, culture ethnicity, refugees, piracy, terrorism etc.) | 20 | 9[2] | 4 |

1. Data for SDSC were collated by Helen Wilson, other data by Michael Shaik.
2. Six on terrorism.

## ANU Conferences

The conferences run by SDSC, PRC and IR provide another indicator of the evolving security agenda of the ANU research community. Academic specialists from outside Canberra and from overseas present papers at these conferences and attendees come from all over the country. Conference proceedings are usually published in the in-house publications programs. Since the list does not fit easily with the above categories it is simply presented in toto.

*1983*

> Asian Perspectives on International Security (SDSC)
> Security Problems of NE Asia (SDSC)
> Civilian Infrastructure of Australian Defence (SDSC)

*1984*

> Australian and New Zealand Security (SDSC)

*1985*

> Forty Years On: Studies of World Change in the Four Decades after 1945 (IR)
> The Future of Arms Control (SDSC)

*1986*

 Air Power in the Defence of Australia (SDSC)

 International Workshop on Global Monitoring (PRC)

*1987*

 The Changing South Pacific and Implications for Australian Policy (IR)

 Security and Arms Control in the North Pacific (PRC and SDSC)

*1988*

 Soviet in the Pacific in the 1990s (SDSC)

 Australia and the World (SDSC)

*1989*

 New Directions in International Relations: Implications for Australia (IR)

 Australia and the Fourth NPT Review Conference (PRC)

 Women, Race, Ethnicity and the State in Australia (PRC)

 A New Security Dialogue for the Pacific (PRC) (Hawaii)

 Implications of New Technology for Australia and Regional Security (SDSC)

*1990*

 India's Strategic Future (SDSC)

 Security and Prosperity in Pacific Asia: Beyond the Cold War (ISIS, Malaysia-SDSC)

 Australia's Regional Security (IR)

 Australia and the Northeast Asian Ascendancy (IR)

 Women and Militarisation in the Asia-Pacific Region (PRC)

 Cooperative Security in the Pacific in the 1990s (PRC) (Hawaii)

*1991*

 Naval Confidence Building Regimes for the Asia-Pacific Region (PRC / ISIS Malaysia) (Kuala Lumpur)

 Biological Weapons Conventional Workshop (PRC)

 Korea 1991 Workshop (IR/Northeast Asia Program (NEA))

 Managing International Economic Relations in the Pacific in 1990s (IR)

 Strategic Studies in a Changing World (SDSC)

 Australia and Space (SDSC)

*1992*

 Security and the Korean Peninsula in the 1990s (IR)

 Arms Control in the Post–Cold War World (PRC)

 The Post–Cold War International Order (IR)

 The New Korean State: Post–Democratic Politics and Policy (NEA with the Monash Asia Institute and the Asia Research Institute, Murdoch University)

*1993*

 Taiwan's Changing Role in Asia-Pacific Region (NEA)

 Cooperative Economic and Security Regimes in the Asia-Pacific: Agendas for the 1990s (IR)

 China as a Great Power in the Asia-Pacific: Myths, Realities and Challenges (NEA / SDSC)

# APPENDIX 4
## Research Questions

The research questions which currently characterize the field:

* Australian defense policy (including alternative defense postures)
* Australia and regional defense cooperation
* Australia's alliance relationships in the post–Cold War world
* the emerging global security order and its implications for the region
* the emerging regional security order
* the regional military buildup
* confidence building regimes for the region
* regional maritime security (including piracy, poaching, drug running, refugees)
* nuclear and missile proliferation in Northeast Asia and South Asia
* nuclear-weapon free zones
* comparison of Australian and Asian perceptions of security, including the cultural determinants of security perceptions
* ethnonationalist conflict in the region
* the declining utility of aggression as a mode of statecraft in the region
* the economic growth democracy nexus and its security implications
* the evolution of cooperative regimes in the Asia-Pacific—economic and security
* the long-term security implications of rapid, but uneven, economic change, population growth, refugees and environmental change
* peacekeeping
* preventive diplomacy
* concepts of security
* implications of the proposals in the UN's *An Agenda for Peace* and Gareth Evans *Cooperating for Peace* for national and regional security
* ongoing studies of particular regional conflict/security issues: e.g., Cambodia, East Timor, the Spratlys, the Koreas, human rights, etc.

# APPENDIX 5
## Universities Offering Asia-Pacific Security or Related Studies

The following universities offer courses which deal, in whole or in part, with Asia-Pacific security issues:

### MA Programs

* Griffith University: an MA course
* Flinders University: a unit on nuclear proliferation will be on offer in the new 1994 MA program
* The Australian Defence Force Academy: offers an MA course
* The University of Queensland: offers an MA unit in Asia-Pacific security
* University of New England is offering an MA in Defence Studies
* Deakin University: offers MA programs in IR (forthcoming) and Defence Studies

### Undergraduate Programs

* La Trobe University: offers an interdisciplinary undergraduate program in Peace Studies
* Griffith University has a number of undergraduate units
* University of New South Wales: a new undergraduate course on the Asia-Pacific which includes security issues and a new course in diplomatic studies

# Asia Pacific Security Studies in Canada

DAVID B. DEWITT
and
BRIAN L. JOB

## Introduction and Overview[1]

For the last several years, Canada has pursued strategies to advance progress towards the nurturing and formation of a security community in the Asia Pacific. Its activities have sought to promote comprehensive dialogue, including the "non-like-minded," and to work closely with Asian partners to enhance the development of regional and subregional mechanisms to facilitate confidence building. An important feature of these efforts has been a reliance on the so-called "track two" approaches, which have sought to capitalize on resources in the academic and private sectors in Canada and to foster channels in which individuals inside and outside of government could engage in unconstrained interchange. These efforts have begun to have an impact, both inside Canada and within the region. However, the question remains as to whether or not, in times beset by domestic political uncertainty and extreme budgetary pressures, a proactive Canadian posture towards an Asia Pacific security agenda can be sustained.

"Security studies" in Canada, that is the activities of teaching, analysis, research and writing concerned with national and international security in private, governmental and advanced educational institutional settings, have largely reflected the same geopolitical and cultural factors which have shaped the national foreign policy and defense policy agendas. They have been oriented primarily towards the Euro-Atlantic, the NATO alliance partnership, and Cold War deterrence strategies and have been heavily influenced in terms of training, theory, method and substance by the United States. There are, however, certain distinctive elements of the examination of security in Canada. In substantive terms, these have been focused upon policy-oriented research and training on conflict resolution, peacekeeping, arms control and verification—representative and supportive of the multilateralist strain in Canadian foreign policy. Often, this work has been done within a small, activist community of nongovernmental organizations and institutes. But, again, matters of relative scale and "national style" come into play. The relevant Canadian university community is quite small; there is limited private/public foundation support for policy-oriented research; the Canadian academic, policy research and governmental official communities have not developed working relationships (for better or worse), such as those operative in Canberra, Seoul, Tokyo or Washington.

Alternately, from the perspective of someone looking ahead to the demands on those in security studies in the post–Cold War future, there are attractive features and great potential within the Canadian context. The baggage of the Cold War has been quickly discarded. Utilizing the broader definition of cooperative security has served to expand both the participants and audience. Several Canadian institutions do possess the critical mass of human resources and facilities to pursue an innovative agenda of security studies on the Asia Pacific, especially if key partnership relations with relevant regional institutions are developed. Finally, Ottawa's willingness to support and to cooperate with track two agendas and activities involving academics, experts, and officials in their unofficial roles, has proven and presumably should continue to prove fruitful in the regional and national contexts for Asia Pacific security affairs.

This paper is organized to cover a dual mandate: to survey the impact of the end of the Cold War on the field of security studies in Canada, and to delineate the needs and priorities, at national and regional levels, for furthering Asia Pacific security studies into the next century. Prevailing perceptions of national security and security interests, including the emergent post–Cold War attention to adoption of a cooperative security perspective, will be briefly reviewed in order to establish the broader context for an overview of security studies in Canada. Here, emphasis will be placed upon drawing broader conclusions and highlighting the characteristics of the Canadian environment most likely to be seen as distinctive by those in other Asia Pacific states. A similar emphasis is placed in the following section, which is a discussion of the nexus in Canada between the nongovernmental security studies community and those in the policy making and official communities in Ottawa.

The balance of the paper focuses upon Canada's orientation towards, and involvement in and with, the Asia Pacific.[2] The crucial issues are whether or not, and to what end, Canada can sustain its recently developed levels of interest and energy in Asia Pacific security affairs, seen in both official and security studies contexts. We look at the increasing importance and impact of the Pacific region on Canada and at the manner in which this has been recognized in thinking about Canadian interests in Asia Pacific security and policies to pursue those interests, (e.g., in the ASEAN process, through its development assistance programs, and regionally oriented arms control and conflict management activities). Finally, security studies in Canada relevant to Asia Pacific, per se, are discussed, as well as the various needs and priorities within Canada, and on regional or subregional bases.

## Canadian Security and Security Interests

Since 1945 Canada has sought to play the role of an activist, middle-power in international affairs. The central premises of its foreign policy have been membership in the Euro-Atlantic alliance community, maintenance of its relationship with the United States, support for an open international economy, and advancement, through multilateral avenues, of a wide range of confidence building and conflict resolution approaches aimed at crisis management, dampening proliferation and peacefully resolving regional conflicts. The exigencies of the Cold War threat environment shaped Canadian understandings of its primary security interests, these being geographically focused upon Europe and upon access to North America through the air and the Atlantic Ocean and, in turn, functionally promoted through active Canadian participation in the Western alliance, including the stationing of forces abroad and a close Canadian-US partnership on continental defense. Sovereignty protection per se, i.e., the patrolling of Canadian territorial waters and monitoring of Canadian maritime resources, has only risen in the public's eyes as a security concern in the last two decades and somewhat paradoxically has tended to emerge as a pitting of Canadian interests against those of some of its closest allies.

Being perceived as having an independent identity in world affairs has been, and remains, of central concern to Canada. In order to preserve and advance this identity, successive Canadian governments have tended to favor multilateralist and regionalist approaches to political, security and economic problems and have adopted substantive policy agendas in the security domain that emphasized consultation, peacekeeping, arms control and nonproliferation, i.e., tactics aimed at mitigating the central tensions of the Cold War and moderating the stark ideological images of adversaries and "non-like-minded." Thus, Canadian participation in multilateral organizations, especially the United Nations, stems not only from a deep substantive concern over these issues but also a conviction that Canadian interests are more successfully advanced in multilateral forums. In these, as opposed to bilateral contexts, middle- and small-powers are viewed as having a greater opportunity through their collective action to influence and to assuage unilateral great-power interests. This logic has, of course, been particularly important in Canadian/US economic and political relations. It has also led to Canadians adopting a broader perspective on "security" relationships that extended beyond the narrowly military.[3]

The end of the Cold War, however, found Canada in a somewhat unusual position in the international security context. On the one hand, the disappearance of the Soviet threat swept away the rationale for much of Canada's traditional defense policy and defense deployments.[4] In 1992, the decision was taken to close Canadian bases in Europe and to return forward-based troops home. Although this was largely for budgetary reasons, it was more important in its symbolic reversal of a central tenant of postwar security policy. Demands for a peace dividend and domestic budget relief have begun to erode the Canadian Forces' capital equipment acquisition plans and priorities, which were characterized in the rhetoric of domestic political debate as artifacts of a Cold War mentality. Current defense policy statements focus upon risks in a new and less certain threat environment, highlight the regionalized character of the emerging post–Cold War security order, accent the importance of protection of Canadian sovereignty, and emphasize Canadian peacekeeping efforts. But, pending the promised, wholesale review of Canadian defense and armed forces by the newly elected Liberal government, there exists no clear articulation of defense priorities and policies.

On the other hand, because of the distinctive features of its foreign and security relations during the Cold War period, Canada could find itself well-positioned to further its middle-power role in the current and future international system. There is, in essence, a smaller legacy of Cold War mind-set and doctrine to dispel in Canada than in most other Western alliance states. Thus, while seen as a contributing ally, Canada is also known for its disavowal of nuclear roles and capabilities for itself, for its advancement of non-self-serving strategies to dampen proliferation of NBC weapons and for its pursuit of policies that envisage security enhancement as involving political, economic and social dimensions and strategies beyond deterrence. Through its active participation in regional and multilateral forums, it has built a reputation as a state with few, if any, vested interests in regional conflicts and as a state that, as a result of its having to manage a sometimes difficult but necessarily close relationship with its neighboring superpower, is an effective operator in multilateral contexts. Thus, as issues of conflict management, confidence building, peacekeeping, and nonproliferation take on newly realized importance on the agendas of major powers and of regional and global institutions, Canadian experience and expertise has been recognized and called upon.[5]

For those responsible for the design and implementation of Canada's activist foreign policy agenda of the last five decades, namely the ministers and mandarins of the Department of External Affairs and International Trade Canada (EAITC),[6] the emerging character of the new world order has reinforced their tendency to view security as a broadly based concept and to see military policies as only a single facet of what are Canadian security interests, broadly conceived. To this end, the phrase "cooperative security" has been adopted by Ottawa as a term designed to highlight to Canadians the distinctive character of the new world order and, of perhaps even greater significance, to provide a descriptive label for Canadian foreign policy initiatives in regional and global forums. Cooperative security, therefore, has numerous aspects: One is that security must be viewed as "mutual security"; it can not be attained unilaterally by any state. Threats to security arise not only in interstate interrelations but also from domestic and regional instabilities caused by tensions of an ethnic or nationalist nature and by sharp disparities in conditions of life. Security interests are not separable from economic interests, especially insofar as maintenance of political stability is necessary for the advancement of domestic, and often regional, growth. Critical as well is the maintenance of open international economic relations. In addition, the security agenda is broadened to include so-called unconventional or nontraditional security threats such as environmental degradation, drug trafficking and the irregular movement of peoples.[7] And, in what has proven to be a somewhat more controversial position when posited by Canadian officials in international forums, the advancement of cooperative security is seen to require, on domestic levels, the implementation of "principles of good governance" and "securing democracy and respect for human values."[8]

The notion of "cooperative security" is important to the understanding of contemporary Canadian security relations. It has had impact on policy-making and policy implementation. The consensus surrounding these ideas appears in fact sufficient to transcend changes of government. However, the possible adoption of this concept as a leitmotif for Canadian policy also highlights a critical dilemma, namely that Canada does not possess the human and fiscal resources to broadly implement any full agenda of cooperative security. While singular concentration upon Europe is no longer viable, nor can Canada spread its efforts across all other regions or subregions or in all other multilateral forums. Making choices and establishing selective priorities, however, has proven difficult for Canada—with its inclinations towards global activism and a foreign policy tradition of presence, albeit with a Eurocentricist cast.

## Security Studies in Canada

There is a symbiotic relationship between the character of a state's foreign and security policies and the character of security studies, broadly conceived, within that state, both shaped by the same geopolitical and cultural biases. Certainly, this is true for Canada, where one does find a Canadian "style" of security studies. This is true not only in approach and content, but also in reflecting factors such as the relative scale of available human and financial resources in comparison to countries with longer established and larger institutional capacities, and national attitudes about the appropriate relationships among private, public, academic and governmental actors in the conduct and formation of foreign policy.

When assessing the current status of Canadian security studies, it is important, therefore, to keep in mind its relatively short history,[9] the relative size of the overall institutional bases from which it springs and the implications of geographic dispersion. All but several of Canada's approximately fifty universities were built during the last seventy-five years. While independent in programmatic terms, Canadian universities are state-supported, largely through provincial government funding. As far as matters of scale are concerned, Canadians tend to compare themselves to the United States, with the index of comparison being roughly 1:10. But as regards university resources, the United States, with its premier private institutions and network of large state universities, has established an advantage that is substantially in excess of the usual bilateral ratio. On the other hand, compared to their counterparts in the United Kingdom, funding cuts for Canadian universities have not yet become extreme. For those looking across the Pacific, Canadian universities present an attractive training and research environment with their established excellence in relevant technical sciences, quality professional schools, strong programs in the social sciences and overall unrestricted research climate.

By the 1970s most Canadian universities offered curriculums covering the range of subjects relevant to security studies, including international relations theory, Canadian foreign and defense policy, international political economy and the history of war. Similarly, most schools had some capacity to offer specialized "area studies" work, including language training, works on the countries and regions encompassed by the OECD, on the Communist world and on parts of the so-called developing world, notably those within the Commonwealth and Francophone blocs. However, while these represented what could be seen as necessary background or ancillary programs to security studies, they did not represent a solid core of security studies, per se.

## The Military and Strategic Studies Program (MSSP)

The establishment in 1971 of the Military and Strategic Studies Program (MSSP) by the Department of National Defence provided the key impetus and resources for the creation and maintenance of the field of security studies on a national basis in Canada. Without the program, work on security studies would have certainly proceeded through the efforts of individual scholars at separate institutions, but without the synergism and continuity provided by the operation of a network of security studies programs in universities across the country. Indeed, in many of its key aspects the MSSP can be seen as a model program of its type, especially for a middle-sized country with limited resources that wishes to promote security studies in multiple institutions not affiliated with, or directed by, the government itself. Furthermore, anticipating the latter sections of this paper, the national security studies picture of the future in Canada (including its capacities regarding the Asia Pacific) will be significantly affected by the health and direction of the program.

The MSSP is administered through the Office of the Assistant Deputy Minister for Policy, with a national advisory committee composed of academics, department officials and representatives from the armed forces and the public sector. The purpose of the program is to promote teaching, research and public education to advance understanding of the political, historical, social and technical aspects of international security questions, with emphasis upon those questions that are relevant to the interests of Canada. To this end, the MSSP has funded, on a five-year cyclical basis, a set of strategic studies centers at Canadian universities—eight centers until 1986, up to fourteen centers since the resources for the program were approximately tripled in that year. Grants to these centers have ranged from Can. $60,000 to $135,000 annually, supporting a broad range of curriculum, teaching, fellowship, library and faculty research activities as well as serving as a multiplier effect by providing the seed-monies necessary to obtain grants from other sources. The faculty associated with these programs supervise the bulk of the graduate students in Canada doing thesis research on security-related topics.[10]

The MSS Program has a further direct impact on facilitating security studies by Canadian students through the funding of a national competition for graduate and postdoctoral fellowships.[11] Of the roughly Can. $2 million currently expended on the MSS Program, about one-quarter is allocated to this end. While this scholarship program is only open to Canadians, one of its important features is that it funds Canadians doing graduate work abroad, thus enabling each year a small number of the best and brightest to study at premier institutions in the United States and Europe. Over the years, increasing numbers of graduates from MSSP-supported undergraduate and MA programs and scholarships have gone on to careers in governmental service, in External Affairs or in Defence. Many of the current faculty of security studies in Canadian institutions, while not necessarily receiving their PhD's at Canadian schools, did utilize MSSP postdoctoral fellowships as the vehicles to start their careers and to gain their university positions.

Over the twenty years or so that the MSSP has been operating, there has been a marked increase in the quality of research and analysis, the level of debate and the role of public involvement in issues related to international politics in general, and Canada's role in international peace and security issues in particular. Thus, there appears to be a general agreement in both academic and governmental circles, that the MSS Program has been and continues to be successful. Certainly, for a relatively small investment by a single federal department, there has been a return far exceeding initial expectations.

## The Substantive Scope of Security Studies

Three observations are in order concerning the substantive scope of security studies in Canada. First, the bulk of work has focused on the traditional concerns: the operation of the Western alliance, the strategies and policies of the United States, including its continental defense partnership; and multilateral approaches to peace and security. Somewhat paradoxically albeit perhaps typically Canadian, relatively little critical attention has been focused upon Canadian security interests and defense policy, per se.

Second, while the substance and direction of Canadian security studies have not been "radical" in character or challenging of the basic parameters of the Cold War system, Canadian scholars have pursued somewhat distinctive avenues within the mainstream. Thus, for instance, prominent Canadian scholars are known for advocating reassurance strategies as more effective than traditional deterrence strategies, for focusing upon preventing accidental war and the avoidance and control of international crises, and for inclusion of ideological adversaries in confidence building processes. There also always has been a peace studies and peace advocacy tradition in Canada, pursued by a few academics and groups of dedicated citizens, but widely respected by political and public leaders. These points being made, however, the end of the Cold War in 1989 did not result in a rapid transformation of the foci of security studies. The broader implications of a cooperative security perspective, such as the relevance of resource scarcities and population movement, for peace and security are being recognized but there has not been sustained research output within the securities studies community on these topics to date.

It is interesting to note that while in many disciplines and on questions that concern them there would be a disctinctive outline exhibited by Canada's Francophone academic community, concerning security studies this does not appear to be the case. Other than through some greater attention in writings at the theoretical level regarding the international system to the European, especially French, political sociological tradition, as far as the choice of topics and the manner of their study, security studies scholarship by Francophone Canadians appears essentially similar to that done by their Anglophone counterparts.[12]

Third, while Canadian universities have been home to the development of research and the teaching of expertise in technical areas relevant to aspects of international peace and security concerns, unlike what has occurred in the United States the security studies community in Canada engages few if any natural or physical scientists, engineers or mathematicians. Security studies has remained largely the purview of social scientists, particularly political scientists. On the other hand, the Canadian government itself does call upon technical scientists, many at universities, for guidance and research in areas such as verification, communication, settlement of territorial disputes and the control of proliferation of NBC weapons.

## Some Concerns

Over the past decade or so, the Canadian research community in security studies is doing rather well. There is a base network of security studies programs at Canadian universities whose short-term future appears relatively secure. There is scholarship support for students pursuing advanced degrees in security-related fields. However, this being said, certain features of the Canadian context are concerning when one assesses the future.

First, and in the scheme of things, a minor point: There are relatively few specifically Canadian outlets for research and commentary on security studies. In part, this reflects the relative size of the Canadian population and the subset of readers who would follow informed writing on international affairs. In part, it also reflects the fact that most Canadian academics chose, for career advancement purposes and to reach specific audiences of specialists, to publish either in book form or in the major academic journals in their field. For security studies, therefore, in addition to the major university and commercial presses, this means publication in *International Security*, *World Politics*, *International Studies Quarterly*, and *Journal of Conflict Resolution*—all US-based journals—and *Survival*, *Adelphi Papers*, *Review of International Studies*, and *Millennium*, all published in the United Kingdom. The Canadian quarterlies, *International Journal* and *Études internationales*, serve respectively Anglophone and Francophone audiences; however, they only occasionally carry articles on international security. A newly established journal, *Canadian Foreign Policy*, while not exclusively devoted to this purpose may come to be the niche for work specifically concerning Canadian security.[13]

Much more important is prognosis regarding the availability of financial resources to sustain a "cooperative security" studies agenda into the future. The public purse in Canada, basically the key source of educational funds in this country, is dramatically tightening. Institutional growth has basically come to a halt. Ironically, this comes at a time when there are outstanding young PhD's being produced in Canada (or Canadians abroad). Yet, there are virtually no university or public service openings to provide them proper professional employment and career prospects. There are no sources in Canada for funding to create new faculty appointments, and the raising of private endowments for such purposes is a strategy which Canadian universities have only recently begun to adopt.[14] Thus, with an effective cap on the talent pool, one is essentially stuck with the current configuration of faculty just at the time when the demand has arisen for the study of a new security studies agenda by persons with recent training and relevant field research experience, technical training or language skills.

These circumstances are exacerbated by two structural features of the Canadian context: the fact that there are very few sources of long-term funding for research programs; and the fact that, unlike most other countries, within Canada there are no substantial private or quasi-private research institutes with sustained and assured funding. With the exception of the DND-MSSP competitions award, neither Canadian foundations nor government-funded research programs provide sustained, long-term financial support for research in one or more areas of security studies.[15]

In Canada, one finds neither large, private foundations (such as the US-based Ford or MacArthur Foundations) with the resources to sustain long-term public policy, training and research programs, nor research institutes with endowments or major, *long-term* funding from governmental or a mix of governmental and private sources (such as the US Institute of Peace, the East-West Center or the foundations in Japan and Korea.) Only in exceptional instances are Canadians or Canadian institutions eligible to apply for funding from non-Canadian foundations. The result is a combination of a relative dearth of public policy oriented security studies research in Canada (equivalent for instance to that produced by the Brookings Institute), and an absence of research positions for experts working outside academia on security questions.[16] The private sector in Canada has traditionally been adverse to providing funding to public policy institutes and think tanks.[17]

## The Interrelations Among Branches of Government and the Security Studies Community

A country's security community, i.e., all those who have an interest in the nature of security and defense policies and their various elements, extends across academia, private and public institutes and various branches of government including the armed forces. In many countries, this is a close-knit community, perhaps even a closed community. Often there is a relatively constant flow of individuals from one role to another, given changes of government and the vagaries of politics. There is also often substantial reliance by government upon the advice and expertise of outsiders, not only on technical issues such as chemical or biological weaponry but also on the formation of policy itself, e.g., as in the process leading to the latest Australian white paper. Thus, it is somewhat odd, that in a middle-power like Canada, with a relatively small security community to start with, there are fewer linkages among its components, in and out of government, than might be expected.

Canada's civil service, especially in its elite branches, is modeled in the British tradition. The majority of professional appointments are made to young persons with strong backgrounds in the humanities and social sciences, often with postgraduate training in one of those disciplines or in law. The aim, especially in the foreign service, is to mold persons as generalists, rather than specialists. Individuals are rotated from position to position every three years or so. This is done presumably to avoid pitfalls of narrowness and policy rigidity. On the other hand, it means that it is difficult to sustain and build pockets of expertise within the bureaucracy. Unlike the United States, there are relatively few political appointments at any level of the public service. Also, there is very little lateral movement in Canada between government service and the academic and private sectors.

The two branches of the Canadian government with key responsibility for national security are the Department of External Affairs and International Trade

Canada and the Department of National Defence. They are, however, quite distinct bureaucratic entities which operate separately in many ways. The key to understanding their relationship is the knowledge that, within Canada, defense policy has always been viewed as derivative to and in service of foreign policy. Although officials in both departments regularly consult across departmental boundaries on operational matters, overall international peace and security policy is the purview of External Affairs. Even on matters requiring substantial technical knowledge such as peacekeeping or verification, for example, EAITC has established offices within its own organization to take the lead on policy development and be able to participate whenever appropriate in field operations.

There are also differentiations between these two departments in terms of their geographical and functional orientations which are also important. With its aspirations to sustain a global foreign policy, External Affairs always has maintained a balance between geographic and functional divisions—strength in both being essential for pursuing the Canadian agenda of engaged regionalism and multilateralism. Of its regional bureaus, those of the United States and Europe have held preeminent positions, responsible for Canada's key bilateral relations. On the functional side, trade, legal, international organizations, and international security have remained among the key divisions, and the department has invested heavily in the personnel commitments necessary to sustain the technical expertise required in key areas such as arms control and nonproliferation of weapons of mass destruction. While maintaining a small Policy Planning Staff until recently, the department has not given it a priority position. This is perhaps due to a combination of factors: a tradition of strong ministers with their own vision; the dominance of a core of key departmental mandarins, and the general attitude that as a department of generalists, planning is not a separable function.

Juxtaposed to the Department of External Affairs, the Department of National Defence presents a quite different picture. After allowing for the fact that it exercises its functional responsibilities on an altogether different dimension, there are comparative differences in the operating tone of its bureaucracy, its regional emphasis and its structure. The Canadian Forces are modeled after their British antecedents; that is, there is a strong ethos in support of a professional military. Thus, while the department draws its officer corps primarily from Canada's three military colleges or from graduates of civilian universities, promotion and advancement are predominantly based on service and experience. Unlike the United States, for instance, the obtaining of postgraduate degrees by officers is not yet required nor necessarily encouraged by senior ranks. On the other hand, its high professional standards, its relatively small size, and its great emphasis upon training ensure that the Canadian Forces have bilingual language capabilities, and high levels of technical training in military, organizational and logistical skills. This has allowed the continuation, even in spite of budget cutbacks and disappointments concerning procurement programs, of a belief that the Canadian armed forces must be, and are, capable of employing their skills anywhere in the world at a moment's notice—witness Canadian involvement in every United Nations peacekeeping operation.

The geographical priorities of DND have followed naturally from the nature of the three priorities of Canadian postwar defense policy, i.e., Euro-Atlantic collective defense, North American continental defense, and the "out-of-area" contingencies pursued principally through the United Nations.[18] Thus, defense planning has focused on European theater commitments and on continental defense, with doctrine, procurement decisions and force structure following accordingly. As a result, regions such as the Asia Pacific arena have been "over the horizon"—an American sea and responsibility—from DND's perspective. The result is that the department has maintained limited capacities for regional analysis beyond the European theater.

Since WW II, the Department of National Defence has maintained its own research and strategic analysis branches for these purposes. In organizational terms, these have evolved from the wartime Defence Research Board into a division between a set of technical research facilities (Defence Research Establishments) focusing upon chemical weapons, oceanography, etc., and the ORAE (Operational Research and Analysis Establishment) which is responsible for strategic and regional analyses. Recent reorganization has taken place to the effect that the ORAE is no longer an autonomous agency; it now reports to the ADM Policy. In light of this reform, i.e., its symbolic implications, as well as the general cuts to funding and personnel experienced throughout the department, whether or not the department will maintain and encourage an in-house unit able to produce high-quality analyses—analyses which are "independent" both in terms of their ability to question accepted departmental wisdom and in terms of their being more than synthesis of otherwise easily available information—remains to be seen.

The nexus between the Canadian government (that is, officials within EAITC and DND) and the nongovernmental security studies community is somewhat ambiguous. Certainly, it is not equivalent to the models found in other Asia Pacific partners, e.g., the "partnership" relationship of Australia, the "revolving-door" model of the United States, or the gentle or rigid co-optation that exists in other countries. Canadian officials are skeptical of the value of opening their files and their decision-making processes to the scrutiny and input of outsiders.[19] They also appear skeptical of academic research; even when it is intended to have policy relevance, it is often viewed as overly theoretical and conceptual, at times empirically incomplete and/or dated. On an informal, ad hoc basis, officials in both departments do draw informally on academics and other nongovernmental experts, usually by commissioning academics to undertake studies on a particular topic on quite short notice. Occasionally, officials receive brief study leaves which are taken at Canadian universities. As noted earlier, lateral movement in either direction, unlike in many other countries is very uncommon.

As noted in the previous section, EAITC and DND, however, remain the key sources of discretionary funds to support academic research on security studies. These funds are granted through a competitive and arm's-length process through two programs: the MSS Program in DND and the Cooperative Security Competition Program (CSCP) in EAITC[20]—whose origins, purpose, and size deserve specific comment.

As for the bottom line concerning whether or not research done through the MSSP or CSCP sponsorship has a significant impact by informing policy and policy formation within their respective parent departments in the Canadian government, one could at best give a guardedly positive response. In general terms both EAITC and DND view with reservation their relationship, or potential relationships, with the academic and NGO communities. While some might prefer to develop along the lines of the Australian "partnership" model, overall there appears to be agreement about the advantages and cultural preferences for both sides to conduct themselves at arm's length from each other.

There are, however, certain specific areas where strong professional relationships between the government and sectors of academia have developed, to their mutual benefit. These are the functional areas of international security—e.g., arms control—areas in other words, in which state-of-the-art technical, practical, or regional area studies expertise is required in order to conduct effective and innovative policy initiatives. For example, since the early days of the CSCE and the CFE, Canada has developed widely recognized expertise in the broad area of confidence and security building measures—policies, instruments, and practice. EAITC, along with DND, have sponsored researchers at numerous Canadian universities working, for example, in the general area of verification: on satellite, air and seismic surveillance; on legal issues including space, air and maritime law; on the international politics of decision making, threat perception, confidence building instruments and procedures; on the formal (mathematical) modeling of the implementation and verification of agreements. The Verification Research Unit (VRU) of the Department of External Affairs has, through this strategy, become internationally noted and respected. Another recent contractual arrangement was the underwriting of the North Pacific Cooperative Security Dialogue (NPCSD) project housed at York University with the mandate to conduct a three-year program of research, exchange and workshops drawing on both academic and other experts from the seven North Pacific countries and other interested actors. In the case of both the VRU and the NPCSD, it is clear the arrangements undertaken by the Canadian government to involve nongovernmental experts provided results used by both itself, other governments and international agencies in the formulation of policy.

Before concluding this section, mention needs be made of Canada's track record and human resource base, in government and in institutes and universities, in the area of international development. By facilitating political, economic and social stability in many countries in the so-called developing world, Canadian aid programs have been relevant to the promotion of peace and security. Furthermore, Canada has established strong credentials in the aid program formulation and delivery fields with its International Development Research Centre and Canadian International Development Agency (CIDA). While not mandated to address issues of peace and security per se, it is increasingly realized in Canada that their work relates to the enhancement of national, state and regional security—in keeping with the understanding of security encompassed in the cooperative security concept. Thus, while CIDA has and will always support both field work and research in a range of disciplines viewed as linked directly to their principal focus on development, it has begun in recent years to sponsor work exploring the linkages between modes of governance (e.g., militarization, democratization and extension of human rights) and development, clearly areas emerging as critical to long-term sustainability of peace and security. Two of the primary regional foci for such work are Southeast Asia and South Asia, as well as the oceans around them.[21]

In summary, while the overall picture of government-academic relations concerning security studies leaves room for improvement, nevertheless one can point to significant developments and accomplishments. Within both EAITC and DND, the younger generation of officials (whether civilian or in uniform) are more aware of and comfortable with the potential positive roles of outside experts. The two funding programs—DND/MSSP and EAITC/CSCP—mentioned in this survey (and others in related areas, such as the Pacific 2000 Fund, the Canada-ASEAN Centre programs, CIDA and IDRC support and NATO Fellowships) do provide Canadian academics and experts with opportunities to conduct policy relevant research.[22] Although the tradition of policy-making in Canada, especially on security matters, is top-down and in-house, there is a constant effort to find ways, often informal, to exchange views and to consult in areas of mutual interest and where there is appropriate expertise. While the absence of lateral mobility hinders the development of trust and confidence in how the components of the security studies community view each other, and while it stifles the introduction of ideas and methods which challenge conventional wisdom, the Canadian community is sufficiently small that there are opportunities for the aggressive and creative academic interested in policy relevant issues to engage counterparts in government and at times even to be heard. Finally, in those areas where political and/or bureaucratic elites perceive the value of bringing scholars into the process, the results usually are welcomed by both. The recent experiences in the NPCSD and the VRU, along with the decade-old effort with the Canadian Consultative Group on Disarmament and Arms Control Affairs, provide sufficient evidence to be encouraged about the future prospects for an improved and still more active relationship between the government, its officials and outside experts and academics.

# Canada and the Asia Pacific

Increasingly, Canadians are beginning to appreciate the opportunities and obligations afforded them by virtue of being a Pacific state with human and material ties to Asia. However, this realization has been slow in coming. Throughout most of its history Canada has been oriented towards the Atlantic, the European continent beyond it, and the United States to the south. The Canadian heritage is primarily European; the bulk of Canada's population resides in the eastern half of the country. Its demographic center of gravity rests in Southern Ontario and Quebec within close proximity to the United States. The Canadian economy was structured first through its relationships with Europe and, in the twentieth century, through the dominant presence of the United States, which continues to account for roughly three-quarters of Canada's trade. Foreign direct investment is similarly skewed towards the United States, and Canadian economic policy in general is of necessity reactive to US influence. Canadian foreign relations, after the cutting of colonial ties, have been primarily Eurocentric within the larger framework of association with the United States. Canadian security policy has been shaped by the perceived priority of being called upon to defend the Western

European landmass. Indeed, throughout the post–WW II era, Asia and the Pacific were essentially viewed by Canadians through Euro-Atlanticist, Cold War lenses, with the central feature of this region being the United States and its agenda of reconstruction, containment and power projection.

However, on all of these dimensions an Asian factor is becoming more salient.[23] In a largely stagnant global economic picture, Canadians recognize that Asia, as the one region of dynamic growth, will be the engine for economic growth in the coming decades. Canadian trade with Asia has for the last decade roughly equaled or surpassed Canadian trade with Europe. Business interests including investment between Asia and Canada have increased in absolute and relative terms to become second only to Canada's economic and commercial relations with the United States. As well, the Asian fact has increasingly taken on a human face within Canadian society. While Asians have been finding their way to Canada since the turn of the century, in the last decade their numbers as immigrants and refugees have swelled to the point where they constitute the largest source of population influx to this country (over 100,000 annually). Their presence, in turn, is being increasingly felt in the cultural, economic, and social lives of the urban centers in which they live, mainly in Ontario and British Columbia. As Canadians of Asian background become more involved within the political process, their interests in economic, social, religious and political conditions with the states to which they retain cultural and family ties will correspondingly have an impact upon the federal government's foreign policy agenda.[24]

Canada's elected leaders, in turn, are coming to terms with the Asia Pacific. The Canadian government realizes that if it does not engage in the Asia Pacific, it will simply be passed by and left out. The problem, however, is how to engage effectively; that is, how to articulate Canadian interests in the region, how to advance these interests on economic, political and security dimensions; and how to sustain the attention of Asian states and maintain productive relations with them. The Canadian government has attempted to do so in the past and largely failed. Canada needs to dispel its reputation for being an inattentive and intermittent participant in regional affairs, and therefore a marginal player in Asian eyes. To be taken seriously, its initiatives must be thoughtful and designed to take advantage of perceived Canadian "comparative advantages." Canada cannot take up a predetermined role for itself in the region or its subregions; on the other hand, Asian partners are receptive to Canadian involvement and to Canadian perspectives on, and preferred modes of dealing with, international problems.

## Asia Pacific and the Canadian Government

Canada's instinctive reaction has been to look to multilateralist and regionalist, rather than bilateral, approaches for advancing its interests in the Asia Pacific region. The larger context for dealing with regional political/security questions traditionally has been within the rubric of the United Nations. Thus, Canada has supported, through its diplomacy and commitment of human and fiscal resources, peacekeeping and disarmament/proliferation agendas vis-à-vis Asia, for example, in the joint supervisory commissions in Indo-China, in its role in the Korean War and in promoting the adoption of IAEA, MTCR, and UN arms transfer registry provisions by Asian states. On security matters more generally, Canada has engaged itself to the full extent possible in the ASEAN PMC process and more recently in the SOM and development of the Regional Forum, as well as in other subregional processes such as the quadrilateral meetings of planning staffs. There are also a host of environmental, maritime resource and oceans management regimes focusing attention in whole or in part on the Pacific (or the Arctic) in which Canada takes an active role. On economic fronts, Canada's aims have been to preserve as open an economy as possible across the Pacific and within Asia. It has therefore actively supported all efforts to create multilateral mechanisms, e.g., PECC, APEC, and PBEC, to facilitate Asia Pacific economic relations and understandably has been particularly sensitive about any initiatives put forward by Asia Pacific states which might exclude North American or Canadian membership and participation.[25]

Ottawa's bilateral relations with key Asian states, namely Japan, China, and Russia, extend beyond the last hundred years. China always has held a particular fascination for Canadians; but this has not always translated into a particularly effective diplomatic relationship with the Chinese government.[26] On the other hand, while economic ties with Japan have been much more important (Japan currently accounts for over half of Canada's trade with Asia), Canada has not developed a commensurate understanding of this country and of how to conduct relations with its government. Russia, of course, came to be viewed in Canadian eyes as the key adversary of the Cold War, the Pacific character of this relationship for Ottawa largely defined in terms of Soviet military threat. However, there persisted in Canadian foreign policy during this era a strain of independence vis-à-vis the dominant and monolithic interpretation of Communism emanating from the United States. Through the influence of seasoned individual diplomats with Asian experience, Canada was more prone to recognize the indigenous character of Asian revolutionary societies as well as to appreciate the long-term payoff in engagement with non-like-minded players. Thus, Canada recognized the People's Republic of China, it traded with China and Russia despite US views of such ties, and it exercised a dissenting voice, albeit not a vigorous one, on US involvement in Vietnam. The record of these actions left in the minds of Asians the view that Canada could be distinctive from the United States and that it saw the Asian world differently than its superpower neighbor.

Today, two related phenomena have come to redefine Canadian interests in the Asia Pacific. One is the end of the Cold War(s) in Asia, the other is the combination of the forces of economic growth and democratization sweeping through the region. Focusing on the first, since the demise of ideological confrontation there is no longer the prospect, in the short or medium term, of war between any of the region's five major powers (the United States, Russia, Japan, China, and India). What is now of concern are the threats posed by proliferation of high-tech conventional and NBC weapons, by the resurgence of long-standing territorial disputes and attempts to assert sovereignty and by domestic conflict arising from confrontation over ethnicity or economic disparity or both. For Canada, the current environment in the region raises substantial concerns over issues that have traditionally engaged Canadian attention: the lack of viable regional or subregional mechanisms for dialogue and conflict management, the proliferation of dangerous weapons, the protection of human rights and the promotion of effective conflict management mechanisms.

On the economic front, Canada's primary interests are the maintenance of an open international economy and the prevention of regional or internal upheavals that erode the conditions necessary for continued or greater economic prosperity. In this context, in the short term, Canada is concerned that trade and investment flows remain unfettered and that exclusivist regional trading blocs do not arise which do not include Canada or have the potential of discrimination against its economic participation. In the long term, however, economics and security interests are not separable because continued political stability, within and across borders, is seen as dependent upon the achievement of a relatively sustained equal distribution of wealth, a dampening of ethnic and religious tensions that tend to undermine the state, progress towards open societies and the protection of human rights, and the employment of environmentally sound, sustainable development practices that secure populations against water and other resource scarcities.

The inseparable quality of economic and of political/military interests is, in essence, what is captured by the notion of "cooperative security"; and it is within this framework that Canada began several years ago to redefine its interests vis-à-vis the Asia Pacific.[27] This was at a time when the emerging parameters of the post-Cold War Asia Pacific security order were just becoming apparent, and there was, on the part of several key regional players, particularly Japan and the United States, a reluctance to accept the idea that the traditional security strategies and bilateral arrangements which had proved successful over the last forty years would not suffice into the future. Without going into the details of the security developments within the region, which are charted elsewhere,[28] suffice it to say that there has been a noticeable change in these attitudes.

Thus, while several years ago Canadian efforts to advance a cooperative security concept and to encourage acceptance of multilateralism were viewed by regional players as intrusive, naive, or at least premature, today most of these same states have come to espouse similar themes. Indeed, in colloquial terms, where Canada once found itself on the forward edge of the wave on these matters, events have virtually overtaken Ottawa to the point where it now has to swim hard simply to keep up with the accelerating pace and scope of regional and subregional developments. It is in this context that the efforts of the nongovernmental security studies communities in Canada, and the relationship between them and Ottawa's policymakers in so-called track two processes, becomes especially important. As will be discussed below, in particular regarding the Canadian initiative known as North Pacific Cooperative Security Dialogue and subsequent regional developments such as the Committee on Security Cooperation in Asia Pacific, Canadian officials, academics and other experts have proceeded in tandem in pursuit of cooperative security objectives in the region.

## The Pacific and the Canadian Military

The Canadian defense establishment has found, within the context of its larger need to adjust to the post–Cold War order, difficulties in coming to terms with Asia Pacific. Canada's security commitments in the Pacific have never approached those in the Atlantic because of its overriding priority of protecting the ocean supply routes to Europe from the Soviet threat, because of its reliance, like Asian states themselves, on the United States to manage the Pacific; and because of a relative lack of resources to sustain substantial forces in its Pacific waters. In the context of peacekeeping and UN-mandated operations, e.g., the Korean War, the supervisory commissions in Indo-China or the more recent missions to Cambodia, the Canadian military has been involved in Asia. Canadian military officers, of course, serve as attachés in Canadian missions, and military personnel regularly visit the region. Canadian naval forces participate in joint RIMPAC exercises. Limited maritime surveillance and coastal patrol activities are undertaken along the Pacific coast. However, these diverse Pacific-related activities—that is, the multilaterally sponsored missions (by definition episodic in nature) and the quasi-diplomatic, training, exercise and patrol activities just noted—do not add up to produce a policy and program of significant or sustained presence in Asia Pacific. As a result, relatively few uniformed officers or civilian defense officials have an intuitive feel for or inclination regarding the Asia Pacific and its regional security concerns.

Prior to 1987 even the most general Canadian defense policy statements tended to ignore the Pacific. It was the white paper of that year which announced that Canada now recognized itself as a "three-ocean country" and set forth commitments to acquire additional resources, including nuclear-powered submarines, to effectuate a greater presence, mainly for sovereignty protection, and increasingly in the Pacific and the Arctic. However, the policy outlook and associated procurement and deployment agendas in this white paper were not implemented. The end of the Cold War undercut the rationale of the former and the pressures of budget cuts decimated much of the latter. This being said, naval procurement programs for new frigates and for smaller, coastal patrol-type vessels have gone forward, albeit for fewer numbers and over longer periods of time than planned.[29] Official statements of 1991 and 1992 reaffirmed that efforts were going forward to bring about "balance" between Pacific and Atlantic deployments, which is taking place.

It remains, however, a bit difficult to see just how Asia Pacific might be brought within the department's horizons. The traditional logic of the military—that is, the logic of threat determining commitment and targetted force deployment—does not apply. There are no security threats to Canada from Asia that could be addressed through military presence in the region. The "threats" to Canadian interests concerning the Pacific instead are of two distinct sorts—threats to sovereignty arising from challenges to Canadian ocean borders and to regulation and protection of ocean resources, and threats to peace and stability in the region calling for multilateral, cooperative security responses. But both of these are concerns for which it is difficult to plan and equip, especially since quite different equipment configurations could be required, depending on the scenarios and contingencies seen as most likely and relevant for Canadian response. Directions and choices have to be first spelled out at the policy level before military planners can proceed intelligently. In the absence of an overall planning framework (one is promised from the defense review to be undertaken by the new government), the Canadian public, Canadian politicians, and the Canadian

Forces are going to continue to be frustrated, both with each other domestically and vis-à-vis others in the region.

## Track Two Diplomacy: The NPCSD and the Future

In 1990, the Canadian government took decisions to take on a more active role in the Asia Pacific. Then Secretary of State Joe Clark began to promote what was labeled a "Canadian initiative for a North Pacific Cooperative Security Dialogue (NPCSD)."[30] The basic thrust of this initiative was to assert a Canadian presence in the region "commensurate with its political and economic interests and its proven multilateral capabilities," and to act to rectify what Canada saw as the emerging post–Cold War institutional vacuum in the North Pacific—a subregion in which tensions over security involving four great powers and over half the world's population were becoming acute. In effect, the object of Clark's initiative was to nurture the creation of a security community in Northeast Asia/North Pacific through the development of dialogue among all the seven states of the subregion, specifically to include non-like-minded states like North Korea. The NPCSD unfolded over the course of the next two years, coordinated through an NPCSD Research Program administered from York University (Toronto). A set of workshops in Canadian and Asia Pacific venues, involving experts and government officials acting in their private capacities, took place and a series of working papers were produced. Significantly, during this period, the attitude of Asia Pacific states, especially the United States and Japan, progressed from being openly negative to being quietly supportive of the prospect of multilateral consideration of security issues. With more recent events and the transition to new governments in these two states, the stance of the Asia Pacific states towards, and willingness to participate in, multilateral dialogue processes has changed dramatically—witness not only the ASEAN process itself, but also a virtual outbreak of multilateral dialogue and consultation initiatives focusing upon subregional groupings and/or upon specific functional topics. Among other things, current efforts to establish the Committee on Security Cooperation in Asia Pacific (CSCAP and its associated national committees and working groups—somewhat analogous to PECC) can be seen as drawing upon the success of the NPCSD.[31] Certainly, for Canada, the willingness of Asia Pacific partners to involve Canadians in such regional and subregional institution building can appropriately be viewed as a legacy of their experiences in the NPCSD.[32]

In substantive terms, the NPCSD initiative increased the breadth and level of sophistication of understanding across the range of factors encompassed by the notion of cooperative security. The conduct of the NPCSD established Canadian credentials as an engaged player, not only in subregional but also in regional security. Although for a brief period it appeared to outsiders that Ottawa may have failed to pick up the ball with the official conclusion of the NPCSD process, more recent developments surrounding ASEAN, CSCAP, Northeast Asia/North Pacific initiatives, the South China Sea, and UN activities in the Asia Pacific have provided Canada with opportunities to sustain an active role, if not an "out front," initiating role in the evolution of the Asia Pacific security order.[33]

The NPCSD may be best remembered by Asia Pacific states for its practical lessons concerning the efficacy and organization of track two processes. First, there could be two different, ongoing avenues of movement towards the goals of an NPCSD or similar regionalist project—one propelled by governmental officials pursuing officially stated policies, the other propelled by academics and other experts. Second, once these two tracks were set in motion, one—usually the second—could take on a life of its own, i.e., proceed quite separately and get somewhat ahead or out front of an official process involved in the same overall initiative. Third, the "blending" of the two tracks could be most productive. That is, the most useful collective interaction could take place when academics and experts worked together with government officials, who participated in meetings *in their private capacities*, i.e., they were not bound to put forward their governments standard policy line, and they could try out arguments and initiatives which could not be carried on through official modes of communication. The track two approach proved to have significant advantages for facilitating progress on the multilateral security agenda. It allowed free-ranging discussion of wide ranges of options and ideas, it freed country representatives from having to constantly espouse national positions and it fostered an ethos among the attentive elite within Asia Pacific states that reflected the nascent emergence of a security community. For the foreseeable future, track two processes will be indispensable, especially in the beginning periods of any initiative, for fostering regionalism and multilateralism. Within Canada, the NPCSD seemed to encourage and facilitate a climate of a closer working relationship between officials and NGO experts.

## Asian Studies in Canada

Some brief comments on Asian studies in general in Canada are useful for background purposes. Informed appreciation of Asian approaches to security as seen in their history, their culture, their organization of society is important if one is to understand the policies and events of the near present. This base of knowledge in academic institutions, including the study of the relevant languages, largely resides in what are referred to on North American campuses as the Asian "area studies" programs.[34] Academic programs focusing on the societies and cultures of individual countries in East Asia, especially China and Japan, are more than a century old in at least three universities in Canada. "Area" studies programs defined in terms of East, Southeast and South Asia or, alternatively, "Asia" were established at several Canadian universities in the 1960s and 1970s and often tied to specific departments. Beginning in the 1970s, some sixteen "centers" or institutes have been created with a focus on some portion of Asia. The largest include the University of Toronto-York University, Joint Centre for Asia Pacific Studies, the Institute for Asian Research at the University of British Columbia, the Centre d'études de l'Asie de l'est at the University of Montreal, and the Centre for Asia Pacific Initiatives at the University of Victoria.

The primary emphasis in department-based programs being upon the study of language and culture, the bulk of their associated faculty are in the humanities, linguistics and history—with China receiving the earliest and greatest attention, followed by Japan (especially in the last decade), South Asia, and Indo-China. On many campuses an isolation or gap has developed between those working in these more "traditional," Asia-specific programs and those faculty in the social sciences, natural, physical, and technical sciences, and professional schools who have become interested in the Asia Pacific as a substantive context in which to do analytic or comparative work. The former have tended to view the latter as unappreciative of the substantial investment in language and field work they believe prerequisite to any "real understanding" of Asian culture. The latter tend to regard the former as so bound up in narrow definitions of specialization within discipline, country and time period, that they have lost a larger perspective and that their approach and even, at times, their knowledge may be irrelevant to the demands of understanding the events and problems of today—feelings which are fueled by the growing appreciation of the postwar importance of the region in global economic and political relations, and the demand for policy-oriented research to inform business and government.[35]

Those doing research and writing on Asian subjects at Canadian universities have tended, if they are in the humanities, to publish their work in monograph form, and if they are in the social sciences, to publish in the major journals of Asian studies which, with few exceptions, emanate from the United States. One important exception is the journal *Pacific Affairs* based at the University of British Columbia, which has served to bring wider professional acknowledgment to the Canadian presence in this field. A number of the centers or institutes in Canada publish monographs and working papers distributed principally to specialist audiences in North America, Europe and Asia.

With the general increase in Canadian connections across the Pacific, there has been a correspondingly significant rise in the attention paid to the Asia Pacific region as a substantive focal point for studies in the professional, scientific and technical faculties in Canadian universities. Thus, legal studies, maritime law applied to the Pacific, climatology and oceanograpy of Pacific waters, fisheries management, forestry management, business management strategies, demography and the patterns of settlement, communications and mass media, sustainable development, and the delivery of technical assistance, all focused upon Asia or utilizing Asian subject matter as their substantive base have become highly developed on separate Canadian university campuses. Often the faculty associated with such focused research endeavors have developed close individual and institutional arrangements with their counterparts in universities and institutes in Asia. They constitute an important resource base for studying the social, economic and physical conditions and problems which are brought into the purview of "security studies" when conceived more broadly as cooperative security.[36]

In Canada, Asia studies programs, especially those projects that focus upon contemporary affairs and policy-oriented work and/or emphasize training in oral language skills, are expanding. There are funds available for this purpose through the federal government's Pacific 2000 Program, Asia Pacific Foundation (supported through a combination of Canadian government funding, including Pacific 2000 funds), and supplementary funds from Canadian provincial governments and Asian governments. However, these monies are neither large enough nor permanent in nature, thus precluding the much-needed creation of new faculty positions at universities and the establishment of fellowship programs for supporting students. Canadian universities, while not as accustomed or as skilled in raising endowment funds as their American counterparts, are beginning to do so in the Asia studies field—the most successful example to date being the University of British Columbia.

# Security Studies of Asia Pacific in Canada

The number of persons doing work on security studies of the Asia Pacific has traditionally been quite small. Accordingly, the amount of attention in Canadian university classrooms and the quantity of research work done by faculty and graduate students has not been high. However, changes which we regard as important have been set in motion during the last several years. In fact, in light of the relative scale of the security studies community in Canada and the context in which it operates as detailed above, the nature of this change could be termed without exaggeration to be quite dramatic and, we anticipate, to be long-standing. On all dimensions (curriculum, training of graduate students, research activity in and outside of university settings, field research within Asia Pacific, contact with Ottawa, participation in workshops and conferences, track two dialogues, and exchange activity with regional institutions), there have been notable increases concerning Asia Pacific security matters. While it is not possible or productive to provide an exhaustive listing—in fact an adequate national inventory does not exist[37]—three recent developments will be singled out as having greater significance than others. These are (*a*) the change in focus towards cooperative security and the increased attention to Asia Pacific within Canadian security studies programs, especially those within the MSS Program; (*b*) the energizing impact of the North Pacific Cooperative Security Dialogue program, and (*c*) the establishment of the Canadian Consortium on Asia Pacific Security.

In a recent review of the set of Military and Strategic Studies Programs within Canada,[38] it was apparent that the sense of what constitutes security and security studies is moving away from its traditional emphasis on military strategy, weapons and their control, and interstate warfare. Acceptance of the logic underlying the broader definition of cooperative security and the manner in which this redefines Canadian security interests has begun to leave its mark. The emphases on conflict resolution and peacekeeping approaches has been expanded and reoriented in light of the circumstances of the post–Cold War era. So-called "non-traditional" uses of the armed forces and responses to "unconventional" security threats are being taken up. Substantial attention, more so in curriculums than in research, is being devoted to examining the phenomena of ethnicity, nationalism and religious beliefs as causes of conflict in the contemporary system. Past and ongoing work on these subjects by experts outside the usual self-defined security studies academic cohort—that is, work in area studies programs and in fields such as sociology, anthropology and human geography—is being integrated into the security studies curriculums around the country and is influencing the design and direction of research programs. Most importantly for our purposes, the "regional" characteristics of the work being done is changing. Not only is there increased analytical attention to the phenomena of regional conflict and regional and subregional mechanisms for promoting peaceful change, there is also apparent a redressing of the balance, or rather imbalance, of attention given towards the so-called Third World, especially the relevant subregions in the Asia and Pacific region.

The intellectual shifts described above are leading to important synergisms, most apparent in the manner in which graduate students are designing their programs and research theses. Many have come to recognize the value of developing and complementing expertise (including language skills) about a region or country with functional knowledge and interest in problems of conflict, security, and the joined forces of development and democratization. Thus, there are increasing numbers of younger scholars in Canada (as well as Canadian graduate students abroad) who are pursuing such combinations with an Asia Pacific focus. Cooperative security, maritime defense, nuclear accidents, incidents at sea, confidence building mechanisms (CBMs) in the North Pacific, CBMs on the Korean peninsula, CBMs in Southeast Asia, regional peacekeeping, the role of the United Nations in the region, defense technology transfers, defense industries, military conversion, refugees and security, human rights, civil-military relations and development, environmental degradation and regime stability, and regional arms control are all topics currently under investigation.[39]

Special mention is merited for the success that the NPCSD research program had in broadening understanding of the dimensions of cooperative security as applied to the Asia Pacific. Thus, the implications of population growth and migration, of resource depletion in the oceans and on land, and of degradation of the environment especially in light of urbanization and industrialization were all explored in forums which brought together experts on these subjects from North America with Asian counterparts and with experts on Asia Pacific security. Also, the NPCSD provided a framework for dialogue on the questions of human rights and democratization—touchy subjects for both academics and officials—which when vented through the channels of public diplomacy tend towards deadlock and acrimony.

Maintaining the momentum created by the NPCSD program activity and related events in the region has become a challenge. For Canadian academics and experts, problems have been three-fold. On the one hand, it has been difficult simply to keep up with the pace of "opportunities" presented by the proliferation of academic and track two forums and conferences.[40] There has simply been so much activity that there are, within Canada, insufficient numbers of experts to allow participation and representation in every venue and on every topic. With the recent developments around ASEAN and the formation of CSCAP and its likely formation of subregional working groups, the nature of the problem, as it were, has changed—from one of coverage and keeping track, to one of effective coordination of national-level activities to interface with the track two associated but strictly academic enterprises.[41] Finally, on a the national level, given its decentralized nature and geographic distribution, without a vehicle to both keep track of who is doing what and to circulate research results to people who would not otherwise come across them in their normal disciplinary lives, the Asia Pacific security studies community will simply diffuse. To address these various perceived concerns, an initiative to create a Canadian Consortium on Asia Pacific Security (CANCAPS) has been undertaken to redress the problems of community building, information sharing, and distribution of research results identifiedabove.[42] It is likely that the consortium will function parallel to and in support of the Canadian national committee to CSCAP and its associated working groups.

Thus, on many fronts, there appears to be considerable potential for development of Asia Pacific security studies in Canada. There is enthusiasm, there is an increasing talent pool of expertise, there are elements in place for an effective relationship between academic and governmental components allowing the pursuit of both their natural complementary and separate interests. CANCAPS may provide useful solutions to certain coordination and information distribution problems. However, a number of important structural concerns and challenges remain to be addressed.

# Looking to the Future

## *Five Premises*

It is our view that the future development of security studies communities within Canada and across the Asia Pacific should proceed on the basis of the following five premises:

First, the principles of multilateralism, regionalism, inclusion and cooperative security are being increasingly validated in the regional and subregional processes of the post–Cold War Asia Pacific. These same perspectives are the historically proven bases of Canadian diplomacy and security studies. Canadians, therefore, have traditions of scholarship and experience, especially in functional areas such as peacekeeping, which are relevant to participation in the contemporary Asia Pacific.

Regionalist and multilateralist approaches play to the strengths of the Canadian research community and to the proclivities and capabilities of those officials responsible for international security issues. Such approaches serve to constrain the preeminence of dominant powers, introduce counterweights to any tendencies towards unilateralism, and ensure that all members of the regional or subregional systems have their viewpoints considered, both at the diplomatic table and in the scholarly agenda. In both contexts, Canadian experience has been shaped by its attempts to advance its interests in tandem with a superpower neighbor. As a result, there has been a consistent sensitivity towards allowing the dominant ethos within a region to define its own membership. Thus, Canadian security studies experts have worked hard to avoid the presumptive attitude that European-proven institutional modes will provide salutary relief to the Asia Pacific circumstances.

From this rationale it is easy to understand why Canada should continue to pursue a distinct international profile and a relative comparative advantage in the functional areas of international security expertise (normally carried out within some form of multilateral context) such as peacekeeping, verification, confidence building measures, strategies of reassurance, preventive diplomacy, civil-military relations, the creation of legal instruments, and technical assistance and training.

Second, if Canada is to become and remain an engaged participant in security studies of the Asia Pacific, it must more clearly and consistently articulate policies and commitments in ways which are perceived as relevant both by regional actors and by Canadians. For neither constituency will rhetorical gestures satisfactorily substitute for limited but sustained engagement on key issues.

Third, the advancement towards a regional security community or subregional security communities in the Asia Pacific should not be viewed, especially by North American partners, as requiring the homogenization of cultural, national and subregional perspectives. The challenge for those in the security studies communities of their respective states will be to foster mutual understanding of the distinctive ways in which others define the central principles of their international character, e.g., sovereignty, national interest, multilateralism and transparency. Such understanding can be fostered by a series of practical steps, including facilitation of scholarly and diplomatic exchanges.

Fourth, the long-term security of the Asia Pacific is not going to be assured through traditional military means or diplomatic strategizing alone. Rather, it will depend as well, and perhaps more so, on the extent to which processes of economic growth, of identification with community, of popular legitimization of government, and of resource utilization can proceed in synchrony. This is the essence of cooperative security. Fostering this understanding within the Asia Pacific will require expanding the horizons of those in the existing security studies community—in both substantive and longitudinal terms. The longer-term implications for security and well-being of the knowledge of the larger scientific and technical communities concerning the availability and use of human and physical resources need to be understood. This calls for funding, facilities, and research incentives to explore such questions, including through the establishment of research networks that encompass experts currently outside the tradtional military security studies cohorts.

Fifth, regarding resources: At present, human and fiscal resources are limited, particularly within certain countries, and insufficient resources exist for effective and inclusive intraregional or subregional research and exchange. What is necessary is (a) reallocation of current resources to achieve maximal results; (b) recognition of areas where individual states have expertise and some comparative advantage vis-à-vis other regional partners; and (c) the infusion of new resources, focused upon regional and subregional agendas, committed over the next decade.

In effect, from peacekeeping to international institutions, from redefining security to practical issues of verification and arms control, and from a focus on regional security to the linkage with the political economy of development, Canadian scholars and practitioners have understood security and security studies as involving concerns beyond defense, border penetration, or the security of the state—at least not in the traditional terms of military threat. Hence, among Canadian academics as well as officials, broadening the parameters of "security" has been of central concern since well before the tearing down of the Berlin Wall. The concept of "cooperative security" as articulated by Canadian political leaders, officials and scholars is a logical extension of Canadian thinking and policy and is compatible with and an extension of some of the earlier Asian thinking on "comprehesive security."[43]

## *Security Studies of Asia Pacific: What Should Be Done in Canada?*

We have argued that Canadian engagement in questions of Asia Pacific security is best viewed through regionalist/subregionalist lenses, and that Canadian expertise in both official and academic circles already exists or is emerging. What does this augur for the future of Canada's role in the evolving Asia Pacific security order? Our position would be, quite simply, that we should build on our strengths and that in order to make a difference we require creative leadership by political elites, senior public servants, and leading academics supported by resources sufficient to enable sustainable and constructive engagement. Canada requires a political presence which articulates a vision of Canada as a responsible and committed partner in the Asia Pacific arena. Hence, those areas mentioned before—peacekeeping, verification, preventive diplomacy, confidence building measures, negotiation and mediation, maritime surveillance, creation of legal instruments, environmental resource monitoring and management and oceans and fisheries protection—must be advanced on agendas as items where Canada's contributions in some combination of official channels, track two processes and scholarship can be applied. Some of these might lead to special bilateral programs (for example, when a country wishes to consult on peacekeeping operations or when a consortium of scholars works together on a specific research topic), but most would have a (sub)regional context. More importantly, there must be a visible commitment of sufficient resources, including political will, to sustain both an official and a track two presence, e.g., as with the NPCSD.

In more specific terms, we argue that movement along five avenues is essential if both the governmental (that is, official) and the nongovernmental (that is, academic and independent expert) dimensions of Asia Pacific security studies in Canada are going to realize their full potential in the next century.

First of all, there is a fundamental need for Canada's political leaders to produce and follow a clearly stated approach to Canada's definition of and role in international security in general, and for responsible involvement in the Asia Pacific more specifically. Certainly, taking on a role in this region and its subregions resonates with arguments based on mutual benefit, socioeconomic and cultural linkages, political responsibilities and opportunities and a normative consensus. However, within the Canadian context, there are a myriad of demands and competing interests for attention and resource allocation in other areas. The case for the Asia Pacific has to be made carefully and in a sophisticated fashion. Such articulation needs to come from Ottawa; but the groundwork, in terms of research concerning Asia, as well as concerning the Canadian context itself, will necessarily emerge from work largely done in the foreign policy and security studies communities.

The second priority is that the governmental, academic, and private actors in the these Canadian communities work out more effective interrelationships than they have had in the past. On several fronts, developments over the past couple of years have been positive in this regard, specifically concerning the Asia Pacific: the track two components of the NPCSD, the increased openness and willingness to engage in debate shown by officials in EAITC responsible for Asia, the sustained support for expert consultation and research in the fields of disarmament, verification and surveillance, peacekeeping, and the support for the creation of CANCAPS. But, as noted earlier, certain barriers persist between official and experts outside government which can impede their effective cooperation and collaboration.

The third recommendation concerns a somewhat more ephemeral matter—namely, that what is needed in both government and academia are individuals whose perspective, training and inclination would lead them to be labeled "regionalists" (as opposed to being known as area studies experts or functional security experts). One does not often find, in either academic or governmental circles, individuals with training, experience and attitudes that are congruent with their assigned task of advancing "regional" security. But it is exactly this blending of the area expert with the functional expert, in effect creating a "regionalist" or "subregionalist," that is required for the future. To a certain degree, Canadian proclivities and skills likely are attuned to such an approach because, given the structural parameters of Canada's international security role, it has been necessary to emphasize approaches with regionalist and multilateralist tacks, which alternately challenge and complement the dominant north-north/east-west conceptions of international politics and security studies.

However, the intellectual and bureaucratic forces offering impediments to moving towards "regionalists" in both governmental and academic positions should not be underestimated. EAITC, with its tradition of producing generalists, has not normally encouraged the development of real country experts. Even regional expertise is less present than some would argue should be the case. An obvious implication, if this analysis is sound, is that the Canadian government should begin to encourage and to reward officials, both in EAITC and DND, who would wish to combine regional expertise with functional concentration. Officers (both diplomats and military) should receive appropriate language training and have their careers move them through the principal countries of the region as well as to Ottawa and to one or another appropriate international or multilateral institution. In practical terms, what this argues for is a regional diplomat (one who can manage political, security and economic functions) supported by a regional military expert (having multilateral experience) on career paths which ensure regular rotation through the region when outside Canada and being kept involved in regional issues when at headquarters.

It is no less difficult to imagine the training of a "regionalist" on the academic side of the security studies community, although the merits of the case for doing so are equally strong. Graduate training is structured in terms of time and especially of available resources so that the student will have an inevitable choice between concentrating upon language acquisition (if necessary) and field work or concentrating upon acquiring state-of-the-art knowledge in a functional or theoretical area of study. Once in professional ranks, the pressures to produce specialized works in one's field are overriding until mid-career stage, at which point acquiring new training or skills is not feasible. Thus, there continues, for example, the perpetuation of area studies (read single country) experts on the one hand, and functional experts (e.g., defense policy, arms control, nonproliferation, peacekeeping, and low intensity conflict) on the other. Two courses of action could lead to remedying this structurally induced situation. The first is the fostering of joint research by teams of individual researchers drawn together on the basis of the complementarity, rather than the similarity, of their backgrounds and perspectives on security studies questions. The second is the funding of early to mid-career fellowship programs to give persons a minimum of two years time to acquire either training or field experience.[44]

Fourth is the matter of resource allocation, a delicate issue in the Canadian context. The call for greater funding, especially from the federal government, is largely agreed upon. From the perspective of the university-based research community, increases are necessary to ensure that sufficient funds are allocated to both teaching and research programs so that the next generation will have both the necessary language and cultural skills to understand and to appreciate the world of the twenty-first century, and the theoretical, conceptual, methodological, and analytic capabilities to undertake meaningful research and to impart sensitive and thoughtful recommendations. What is more controversial, although also necessary in our view, is that investment of resources be concentrated in a select number of centers of excellence. Rather than allocating money across a set of centers whose existence is mandated on the basis of regional distribution, or distributing a grant program across a myriad of small grants, better to award a select number of larger grants, over a longer period of time, to a select number of security studies centers or institutes.[45] Without such a "vertical" commitment, we would argue that it is improbable that the education and industrial sectors can alone sustain a sophisticated capability in the increasingly difficult and complex arena of regional security studies.

The fifth avenue concerns the need to erode the barriers among what have been traditionally isolated components on the Canadian scene. Thus, the self-isolation that has arisen between established Asian studies programs and their members and the social scientist community (including security studies) and their research programs is counterproductive and needs to be bridged wherever warranted. With the recognition by social scientists that security concerns have cultural and societal roots and that technical solutions to economic and physical problems of the environment can not succeed if advanced in ways that are insensitive to cultural mores, the basis for building bridges is becoming more apparent, and more effective collaboration is being undertaken. Similarly, there is increased activity on the part of people in the security studies field of the need to call upon the expertise of those in the natural, physical and human sciences (such as medicine and demography) to inform their teaching and writing about current and future security problems in the Asia Pacific. What was sufficient several years ago, namely the passing reference to the importance of the environment, for example, is no longer so. Consciousness has been raised, and it is time for concerted collaborative efforts. Following is a list of recommendations regarding the establishment of an infrastructure, program, and necessary changes which would be sufficient to achieve a viable future in Asia Pacific security studies:

## Recommendations—Canadian Infrastructure

1. The creation and sustaining of a consortium of individual scholars, institutions and other experts and parties within Canada committed to research and related track two activities on Asia Pacific cooperative security (i.e., CANCAPS).

2. The creation of an endowed research and scholarship program—the Foundation for Asia Pacific Security Studies in Canada—with a minimum ten year commitment to underwrite research, (re)training and scholarships, with support drawn primarily from the federal government (e.g., EAITC Pacific 2000 funds, Human Resources Development, and/or Canadian Heritage) but with participation from private foundations, the business sector and the provincial governments, with the intention to mirror, both in scope and imagination, Canada's recent federally funded commitment to Eastern Europe.

3. The establishment of a National Advisory Council on Asia Pacific Security Studies in Canada to oversee the creation and program management of the foundation and of its emergent ancillary programs.

4. The secured funding of a number of university-based "centers of excellence" focusing on Asia Pacific cooperative security studies, with funding coming from a combination of the newly established and newly funded foundation and the already existing Cooperative Security Competitions Program (EAITC) and the Miitary and Strategic Studies Program (DND).

## Recommendations—Canadian Programs

1. Mid-career exchange and secondments—among universities, other research organizations, and government—within Canada (i.e., lateral movement) and between Canada and our partners in the Asia Pacific region, with a focus on the development of regional expertise.

2. Canadian graduate fellowships specifically for dissertation field research on Asia Pacific regional or subregional cooperative security issues.

3. Graduate student field placements whereby students from throughout Asia Pacific could undertake course work or specialized study and research at Canadian institutions while Canadians would have enhanced opportunities to undertake work within the larger region.

4. Area and language training: for undergraduate and graduate students to include an overseas component; for both young and more established scholars with functional (e.g., international relations and security studies) expertise, to provide a two-year paid leave of absence to permit both language development at a professional level of competence and familiarity with a (sub)regional context.

5. Through the newly created Foundation for Asia Pacific Security Studies in Canada, to establish a number of (sub)regional task forces to undertake basic collaborative research on priority areas identified by the cooperative security conceputalization (i.e., areas deemed important for preventive diplomacy, reassurance and transparency), not unlike the initial NPCSD concept but with a longer time horizon and more explict commitment to policy relevant fundamental research.

6. Through the foundation, to provide opportunities for outstanding young scholars and scientists to work with or in the laboratory of a senior scholar in a discipline and on a topic which would complement the existing expertise and contribute towards refining and operationalizing the newer and more problematic areas of cooperative security (e.g., a security studies expert working with a human geographer on the relationship between population dynamics—growth, migration, inequalites, resource accessibility, etc.—and regime security or interstate tensions; an expert on arms control working with scientists involved in developing new means of nonintrusive passive detection; or an expert on maritime law working in an environmental studies laboratory on the basic issues of ocean resource management and pollution).

## Security Studies of Asia Pacific: What Should Be Done in Regional and Subregional Contexts?

The assumption of this paper has been, of course, that current trends towards openness at national levels, inclusiveness in regional dialogue, and advancement of multilateral approaches to dealing with regional and subregional security questions in Asia Pacific are progressive ones which should be sustained and enhanced. The following brief comments, therefore, are written from this perspective and speak largely to what might be done concerning the nongovernmental dimensions of an Asia Pacific security studies community. We have identified five main areas of concern.

First, and most briefly since it appears to us to be self-evident, is the necessity to structure and promote a security studies community that is inclusive of all perspectives and national viewpoints. Oddly perhaps, at present this principle seems further advanced in the practice of Asia Pacific regional and subregional diplomacy than in, and among, the nongovernmental institutions of the Asia Pacific security studies community or within the larger group of individual university-based scholars and graduate students.

The second is fostering appreciation for the realistic potential of regionalist and subregionalist approaches to security issues in the Asia Pacific. For some this will involve gaining a fuller understanding of the substantive experience of others and of other parts of the international community in solving their security problems. While simple analogies and simplistic transfers of ideas and modes of institutionalization from one region to another will not work, neither is it wise for those in Asia Pacific security studies not to be aware of the logic and substance of regional and subregional multilateralism that have already proceeded in other environments. However, there is also a need to come to terms with the limits of regionalism and multilateralism. Within the Asia Pacific context, for the foreseeable future, certain parameters of the security order will be sustained through bilateral relations. Arguing against these is counterproductive and alienating; arguing for gaining an understanding of how bilateral and multilateral agendas might be most effectively combined by nations to advance their long-term security interests is a positive way of approaching this issue—one that should be taken up more by those in security studies.

Sorting out which issues are most appropriately dealt with in different contexts is a process that will require careful attention. Further, there is the need to ascertain which sets of intellectual puzzles and of policy-oriented concerns should engage those researchers concentrating on regional or subregional security issues. If we accept the premises of cooperative security and are sensitive to the changing political security complex within the Asia Pacific region, then preventive diplomacy, with all that that entails, should emerge as a foremost area of concentration. This would draw on the idea that mutual reassurance (rather than deterrence or adversarially structured confidence building measures) should become a singularly important topic, as would the derivative functional issues of transparency, verification, peace enhancement, etc. It also would lead to a consideration of how best to develop military doctrine and procedures which would best conform to these tasks; for example, developing a strong peacekeeping and conflict management and resolution capability.

Third is the promotion of the broader conception of security envisaged in the term "cooperative security," to utilize the language of this paper.[46] Enough has been said above on this point. Note, however, the implications for doing so for a "cooperative security studies" community at the regional or subregional level: (*a*) emphasis on a longer, rather than shorter, time horizon; (*b*) engagement of experts from areas of the human and technical sciences not normally found in traditional security studies networks; and (*c*) a need to be willing to address what some individual states may regard as contentious or delicate matters, e.g., the effects of rapid economic growth and creation of economic disparities on political stability, or the erosion of the separation of what has been traditionally seen as the borders between the domestic and the international.

Fourth, creating a security community in Asia Pacific or its subregions should not be viewed as an exercise either in a simple adoption of out-of-area values or in an attempt to move towards some unidimensional security culture. A security community involves more than mere coexistence, but it need not imply homogenization across national entities, nor homogenization across regions or subregions. Concepts and tactics that worked in one environment may never be applicable in another. Thus, for instance, certain Asian security studies experts argue that advocacy of confidence building measures (CBMs) may not be appropriate to the Asia Pacific context. This is because for them CBMs arise from the Cold War context of amelioration of relations between directly threatenting adversaries. For these persons, what is called for instead is "mutual reassurance"—the promotion of greater understanding of others perceptions of their needs for security, of their definitions of sovereignty, and of their understanding of the implications of transparency.

Fifth is the need to promote at both national and regional levels security studies communities which maintain productive relationships with their respective governments and regional/subregional interstate governmental institutions. Nurturing and sustaining such relationships is a delicate matter. On the one hand, firm co-optation or complete control of the intellectual agenda of security studies by governments or institutions is self-defeating. It destroys the capacity for criticism, interchange, and development of new ideas necessary ultimately for the survival of the institutional master. On the other hand, a security studies community which is not informed about, and attentive to, the realities of the regional environment or which persists in ideologically oriented work or work given over to abstraction is of little use either. Theory does not advance in ignorance of substance. Among Asia Pacific countries there are already many different national models of relationships with nongovernmental security studies communities. Some clearly provide examples of practices worth pursuing in other states.

When it comes to fostering what might be termed a regional or subregional security studies community, it would appear desirable for (a) national participants to be able to be as informed about but as unconstrained as possible by their government's viewpoints, (b) for research agendas to be set in fashions that facilitate the airing and exploration of all points of view, and (c) for resource allocation to be undertaken in such a way that all participants can do so on an equivalent basis. In essence, this will mean a purposeful uneven distribution of resources. Expecting scholars from poorer environments to participate as equals implies providing sufficient resources for research assistants, for library materials, and for field work to enable them to work as effectively as their counterparts elsewhere. It also suggests creating means to facilitate equitable within-region exchange programs, ensuring that the movement of scholars involves all as both home and host.

What might be done in practical terms? We presume that several of the strategies proposed for the Canadian context have their regional or subregional equivalents: for example, promoting better relationships between country experts, technical scientists and security studies and better relationships between governmental and nongovernmental communities; formation of cross-national research networks and cross-national research teams and projects; etc. But at the regional or subregional level, the question of resources becomes more difficult since it devolves to two issues: (a) resource sharing agreements across states, or (b) creation of pools of resources, from private, quasi-private, or governmental sources.

Resource sharing across states goes on already, of course. Some countries like the United States make available relatively large amounts of funds to facilitate the work of their own nationals and of those of other select countries. While the distribution of resources may continue to be skewed, with the accelerated economic performance and increased openness of many East Asian states, more resources and opportunities for development of regional/subregional security studies should be coming on-line in the near future. What are also needed are more creative arrangements and mechanisms which effectively capitalize on the different sorts of resources different countries have to offer. What is needed is are regionwide or subregional mechanisms with the funds and administrative capacities to "broker" such arrangements. Thus, for example, Canada has relatively few funds available to give directly to individuals from other countries. It does, however, have an attractive base of universities at which to study for degrees or to undertake independent research or mid-career retraining. Hence, arrangements could be developed whereby Canadian host institutions provided infrastructural support (i.e., research and support facilities or waiving of tuition costs), the individual's home country provided return air transportation, and the Asia Pacific "funding consortium" underwrote the salaries and/or living expenses of individuals coming to Canada.

There is still another avenue available for the promotion of security studies communities: the creation of regional or subregional institutes which transcend national boundaries.[47] There are a number of important functions that such an institution could provide, if it had adequate resources: for example, facilitation of mid-career and junior-career secondments from the governments and universities of one country to another; the provision of mid-career (re)training fellowships; the underwriting of research projects which bring together scholars from different countries for extended working periods; the editing and production of working papers and a journal of Asia Pacific security studies; the underwriting of work that addresses the conceptual underpinnings of a "cooperative security community." However, there also are very serious potential costs. The creation of a large physical establishment for such an institute or institutes is difficult, not only because of the symbolic politics involved in determining location but also because of the heavy infrastructural investments required. Only a very few countries within Asia Pacific currently could afford to support and enhance, either financially or with high calibre personnel, both their own national programs and institutions as well the creation of one or more transnational institutes.

## Recommendations—Infrastructure

1. The creation of a consortium of scholars and other experts on Asia Pacific security committed to facilitating the development of Asia Pacific security studies and to promote and sustain track two processes throughout the Asia Pacific (i.e., CSCAP).

2. The creation of the Program on Asia Pacific Security Studies (PAPSS), having the financial resources, professional expertise, and independence to undertake and/or to facilitate regionwide scholarship, research, and exchange programs, including institutional, programmatic and individual networking as well as information dissemination.

3. The establishment of an Advisory Council on Asia Pacific Security Studies to serve as the governing council to PAPSS, to work with foundations, governments, and nongovernmental agencies on establishing and managing the priorities and programs of a coordinated effort to further Asia Pacific security, and to provide guidance and institutional support to the track two processes undertaken through CSCAP.

4. PAPSS to have a professional secretariat but—at least initially—no institutional base outside of the secretariat, with its advisory council being responsible for the allocation of resources and the setting of PAPSS priorities and missions.

5. PAPSS should be funded by a formula which provides equal opportunity for all Asia Pacific countries to participate and, at the same time, draws on the financial and other supports afforded by leading international private foundations; funding sufficient to endow this program for an initial ten-year period.

## Recommendations—Programs

Finally, we include recommendations for regional and subregional programs:

1. Postdoctoral fellowships providing training in complementary fields relevant to cooperative security definitions and long-term priorities, these to be made available on a competitive basis throughout the Asia Pacific region with an effort to ensure that all participating countries regularly have their own young scholars circulating and also receive equivalent scholars from throughout the region.

2. The creation of multinational research teams, facilitated by initial PAPSS support, in which at least one-half of all members have not had their PhD's for more than five years, to undertake basic research relevant to the evolving security concerns of one or more aspects/parts of the region or a subregion.

3. Doctoral and postdoctoral fellowships enabling long-term (minimum one year) field work, including advanced course work and language study where relevant, as well as primary research.

4. The creation of a professional journal on Asia Pacific security, managed and sponsored by PAPSS, with an international advisory board (perhaps drawn from the PAPSS Advisory Council) and co-edited by three scholars, one from Southeast Asia, one from Northeast Asia, and a third non-Asian.

5. The creation of an Asia Pacific equivalent to the Rhodes Scholarship program, targeting "the best and the brightest" young persons throughout the region with interests in any aspect of cooperative security, broadly conceived, for prestigious "two plus" years of support at any of the leading universities throughout the region which have agreed to contribute "in kind" support and have the necessary prerequisites to facilitate first-rate postgraduate education; to be managed by PAPSS with its secretariat facilitating the competition and evaluation process.

# Conclusions

It is evident that security studies in Canada have developed over the last twenty years into a core component of the international relations and foreign policy teaching and research communities. Similarly, area studies, in this case on the countries of the Asia and Pacific region, also have become well established within many Canadian universities. Today, in the uncertain transition after the Cold War, there is both the need and the opportunity to bring these two substantive and methodological disciplines more closely together in support of the development of regional cooperative security studies and practice in the Asia Pacific arena.

In both the official and research communities, Canada has developed expertise in creative policy development and conceptualization as well as in specialized instruments and areas of functional capabilities. Canada has the potential to provide a sustained positive contribution to the furthering of Asia Pacific security—in terms of research and teaching as well as in practice—and thereby confirm its place as an Asia Pacific country. But this will require enhanced investment in people and in institutions and a commitment that is both visible and sustained.

# Notes

1. This is an abridged version of a paper presented at the meetings on "The Future of Asia Pacific Security Studies and Exchange Activities" held in Bali, December 12–15, 1993. The authors acknowledge the research assistance provided by Wilma Suen and the comments and information provided them by Yoshi Kawasaki, Frank Langdon, Shannon Selin, and Elizabeth Speed. The authors acknowledge the support of the Cooperative Security Competition Program of the Department of External Affairs and International Trade Canada and of the Military and Strategic Studies Program at both the York University Centre for International and Strategic Studies and the Institute of International Relations at UBC. The views expressed in the paper are the authors' and do not represent the views of any institution or program. Any errors are the responsibilities of the authors.

2. We recognize that there is an ongoing debate over how best to define the Asia Pacific arena. We have decided to focus on East or Eastern Asia, and include in that discussion the additional principal countries in the South Pacific and the North Pacific. We recognize that countries in each of these two main subregions variously have strong linkages with countries in the other subregion. Hence, on some issues researchers and policymakers must be prepared to integrate across subregions or at least to factor into their thinking the broader regional context.

3. Thus, for Canada, NATO was always viewed as more than simply a military alliance; it was seen since its inception as a community-building institution whose goals extended beyond deterrence to advancing an understanding of common security among members based on underlying economic, political and social interests. Towards this end, Canadian efforts were important in leading to Article 2 of the Charter of the North Atlantic Treaty Organization and later to the Harmel Report of 1967.

4. The publication of the defense white paper of 1987, the first in over fifteen years, proved to be the victim of poor timing. The 1987 document was couched in what was (for Canadians) fairly harsh Cold War rhetoric. With the transformation of the international security system shortly thereafter, the white paper came to be viewed as a document for another era and was essentially shelved.

5. Thus Canada has been involved in every UN peacekeeping venture and continues to be the largest contributor to forces in difficult venues such as in the former Yugoslavia.

6. When the Liberal government of Jean Chrétien took office in late 1993, the name of the department was changed to become the Department of Foreign Affairs and International Trade (DFAIT). Given the time of writing of this paper and the periods of policy and policy-making being discussed, the former name and acronym will be maintained.

7. For a detailed treatment of the Canadian understanding of "cooperative security" plus a discussion as to how this relates to concepts advanced in the Asia Pacific context, such as the notion of "comprehensive security" as advanced by a number of East Asian countries, see David Dewitt, "Common, Comprehensive, and Cooperative Security in Asia Pacific," *The Pacific Review* (January 1994), based on a paper initially prepared for and presented to the Seventh Annual Asia Pacific Roundtable, Kuala Lumpur, June 6–9, 1993.

8. See "Foreign Policy Themes and Priorities, 1991–92 Update," Policy Planning Staff, Department of External Affairs and International Trade Canada, Ottawa, December 1991.

9. Indeed, R.J. Sutherland, writing some thirty years ago and reflecting upon the state of the art of the literature concerning Canada's security interests and defense policies, and the underlying premises and arguments which it represented or perhaps failed to represent, concluded that "Canada has no particular tradition of strategic calculation." (See his "Canada's Long-Term Strategic Situation," *International Journal* 17 (1961/62), p. 19.)

10. In 1992, this was more than 110 masters students and over 50 PhD students.

11. The Social Sciences and Humanities Research Council (SSHRC) is the major source of PhD graduate fellowship funds in Canada, operating programs in all of the major disciplines, including political science and history, but not international relations per se. Thus, some PhD students working on international or domestic security questions will be funded under the SSHRC rubric or much smaller programs such as the Barton Fellowship program. The MSS Program remains the sole source for MA level scholarship support.

12. The major journal for French-language scholarship in Canada is *Études internationales* which is published by the Centre québécois de relations internationales (CQRI) located at Laval University in Québec. The work of Albert Legault, the director of the CQRI, gives some sense of the strength and flavor of Francophone scholarship in international relations. See, for instance, his *The End of a Military Century* (Ottawa: International Development Research Centre, 1993); and his volume with Michel Fortmann, *Une diplomatie de l'espoir – Le Canada et le désarmement 1945–1988 (Québec: Les Presses de l'Université Laval, 1989)*.

13. It is somewhat surprizing, therefore, that the MSS Program has not organized any regularized production and distribution of working papers on security issues. Also, it is unfortunate that with the demise of the Canadian Institute of International Peace and Security (CIIPS) came also the end to the publication of the institute's high-quality, magazine-type publication devoted to informing the attentive public at home, and abroad, of the Canadian perspective on international affairs.

14. In the last several years endowment campaigns have been undertaken at several major Canadian universities. These have had some success in raising funds to endow chairs or programs in areas ancilliary to security studies, e.g. law, commerce, and Asian studies.

15. Grants usually run on an annual basis, sometimes for two or three years. Amounts vary, but rarely do they exceed $250,000 over three years, and even that limit is the exception. Most awards are much smaller, usually in the $7,500 to $35,000 range, and do not allow sustained contributions to infrastructure or institution building. Overall, there are only occasional opportunities to compete for Canadian financial aid in support of longer-term primary research, whether this involves one or a number of scholars.

16. One such institute should be noted, the Canadian Centre for Global Security, which over the years has produced work of high quality, particularly on issues concerning arms control and disarmament. However, without any secure funding base, the center can not undertake a long-term, independent research program.

17. The former Conservative government dismantled most all of the existing policy research institutes and councils in Canada, including the CIIPS—the relatively new, high profile research, policy, and funding institute focused upon foreign policy and international affairs. Whether or not the new Liberal government renews these institutions, as has been intimated regarding the international relations area, remains to be seen.

18. For a selection of articles which provide an overview of this with a focus on post–Cold War challenges, see *Canadian Defence Quarterly* 21:1 (Special No. 2/1991), David Dewitt and David Leyton-Brown, guest editors. The articles by Brian Job, "Canadian Defence Policy in the Pacific: Relevance, Commitments, and Capabilities," and by David Dewitt, "Canadian Defence Policy: Regional Conflicts, Peacekeeping, and Stability Operations," are most relevant for the principal focus of this paper.

19. For those scholars wishing to work with archives or on subjects in which access to individuals and/or files in either department is necessary, Canadian law is, in principle, restrictive. However, in practice the relatively small size of the Canadian academic and official communities and the mutual benefit often perceived by the work undertaken tends in most cases to override many of the formal constraints. In other cases, scholars have often found that they can access the documents they desire through the archives of other countries. Indeed often a Canadian policy document concerning NATO or North American security matters can be more easily obtained through US archives in Washington than in Ottawa.

20. The Cooperative Security Program represents the legacy of CIIPS which was terminated in 1992 after a short existence of seven years. Although the Cooperative Security Program's budget is not insignificant (currently Can. $2.1 million annually, with an additional $200,000 for student scholarships), it clearly is designed not to replicate or recreate the form or the output of its predecessor.

21. Particular note should be given to the CIDA-sponsored Asia Pacific Oceans Council, an umbrella for a set of projects involving the conduct of research and the enhancement of expert and institutional resources in Asian states concerning the management of maritime disputes and the monitoring and management of ocean fisheries. Particularly important have been a set of workshops sponsored by Canadian experts bringing together, in a track two context, experts and officials in their private capacities, to exchange views and frame alternatives for the settlement of the conflicting territorial claims in the South China Sea.

22. Between the two of them, roughly Can. $ 4.5 million annually in government funds is being spent on furthering work outside of government on international relations, much of it on security studies.

23. See Brian Job and Frank Langdon, "Canada and the Pacific," in F. Hampson and C. Maule, eds., *Canada Among Nations, 1993–94: Global Jeopardy* (Ottawa: Carleton University Press, 1993), chapter 14.

24. Confirmation of this trend may be found in the actions of the newly elected (November, 1993) Liberal government which has created the position of Secretary of State for Asia, just below Cabinet rank, and appointed an Asian Canadian to fill it. In addition, the Parliamentary Secretary for Foreign Affairs has recently been named and is a Asian Canadian as well.

25. A detailed analysis of the history and progress of multilateral, nongovernmental organizations in the region is provided by Lawrence Woods, *Nongovernmental Diplomacy and the Pacific Economic Cooperation Movement* (Vancouver: University of British Columbia Press, 1993).

26. For a review of Canada's foreign relations with China see the recently published volume by Paul M. Evans and B. Michael Frolic, ed., *Reluctant Adversaries: Canada and the People's Republic of China 1949–1970 (Toronto: University of Toronto Press, 1991).*

27. The most visible starting point was Secretary of State Joe Clarke's speech to the UN General Assembly of September 1990.

28. For an overview of a Canadian perspective, see David Dewitt and Paul Evans, "The Changing Dynamics of Asia Pacific Security: A Canadian Perspective," NPCSD

Working Paper, no. 3, Centre for International and Strategic Studies, York University, Toronto, January 1992.

29. Following their election in 1993, the Liberal government cancelled procurement of the new helicopters which had been designed to provide wide-range, sophisticated ASW capability for the frigates. This was an important decision, not only for its financial implications, but also for its messages (symbolic and real) regarding the post–Cold War role of the forces.

30. See Stewart Henderson, "Canada and Asia Pacific Security: The North Pacific Cooperative Security Dialogue, Recent Trends," External Affairs and International Trade Canada, Policy Planning Staff Paper 92/3, Ottawa, January 1992; simultaneously published as NPCSD Working Paper, no. 1, Centre for International and Strategic Studies, York University, Toronto.

31. Paul M. Evans, "The Council for Security Cooperation in Asia Pacific: Context and Prospects," *Pacific Review*, Summer 1994 (forthcoming).

32. Ironically, just at the time NPCSD gave evidence of some substantial successes, Ottawa terminated the initiative. Shortly thereafter, Washington undertook to establish its own university-coordinated track two program on North Pacific multilateral security, with Canada excluded from the proceedings.

33. See the *Agenda for Cooperative Security in the North Pacific* edited by David Dewitt and Paul Evans, a conference report of the final meeting of the NPCSD which provides an indication of the various dialogue channels opened, or opening up, in Asia Pacific. Toronto: York University, Centre for International and Strategic Studies, July, 1993.

34. The word "program" is used here to refer to the overall configuration of faculty focused upon the study of Asian countries on a campus, i.e., usually a group of faculty who self-identify across their respective departmental homes. Some universities have specifically constituted and separate faculty units of Asian studies to which the term "program" is applied in a more narrow sense.

35. Despite the efforts of several of the area-based research centers to bridge the gap, the greater public appreciation for the relevance of the Asia Pacific has led, in some instances, to a heightening of fractions on university campuses over the relative priorities and resource allocations to be given various teaching and research components. However, the long-term trend towards a more contemporary orientation and towards more inclusion of social science concerns and modes of research is likely to be irreversible and, in our view, a positive development.

36. This is not to engage the argument as to whether or not work of this sort, e.g., on the environment, constitutes the study of security per se. Rather it is to argue that informed knowledge of such topics is essential to those attempting to assess the impact of social, economic, or environmental change upon the security perceptions and policies of peoples and states. A good example in the Asian context would be the importance of the understanding about ocean resources and maritime territorial disputes in the South China Sea that could be provided by resource economists and legal experts to the security studies scholar studying China's security policies and the implications of China's force configuration.

37. Recent efforts by one of the authors has shown that such an inventory cannot be created by assembling information available through present institutional bases. Creation of such an inventory is to be a key activity of the newly established Canadian Consortium on Asia Pacific Security.

39. One of the authors examined the annual reports of the MSS Programs across Canada for the two years 1987 and 1992, attentive to the apparent changes in the

curriculums, graduate student theses, and faculty research projects between these two dates. The significant nodes within the MSSP network of security studies centers which focus upon the Asia Pacific are at the University of Victoria, the University of British Columbia, York University, Carleton University, and Laval. Five years ago, this could be said of only one center.

39. The role of the Cooperative Security Competition Fund in providing short-term support for Asia Pacific policy-oriented research should be noted. However, it was not possible for this paper to do a systematic review of the relative and absolute numbers of projects and amounts of funds devoted to Asia Pacific topics.

40. See chapter 15 of this volume by Paul Evans which provides an account of the regularized conferences, workshops, and dialogue activities underway in the Asia Pacific over the last several years.

41. This is, in some ways, a set of processes similar to those found with PECC. However, Canada's relative lack of success in bringing into play a national network of NGOs and business people around PECC is not a model for a subsequent CSCAP "member committee" process.

42. This is a further example of the interest in government in facilitating the development of Canadian expertise in Asia Pacific security studies. CANCAPS was set up with a one-year start-up grant provided by the Pacific 2000 Fund within EAITC. The consortium is intended to be a quasi-institutional means to bring together existing and newly developing expertise from both the research and policy communities in a track two format.

43. See David Dewitt, "Common, Comprehensive, and Cooperative Security in Asia Pacific," as referred to in note 7. Note, however, that usage of the terms associated with cooperative security does not necessarily imply a similar logic. For example, an American presentation which appropriates the term but *not* the logic, instead reflecting a perspective of a superpower's search for new touchstones in the post–Cold War era, is Ashton B. Carter, William J. Perry, and John D. Steinbruner, *A New Concept of Cooperative Security* (Washington, D.C.: The Brookings Institution, 1992).

44. Such a program would admittedly be expensive but should be attempted in light of the success of the MacArthur Foundation's program and the AAAS fellowship program, the latter designed for social scientists wishing to acquire training in the hard sciences relevant to arms control, and vice versa, the former less restrictive in providing training to extraordinarily able young persons who wish to take up work in areas that would allow them to do more innovative security studies work.

45. A call for select centers of excellence does not mean that accountability would be lost. In fact, the opposite is likely to be the case. As matters now stand, the performance of institutions may begin to count for less than their regional, or other, representative character. In a program of very small grants, there is little need or capacity for evaluation because each individual award accounts for such a small amount of the pie.

46. Reference should also be made to the notions of comprehensive security and common security. While these terms share much of the meaning of cooperative security, there are some subtle but important differences among them, both in terms of their conceptual connotations for scholars and their use in practice by officials of different Asia Pacific states. See Geoffrey Wiseman's "Common Security in the Asia Pacific Region," *The Pacific Review*, vol. 5, no. 1, pp. 42–59, and Dewitt, note 7.

47. Among many observers, not least those in the subregion itself, the Northeast Asia/North Pacific subregion is seen to be of particular importance on matters of military security, economic development and political capacity.

# China's Asia-Pacific Security Studies

## CHEN QIMAO

This paper attempts to offer a brief description of the current state of the Asia-Pacific security research in China, including China's assessment on the post–Cold War Asia-Pacific security situation, and transformation of some relevant perceptions. To begin with, it is very advisable to compare briefly China's security research with those of the Western countries, so that China's Asia-Pacific security studies can be better understood.

Since 1840, China, a great country notwithstanding, has been invaded by foreign powers. Even after the founding of the People's Republic of China in 1949, China still experienced quite a long period of foreign threat. Therefore, China has come to attach great importance to national security issues and has put the preservation of national sovereignty and security as a top priority. At the same time, as one of the Asian countries, China is particularly concerned with the research of Asia-Pacific security issues. But China's approach to security issues bears some different features, as compared with those of Western countries, which can be mainly listed as follows:

First, in contrast with the West, security as a concept in China is more inclusive and the human factor is given more importance in this respect. Since the time of the ancient Chinese strategist Sun Tzu (B.C. 770–476),[1] Chinese strategists have viewed security issues not only in terms of purely military considerations but also in terms of various other factors such as politics, economics, psychology and ethics. The support of the people is often deemed a more crucial factor in winning a war than the sophistication of weaponry. It was assumed, and is inherited by the Chinese contemporary security specialists, that the correct strategic decision, flexible tactics and moral righteousness can offset the opponent's tactical advantages.

Second, during the long revolutionary period before the founding of the People's Republic of China, China had formed its own specific military and political strategy and tactics to defeat its opponents. And since the birth of new China, China has accumulated much practical diplomatic and political experience, thus forming a unique strategy and tactics in maintaining national sovereignty and security. This special strategy and tactics are based on Mao Tse-Tung's doctrine "On Contradictions" which assumes that the world is inundated by contradictions and a complex composition of everlasting changes and metamorphosis. Various contradictions in turn influence each other and give rise to a major one, but vary in different phases. Armed with this doctrine, Chinese leaders and specialists can more often than not be successful in making an original assessment of the emerging situations with macrocosmic and holistic approaches, which have always tallied with the actual situation afterwards. For example, when the Soviet Union was disintegrating and East Europe was undergoing a drastic change, many Western scholars predicted that socialist China would follow suit in no time. Deng Xiaoping, however, pointed out that one should not be too pessimistic and disappointed about the situation, "The world contradictions are great in number and large in size, some profound ones have just been revealed." In addition, he elucidated that the chance for China's development does exist and the problem is the ability to seize it.[2] A good many Chinese scholars made similar assessments at the same time, and their analyses were also proven correct by the resulting facts.

Thirdly, with the adoption of open policy after 1978, and with more academic exchanges, the Chinese specialists have begun to pay attention to the study of Western security doctrines. Many useful Western concepts in security studies, such as arms control, confidence building, conflict prevention, etc., have been introduced to China, greatly enriching its security studies. But, up to the present, Chinese security research, with military strategy studies as an exception, has not yet separated from political science and fails to become a special academic subject as in the West. Therefore, China's security research still links itself to the research of international politics and economics, regional and country-specific studies, and is relatively weak in specific security topics such as arms control, confidence building measures, conflict prevention and peacekeeping actions, etc. The weakness in security research has in turn restricted the training of security specialists, thus presenting difficulties for a paper such as this. But it is just this fact that reflects the strong points as well as the weak points of China's security research—strong points in the sense of a holistic approach to strategic analysis and weak points in research on special areas in security issues.

## China's Asia-Pacific Security Research Institutions

China's Asia-Pacific security research institutions can be generally categorized as follows:

The first category of research institutions belongs to the Ministry of Foreign Affairs and the military. They include research departments, relevant regional departments (Department of Asia, Department of America, Department of Russia, Central Asia and Eastern Europe), and an International Department under the Ministry of Foreign Affairs and relevant bureaus and departments under the Ministry of Defense, the Ministry of State Security, and the Headquarters of the People's Liberation Army's General Staff, and so forth. At the request of their respective superior leadership, these institutions engage mainly in investigating and researching relevant security issues in assigned areas, in making the policy suggestions and countermeasure suggestions, and in drafting various documents and speeches for their leaders. Advantages can be identified in that these institutions are in close proximity to the policymakers and these institutions have access to varied first-hand materials. Their suggestions are of certain authority and they can exert direct impact on policymakers. Disadvantages can also be recognized in that their research findings tend to be restricted within immediate current affairs and a lack of strategic and forward-looking ability. Therefore, their research is often restrained by the current policies resulting in the absence of creativity.

The second category should be professional research institutes of international relations which are closely related with the government and the military. These are China's principal think tanks in Asia-Pacific security research. Some of those institutes belong directly to certain departments under the government or the army; others don't, but have close relations with those departments and are commissioned to do research work on certain subjects. They engage mainly in policy and strategic research and in investigation on some broad issues. Their opinions have a certain impact on policymakers. But they are weak in theoretical training; their security research needs more concreteness and depth. The following is an introduction of some principal professional research institutes of international relations:

1. China Center for International Studies (CCIS). The CCIS was first created in 1982 by Huan Xiang, the late eminent diplomat and international affairs specialist. The former name for the institute was the "Center of International Studies of the State Council," and was changed to the present name in 1988. The CCIS is a research and consultative institute on international affairs, foreign policy and security strategy. It specializes in important current world issues of a political, economic, and/or security nature. At the same time, it undertakes long- and medium-term predictions on international situations and comprehensive research on international security. The Department of International Strategy and Security has been set up under the guidance of the CCIS, which, as far as I know, is the only department of this kind among institutes of international relations in China. In the lifetime of Huang Xiang, the CCIS made several important policy suggestions on issues such as Chinese foreign policy readjustment in 1980s from "one line" in resisting Soviet expansionism to independent foreign policy of peace and the need to strengthen Asia-Pacific security research. These suggestions were highly appreciated and then adopted by the decision-making authorities. The former Chinese representative to the United Nations, Ambassador Li Luye is the incumbent director general of the CCIS.

2. Institute for Contemporary International Relations (ICIR). The ICIR has a staff of 400, of which more than 300 are researchers, and is the largest institute on international studies in China. It is powerful in research undertakings and has a library with a big collection of books and other information resources. Preparations for its establishment began back in 1965 and academic contacts with foreign counterparts have been expanding ever since 1980. It is now under the leadership of the relevant foreign affairs departments of the State Council and is commissioned by the latter to undertake research and consultation work. The ICIR places emphasis on the research of international political trends and security strategy and submits regular analytic reports and various investigation reports to the leadership with high appreciation. Shen Qurong is the incumbent director of the institute.

3. China Institute of International Studies (CIIS) was established in 1956. It was originally named as the Institute of International Relations and was later renamed as the Institute of International Studies. The present name has been used since 1987. The CIIS belongs to the Ministry of Foreign Affairs, and is the latter's principal think tank. It conducts research mainly on strategic issues such as international politics and world economy. Now it has a staff of nearly 100 with diplomats in rotation. The incumbent director, Yang Chengxu, is the former director of the Research Department of the Ministry of Foreign Affairs.

4. Shanghai Institute for International Studies (SIIS) was established in 1960 and was closed in 1966 due to the "Great Cultural Revolution." It was resumed in 1978. It has now a staff of approximately 100. According to the directive of the State Council in 1964, SIIS placed emphasis on research of North American and West European politics. It has also strengthened its research on Asia-Pacific regional politics, economics and security issues since the 1980s. In recent years, SIIS has focused its research on China's post–Cold War international environment and China's surrounding countries and regions. It has made some important suggestions on the issues of breaking sanctions imposed on China, developing relations with ASEAN countries and other neighboring countries, the Nansha Islands disputes and the Sino-US relations, which drew attentions to the decision-making authorities. SIIS receives the majority of its budget from the Shanghai municipal government. I had the honor to preside over the SIIS for ten years from 1981 to 1991. Professor Chen Peiyao is the incumbent president.

5. China Institute for International Strategic Studies (CIISS) was established in 1979 with its original name being the Beijing Institute for International Strategic Studies. The present name was adopted in 1992. The CIISS is a nonofficial research institute, despite its close links with the military. The first director of CIISS is General Wu XiuQuan, the ex-deputy chief of General Staff of the People's Liberation Army. The incumbent director is General Xu Xin, also the ex-deputy chief of General Staff of the PLA. CIISS mainly undertakes research on international strategic situations, international security, world politics and economics and regional issues. The majority of the present 100 and more full-time and part-time researchers are retired army officers or officers on the active list.

6. Department of Strategic Studies of the Academy of Military Science (AMS). The AMS is the largest military research institution in China. The Department of Strategic Studies (DSS) concentrates on security strategy research. The DSS has a staff of more than eighty which compose three offices—Office of Defense Strategy, Office of Basic Theory and Office of the Ancient Art of War, whose research findings are mainly circulated for military leaders as reference for decision making.

7. Institute for Strategic Studies (ISS) of the National Defense University (NDU) has about twenty research fellows who, in recent years, have paid more attention to research on such issues as the changes of the Asia-Pacific situation, the regional international relations, security mechanisms, arms

control and the changes of foreign military theories as reference for military leaders.

8. Center for Peace and Development studies (CPDS) is a nonofficial institute of international studies. It specializes in the issues of peace, security and development. The CPDS maintains a staff of approximately forty full-time and part-time people, and is funded mainly by the China Association for International Friendly Contact (CAIFC).

9. Institute for Peace and Development Studies (IPDS) was established in 1985. The IPDS is a new type and nongovernment research institute. Director Hu Gang is a young entrepreneur. The majority of the budget is funded with the profits gained by his enterprise—Shanghai Modern Social Science Consulting Corporation. The IPDS has hosted a number of influential conferences on Asia-Pacific security and other international issues.

The third category should include institutions of international and regional studies affiliated with the China Academy of Social Science (CASS) and some provincial and municipal academies of social science. The China Academy of Social Science (CASS) is China's largest national social science research institution. It consists of an Institute of World Economics and Politics (IWEP) and seven institutes of regional studies. Besides the IWEP, the Institute of Asia-Pacific Studies, Institute of Japanese Studies, Institute of American Studies and Institute of East European, Russian and Central Asian Studies also devote part of their research work to Asia-Pacific studies. There are also several institutes of Asia-Pacific regional studies under some of the provincial and municipal social science academies, such as the Institute of Asia-Pacific Studies located in Shanghai, the Institutes of Southeast Asian Studies located in Yunnan and in Fujian. These institutes place emphasis on comprehensive research over the politics, culture, society and history of relevant regions and countries. The strong point of these institutes is that they concentrate on academic orientation, and do research more systematically, and their research findings are deemed valuable to the government in policy-making, teaching and so forth. But they are relatively weak in combining their research with the current international practical struggles, and they do not focus on security studies. Nevertheless, certain experts in those institutes do put forth some important suggestions in concern with specific national security issues. For example, the Institute of American Studies has pursued systematic research on the history of Sino-US relations (including US-Taiwan relations) and put forward corresponding policy suggestions. The Institute of Southeast Asian Studies of Yunnan Social Science Academy, located in Kunmin, has a profound knowledge about Indo-China, Myanmar and Thailand. The Foreign Ministry often consults with them in dealing with issues related to those countries.

The fourth category covers departments and institutes affiliated to universities. There are three universities, namely, Beijing University, People's University and Fudan University, where there are departments of international politics. A number of universities set up institutes of international and regional studies, such as the Institute of International Relations at Beijing University, Center of International Studies at Nankai University, the Institute of USA and Canada at

Wuhan University, the Institute of International Studies at East China Normal University and the Institute of International Studies at Shanghai University of International Relations, and so forth. Those institutes are generally oriented to teaching, and mainly focus on theories of international relations, history of modern international relations, and basic situations on relevant countries and regions. Since they hardly have timely access to certain first-hand information on international struggles due to the current Chinese educational system, most of them do not enlist international trends and foreign policies in their research scope. However, those universities have many excellent scholars who are very active in the international academic community and quite informed of the knowledge of relevant Asia-Pacific countries; therefore, they are always able to put forward important suggestions on Asia-Pacific security issues. Especially in recent years, there have been many young scholars, including some with PhDs from American and European universities. One good example is Dr. Shen Dingli, a young scholar in the Center for American Studies of Fudan University, whose original major was physics, but who, after studying at Princeton University for several years, is now pursuing a joint disarmament project with professors at Princeton. He tries to combine his knowledge on physics with nuclear disarmament. In the early 1980s, the universities were considered as peripheral members of Asia-Pacific security studies, but since the late 1980s, this situation has changed significantly.

The first two categories of Asia-Pacific security studies institutes mentioned above are located in Beijing, except for Shanghai Institute for International Studies, and the Institute of Peace and Development Studies, both of which are located in Shanghai. The other two categories are distributed across the country. They are either under the leadership of or supported by central and local governments without leading centers or coordination centers at the national level. Soon after its establishment in early 1980s, the Center of International Studies had tried to coordinate the international studies of the State Council in China but failed due to the enormous size of the country and complicated conditions. The present practices are as follows:

1. Hosted by the China Center of International Studies, conferences on international situations have been held annually in December since 1989. Directors and well-known specialists from all of the relevant institutes in China are invited to attend the conferences. Asia-Pacific security has been the constant topic in those conferences. Conferences of this kind are held irregularly by other institutes. For example, in August 1993, the Institute of Peace and Development Studies sponsored a symposium on international studies at Yantai, Shandong Province. The leaders of all institutes of international studies were invited to the symposium. Issues of post–Cold War international situations and strengthening international studies were the major topics of the symposium, among which issues such as Asia-Pacific security and Chinese security policy were also discussed.

2. All kinds of national and local associations and societies of international studies such as the Society of World Economy, the Society of American Studies, the Society of Japanese Studies, Shanghai Society of International

Relations, and so forth, often hold academic symposiums aimed at exchanging ideas, or coordinating topics and research. These symposiums are basically academically oriented, though sometimes hot issues like China's security are also discussed.

3. Since 1983, the State Council has set aside funds for the Foundation of Social Sciences (FSS). The FSS is composed of different academic evaluation teams, each organized on a disciplinary basis, of which international relations is one. Key projects of state social sciences are selected every five years, while ordinary projects are selected additionally every year. The themes of both key projects and ordinary projects are set by the leading committee of FSS, and then all projects are competed for among universities and research institutes. The final choice will be made by relevant evaluation teams. A number of the projects on international relations are related to Asia-Pacific security.

## Publications

In China since 1979, research has been independent and free from government intervention but publication has been somewhat limited. In the research area, government encourages emancipated thinking, seeking truth from facts, free expression of ideas and views and free discussion. In terms of publications, the regulation is that opinions that differ from to the government's current foreign policy are permitted to be published in classified journals and documents which are circulated in a specific circle, but not allowed to be published in newspapers and open journals. In addition, since Asia-Pacific security issues are closely related to China's national security, a lot of research findings of Asia-Pacific security are regarded as secret. The professional institutions, as included in the second category mentioned earlier, and institutes affiliated to social science academies have compiled a considerable amount of classified materials and documents concerning Asia-Pacific security in terms of policy suggestions, tendency analysis, discrete topics, comprehensive reports and so on. They are mainly selected as reference for leadership and relevant government departments. I am sorry I can not go into further details.

It is impossible to assess the specific impact of the research results on policy-making. But it can be certain that as the old generation of veteran revolutionaries gradually recede from the political arena and a new generation of leaders, mainly grown up from technocrats, come into power that the influence of think tanks in policy-making will be on the rise. For example, when dramatic changes occurred in the Soviet Union and East Europe a couple of years ago, top leaders, including General Secretary Jiang Zemin, called for several meetings with relevant specialists and listened to their opinions. Sometimes the top leaders would create topics and seek advisories from relevant specialists. In recent years, China has made great achievements in carrying out omnidimensional diplomatic policy, improving relations with neighboring countries, breaking sanctions imposed by Western countries, and Chinese international studies specialists have made their contributions to these achievements.

The following are some of the main published periodicals concerning Asia-Pacific security research:

1. *International Studies* is a quarterly that started publication in 1959, and is edited and published by the China Institute of International Studies. Articles about Asia-Pacific security carried in recent issues are: "Seeking for a New Political Order in the Asia-Pacific Region" (no. 1, 1992); "Adjustment of the US Asia-Pacific Strategy" (no. 2, 1992); "Asia-Pacific Regional Situation and China's Good-neighbor Policy" (no. 4, 1993), etc.

2. *Contemporary International Relations,* started publication in October 1981, and since 1993 has become a monthly. It is edited and published by the Institute of Contemporary International Relations. Articles about Asia-Pacific security carried in recent issues are: "Asia-Pacific Security Situation and Different Concepts of Security Mechanism" (May 1993); "The US: Its New Asia-Pacific Strategy and Policy Trends" (no. 2, 1992); "Northeast Asia: Features of the Security Environment and its Sensibility" (no. 6, 1992); "Initial Analysis of the Situation in the Asia-Pacific Region in the 1990s" (no. 6, 1992); "Nuclear Issues on Korean Peninsula" (September 1993).

3. *International Strategic Studies* is a quarterly edited and published by the China Society of International Strategic Studies. Articles about Asia-Pacific security carried in recent issues are "New Situation of Arms Control and Disarmament in Asia-Pacific Region and China's Policy" (January 1993); "Inquiry of Asia-Pacific Regional Situation and Security Issues" (January 1993); "China's Defensive Strategy under New Situation" (September 1993).

4. *Peace and Development* is a quarterly edited and published by the Center of Peace and Development Studies. Examples of articles about Asia-Pacific security carried in recent issues are "Prospects of Changes and Development in the Asia-Pacific Regional Security Situation" (no. 1, 1993); "Northeast Asian Regional Security Situation" (no. 4, 1992), etc.

5. *SIIS Papers and Research Reports* is published irregularly and is comprised of selected papers edited by the Shanghai Institute for International Studies. Articles about Asia-Pacific security carried in recent issues are "Features and Tendencies of Change in Asia-Pacific Power Configuration" (February 1991); "Asia-Pacific Security in the 1990s and China's Policy Response" (January 1993); and "An Approach on the Solution of Nansha Islands Disputes" (January 1991).

6. *Asia-Pacific Studies* is a bimonthly edited and published jointly by the Institute of Asia-Pacific Studies, the China Academy of Social Science and the China Association of Asia-Pacific Studies. Some articles about Asia-Pacific security carried in recent issues are "Security Environment and Arms Control in Asia-Pacific Regions" (March 1992); and "Trends of Adjustment of the US Asia-Pacific Strategy" (May 1992).

7. *Asia-Pacific Forum* is a bimonthly edited and published by the Institute of Asia-Pacific Studies, Shanghai Academy of Social Sciences. Examples of articles about Asia-Pacific security carried in recent issues are "Asia-Pacific

Regional Security Configuration in the 1990s and China's Policy Response" (January 1993); "Sino-US Relations: From the View of Asia-Pacific Security Configuration" (March 1993); and "Disputes on Nansha Islands and the Prospects of Their Solution (no. 6, 1992).

8. *Southeast Asian Studies* is a quarterly edited and published by the Institute of Southeast Asian Studies, Yunnan Academy of Social Science. Articles about Asia-Pacific security carried in recent issues are "Review of Arms Trade in Asia-Pacific Regions"; "A Glance of Arms Control in Asia-Pacific Regions" (January 1993).

Readers of the above-mentioned journals are mainly composed of relevant government officials, intellectuals of universities and science research institutions, and those who are interested in international studies. They are mostly published in Chinese, except a few with English index and summaries, such as *International Studies, Contemporary International Relations*, and *SIIS Papers and Research Reports*. China Institute of International Studies, Institute of Contemporary International Relations and Shanghai Institute for International Studies publish some English papers on an irregular basis.

The popular journals of international studies published in China at present are *World Affairs*, and *International Outlook*. Both are biweekly publications. The former is edited and published by the World Affairs Publishing House. The journal has a history of more than sixty years with a circulation of 100,000 or more. The latter is published by SIIS and has a history of ten years with a circulation of 40,000–50,000. Those two journals frequently brief their readers on situations on Asia-Pacific security, which include big-power relations in the region, arms race and arms control situations, hot spot conflicts, political and economic information of relevant countries, China's relations with other Asia-Pacific countries, and so on.

# The Training of Security Specialists

As described earlier, in China international security studies has not yet disassociated from the discipline of international politics as an independent discipline, except in the army. This fact has somehow influenced the training of security specialists.

At present, the young generation of Asia-Pacific security specialists are mainly trained by the following institutions:

1. Professional institutes and colleges, of which three are on a national level:

   a) The National Defense University (NDU) is the institution of highest learning in the army, which was set up by merging the PLA Military Academy, PLA Political Academy and PLA Logistics Academy. Its task is to train senior commanders and researchers of strategic studies and staffs for the three services. Asia-Pacific security specialists is the main training purpose of its strategic studies program.

b)  Foreign Affairs College (FAC), directly under the leadership of the MFA, is an institution of high learning that trains diplomats, foreign affairs personnel and international studies specialists. It was established in 1955 according to the suggestion of the late Premier Zhou Enlai, and was presided over by its first president, the then Vice Premier and Foreign Minister Chen Yi. Some of the graduates were distributed to serve in the foreign affairs departments, and others to serve in institutions of international studies.

c)  The Institute of International Relations (IIR) mainly fosters and trains political science and foreign affairs specialists with foreign language skills. The graduates are distributed to relevant foreign affairs sections undertaking practical work or research work.

All the three above-mentioned institutes are located in Beijing. Similar institutes, but of smaller scale, are set up beyond Beijing.

2.  Most of the departments of international politics and departments of foreign languages under universities undertake the doctoral and master degree programs. A lot of the graduates are assigned to research institutes undertaking research work concerning Asia-Pacific affairs.

3.  Postgraduate programs operated by professional research institutes and institutes under academies of social sciences. Since 1980, the Chinese Academy of Social Sciences and a number of local equivalents have offered postgraduate programs leading to a master's degree and doctoral degree for the study of international politics, economic and regional researches. As a result, a large number of talents on Asia-Pacific security affairs have been fostered. Professional research institutes are doing the same but started a bit later. Three points are basically observed in the training:

1.  Marxism and Mao Zhedong Thought are still stressed as guiding principles, but students are advised that Marxism should not be treated as dogma, rather it should be used as a weapon or methodology. The emphasis is laid on seeking truth through facts, which as Deng Xiaoping explained, is the soul of Marxism. At the same time, much importance is attached to absorbing the essence of traditional Chinese strategic theories and Western strategic theories as well as the former Soviet Union's strategic theories.

2.  It stresses the combination of theory with practice. This is especially obvious in those professional research institutes at Beijing, whose researchers are frequently on the rotation with government officials, ex-ambassadors and other diplomats, who always take positions in research institutes and vice versa. This process is particularly effective for the training of security experts. But it is almost unavailable for the local research institutes.

3.  The combination of domestic training with studying abroad. Since the 1980s, most of China's international and Asia-Pacific security research institutes granted by the government and some foreign foundations, have dispatched a great number of middle-aged and young international politics and security researchers to the universities and research institutes in the United States,

Japan, Germany, Britain and other countries for further education or to serve as guest scholars. This is most helpful for the training of a great many security experts who will be well informed in international and Asia-Pacific affairs. Many of them, after return, become professors, associate professors, and directors of research departments. Several new courses, such as Western International Relations Theory, Western Diplomacy Theory and Security Defense are introduced to political science departments by them. In terms of methods, the most effective is the one-year term of visiting scholars and the one- or two-year term of postgraduate programs, such as the postgraduate program offered by Fletcher School at Tufts University for young diplomats, and the one-year master degree program operated by SAIS at Johns Hopkins University. Study in a doctoral degree program can acquire systematic knowledge, though its term is too protracted and some students, after finishing their programs, cannot always return to China as scheduled due to various reasons, so that the result is not as good as expected. On the other hand, a term too short (e.g., three months) makes it difficult for guest researchers to reach their goal. They always have to return to China just when they have learned something and made a good beginning to their projects.

In regard to procuring various foreign journals, research findings and other sources of Asia-Pacific security affairs, the professional research institutes are in a better position than some other institutes as they possess more financial means and some have special purchasing channels. The research institutes of the academies of social sciences are not as well off. These university-affiliate institutes purchase less foreign journals because of financial difficulties. Listening to foreign broadcasts is no longer a problem at present.

## External Exchanges

Since the implementation of reform and open policy in 1979, a boom of external exchanges has been witnessed in China's international studies institutes. It can be said, in a sense, that those institutes have been playing the leading role in China's external cultural and academic exchanges. Professional research institutes and institutes under the academies of social science and universities have all established two-way academic exchange relations with their foreign counterparts. Those exchanges include exchanging visits and information sources and holding academic conferences. Many conferences are concerned with Asia-Pacific security. It has been a common practice that senior specialists are invited to various international conferences discussing Asia-Pacific politics and security issues.

In recent years, some relevant research institutes have held several large-scale conferences on Asia-Pacific security at Beijing, Shanghai and other localities, among which some more influential conferences are as follows:

In September 1991, the Chinese Academy of Social Science, China Center of International Studies and China Institute of International Studies jointly convened the symposium of New International Order, which was attended by specialists and scholars from more than twenty nations. One special section was set for discussion on the Asia-Pacific regional security situation and the establishing of new political order in the region.

In August 1992, the China Center of International Studies convened, in Beijing, the international conference titled "Change of Asia-Pacific Power Configuration in the 1990s: Security, Cooperation and Development," on which Asia-Pacific security issues was the key topic.

In August 1992, SIIS and the UN Disarmament Department jointly held the conference "Asia-Pacific Regional Security and Disarmament." More than sixty people including senior officials and experts from eighteen nations attended the conference in Shanghai. Foreign Minister Qian Qiceng made the keynote speech on the meeting.

In November 1992, the Institute of Peace and Development held in Shanghai the Conference of Northeast Asia Security and Development. Forty-odd specialists from six countries attended the meeting.

In July 1993, the China Research Association of Strategy and Management under the support of the Department of Strategic Research at the Academy of Military Science sponsored together with the Chinese Center of International Studies and the Atlantic Council of the US (ACUS), a conference in Pejing titled "East Asian Cooperation and Development in the Coming Decade." The conference was attended by Mr. Hawke, former premier of Australia, Mr. Chutchai Choonhawan, the former premier of Thailand and many distinguished specialists, scholars and entrepreneurs. Apart from the discussion on the change in post–Cold War East Asian configuration by the conference, Asia-Pacific security was specifically discussed at one of the group meetings.

It is reported that the Chinese Center of International Studies will convene a large international conference in Beijing in mid-1994 on Asia-Pacific securities issues.

## Assessment by Chinese Experts on the Post–Cold War Asia-Pacific Security Situation

1. In the fall of 1989, when dramatic changes took place in the Eastern European countries, Deng Xiaoping[3] gave three important advices: One was to observe the situation cool-mindedly; the second was to secure our own front line; and the third was to handle all incidents with calmness. He also advised that China should not be involved in international ideological debates,[4] but rather we should concentrate our energy to do a better job domestically. All these points are very important for China's recent security studies. They gave an impetus for more pragmatism, hard data and first-hand materials collecting, overhauling the real situation no matter how serious it is, seeking and telling the truth. Of course, time and again, there are some ideologic interventions from the leftist trends, but it's not the mainstream. The mainstream in security studies is more pragmatism and more realism. That's why China's security experts could make correct assessments on China's international environment in recent years and committed no big mistakes.

2. Most people are optimistic on the present situation of the Asia-Pacific region. In the wake of the end of a bipolar power configuration, the formerly rela-

tively stable Europe is beset by various turmoils while the formerly regional-war-ridden Asia enjoys relative political stability and economic boom. The two regions present a striking contrast which is a striking feature in the post–Cold War situation.

3.  It is conceived that the occurrence of a relatively stable political situation in the Asia-Pacific region is not accidental and the reasons are as follows:

    a)  The Yalta system was not so complete and consolidated in the Asia-Pacific region as in Europe. In Europe, many historically inherited contradictions and disputes had been long covered by confrontation of a bipolar power configuration based on the Yalta system. Those contradictions and disputes erupted as the bipolar power configuration had ended. This has lead to new turmoil and hot spots. In the Asia-Pacific region, however, the Yalta system was broken through by the Chinese revolution in the late 1940s and the Asian national liberation movements in the 1950s wherefore many contradictions had already been exposed and unfolded. Several relatively large-scale wars took place successively in the Asia-Pacific region in the post–Cold War era. Thus, some contradictions were settled, and some are in the course of settlement or alleviation. On that account, the end of the bipolar power configuration had less impact on the Asia-Pacific region.

    b)  Thanks to postwar political and economic development, the Asia-Pacific region has in fact already formed several relatively <u>balanced and mutually checked</u> centers as of the United States, Japan, China, Russia, ASEAN and so forth.

    c)  Many Asia-Pacific nations and areas have developed an idiosyncratic East Asian mode from their own economic development, which has resulted in continuously high economic growth, and thus provided a base for relative stability in the Asia-Pacific region and made it possible, at the same time, for the occurrence of a benign circle in which economic growth and political security are mutually encouraged.

4.  On the other hand, it should not be ignored that unstable elements still remain in Asia-Pacific regions, namely

    a)  Historical legacies left by the Cold War, of which the most salient is the serious military confrontation on the Korean peninsula that has not been fundamentally settled and will probably be intensified again. The Cambodian issue might also experience some setbacks.

    b)  Historical disputes on territorial lands and seas between some Asia-Pacific countries, such as disputes over the sovereignty of the Nansha Islands (Sprataly Islands), disputes over the Northern Territories between Russia and Japan, disputes over territorial lands and seas among Southeast Asian countries and so on.

    c)  Relations between big powers in the region have not yet been stabilized. Frictions of different natures and degrees exist between China and the

United States, between the United States and Japan and between Japan and Russia, and they are yet to be adjusted.

d)   A number of countries in the region are at present in a political and economic transition period and face a succession of problems.

Some unstable elements may emerge and intensify or even turn into turmoil especially if some big powers intervene in those countries' domestic affairs inappropriately. It should not be neglected that those unstable elements will lead to uncertainty in Asia-Pacific region. These unstable elements, if handled improperly, might jeopardize the politically stable and economically prosperous situation in the present Asia-Pacific region.

5.   Under the current situation, it is much desired and opportune to step up the research and exchanges of Asia-Pacific security.

## Shifts in the Chinese Security Concepts in the Wake of the End of the Cold War

1.   Given the lesson that the Soviet Union, a superpower as such, collapsed without war, China places particular emphasis on security in its comprehensive senses, namely, economic construction, political stability, national unity, law and order, and building of a spiritual civilization. In late 1991 when the Soviet Union was going to disintegrate, the Chinese specialists had discussed what the main threat might be and where it would come from after the end of the Cold War. Many specialists suggested that the main threat to China might come from multilevel economic and scientific challenges. They concluded that if China could not develop its economy and science and technology steadily, sustainably and rapidly, so as to reduce the gap between itself and the West and the four Asian NIEs gradually, and if China's economy lagged behind the neighboring ASEAN countries, or if things got even worse so that China's economy suffered from stagnation or hyperinflation, the Chinese populace would doubt the viability of building socialism with Chinese characteristics. With that in mind, it was seen that the economic crisis would turn into a political one.[5] This opinion conforms to the spirit of Deng Xiaoping's speech in his southern trip in the spring of 1992, in which he emphasized the speeding up of reform and opening up as well as modernization. He pointed out that the economy in some neighboring countries and areas had been developing more rapidly than in China. Thus, if China remained underdeveloped or developed very slowly, people would compare by themselves and would become dissatisfied. He warned that if China did not stick to socialism, did not reform and open to the outside world, did not develop the economy and improve the peoples' lives, China would definitely begin to slide into oblivion.[6] Deng's speech reflects the Chinese new security concept after learning the lessons of the collapse of the Soviet Union.

2.   China attaches more importance to the research on the surrounding environment and the relations between China and neighboring countries. China also

puts more emphasis on the developing of friendly relations with neighboring countries.

3.  China pays more attention to the research on the big-power's Asia-Pacific security policies in search of a common position and in discerning differences. At present, China particularly emphasizes the research on the Clinton administration's Asia-Pacific policy which is yet to take shape, and the research on Clinton's implication and intention of his "Asia-Pacific Community" concept. This demonstrates that China seeks the prospect of establishing stable relations with big powers in the Asia-Pacific regions.

4.  China adopts a cautiously positive position towards the gradual establishment of an Asia-Pacific security mechanism. As is known to all, China had been critical to the Asia collective security system proposed by Brezhnev through Gorbachev. As of now, China still distinguishes the Asia-Pacific region from Europe and rejects copying the CSCE model. China holds that the condition is not ripe for immediate building of an Asia-Pacific security mechanism. China considers it significant and necessary, at the present stage, to set up a forum for multichanneled, multilayered dialogues and consultations on security. China has already decided to attend, upon invitation, the ASEAN-initiated regional forum. China also favors active dialogues with relevant countries on security issues in the region and the research and probe on gradual establishment of a security mechanism.

5.  China is moderately positive towards the UN role in maintaining world stability and peace including the UN peacekeeping activities. For instance, China is basically positive towards the UN peacekeeping action in Cambodia and actively joined the actions by dispatching personnel. Besides, China voted in favor of the UN humanitarian securing actions in Somalia. But, conceivably, China holds a reserved attitude towards some UN peacekeeping actions and thus abstains from voting on some cases. China opposes interference in the domestic politics of other countries.

6.  China attaches great importance to the establishment of international order. As early as December 1988, Deng Xiaoping initiated the establishment of a new international order on the basis of five peace and coexistence principles.[7] Later on, other Chinese leaders reiterated the initiative on many occasions. Chinese scholars and specialists have conducted a great deal of research and held many discussions on the matter. Some scholars attempted to research the feasibility of establishing a new political order first in the Asia-Pacific region, in view of the fact that the post–Cold War world situation is characterized by complexity, unrest and disparity as against relative political stability and economic prosperity in the Asia-Pacific region.[8]

# Key Topics on Asia-Pacific Security in Current Research

According to incomplete sources, the main research topics currently undertaken by relevant research institutions in China on Asia-Pacific security are as follows:

1. Changes in the post–Cold War world configuration and its impact on the Asia-Pacific region
2. Power structure and great-power relations in the Asia-Pacific region after the Cold War
3. Clinton administration's Asia-Pacific security strategy—Clinton's concept of the "Asia-Pacific Community"
4. Japan's trends after the formation of Morihiro Hosokawa's cabinet
5. Establishing dialogue mechanism on Asia-Pacific security
6. Arms control in the Asia-Pacific region
7. Issues on the Korean peninsula
8. China's surrounding environment and its relations with neighboring countries, including China's border disputes with some neighboring countries and the Nansha (Sprataly) Islands issue
9. Sino-US relations
10. Economic security

## Difficulties in Stepping Up Research on Asia-Pacific Security

Presently, the budget difficulties are the greatest problem facing Chinese institutions of Asia-Pacific security studies. Most Chinese institutes are funded by the government. Since China is now in its initial stage of transition from planned economy to socialist market economy, the financial situation of the central government is relatively difficult. Therefore, many research institutes funded by the government are in a difficult situation. Moreover, Chinese enterprises have not yet developed to the degree of the transnational corporations in developed countries. Quite a number of state-run companies are themselves in financial straits. These state-owned companies have neither the desire nor the capacity to grant research monies to institutes. This, combined with inflationary pressure, means that most institutes are suffering from financial difficulties which will inevitably hinder not only the strengthening of research work but also the well-being of academic exchanges, the securing and accumulating of informational materials, as well as the stability of the pool of researchers. For example, the price of flight tickets from Shanghai to Beijing have doubled and redoubled; thus the institutes have to control the number of times researchers are allowed to attend academic meetings. And some young researchers with excellent foreign language abilities have quit their jobs to find jobs in joint ventures or foreign-owned corporations, due to the sharp salary differences between institutes and foreign-invested corporations. The recruitment of students for graduate programs is difficult for the same reasons. Some research institutions, for the sake of getting rid of financial difficulty, operate tertiary industries but few succeed. Some foreign foundations, such as the Ford Foundation (USA), the Asian Foundation (USA) and the US Committee of International Relations Studies with the People's Republic of China (CIRSPRC) and the Japanese Foundation of International Exchanges have granted a great deal to Chinese research institutions. But, unfortunately, for various reasons, these grants have decreased in recent years. Owing to financial restrictions, external exchanges are confined to a few countries such as the United States, Japan and Germany. Little exchange is under way with ASEAN countries, Australia, New Zealand and Canada, and this will inextricably check the research on Asia-Pacific security.

Perhaps one way to resolve the budgetary difficulties is to establish some foundations. One example is the Foundation for International and Strategic Studies in Beijing, which was established in June 1989, with Chen Chu, the former vice foreign minister as its president. So far it had granted several research projects and academic activities, but its role is still limited due to lack of more finance resources. Under the support of relevant leadership, the China Center of International Studies and some other institutes are trying to raise funds to set up a foundation of international studies. As China is now transforming to a market economy, the possibility for establishing successful foundations to support the security studies is increasing. The big foundations in industrial countries may consider this new alternative instead of granting to individual institutions or projects.

# Afterword

As mentioned above, the strength of China's security research is its holistic approach to strategic analysis, while the weakness resides in its lack of deep and systematic research on specific issues in the field of security affairs, which is partly due to the shortage of experts in the field. Under the new situation after the end of Cold War, China is strengthening research on Asia-Pacific security, and trying to maintain its own advantages while overcoming disadvantages. It does this by drawing on foreign experiences, especially those of developed countries and by making an effort to build a security discipline with Chinese characteristics which accords with the demands of post–Cold War situational developments. At the same time, Chinese research institutions will zealously engage in exchanges and cooperations with foreign counterparts and expect their support.

## Notes

1. Sun Tzu was the famous Chinese strategist of the late Spring and Autumn period. His works *Sun Tzu's Arts of War* is of great influence and has been translated into many languages.

2. *Selected Works of Deng Xiaoping*, vol.3 (Beijing: People's Publishing House, 1993), pp. 354, 363, 375.

3. Ibid., p. 321.

4. Ibid., p. 353.

5. "New Approaches in China's Foreign Policy: The Post–Cold War Era," *Asian Survey*, vol. XXXIII, no. 3, March 1993.

6. "Main Points in the Speech in Wuchang, Shenzhen, Zhuhai, Shanghai and So On," *Deng Xiaoping's Collections of Essays*, vol. 3.

7. *Selected Works of Deng Xiaoping*, vol. 3, pp. 281–83.

8. "Inquiry on Establishing New Political Order in Asia-Pacific Region," *International Studies*, no. 1, 1992.

# Asia/Pacific Security Studies in Europe

## GERALD SEGAL

N o, Europe is not all that far from Asia/Pacific. Brussels is considerably closer to Bali than is Los Angeles or Vancouver. If we are measuring European involvement with Asia/Pacific in terms of trade, East Asians will know that the likes of Germany, Britain and France rank among their top traders and European markets are taking an increasing share of exports while North American markets decline as a percentage of total exports. In short, Europe matters to East Asians and after a period of post-colonial decline, its importance is increasing.

This Eurasian reality, as unpalatable as it may be to Pacific enthusiasts, explains why the first book to be written on arms control in East Asia came out of Europe and why the leading Pacific studies journal covering security issues is based in London.[1] Apart from the concentration of expertise in the United States and Australia, Europe has the largest community of Asia/Pacific security specialists and is ranked with the Americans and Australians as one of the best places for young scholars to train.

The explanation for the continuing European role is a complex mix of historical tradition, long-standing and cutting-edge research in security studies, and a more recent concern with defining a broader sense of European global interests. The result is a community of specialists of the highest caliber, and yet one that often has to struggle with the excesses of Pacific-chic that sometimes excludes Europeans from discussions about Pacific security. If there is a common thread to analysis in Europe about Asia/Pacific security, it is that the subject should not be left to the Pacific enthusiasts in the region. What takes place in Asia/Pacific is of concern to the world at large, and what takes place in the world at large should be of concern to people in Asia/Pacific. In this respect at least, Europeans are generally committed to trilateralism among specialists and in government policies. Therefore it is all the more sad that such multilateralism is often interpreted as an attempt to impose Eurocentric or mid-Atlantic notions of security on Asia/Pacific. In reality, Europeans have mostly transcended the imperial phase of thinking about Asia/Pacific, even if many Asians have not yet done so. This is all the more reason to strengthen the Eurasian leg of the trilateral system.

# Perceiving Asia/Pacific

At the outset it must be acknowledged that the term "European" must be used with great caution, especially when talking about perceptions and even more so in the post–Maastricht era. Europeans are only now learning to be less glib and confident about their supposed unity of mind and purpose. There are vast differences between a British view of Europe that sees the region more as one part of a globally interdependent world, and a French perspective that is determined to drive towards a federal Europe. These differences are naturally reflected in views of Asia/Pacific, for Britain welcomes East Asian foreign direct investment while others in Europe tend to fret about a "Yellow Peril."[2] These differences have their roots in varying experiences and perceptions that stretch back several hundred years.

## *Imperial Ties*

A useful starting point is the fact that Europeans used to dominate much of Asia/Pacific. For centuries the international relations of Asia was little more than an extension of European great-power politics. Britain settled and ruled the North American Pacific and much of the South Pacific. They opened China and governed much of Southeast Asia. France and the Netherlands had much smaller empires in Asia/Pacific, nearly all of which is now gone. Russia has still not given up the territory it colonized in the east, and Britain is about to surrender its last significant holding to China in 1997 (and so will Portugal in 1999). Significantly, Germany has no imperial baggage and therefore an easier task in building normal relations in Asia/Pacific.

The legacy of imperialism for Europeans can be found on many levels. For one thing there are important minority populations in Europe which reflect the colonial heritage. In Britain this is more true for South than East Asia, and issues are often wrapped up in wider aspects of Commonwealth politics. In France, Indo-Chinese issues were of the highest importance in the 1950s, but now only echo in disputes about war crimes or a determination to play an active role in a settlement in Cambodia.[3] France has also had a special interest in South Pacific issues and in part because of the placement of its nuclear testing site there, the South Pacific has figured in much French geopolitical writing. Naturally, this has been associated with more conservative politics, as seen in the operation of L'Institute du Pacifique in Paris.[4] The Netherlands and Portugal take a prominent role in urging tough EC action against Indonesia for violations of human rights, in large part because of a sense of a post-colonial guilty conscience.

The only country where imperial issues still resonate at the highest levels is Britain, where Hong Kong raises complex issues of responsibility. Policies on immigration, attitudes to Communism after the Cold War, and business interests, combine into the volatile politics of today. Governor Chris Patten is one of Britain's most senior politicians and his activities on the other side of Eurasia are often front-page news from London to Edinburgh. As Britain has begun to internationalize the Hong Kong issue, relations with China have suffered and relations with others in East Asia (most notably the Japanese) have taken on new importance.[5]

But Hong Kong will be returned to China in 1997 and soon after the intensity will fade from this issue. Only then will Europeans be more-or-less free of their imperial legacy in Asia/Pacific. By then most officials who ruled in the east will have retired or died. The pattern of trade relations for all Europeans has already passed into a post-imperial phase with the major trading partners being the major trading states of East Asia rather than those who had colonial connections.

In security terms, little has been left of imperial times for several decades. Britain has long since moved east of Suez and the garrison in Hong Kong will be removed on July 1, 1997. French and British ships still operate in the Pacific but sporadically and in small numbers. The curious resilience of the Five Power Defence Arrangements linking Commonwealth states with Britain owes more to Southeast Asian's desire to retain what is essentially a confidence building regime.[6] The resilience is made all the more curious by the fact that there is no other multilateral security arrangement in Asia/Pacific. Some states in the region have contributed to multilateral security operations such as the Gulf War of 1990–91, but they did so effectively under NATO standard operating procedures and because of broader political commitments to Western security interests. Such operations have nothing to do with European imperial legacies except in that FPDA exercises helped some Commonwealth states fit more easily into NATO procedures.

Germany, which was notable for its absence of colonies in Asia/Pacific could be said to be a special case among European great powers. Cynics might note that German scholars have specialized in Japanese studies, but a less cynical explanation probably has to do with the primacy of economic relations and pragmatism in the postwar policies of both states.[7] In fact, German studies and policies concerns in the region have paid most attention to China and that focus seems set to grow as the China market looms ever larger. Unlike Britain and to some extent France, German economic pragmatism has led them to be relatively unconcerned with human rights issues in China. But to a large extent it is true that Europeans increasingly see Asia/Pacific primarily in economic terms. What remains uncertain is whether there are security implications to be derived from the importance of Asia/Pacific for the global market economy.

## Cold War Attitudes

The fading of differences among Europeans because of differing colonial legacies has taken decades to develop to the point where they are of little importance. But the Cold War has only recently ended and its impact might have been expected to take longer to fade. However, because the Cold War was always applied in a different way in East Asia, and because the Europeans had far too much on which to focus closer to home, Europeans have not worried as much about the Cold War in Asia/Pacific.

Europeans certainly noted that NATO prospered in part because Communists conveniently fought with Americans in Asia (Korea and Vietnam), and therefore strengthened the American resolve to help defend Europeans. When Asian tensions drove the United States to extreme attitudes, as in relations with China or the war in Vietnam, Europeans fretted that the United States might lose sight of the main struggle in Europe. Thus Europeans such as Britain and France were ahead of the United States in dealing with Communist China, but tugged at American coattails when the United States wanted to dash into bed with China, all in the cause of upsetting the Soviet Union. Europeans demonstrated on the streets in larger numbers and far earlier than Americans in protest at the war in Vietnam. Americans tended to see the war as an East-West struggle, but Europeans who had their own vociferous Communist parties saw the war as mainly civil strife.

By the time the Cold War ended, Europeans had long since come to see East Asia in regional rather than global terms. By the time the Cold War overlay was lifted from East Asia, Europeans were quicker to see that there was a massive power vacuum. Whereas Americans saw the vacuum as largely a function of the ending of the Cold War, Europeans recognized that the gap was really far larger—it was the result of several hundred years of European domination of East Asian international relations.[8] Unlike Europe where living memory provided clues to a natural balance of power, in East Asia one had to go back several hundred years to find an indigenous pattern of international relations.[9]

The fact that the ancient pattern of relations was one of Chinese domination, at least as long as China was unified and strong, led many Europeans to see post–Cold War East Asia as potentially dominated by China. Europeans were quicker than the Americans to focus on China as the rising power of East Asia and see Japan in a new light as a state under pressure. China's sudden emergence as the EU's third largest source of imports in the 1990s accentuated this assessment. EU states had fewer overt disputes with China such as the American debate over MFN status, but Europeans were tougher about restricting arms sales to China and in being willing to sell arms to Taiwan.[10]

This is not to argue that Europeans were prepared to play a leading role in developing security relations with East Asia. Pressing problems in Europe, ranging from Maastricht to Bosnia, ensured that diplomats had little time for Asian issues. Europeans played an active role in the UN effort in Cambodia, spurred on by a special French sense of responsibility. France and Britain were also very much engaged in the IAEA and UN efforts to halt the North Korean nuclear weapons project. If anything, the European nuclear powers were more anxious than most to take a tough line, fearing further nuclear proliferation in Ukraine and North Africa.

One form of engagement by Europeans that seems to be particularly resented by residents of Asia/Pacific is reference to "European lessons" for Asia/Pacific. To be fair, it is most often non-Europeans who suggest there are lessons, and Europeans who point out the differences—hence the belief in Asia/Pacific that APEU has a grand future just when Europeans are rethinking their own institutions. And yet it does seem clear that some of the mechanisms of European security are applicable in Asia, just as science is not culture bound.[11]

One dog which did not bark (so far) was the European linkage to Central Asia. With the collapse of the Soviet Union, the CSCE and NACC now extended into Central Asia—an evident absurdity for essentially European or North Atlantic institutions. Would Europeans become involved in settling disputes in Central Asia? In a relatively short time the answer was no, at least not in any important way. Europeans that could not end fighting in the Balkans would not try to do so in Tadjikistan. The result was also a relative neglect of the risks of nuclear proliferation in Kazakhstan, erroneously seeing the issue as a footnote to the problem of Ukraine.

Nor did Europeans seem inclined to do much about the growing post–Cold War concern with arms transfers to East Asia. European defense manufacturers needed the markets, just like the Americans, and seemed to care little for efforts to control the trade. Paltry efforts were made at the P-5 level to deal with transfers to the Middle East, but nothing was done about East Asia. Or more accurately, the response was to step up efforts to sell in East Asia. Britain and France were most active in this respect, although Germany also became an important player. French sales to Taiwan preceded and followed the American F-16 deal with Taiwan as France pioneered pragmatism in arms sales policy. The Netherlands buckled under Chinese pressure not to sell ships to Taiwan, and France agreed in 1994 to refrain from future sales. Britain, in its more robust attitude towards China, actively encouraged British Aerospace to join forces with Taiwanese producers, although the deal fell through for commercial reasons to do with transfer of technology. Apart from the specific problems of Taiwan, East Asians will find few problems in buying what they want from Europe. Europeans will explain this cavalier attitude to East Asian security on the grounds of commercial good sense and political pragmatism. Asia/Pacific is seen as a market and not a security problem.

## New Issues, New Perspectives

One obvious change from the Cold War days is the potential to broaden the scope of European attitudes towards Asia by bringing in the East European perspective. It has long been acknowledged that excellent talent exists in the east, but it was distorted by the exigencies of the Cold War. It was rare for Western journals to publish the work of East Europeans before the end of the Cold War. Now, East European specialists are seen on the conference circuit and their government's archives are being explored for new data. Sadly, Russia has closed access to its full set of Chinese Communist Party documents, after a brief glimpse was given in the first months of the 1991 revolution. One of the major tasks for European scholarship and experts will be to integrate their colleagues from the east, although so far there is little that has been done in an organized fashion.[12]

Given the variegated views of Asia/Pacific, it is not surprising that Europeans are fairly relaxed about their definition of the region and its security issues in the post–Cold War world. Problems of definition that plague conferences and institutions in Asia/Pacific are of little concern to Europeans, some of whom still refer to the region as "the Far East." The mainstream European view, as reflected in the organization of most European foreign ministries, is that we are mostly concerned with East Asia (from Burma to Japan). The South Pacific often gets slipped in to that group, but even the likes of Australia rate little more attention than Luxembourg (apart from in the British perspective). Russia is a factor, but is seen as a European power. Canada, especially for Britain and France, has obvious importance but in Atlantic terms.

The United States is of obvious importance, but little attention is paid to its Pacific perspective. Excessive and distorting American rhetoric about the decline of Europe and the rise of the Pacific for Americans, is seen to be undermined by recent policy. Why else do Americans send troops to the Gulf and Somalia, make noise about Bosnia and not Burma, and join with Europeans to denounce Asian attempts to narrow the definition of international human rights. Europeans have plenty of experience in coping with American fads and self-delusions. Asia is a trade partner for the Americans, but it is also a trade problem. Europeans are allies who fight alongside Americans when push comes to shove.

Thus if there is something distinctive about European views of Asia/Pacific, it is to argue against excessive optimism about the creation of a trans-Pacific community. As Eurasian trade grows faster than trans-Pacific trade, this line of argument will grow. Europeans will see East Asia primarily in trade terms. To the extent that trade patterns are affected by level and forms of domestic economic and social development, Europeans will be mainly concerned with trends in these areas.

Much further down the list of European priorities is a concern with conflict and military security. East Asians were never seen as terribly useful in terms of security in the Cold War and the demise of the Soviet Union makes East Asian security of even less concern. No East Asian state poses a security threat to Europe and in that sense this is an age of less rather than more interdependence in security terms. European geopoliticians might even be so bold as to argue that a rising China that worries Japan and other East Asians is "a good thing," at least if the conflict remains cold. As a result East Asian trading rivals will be forced to spend more on defense and will be weakened as a result. Markets will be opened for European arms. European favors will be sought by those such as Japan seeking a counterbalance to China.

Such calculations have so far not yet emerged from the policy planning staffs of European foreign ministries, but the issues are floating in the policy ether. They are balanced by worries about potential damage to the global market economy on which all Europeans depend for their prosperity. But Europeans will not be bothered very much if small conflicts continue in East Asia. Cambodia has faded from the front pages and the locals will be left to sort out their own local difficulties. Southeast Asia will be seen as a market, with or without Cambodia.

Disputes in the South China Sea will stimulate more worry, as will threats to Taiwan. The dividing line will be the use of force, for anything short of that will not arouse much interest in a Europe that has more hot wars than any other region. Whether Europeans would help defend Taiwan or anyone else who came under the Chinese gun is impossible to resolve at this stage. War games played by European officials suggest the surprising conclusion that they would help the United States defend an open trading system, even with the use of force. But so long as Americans sell arms with little discrimination in the region, Europeans will do so as well. As a result, prospects for arms control are severely limited.

Perhaps the one issue in the security sphere that arouses much more European interest, albeit not at the popular level, is the risk of nuclear proliferation in Northeast Asia. France and Britain in particular can be expected to remain very active in pushing for a nonnuclear solution. But the proliferation issue is seen more as a global than regional problem. Europeans have no problem in seeing at least certain security issues in global, for they can lay claim to having invented the idea of global security in the first place. For this reason, Europeans are also more inclined than Americans to see environmental issues as having implications for global security. Europeans are aware that although they are among the most environmentally responsible states in the world, all their efforts are for nought if the Americans and East Asians do not become more aware of their responsibilities.[13]

In sum, Europeans have a distinctive view of Asia/Pacific security. It is obviously relatively detached and pragmatic, but it also sees security in its wider economic, social and environmental sense. These perceptions are shaped by European experience, and also by a stronger commitment to multilateralism than is seen in most of Asia/Pacific. If there are natural partners in perceptions it is with the Canadians and Australians—perhaps not surprising considering the location and history of these states.

## Who Are the Specialists and What Do They Do?

The structure of the European analytical community in Asia/Pacific security studies is little different from the norm in the Western world.[14] The bulk of the expertise is drawn from the academic community. Talent is often nurtured in the academic world and then fed into jobs in the business and government worlds. There are few specialists who restrict themselves to security studies, however broadly defined, if only because the priority in Europe is in seeing East Asian states as trading partners. Virtually every specialist can speak some of the dialects of economics.

In fact, real differences in language competence constitute a crucial issue in the field. In the toughest case, China studies, it is remarkable how few specialists have sufficient command of the language to use it for interviews. This is a less serious problem when dealing with external security issues but it is more serious when focusing on internal affairs. The problem is less apparent in Japanese studies. As one gets down to the cases of smaller states, there is more impressive language competence.

Area studies, in Europe as elsewhere, has traditionally put much stress on language competence and yet this can be a problem in foreign and security policy studies. Especially in the case of Chinese and Japanese studies, the tendency is for analysts to adopt and internalize the myths of national uniqueness. China and Japan specialists seem to have particular problems in stepping outside mind-sets of their own chosen country of study. Thus analysis of bilateral and multilateral issues are often biased and unrecognizable to students of the other countries involved.[15] Analysis of Sino-Soviet or Soviet-Japanese relations often suffered from these problems. Narrow area studies training also made it harder to produce genuine students of the international relations of a region. This problem is as true in North America as in Europe, and even more true in East Asia itself. Perhaps that is why the likes of Michael Leifer, Hanns Maull or François Godement, all of which manage to combine fine scholarship and analysis on area studies and international relations, stand out so clearly. Needless to say there are even deeper problems when one focuses on the specific problems of security studies where it is much harder to find individuals who mix expertise in area studies and defense policy. The positive side of this problem is that analysis has tended to avoid the arcane hardware debates of those who studied nuclear weapons issues. And yet the thirst for the obscure detail is manifest in the field, usually in the form of petty detail about personality politics.

A related issue to the language problem is the difficulty in creating an integrated community on a Europe-wide basis. The lingua-franca is obviously English. Nonnative-English speakers vary in competence, with the Dutch or Scandinavians often speaking more intelligibly than the jargon-obsessed native-English speakers. This is of course more an American than an English disease. Passable fluency in English makes conferences workable and translation is rarely used. The European Consortium for Political Research works in English. Conferences among institutes and involving government officials most often operates in English, even when native-English speakers are not present.

By far the largest proportion of publication takes place in English, if only because it provides access to the wider communities beyond Europe. French and German books and articles are published, but few are ever translated. *Aussen Politik* which publishes an English version is unique.[16] Ideas are diffused into the wider community through conferences and by making a special effort to publish in English.[17] Institutes and journals devote nowhere near enough money for translation. Far more work can be done on a collaborative basis and yet cooperation remains remarkably sporadic. Area studies organizations have some mechanisms for cooperation within Europe but they are usually confined to annual conferences grouping linguists with literature specialists and only a smattering of economic and political studies. There is much scope for specific projects in the security sphere involving scholars in a number of European countries. Logistics problems in the new Europe are much reduced but funding has not yet been organized to deal with the problem. Special efforts are underway in both Germany and Britain to bring the academic communities together in Europe. On the more positive side, it should be noted that Europeans have a regular process of exchange that links academics with government and business. There is nothing special about the "track two" approach because it takes place regularly, although it is curious that there is still much less job-swapping between government and academia than compared to the American case.[18]

It remains an annoying curiosity that collaborative work is more often done between specialists in individual EU countries and colleagues in Asia/Pacific or North America. This is especially true in Britain where trans-Atlantic links are the most highly developed. Specialists in European countries all have their own bilateral links with Asia/Pacific but it is rare of individual East Asian countries to deal with a consortium of European specialists. Taiwan has been a notable exception in its regular meetings with European China specialists.[19] In general, it is a decent guess that most Asia/Pacific institutes or specialists have a database of European specialists which looks remarkably similar. Certainly European institutes and specialists will have common contacts in Asia/Pacific, varying only by the field of study.

Given the relative absence of a single European market in Asia/Pacific studies, it is not surprising that the movement of labor is restricted. While people travel often for conferences—it is easier and faster to get from London to Bonn than London to Manchester—people rarely take jobs in other countries. Labor practices and regulations are part of the problem although nationally based networks of contacts is an even more potent explanation for immobility. Jean Pierre Cabestan traveled each week from Paris to London to teach a course on modern China at SOAS in recent years, but he is an exception that proves the rule, and in any case did not live in London. Reinhard Drifte moved from Germany (and Switzerland) to London (and eventually Newcastle) to work on East Asian security, but he too is a rarity. Some, such as Hanns Maull of Germany have worked for a year in London, but few stay on or are expected to stay on. Rare is the case of Jean Pierre Lehman—now in Stockholm but once in Scotland and Paris. His fluency in many languages and disciplines is a rarity that makes mobility possible. Of course, apart from the field of European studies, such immobility is commonplace.

Far more mobility is seen in the movement of people in and out of the EC, and especially in and out of Britain where language problems are minimal; hence the British loss of Andrew Mack to Australia, the British gain from Australia of Robert O'Neill to the IISS and then Oxford, or the recent Swedish gain of Australia's Trevor Findlay to SIPRI. One dare not draw up a balance sheet of such transactions. Trans-Atlantic trade has been commonplace for years—a category that includes the author of this paper.

The literature in the field reflects these diverse trends. Most publications are written in national languages and essentially for national markets. Only the English-language journals have wide circulation outside the home country. Not surprisingly, the English-language journals are best known in Asia/Pacific and beyond. Europe is the home to the world's most prestigious China journal, *The China Quarterly*, edited by an American (David Shambaugh) at SOAS in London. Until recently, *The China Quarterly* had little coverage of security issues, but the current editor has a personal interest in the subject and matters are changing. Sadly, his American nationality means most authors are sought across the Atlantic. Europe is also home to the only policy-oriented journal on Asia/Pacific issues which has taken a leading role on security issues, *The Pacific Review*.[20] These publications are global in their perspective in that they provide outlets for Americans and Asians as well as Europeans. There are a whole series of leading international relations journals in Britain and elsewhere in Europe—by far the largest concentration outside the United States. In many dimensions of the international relations field, European research is at the cutting edge.

The publication of books follows a similar pattern. National publishers in German and French have virtually no reach beyond the national territory. Books in English are mainly published in Britain, and often by publishers of world standard. Several British publishers have a leading role in Asia/Pacific studies with wide distribution networks in Asia/Pacific. Many authors from the region publish in London and Routledge is the only publisher with a series dedicated to Asian security issues (edited by Michael Leifer of the London School of Economics).

Just as Asians come to London to publish, so they come to London and other parts of Europe to study. Oxford and the LSE are crammed with talented Asians seeking a prestigious degree with the assistance of big-name supervisors. Unlike many American schools, British universities retain active and regular supervision of graduate students. Asians also study in continental Europe but the absence of training in English remains a block on the potential for the expansion of this service sector industry. The result in the longer term is continuing preeminence for British scholarship on Asia/Pacific in Europe because of the resulting closer exchanges with returning students and future policymakers.

Library and general research facilities in Europe are often first class, although concentrated in one or two centers in each country. Paris and London each have notable concentrations of talent and not surprisingly often figure on the travel schedules of visiting East Asians. For some unfathomable reason most visits are in the May–October period.

Passing mention should be made of press coverage of Asia/Pacific issues in Europe. Europe is home to some of the best coverage of the region, and certainly better than what one gets even in the quality American media. Radio and now television coverage by the British Broadcasting Corporation has long been peerless, but smaller operations such as Deutsche Welle and Radio France International also cover Asia well. In the print media, French and British quality papers maintain a web of stringers and staff specialists. L'Institute du Pacifique produces a useful biweekly survey of the French and English press on Asian issues. Among the weekly press, *The Economist* remains the world's most influential paper, and claims to have "introduced" the Japanese and now the Chinese miracle economies to the wider world. It has a weekly section dedicated to Asian news, but like the *International Herald Tribune* (a daily paper edited in Paris) is more international in character and just happens to be edited in Europe. Sadly, *The Asian Wall Street Journal* is not available on the day of publication in Europe, but *The Far Eastern Economic Review* is widely read.

Training functions can also be seen in a wider context, for European governments were often instrumental in setting up government ministries in various Asia/Pacific countries. Although there is nothing like the EU schemes for know-how transfer to Eastern Europe, much the same was achieved more informally in the context of colonial policy. Although American influence remains dominant in Korea, Japan and Taiwan, British influence in shaping institutions in Southeast Asia is more apparent. Of course the passage of time since independence has meant that most of the specific people trained for government have now worked their way out of the system, but traditions linger on. European governments are looking for ways to renew this strain of influence through new exchange programs. Shorter-term training at staff colleges for military officers still takes place.

Interaction between European specialists and East Asians is frequent and diverse. Indeed, it is far more common to meet a fellow European in East Asia at a conference than in Europe. This is especially so in the winter when nothing attracts European participants like a conference in Perth or Bali. European institutes, like their American counterparts, enjoy running regular meetings in the region as a way to bring together specialists. But few such meetings involve a wide range of European specialists, even if they often bring in a wide range of local East Asians. Notable exceptions are the likes of the London-based International Institute for Strategic Studies which has an international membership and a powerful group of ordinary members and council members from East Asia and North America.

In sum, European studies on Asia/Pacific security remain among the best in the world. Contact with the target region is adequate, but could always be improved. The main lacunae are in contacts among Europeans, but this problem can be addressed by developing both direct communications as well as indirectly by broadening contacts with people in the Asia/Pacific. The latter question will now be addressed in the final section.

## Priorities and Gaps

In the "good old days" of the Cold War one could justify almost any study as being relevant to the central security issue of the East-West rivalry. When wars broke out in Korea strategists worried about Chinese hordes, and then when the Vietnam war dragged on for decades, Europeans had no trouble in supporting a branch of security studies focused on Asia/Pacific. In the era of East-West detente there was always the great power triangle to sustain the geopoliticians, and then inter-Communist wars in Indo-China. Only in the dying days of the Cold War did analysts catch the bug of arms control, and because Americans seemed reluctant to embrace the notion of Asia/Pacific arms control, the field was pioneered by Europeans and Australians. Thus in the Cold War phase of Asia/Pacific security studies, Europeans had an important role to play. The fact that the study of European security was so highly developed and many European countries had some of the leading Asia/Pacific area specialists, meant that the basis for a vibrant global community looked set to remain for some time.

And yet, many of these certainties about high-quality research might now be challenged. Security is far less obviously interdependent, despite the clichés about a global village. Europeans are hard to persuade that they should care very much about tension in the South China Sea let alone carnage in Cambodia. The war in Bosnia, along with less well reported conflicts in the Caucasus, has left Europeans more isolationist about security issues. Americans are also drifting in this direction, despite the rhetoric of internationalism. As a result, a young European scholar seeking to make a name in the security studies field is more likely to choose a topic closer to home.

Exceptions to this trend are likely to be those with an interest in issues with an inherently global character, for example arms transfers, nuclear proliferation, or perhaps environmental security. Even the trendy subject of migration studies remains essentially a subject for regional specialists. Other fashionable subjects such as peacekeeping have an Asian dimension, but it is increasingly clear that peacekeeping operations succeed or fail because of local conditions, and are thus best handled by regional specialists.[21]

Alas Asia/Pacific regional specialists in Europe have a declining interest in security studies. Asia/Pacific studies is attractive for the current crop of students because of the success of the Japanese economy, the new models of the NICs, and most recently the prospect of China as the world's largest economy. Most people want to know why these economies succeed and how they might affect the global market economy. There is not much interest in ethnic disputes, potential resource wars, or putative arms races. Students will be better paid by their governments and industries to study economic rather than security issues. The risk is that the

Asia/Pacific security studies field may be left to refugees from the strategic arms control field who lack much regional expertise but who love to scare us with data on weapons capabilities and worst-case scenarios. What is to be done?

For the time being, the talent in Europe for high-quality analysis of Asia/Pacific security is still secure and in place. At a time of wild fluctuation in North American assessments of the future of Japan or China, it is especially important that much European analysis is more dispassionate. Europeans have far more experience of dealing with balance and concert of power. There is much that could benefit the trans-Pacific debates if more is made of talent in the Eurasian leg and experience in the trans-Atlantic leg of the trilateral stool.

It is obvious where this line of analysis is going—the need to strengthen Eurasian cooperation in East Asian security studies. These are arguments that specialists will also recognize in terms of the global market economy. I have argued at length elsewhere why thinking Pacific in a narrow and exclusionary sense is passé and potentially dangerous.[22] Because we all rely on the success of an open global market economy, it must be preferable to have more open multi-lateralism. Most East Asian states have ambassadors to the EU but the EU is excluded even as an observer from APEC. Of course the EU is one of the dialogue partners in the ASEAN PMC process. It would be a source of some concern to Europeans if the dialogue on East Asian security takes on a greater character of Asia/Pacific discussions that excludes Europeans. The CSCAP process certainly seems headed in this APEC-like direction.

Such a direction for Asia/Pacific security studies is regrettable for a number of reasons. Most important is the fact that few, if any issues are best handled on such a regionwide basis. Most security issues are subregional. Does it really make sense to involve North or South Koreans in a discussion of the Spratly islands? Other issues are global in importance, for example nuclear proliferation, conventional arms transfers, or environmental risks. It would be ironic that just at the time when regionwide bodies such as the CSCE are fading in importance, Asia/Pacific thinkers should be gravitating to such old ideas. [23]

The regionwide strategy would also lose the best of the talent that is available outside the region. This is not just a matter of pleading the case of Europeans with expertise on the region, it is also a matter of making analysis easier by finding somewhat more detached perspectives. For example, the best (most objective) analysis of Sino-American or Japanese-American relations is more likely to come from a European than an American. From the European perspective, the future agenda for research needs to include both subjects where there is a European interest, but also general issues of relevance to the wider world. Often these issues are combined, for example when considering the risks of closed economic regionalism or the dangers of nuclear proliferation or environmental mismanagement.

The bottom line is the need for a genuinely international effort to study security issues in the Asia/Pacific. My guess is that few issues worthy of study will be regionwide, with most being subregional and some being part of a global problem. In fact, what is needed is an Asia/Pacific version of the International Institute for Strategic Studies, (although the resulting acronym would be unfortunate, so it would have to be called something which could be called the

Pacific Security Institute—PSI). As it stands, there are no institutes in the region free of close relations with host governments or their agendas. As a result, the research agenda remains too close to that set by governments. There is a related problem in that some have complained that the ASEAN institutes dominate the field and thus the agenda of research in a CSCAP-world is likely to ignore the concerns of Northeast Asians. No institute in the region has international membership, an international governing council, and international staff. A PSI would need to have all of this, perhaps drawing on one member of staff and one member of council from each Asia/Pacific state. It might be seen as a variation of the think tank of the West European Union based in Paris and headed by John Roper. Visiting fellows could come from a range of countries, including outside of the region. It might also serve as the nodal point for an information network that would link specialists in the field around the world. Such a network could be funded independently of a PSI, but would be more credible if it had an independent institutional base. A PSI could also publish a journal—for it is strange that there is no major Pacific studies journal in East Asia—as well as a monograph series. If it were ambitious a PSI could publish an equivalent of the IISS' *Military Balance* and *Strategic Survey* or SIPRI's Arms Transfer Register for the region every year. There would be obvious gains in terms of transparency and confidence building. The resulting collegiate atmosphere would also help in building confidence.

A PSI would cost money, but not much more than is already provided in scattered and redundant ways around the region. Is there much virtue in someone like the Ford Foundation funding yet another predictable study in an ASEAN country on defense spending or civil-military relations? Money is far better spent on research that has a better chance of being independent and representing the concerns of a wider, less-biased community. What is the point of reinforcing the narrow perspectives and interests that are represented on the governing bodies of many of the CSCAP participants, when one might be able to get more challenging and innovative research from a less culture- or politically bound institution.

A PSI should be based in as neutral a place as there is in Asia/Pacific—perhaps in Hong Kong. Such a choice would have the benefit of also serving as a living confidence building measure for the transition to Chinese rule after 1997. As a result such a venue would allow the security studies community to test their theories on themselves.

## Notes

1. My apologies for this note, but the book is Gerald Segal, ed., *Arms Control in Asia* (London: Macmillan, 1987) and the journal is *The Pacific Review*. See also François Godement, ed., *Le désarmement nucléaire en Asie* (Paris: Masson, 1990).

2. This is a regular, if often uninspired subject for Europeans. See a range of views in Francois Godement, "Europe and Asia: The Missing Link," *Adelphi Paper,* no. 276 (London: IISS, 1993); Brian Bridges, "Europe and Asia," in *Asian Survey*, July 1992; and Gerald Segal, "Europe and Asia/Pacific Security," T.B. Millar and James Walter, eds., *Asian-Pacific Security After the Cold War* (London: Robert Menzies Center, 1992).

3. For a sample see Nicolas Regaud, "Le Cambodge depuis le retrait vietnamien," *Défense Nationale,* May 1990; two articles by François Guilbert in *Politique Etrangère* No. 4 1989, and especially the work of Christian Lechervy, *Les Cambodgiens face à eux-mêmes?* (Grenoble: Ecole de la Paix, 1993).

4. Herve Coutau-Begarie, *Géostratégique du Pacifique* (Paris, IFRI, 1987), Gaston Flosse, "Sécurité du Pacifique Sud," *Défense Nationale,* March 1988; Jean-Pierre Gomane, "La France dans le Pacifique," *Défense Nationale,* March 1988.

5. Gerald Segal, *The Fate of Hong Kong* (London: Simon & Schuster, 1993).

6. Tim Huxley, "Singapore and Malaysia: A Precarious Balance," *The Pacific Review,* no. 2, 1991; and more recently Amitav Acharya, *ASEAN in the Post–Cold War Era* (London: IISS, Adelphi Paper, no. 279, 1993).

7. See, for example, Heinz Eberhard Maul, ed., *Militarmacht Japan?* (iudicium verlag, 1992?) but more especially Hanns W. Maull, *Japan und Europa: Getrennte Welten?* (Frankfurt: Campus Verlag, 1993). The list of contributors for the Maull book reads like the great and the good of the field, but only in Germany.

8. Barry Buzan and Gerald Segal, "Rethinking East Asian Security," *Survival,* no. 2, 1994 (forthcoming).

9. See also echoes of these issues in the French geopolitics discussions. Philippe Moreau Defurges, "Politique et diplomatie-La troisième métamorphose de l'Asie," *Défense Nationale*, April 1989; or Valerie Niquet's work on Sino-Soviet relations, including her "Peking et la dislocation de l'URSS" in *Défense Nationale*, April 1992.

10. This is evident in the summary report of the conference on G-7 policy towards China at Ditchley Park, April 1993. The Ditchley process is of course the pinnacle of "country house diplomacy" pioneered by Europeans. High-level officials and specialists are brought together for a weekend with fine food and spectacular and isolated accommodation in order to discuss important issues of the day. Some of the Ditchley style ambience was used in engineering the Norwegian solution to the Israel-Palestine question in 1993. Such dialogue is notably absent in Asia, although Asians are regularly invited to Ditchley and other such gatherings.

11. For some recent European thought on this subject, see Juergen Rueland, "Europe— A Model for Asia?" *Aussen Politik,* No. 4, 1992; or Eberhard Sandschneider, "Germany—A Model for Chinese Unification," in *Aussen Politk,* no. 1, 1992.

12. An example of collaboration is Yakov Zinberg and Reinhard Drifte, "Chaos in Russia and the Territorial Dispute with Japan," *The Pacific Review,* no. 3, 1993; or the presence of Wolfram Wallraf in the Maull volume. Wallraf's first publication in the West was on common security in *The Pacific Review,* no. 4 in 1989. See also the analysis of Alyson Bailes of the British Foreign and Commonwealth Office, "China and Eastern Europe," *The Pacific Review,* no. 2 , 1990.

13. Hanns Maull, "Japan's Global Environmental Policies," *The Pacific Review*, no. 3, 1991.

14. This is also true in terms of "diversity" issues. Few institutions have a staff, council or membership that is diverse in ethnic terms. It is also a matter of concern that although there are many women in the Asia/Pacific studies field as a whole, they tend to be concentrated in language, literature and sociological studies. The security studies field around the world has few women and even fewer in its branch dealing with Asia/Pacific. On a purely anecdotal basis, I would argue that as regards new talent in all the European countries, France seems set to produce more women specialists in the coming generation. In all countries, this problem will only be properly addressed when the general issue of better representation for women is

tackled. Of course, in East Asia there are often cultural reasons for the depth of the problem.

15. For better analysis, see examples in P. De Beauregard, J.P. Cabestan, J.L. Domenach, F. Godement, J. Goldfien, F. Joyaux, *La Politique Asiatique de la Chine* (Paris: FEDN, 1986).

16. The translation problem seems to be more acute for German than French scholars. Take the case of the recently retired Joachim Glaubitz who works on Russian issues in Asia, whose latest book, *Frende Nachbarn: Tokyo und Moskau* (Baden-Baden, 1992) has been well received but is unlikely to be read much in the wider community.

17. This effort is rarely made a high priority. One notable exception is the work of Jean Luc Domenach at the Centre de Recherche Internationale in Paris who holds regular seminars where non-French specialists are brought to town to lecture. Note also the special efforts of Françoise Mengin to diffuse her work on France and Taiwan in English, *Issues and Studies,* March 1992 and *The Pacific Review*, no. 1, 1991.

18. In Britain, even discussions of Asia/Pacific security regularly operate in this fashion. It is certainly standard operating procedure for Ditchley Park or Wilton Park, as well as the obvious cases of the Royal Institute of International Affairs or the IISS.

19. For example, Yu Ming Shaw, ed., *China and Europe* (Taipei: Institute of International Relations, 1986).

20. Modesty precludes me from describing the strengths of the journal and prudence precludes a discussion of weaknesses, even though the workshop organizers have asked for a bit of both in this paper.

21. This is the implication of Mats Berdal, *Whither UN Peacekeeping* (London: IISS *Adelphi Paper*, no. 281, 1993).

22. Gerald Segal, *Rethinking the Pacific* (Oxford: Clarendon Press, 1990).

23. This is not the place to engage in a full debate about the virtues of CSCAP. The issues are discussed in full by Paul Evans in his article on CSCAP for *The Pacific Review*, no. 2, 1994.

# Security Issues and Studies in Japan

SATOSHI MORIMOTO
and
TSUTOMU KIKUCHI

The end of the Cold War has prompted many nations to reassess their respective security environments and reformulate their security policies. Japan is no exception. In the coming decades, Japan has to reanalyze its emerging new security environment on both regional and global levels and reconceptualize its security policies.

## Japan's Security Policies in the Postwar Era

Since its independence in 1952, under the new constitution in which Japan renounced war as a sovereign right, Japan has pursued its national security within the framework of a US-Japan alliance formulated in 1952 and revised in 1960.

In considering ways to protect Japan's vital security interests, based upon basic principles reflected in a new constitution, successive governments have posed some constraints on themselves. First, the government has maintained its interpretation of the constitution that Japan could not exercise its inherent right of collective self-defense (which is allowed to every state under the United Nations Charter). This means that Japan cannot join in any security system within which Japan may be requested to use military force for the third country (countries). Put differently, Japan could resort to force only in case of aggression against Japan. Second, the Japanese government has taken a strict interpretation on the individual right for self-defense. According to an interpretation by the government, Japan could possess military forces at a minimum level suitable to responding to a possible aggression against Japan. Based upon this interpretation, Japan has taken the "exclusively defense-oriented strategy."

In addition to these constitutional constraints in Japan's postwar defense policy, there exist other constraints which have not necessarily originated in the constitution. First, there are so-called "nonnuclear principles" which means that Japan shall not possess or produce nuclear weapons nor allow nuclear weapons to be introduced into Japanese territory. This firm commitment to a "nonnuclear

Japan" reflects the strong antinuclear feeling among Japanese people who suffered from nuclear bombings during the Second World War.

Another constraint to Japan's defense policy is a restriction on the export of military weapons including military-related technology. Although Japan began to transfer military technology to the United States in 1983 as an exception to the "nontransfer policy," this restrictive policy on transfer of military weapons and military-related technology reflects Japan's firm belief that Japan should restrict its role in the international community to nonmilitary fields.

We may add to the above constraints the government's policy to limit defense expenditure to about 1 percent of Japan's GNP which has been adopted since the mid-1970s.

These constraints reflect, among other things, a deep feeling of guilt about Japan's role in the last war, the changes of regional and international security environments, and attention to the possible reactions of neighboring countries who are deeply apprehensive about Japan's possible rearmament.

## Security Debates in Japan

In the 1950s and 1960s the US-Japan Security Treaty caused serious debates in Japan. Even a revision of the treaty in 1960 to create a more balanced relationship caused strong opposition, including forcing the cancellation of a planned visit by the US president. The Japanese prime minister himself was also forced to resign following the ratification of the revised treaty. During the Vietnam War, the Japanese government faced strong criticisms from the opposition parties and the general public for allowing the United States to use its military facilities located in Japan to support the military operations in Vietnam.

Several factors explain why the Japanese people took such critical views of the US-Japan security alliance during the 1950s and 1960s. First, there remained a strong feeling that Japan was pressed to agree to the treaty by the United States in exchange for the independence and the end of the occupation. In this context, so-called antialliance movements reflected a nationalistic feeling emerging in the Japanese general public. Second, there remained a deep perceptual gap between Japan and the United States on the threat posed by China. The United States regarded China as a major factor threatening peace and stability in the Asian region since the Korean War and refused to recognize the PRC. Japan, however, felt that the tough US policy toward China prevented a normalization between Japan and China. Further, Japan had a deep concern that the hostile policies of the United States toward China might drag Japan into any severe confrontation between the Unites States and China. Thirdly, the Vietnam War, which was unpopular in Japan, prompted Japan to have a feeling that the US-Japan Security Treaty worked to promote US strategic interests in other areas, rather than serving to enhance Japan's security.

Aside from misgivings about the US-Japan Security Treaty, many Japanese felt uncomfortable with the existence of the Japanese Self-Defense Forces. Due to

Japan's expansionism during World War II, they felt that Japan should be totally demilitarized.

## Security Studies in Japan from a Historical Perspective

Before the end of the Pacific War, a large number of experts in both government and private circles had engaged in military studies in order to make a contribution to the national policy aimed at expanding Japan's influence in the neighboring areas. This experience in the prewar era had a grave impact on security studies in postwar Japan. That is, military studies have been regarded as a discipline which contributes to war or war-related matters. As a result of this attitude, military studies have been unduly avoided even in government and academic circles in the period since.

In postwar Japan, debates on national security have centered around the constitutionality of the Self-Defense Forces and the rationale for the US-Japan security alliance. Just as national politics was divided into two major political parties (Liberal Democratic Party and Japan Socialist Party), academics and the general public have been sharply divided into two schools of thought on national security.

One is the so-called "realist school," and the other the "idealist school." The realist group, in considering Japan's security policies, puts the priority on the function of "power" in international relations. It pays primary attention to the concepts of balance of power and power politics. It also places the highest priority on the maintenance of a stable US-Japan security relationship as a basic foundation for Japan's security. According to this school of thought, the basic orientation in Japan to the US-Japan security alliance is not only the product of Japan's choice, but also determined by the structures of the then prevailing international relations. During the Cold War era, the major security threat to Japan came from the Soviet Union and China. And the United States was the only power which Japan could rely upon in the face of grave threats posed by the two Communist giants. In economic terms, Japan lost its traditional market in China and Southeast Asia and was discriminated against by the European countries in terms of Japan's export to their markets. Under these circumstances, the US was the only country which could provide Japan with capital, technology and a huge market for Japan's products without which Japan could not have maintained its economic survival.

In the academic circles specializing in international politics and foreign relations, the number of scholars who took realist views has been small. And it was in 1970s that the realists began to express their views to the general public through the media.[1]

In comparison with the realist school, the idealist school, which advocated Japan being totally demilitarized and taking a neutral position in the East-West confrontation, had much influence in both the academic and media circles. Based upon the deep feeling of guilt about past Japanese expansionism, the group denied the usefulness of military power as a means of Japan's enhancing security. It advocated Japan becoming a peace-loving nonmilitary state in international society. It worried much about the possibility of Japan being brought unintentionally into an East-West confrontation through Japan's security ties with the United States and insisted that Japan should take a neutral position by abolishing security ties between the United States and Japan. As a result, the idealists group have consistently criticized policies advocated by the realist group as those of "obeying US policy."[2]

This sharp division over the basic orientation of Japan's national security policy made it extremely difficult to have fruitful discussions on Japanese security policy in both the national diet and academic circles. In fact, the parties in opposition would not depart from their basic position that the Self-Defense Forces was not allowed to exist under the constitution, and that, therefore, they rejected discussing any details of security policies on the assumption that the SDF existed. For the opposition parties, discussion on security policies could only occur after abolishing the SDF (and the US-Japan Security Treaty).

Against this background, the government was reluctant to expose national security policies to the examination in the national diet, because they provoked not only strong criticisms from the opposition parties but also encouraged mass demonstration movements against government policy. These protests also often caused a suspension of examinations of other important policies and bills which the government had before the diet. As a result of this extraordinary situation, the government tried to avoid discussing national security policies there.

This sharp division over national security policies has had a grave impact on the disputes on national security. One was that the government became extremely cautious about opening the military-related information to the public, worrying about causing political disputes. This extreme cautiousness could be found even among the government officials themselves. In fact, the security related information, particularly related to the management of US-Japan security relations, has been strictly kept only among a handful of officials in charge of the management of the alliance. This resulted in the quite unusual situation that security policies, especially ones related to the US-Japan security relations and the SDF, have rarely been exposed to open discussions even within the Ministry of Foreign Affairs and the Defense Agency. The discussions and examinations to formulate Japan's national security policies, thus, has been monopolized by a small inner-group in charge of them. Other officials, even if they had excellent expertise in defense and security affairs, have not been allowed to engage in the process of policy formulation.

# Changing Threat Perception and Attitude toward Security Issues during the Last Decade

## Changing Threat Perception

In a sense, Japan could then enjoy theological disputes in the relatively stable international system provided by *Pax Americana*. However, with declining US economic power and the gradual reduction of US forward-deployed forces, coupled with the increase of Soviet military forces, debates on security policies in Japan have changed gradually.

Japan's threat perceptions have undergone certain notable changes. From the late 1970s through the 1980s, the Soviet Union's military strength was constantly increased, especially in naval and air forces in the Northwest Pacific. This Soviet military buildup, which turned the Sea of Okhotsk into a "sea bastion," posed grave implications for the stability of the strategic balance in Northeast Asia and the Northwest Pacific. The Soviet Union modernized its Pacific Fleet to the extent that the Soviets could launch a large and long-range offensive in the Pacific. The "Backfire Bombers," new types of aircraft carrier and the SS-20 theater missiles with multiple nuclear warheads were deployed in the Far Eastern theater, thereby causing a grave military challenge to the operation of the United States Seventh Fleet as well as Japan's national security. Furthermore, the deployment of land forces and Mig-23 fighter aircraft in the disputed Northern Territories since 1978 served as a stimulus to raising the threat perception even among the Japanese general public.

This threat perception of the Soviets was combined with an emerging perception that because of economic difficulties the United States might not maintain its military forces deployed on foreign soils. In fact, the US government expressed its intention to reduce its forward defense forces, as indicated in the announcement of the force reduction in Korea during the Carter administration.

In this context, Japan was forced to take more realistic attitudes towards national security. Japan no longer seemed to enjoy the *Pax Americana*. Several measures were, therefore, taken to strengthen the US-Japan Alliance. Guidelines for US-Japan security cooperation were agreed to by the two governments. And based upon these guidelines, various studies were conducted between the two governments, especially by the defense officials. Specific studies were undertaken on joint operation, defense of sea lanes of communications and the strengthening of interoperability. Joint exercises between the SDF and the US Seventh Fleet were increased in number and in scope. In essence, in the face of the increasing threat from the Soviets, Japan decided to pursue its national security interest within a framework of US-Japan cooperation, not through the strengthening Japan's independent power for military operations. This approach was designed not only for the effective military operation but also to minimize concerns among neighbors.

Another development was the provision of the host-nation support for the US forces deployed in Japan, which had been started in 1978. The provision of the host-nation support has been expected to enhance the US military capability in the region, thereby making a great contribution to the stability of the entire region as well as Japan's national security.

The Nakasone government which took power in 1982 was the first Japanese government in the postwar era which tried to present military issues in military terms, not political or economic terms. Although the Nakasone government faced some opposition to its security policies in the national diet, their firm commitment to upgrade US-Japan security relations, coupled with the rising threat perception among the Japanese people, made some contribution to discussing national security issues on a common foundation. The changed attitudes of the Japanese people towards security issues have been evident in the facts that the Japanese people have paid little attention to the use of US military bases in Japan and to the definition of Japan as "a member of the Western Alliance" which successive governments had been reluctant to express publicly.

As a matter of fact, according to the public opinion poll conducted by the Japanese government in 1984, 71.4 percent of the respondents assessed US-Japan security relations in an affirmative way in response to the question of whether or not the treaty was useful for the peace and security of Japan. The poll also indicated that 69 percent of the respondents supported the formula of linking the SDF and the US forces as a means for Japan's security policy. This implies that Japan's defense policies based upon the close cooperation between the SDF and the US forces had a firm foundation among the Japanese people.

Japanese people also have been showing more positive attitudes towards the SDF. According to opinion surveys conducted by the various organizations, the rate supporting the existence of the SDF has constantly increased. In fact, the opinion poll conducted by the government in 1987 indicated that more than 80 percent of the respondents supported the existence of the SDF. To be noted in this context, the increasing support of the SDF among the Japanese people seems to be based upon an assumption that the government would continue to maintain a defensive defense posture and various constraints mostly originating from the constitution. Thus, the most pressing issue of the SDF is no longer whether or not the SDF is allowed to exist under the constitution. Rather, it is to what extent Japan should improve the capability of the SDF within a framework of defensive defense, taking the changing regional and international environments into consideration.

## Changes after the End of the Cold War

The end of the Cold War changed Japan's perception of the security environment in the Asia-Pacific region, although in a more moderate way in comparison to those of European countries. First, the military threat posed by the Soviets (Russia) has sharply decreased, although Japan perceives that Russia has a capability to pose military threat to the world and is, therefore, a potential threat to Japan.

In the Asia-Pacific context, in addition to the decrease of military threat posed by Russia, there were positive signs for regional peace such as the establishment of diplomatic relations between Korea and China and the Soviet Union, the settlement of the Cambodian Conflict (which had been going on for over a decade), and normalization between China and the Soviet Union. Japan has regarded these developments as positive factors making a contribution to the reduction of tensions in the region.[3]

At the same time, however, there still remain many unsolved problems caused by the Cold War such as the tension in the Korean peninsula, China-Taiwan relations and Japan-Russia relations which may destabilize regional stability. Furthermore such historically deep-rooted problems as territorial disputes over the Spratly islands are coming to the surface as a regional security issue. In fact, generally speaking, the relations between two countries having a common border or a sea border are not necessarily stable. Japan perceives that without these problems being handled adequately, the regional security environment might become more unstable.

The future policy directions of the major powers which have been much involved in the regional politics so far are not so clear. First, how will the United States engage in the Asia-Pacific? How will the US military presence which has underpinned the regional stability be changed in the future? If the United States radically reduces the forward-deployed forces in Asia without an accompanying formation of multilateral security arrangements, the Asian regional security environment will certainly become instable.

Second, how will the Russian situation develop? It would not be possible for Russia to return to a traditional expansionist policy in the foreseeable future. However, if the current confusion continues for a long time, it will certainly have a negative impact on the stable regional development. Furthermore, there exists some concern in Japan that an authoritarian regime based on a traditional Russian nationalism may emerge if the current state of confusion continues.

The third question is related to China. At this moment, most of the Japanese experts do not necessarily worry about China's military buildup, like the modernization of its naval forces. The problem about the future of China is that historically China has a strong tendency to take a unilateral action without paying due attention to the possible reactions from neighboring countries. In essence, from a historical point of view China, which had been the only empire in the region, has not pursued its national interest taking account of mutual relations with other countries. Another problem from a long-term perspective is that the economic dynamism now taking place between China and the outside countries may pose a serious challenge to the political system controlled by the Communist parties, thereby causing internal instability in China.

Fourth, how will Japan define its regional and international roles? With the end of the Cold War, there certainly has emerged some concern that Japan might fill in a "power vacuum" created by the withdrawal of major powers' military presence. Some neighboring countries express their concerns about the "militarization of Japan." Although we do not think that the international relations of the Asia-Pacific region will develop on the classical concept of "balance of power," we clearly recognize that such concerns exist in the region. One cause of such concerns about the future militarization of Japan has something to do with the fact that, with the end of the Cold War, the US-Japan security alliance which has so far provided a firm basis for predictability and reliability on Japan's security policies has lost some rationale in terms of maintaining the alliance. The pressing task for Japan in the coming years is, therefore, to make great efforts to formulate a multilateral subregional and regional security framework within which Japan's security policy will be placed, as well as to further strengthen US-Japan relations. Put differently, Japan (and the United States) needs to make more efforts to place US-Japan security relations in a broader regional security framework, thereby increasing predictability of US-Japan relations.

Another security problem facing the region is the spread of military weapons, of mass destruction (both nuclear and conventional). The development and spread of modern military technology has made it easier for developing countries to acquire dangerous weapons threatening regional and global peace. The deterioration of the Russian situation poses such a danger as losing control of military-related high technology. In addition, there is a possibility that China and North Korea may export military weapons to get hard currency.

Given the situations mentioned above, the Asia-Pacific region has to make great efforts to arrange confidence building measures with a view to handling territorial and other disputes and controlling a spread of military weapons and military-related technology.

# New Dimensions in Japan's Security Policy

### *Identifying a Role for Japan in International Affairs*

Now two streams of thought are emerging that relate to Japan's foreign and security policy. Debates have been centered around the question of what Japan should do to make a greater contribution to the peace and stability of regional and international systems. It seems that there still exists a majority of people who advocate that Japan maintain its traditional policies of limiting its regional and international roles to the economic field, taking a low profile in international politics and security affairs and avoiding risk taking as far as possible. An idea of Japan becoming a "global civilian power" is a contemporary version of the traditional attitudes towards international politics and economy, although it is presented in a more sophisticated fashion.[4]

On the other hand, other people (such as Mr. Ichiro Ozawa, former secretary-general of the LDP and one of the most influential power brokers under the current government) advocate that Japan should become a "normal state" and that, as a state taking major responsibilities to manage international affairs, Japan should play more active roles commensurate with its economic power not only in economic management but also in the security affairs. They insist that if Japan refuses to play more active roles and continues to avoid sharing risk taking, Japan will be punished and isolated from the international community. Based upon this perception of Japan's roles, they advocate that Japan should try to become a permanent member at the UN Security Council and more actively participate in the peacekeeping operations under the auspices of the UN.[5]

It is still not clear what these debates will result in. However, there is no denying that the debates are closely related to the realignments of the political parties after the collapse of the "1955 regime" which reflected the Cold War confrontation in a global scene. In this sense, therefore, how the debates on the fundamental questions over Japan's national and international policies develop, will have a grave impact on the future course of Japan, both internally and externally.

### *Strengthening the UN's Security Functions*

The Japanese government has frequently stated that Japanese foreign policy has three pillars: US-Japan relations, the United Nations, and Asian diplomacy. During the Cold War era, however, Japanese foreign and security policies were centered around US-Japan relations because of the structures of the international system, characterized by the East-West confrontation. With the end of theCold War, Japan now puts great emphasis on an Asian diplomacy and the United Nations as well as the United States in foreign policy considerations and practice.

A Japanese approach to the UN indicates a new dimension of Japan's foreign and security policies. One of the arguments on the UN, which were encouraged by the end of the Cold War and the Gulf War, is related to the question of how Japan should play a constructive role for the UN-sponsored peacekeeping operations. Although the government succeeded in passing the PKO Bill at the national diet and sent a peacekeeping force to Cambodia for the first time in Japan's history, the debate over whether or not Japan should participate in the military operations of the United Nations has been consistently going on. The debate is concerned with whether or not Japan should militarily participate in the UN peace activities, and if Japan says yes to that question, then under what conditions.[6]

Other issues relating to strengthening the UN security role are the prevention of military weapons of mass destruction, control of transfers of military-related high-technology and military weapons to adventurous countries, and other areas which demand international cooperation such as protection of the global environment, prevention of a population explosion and prevention of the spread of AIDS.

The second debate over the UN in Japan is related to the function and composition of the Security Council. On one hand, there are people who insist on the function and composition of the UN Security Council having to be reconsidered. As a matter of fact, the current composition of the council reflects international relations as they existed at the end of Second World War, and has not accommodated the changes which have taken place in the postwar world. Some people argue that Japan should exhibit explicitly its intention to become a permanent member of the council and contribute more to UN activities.

On the other hand, others argue that although the security functions of the Security Council have to be enhanced, Japan should take a more cautious approach to the issue of becoming a permanent member because Japan has to answer the question of whether or not it is allowed to join in the military activities conducted under the auspices of the United Nations before becoming a permanent member. Is it politically possible and morally justifiable for Japan to ask other countries to join in the military activities, while itself holding a position that it is not able to send the SDF even under UN auspices?

## *Multilateral Security Dialogues in the Asia-Pacific*

Given the complex situation in the Asia-Pacific region, Japan cannot totally depend for its security upon international organizations like the United Nations, even if its roles and functions in the security field are strengthened. Bilateral and trilateral security arrangements formulated during the Cold War must still make contributions to regional stability.

However, at the same time these security arrangements may need to be reformulated, especially as new types of potential instability are emerging with which security arrangements set up during the Cold War can not deal in an appropriate way.

Both government and academic circles in Japan are now paying more attention to possible multilateral/regional dialogues to deal with security issues in the Asia-Pacific region. The CSCE (Conference on Security and Cooperation in Europe) process in Europe has attracted practical attention in this context.

This increasing attention to multilateral security dialogues does not imply that Japanese security analysts believe that a CSCE-type of arrangement will be realized in this region in the near future. According to experiences in Europe, there are several conditions which must be realized before multilateral security arrangements can be put into practice. First, there must be diplomatic relations among all the parties concerned. Second, it is indispensable that an agreement not to resort to military means to solve disputes be reached among the parties concerned. However, in Asia, diplomatic relations have not yet been established between some of the states and there is the possibility of the use of force to change existing boundaries.

Given these conditions, the possible ways for the Asia-Pacific to proceed with multilateral security framework are two-fold: First, the region can start with a subregion in which the two conditions are satisfied and then expand it into a large area. The other possibility is to utilize economic collaborative elements fully to build a sense of the region.

Since the last war, Japanese foreign and security policies have been centered around the US-Japan Security Treaty. As a result, internal debates on security also centered around this bilateral relationship. The United States will still be of greatest importance in Japan's security, political and economic policies in the foreseeable future.

However, at the same time, there is an emerging recognition in both governmental and academic circles that US-Japan relations have to be reanalyzed and readjusted to the changing international and regional security environment. Moreover, the US-Japan relationship must take into account the possibly emerging multilateral security framework of the region.

There are two types of arguments in this context. One is related to the possible roles of the US-Japan security alliance enhancing regional stability. The alliance connecting the largest economic power and the second largest in the world has been important for regional peace and stability during the Cold War and will still make a contribution to peaceful developments in the region in foreseeable future. However, in order to strengthen the alliance as a key factor for regional stability, the alliance will have to be placed in a broader multilateral regional context. The pressing task is, therefore, to adjust the alliance into the changing international and regional environment.

A second argument is related to the possible role to be played by Japan itself in the security field. Politically and militarily, Japan has taken a low profile since the war. The Japanese government has consistently announced its intention of not becoming a military giant. In effect, Japan has taken a "defensive defense" posture due to concern about the militarization of Japan. On the other hand, Japan's defense expenditure has increased to the level equivalent to that of the GNP of Malaysia or Pakistan, although the Japanese SDF has been structured so as not to be able to carry out a military mission without cooperation of the US forces deployed in the Pacific. The division of labor between Japan and the

United States has been what is symbolically called "the shield and the spear." Japan is the shield and its defense policy is a defensive defense. Nevertheless, due to Japan's great economic power, it is inevitable that neighboring countries have some suspicion of the militarization of Japan in the future.

During the Cold War, most of the feedback in the defense policy field came from the United States. In the post–Cold war, Japan has to explain the rationale for defense policy, and get feedback from not only the United States but also neighboring countries in Asia in order to obtain credibility. It may be increasingly difficult for Japan to gain acceptance of its defense policy from the neighboring countries by relying only upon the US-Japan alliance. This is because how Japan plays a security role in the region will have more and more important regional implications. In addition, the regional countries will not be satisfied with a situation in which Japan's security policies will be subject to the strategic priorities of the United States. Therefore, other ways have to be found to enhance the credibility of defense policies. The multilateral forums/dialogues are quite important for this purpose.[7]

## Definition of Security—Concept of Comprehensive Security

In postwar Japan, security has been defined in a comprehensive way, i.e., not restricted to military aspects. In fact, from the end of the 1970s, the concept of comprehensive security has been officially adopted as a government policy. Behind this conceptualization of security there have existed strong concerns about Japan's economic vulnerabilities, including high dependence on import of vital natural resources and international trade for economic welfare. In particular, the 1973 oil crisis prompted Japan to further recognize its vulnerability in terms of importing vital natural resources. The maintenance of a free international economic system symbolized in the GATT has also been a key factor underlying this concept of comprehensive security.

The concept of comprehensive security has also served as a useful one to reconcile the pacifist feelings among the Japanese people to the increasing requests from the United States to expand Japanese defense capabilities in the 1970s and 1980s due to the rapid increase of the Soviet's military buildup and the decline of the US capability to face the threat originating from Russian military expansion.

Since the late 1970s, Japan has also been aware of the security implication of commercial dealings. This awareness is especially strong among government agencies and private business circles. The immediate event which prompted this was the Japanese purchase of oil produced by Iran which was then under the severe economic sanctions by the United States because of the former's violation of international law (i.e., the kidnapping of US diplomats in Teheran). The purchase of Iranian oil by Japanese trading companies caused serious diplomatic criticisms from Washington. Japan has also been paying more attention to the transfer of military-related and dual-purpose technology to potentially dangerous countries.

The concept of comprehensive security has even stronger popular support in Japan after the end of the Cold War. The emphasis on economic strength or resilience over military attributes is preferred by the Japanese public.

## "Region" in Japan's Security Perception

From the departure point of Japan's concept of comprehensive security, the "region" for Japan's security has actually been defined as global in nature. The maintenance of a free international trading system and the free flow of natural resources, for example, depend upon global security not just one region's.

Still, the region in which Japan has an especially important security concern is, of course, Asia. Japan perceives that without stability in Asia, it could not enjoy its own economic, political and security welfare. In fact, "Asian diplomacy" has always been regarded as one of three major pillars of postwar Japan's foreign policies (the others being the United States and the United Nations).

Within the Asian region, Northeast Asia and Southeast Asia have been regarded as most vital. In addition to a geographical location in which Japan is situated close to such major powers as China and the Soviet union, there have existed conflicts and tensions in the region such as the South-North Korean conflicts, the Japanese-Russian disputes over the Northern Territories and the Soviet's deployment of large-scale offensive weapons. Therefore, Northeast Asia has been, and will be, the most important region for Japan's security considerations.[8]

Southeast Asia has also historically been regarded as a region vitally important for Japan's security. Japan's deepened and widened economic relations with the countries of Southeast Asia and the sea lanes are vitally important for Japan's economic dealings with the world. Without stability of the region, Japan will not enjoy economic developments.

Japan's attention to Asia has been reflected in various diplomatic initiatives taken by the Japanese governments in the postwar era. Prime Minister Miyazawa's speech made in April 1993 in Bangkok was part of these diplomatic efforts. Furthermore, in this context, it should be noted that Japan was eager to promote economic cooperation among the countries of the region, mostly through the allocation of Japan's ODA (Official Development Assistance). In fact, most of Japan's ODA has been allocated to Asia.

Development of the Asian countries through regional economic cooperation has been and will continue to be extremely important to Japan. Japan has been the only industrialized country in Asia in the past century. This unique position induced a sense of mission for Japan to do something for Asia. Needless to say, it is nothing new for a country to possess some sense of mission. Such sentiments have often encouraged countries to play constructive roles for peace and stability of the world. Excessive sense of mission, however, has often resulted in tragic consequences. Japan's behavior before 1945 was a case in point.

Despite its defeat, Japan recovered quickly and became an economic giant. But, since most of the Asian countries had just recently received independence from colonial rule and were in a difficult economic situation, a Japanese sense of mission emerged again. This sense of mission, coupled with a grave gap in economic development between Japan and the rest of Asia and the legacy of the last war, introduced an element of "stress" or "uneasiness" in Japan's foreign policy. In fact, it was extremely difficult for Japan to formulate its relations with the rest of Asia on an equal basis. Japan's relation's with the rest of Asia became inevitably vertical, not horizontal, greatly constraining Japan's postwar diplomacy. The development of the Asian countries, therefore, could "release" Japan from this undue stress and offer an opportunity to establish more equal and mutually beneficial relations between Japan and the rest of Asia, thereby making a contribution to enhancing the stable development of the region.

# Security and Area Studies Relating to the Asia-Pacific Region

## *University Scholars*

For a long time, the departments dealing with politics and international politics have been attached to the faculty of law in most Japanese universities. This is closely related to the fact that political science had been a part of statecraft in the process of Japan's modernization, not a part of social science as in the Western academic circles. Even now, most of the specialists in international politics and security studies belong to the faculty of law.

Due to the postwar strong reluctance to specialize in military-related studies, it was natural that security studies were conducted mainly by political scientists who took more political than military approaches to security affairs.

Echoing the deep division between the government and the opposition parties over Japan's security policy, academic circles were also divided roughly into two groups: one being the so-called realist group, and the other the so-called idealist group.

Disciplines developed in the United States have been introduced in studies of international relations in Japan, especially since the 1970s. In fact, a large number of "theories" of international relations have been imported from the United States into Japan's academic world. Japan is now one of the biggest consumers of books on international relations published in the United States. Furthermore, the number of scholars who have studied in the United States has also been increasing rapidly since the 1970s. However, echoing the pacifist feeling in Japan, military/strategic studies of the United States have rarely been imported, in comparison to peace studies developed in the United States and the North European countries.

With the emergence of Japan as an economic power and the growing awareness of the need to promote security studies, the number of scholars specializing in security studies has been increasing in the recent past, although it is still not sufficient.

Among Asia-Pacific area studies, China studies has a long tradition and, therefore, has a class of scholars in both quality and quantity. In China studies, history and language are the most popular areas of study, though politics and economics also attracts scholars. A recognition of the importance of promoting area studies of the Asia-Pacific region has also grown. In fact, in recent years, many universities established faculties/departments of international relations, and the emphasis has been put on the promotion of area studies. Moreover, some of the major Japanese universities have established faculties of policy studies where more systematic research activities on security and area studies will be conducted.[9]

China studies, general Asian economies, culture and history are listed as popular fields among Japanese scholars, although the scholars of the young generation are now increasingly engaged in Asia-Pacific security studies.

## Government Circles

As already discussed, security policies have been formulated within a small government circle in the postwar era. For example, the management of US-Japan security relations has been mostly handled by a handful of experts of the security division at the Ministry of Foreign Affairs. And there was very little feedback to the policy-making process among them, not only from the outside experts but also from other government agencies. Frankly speaking, the security policies of the postwar era have been monopolized by a small group of people. It was only in the 1980s that a security policy division dealing with non-US security-related matters was established in the Foreign Ministry.

The influence of politicians, scholars and business leaders on the formation of Japan's security policies has been quite limited. Policy coordination over security policies among the relevant government agencies has been restricted to the areas in which other agencies have some jurisdiction. As a small group of experts have actually dominated the decision-making processes of Japan's security policy, there have not been serious bureaucratic wrangles among government authorities over the formation of security policies.

In August 1993 the Foreign Ministry reformed itself based upon the recommendation of a special group comprising scholars, business leaders and ex-government officials, and established a bureau dealing with overall coordination of foreign and security policies, within which a multilateral division was set up. The division deals with multilateral security issues and other security affairs, excluding US-Japan security relations.

Outside organizations and security experts like university professors have had a very limited influence on the decision-making processes of security policy. One of the ways in which outside security experts could have an indirect influence on the formation of security policies has been through their participation in research projects commissioned by the relevant government agencies.

Government agencies dealing with security affairs, such as the Ministry of Foreign Affairs and the Defense Agency, commission a lot of research from outside experts. The purpose of commissioned research is not to gain policy recommendations to immediate problems. Rather, the government agencies expect to have (a) analysis from a long-term perspective, and (b) policy recommendations for issues with which the relevant division could not deal effectively.

# Training Security Experts

## Training in the Universities

Research and training systems to educate students (graduate students) having an interest in security studies have not been well developed in Japan, although some of the universities have been making great efforts to rectify the situation. Thus, whether or not students will get enough training to become security experts depends upon, first of all, their particular supervisors' efforts.

In recent years, many Japanese universities established faculties/departments of international relations. The emphasis at these faculties is mainly on the promotion of area studies (mainly focusing on the Asia-Pacific) as well as international politics and economy. Even at these faculties/departments, education programs for students having an interest in security studies are not well established.

As there are few universities which can provide students with comprehensive security studies in Japan, some of the students having interest in security studies are studying at foreign universities, mostly in America and England. The number of students studying at foreign universities has been increasing. The problem for these students, however, is that because of the small numbers of Japanese university courses dealing with security, it is still difficult for them to get permanent jobs in Japan.

In terms of training young students, it should be noted that the Research Institute of Peace and Security (RIPS) has been conducting a fellowship program for young students (usually postdoctoral fellows). A number of scholars emerged from this program who are now continuing research at various Japanese universities and research organizations.

### Community of Security Experts

The Japanese Association of International Relations (JAIR) has now more than one thousand members. Most of the members of JAIR are university professors. The JAIR has one subcommittee dealing with security affairs among its eighteen research subcommittees. The number of scholars on the subcommittee on security has increased in the last decade. However, their major interests are in the theoretical and historical aspects of security, not focusing on security issues. Furthermore, the dialogues between the subcommittee members and government officials have been quite limited. JAIA publishes its journal, *Kokusaiseiji* (*International Politics*), three times a year.[10]

The largest organization comprising security experts is the Japan Association of Defense Studies. Most of the scholars and analysts of the Defense Academy and the National Institute of Defense Studies are members of the association. The association publishes the journal *Shin-Bouei-Ronsyu* (*New Journal of Defense Studies*).

One of the ways to expand a community of security experts is through participation in research projects conducted and commissioned by government agencies, research institutes and foundations. With the increase of the number of research projects on security and international relations, a community of security experts is gradually expanding in Japan.

The Japan Association of Peace Studies is an organization comprising scholars and journalists specializing in peace studies. They aim at offering alternatives to government policies for peace and security by analyzing factors underlying such issues as militarization of the developing countries and dynamism of military proliferation. Recently concepts developed in Europe, such as "defensive defense" and "nonprovocative defense," were introduced by the association into Japan as alternatives to Japan's security policy. The association publishes a journal *Heiwa Kenkyu* (*Peace Studies*).[11]

## Participation by Security Experts in International Activities

Until recently the number of security experts participating in international activities has been limited. However, now the number is increasing rapidly, although it is still not sufficient. The recent increase has been for both internal and external reasons. Internally, the number of security-related research projects and international conferences sponsored by Japan has increased rapidly. In fact, many research institutes, foundations, government ministries and media organizations have held international conferences on security affairs. Externally, with the emergence of Japan as a major power, many scholars/analysts and government officials have been invited to attend such conferences.

Although most of the international activities done by security experts were in the form of participation in international meetings, recently the occasions for Japanese security experts to join in the joint research with those of foreign countries have been increasing.

The following institutes have been active in promoting international exchanges on security affairs: Japan Institute of International Affairs, Japan Center for International Exchanges, Japan Forum on International Affairs, Institute of Global Peace, Research Institute for Peace and Security, National Institute of Defense Studies.

To be noted in this context is the fact that many foundations in Japan began to support security-related studies and international conferences, although they had been reluctant to do so in the face of the sharp division of public opinion over security affairs. The establishment of the Center for Global Partnership of the Japan Foundation, among others, has greatly contributed in promoting international exchanges in international and security affairs.

## Interrelations between Scholars and Government Officials

Apart from ad hoc or regular contacts between government officials (or politicians) and outside scholars on an individual basis, there are some occasions through which government officials and outside scholars can exchange their frank views on national and international affairs. By way of these occasions, outside experts are able to influence the formation of policy in a direct or an indirect way.[12]

### Government Councils

In the Japanese political system the decision makers (prime minister, foreign minister, etc.) quite often establish special councils to address immediate or mid- and long-term policy agenda. Usually some of the members of the councils are chosen from academic circles. Through examinations, the expertise of the academics could be transplanted into the policy formation process. Taking a few examples, under the Ohira cabinet, the council on a comprehensive security and a Pacific community were established. In the process of examination scholars played key roles and their recommendations were adopted as official policy. And, under the Miyazawa cabinet, a council to study Japan's policy towards the Asia-Pacific region was established. Several scholars participated in policy examination and the making of the policy recommendations to be presented to the prime minister as a basis of his policy initiatives. Most parts of the report by the council were adopted in Miyazawa's speech in Bangkok. The guideline of limiting the defense expenditure to around 1 percent of the GNP was initially proposed by a special council set up by the prime minster, before being adopted as a government policy (1976). And, later, the policy to abolish the guideline was also initially proposed by a (different) special council set up by then prime minister (1983), before becoming a government policy. In the process of examination at the councils, scholars played important roles.

In addition, government agencies often set up study/research groups focusing on specific issues of interest. Usually some of the members are outside scholars.

It is quite difficult to assess and generalize the influence of scholars on policy formation through government councils. To be noted, however, is that these councils have two purposes for the government: first, to provide fresh ideas and policy recommendations which the bureaucracy is not able to produce; second, to authorize policy which is already agreed upon within government circles but needs to be endorsed by a "third" (neutral) party in order to persuade opposition groups.

## Research Projects Commissioned by the Government

Every government agency has its own fund to be used for research. Usually, after the division in charge of research prioritize the proposals presented by the individual divisions, it commissions research projects to outside research organizations (in some cases to individuals). Generally speaking, most of the research projects are commissioned to research institutes over which the ministries concerned have jurisdiction for supervision. That is, many of the research projects of the Foreign Ministry are commissioned to the Japan Institute of International Affairs (JIIA), and those of the Defense Agency to the Research Institute of Peace and Security (RIPS). (Needless to say, most of the research projects by the Defense Agency are commissioned to the National Institute of Defense Studies, a research organization attached to the Defense Agency.) The final reports are presented to the divisions concerned and used as supplements to research conducted by the divisions themselves. The purpose of commissioning research projects to outside organizations is, generally speaking, not to get policy recommendations on matters to which the government must respond immediately, but to have theoretical and broader perspectives about specific issue areas. Therefore, impact of commissioned research on policy formation is usually indirect.

The table below shows the number and the topics of the research projects commissioned by the Foreign Ministry to the JIIA for the last five years (1988–92). (The total is about 80. Some of the projects were counted twice.)

Although these research projects did not necessarily directly focus on security issues, most of them dealt with security as a part of research. And, the number of the projects directly focusing on the security issues (US-Japan security relations, multilateral security arrangements in Asia, etc.) has constantly increased.

Almost all research institutes on international/security affairs do not have enough permanent staff to cope with various research projects. Therefore, outside experts such as university professors usually are requested to engage in the projects.

**Table 6.1**
**Number of Research Projects**
**from the Foreign Ministry to the JIIA**

| | | | |
|---|---|---|---|
| Soviet Union ( Russia) | 21 | Germany | 2 |
| United States | 15 | Far East/Asia | 2 |
| EC/Europe | 6 | Japan's ODA | 2 |
| Eastern Europe | 6 | Indochina | 1 |
| China | 6 | Philippines | 1 |
| US-Japan Relations | 5 | Vietnam | 1 |
| Asia-Pacific | 5 | Singapore | 1 |
| Military Affairs | 4 | Turkey | 1 |
| Korean Peninsula | 4 | Middle East | 1 |
| ASEAN/Southeast Asia | 3 | Northern Europe | 1 |
| | | Others | 3 |

### *Participation of the Government Officials in Study Meetings*

The research projects commissioned by the government provide academics and officials with occasions to exchange frank views. If JIIA's cases are taken as examples, usually the research is conducted through a series of meetings at the institute. Government officials also participate in the meetings, sometimes as full members of the research group. (The Cabinet Office of Information and Research is also conducting research in cooperation with outside scholars as well as their own ones. In addition, they ask outside scholars and experts to present a recommendations and situation analysis on such occasions as the prime minister's visit to foreign countries.)

As another function of the research, it should be pointed out that the research projects provide opportunities for scholars and government officials to have a frank exchange of views, thereby contributing to form a community of security-minded people. In addition, the number of security-related research projects conducted by research institutes themselves or supported by the foundations are gradually increasing.

## Publication on Security Affairs

For the last two decades, especially for the last several years, many books on international relations have been published in Japan. This reflects the fact that both academics and the general public have been paying more attention to international affairs and the role of Japan in the international community. Although most of the works have not necessarily focused on policy issues, a recent notable characteristic is the increase in the number of scholars and analysts who have published excellent scholarly works dealing with regional and international affairs from a mid- and long-term perspective.

Apart from many excellent scholarly works on international affairs, however, it is important in the coming decade that a first-class magazine such as *Foreign Affairs* or *Foreign Policy* in the United States or *International Affairs* in England should be promoted in Japan in order to provide a common forum for the foreign/security policy community including academics, government officials, business leaders and the attentive public. In addition, most Japanese articles are written in Japanese, and it is quite difficult for foreign scholars and government officials to know what arguments/debates are going on in Japan. *Kokusai-Mondai (International Affairs)* and *Japan Review of International Affairs*, published by the Japan Institute of International Affairs, are aiming to be such magazines.

From the point of view of impact on the general public, monthly magazines play an important role. Some of the Japanese popular monthly (and weekly) magazines usually publish articles on international/security affairs and Japanese diplomacy. Among them are *Chuo-Koron* and *Bungei-Shunjyu* which publish articles written from a realistic point of view, and *Sekai* with articles written from a more idealistic point of view. Academics usually publish policy-related issues on international/security affairs in these magazines. Recently, the number of government officials who publish views through these magazines has been increasing.

The Ministry of Foreign Affairs began to publish a monthly magazine (*Gaiko-Forum*) a few years ago. One of the purposes of this publication is to present views of government officials (mostly those of diplomats) to the general public as well as the experts on international affairs.

# Security Studies in Japan—Future Tasks

## *Japan's Security Outlook in the Asia-Pacific and Global Context*

The decline of the US-Russian bipolar system has created a complex and pluralistic world. Furthermore, the pluralization in basic values among the parties concerned has increased the possibility of complex tensions and disputes emerging in the world. In order to cope with this situation effectively, we will always have to keep diplomatic flexibility through active diplomatic initiative and will have to adopt multilateral and multilayered approaches. In the foreseeable future, multiple approaches will be tried in order to manage the international and regional systems, and there will emerge in due course a "soft order" consisting of overlapping parts of multilateral approaches.

We may take a UN-centered approach as in the Gulf War to solve certain security issues. However there will be no assurance that the UN can cope with all conflicts and disputes, as is shown in Somalia and the former Yugoslavia. On the other hand, consensus formation at the subregional level had a crucial impact on the solution of the Cambodia problem. Outside countries like France, Australia and Japan as well as ASEAN also played important roles to solve the problem. Furthermore, the United Nations served in keeping the agreement among the parties in conflict. In the future, it will be difficult to decide in advance which approach and level is most appropriate to cope with an individual conflict. This implies that flexible approaches could be appropriate for the solution of conflicts, and that multilayered approaches such as bilateral, subregional, regional and global ones have to be brought to bear.

Needless to say, it is quite important for the Japanese government and people to understand the fact that security is a function of the international system, not a matter for just one country. Reflecting on the Second World War, in which severe damage was caused to neighboring countries, Japan has consistently pursued a "One-Nation Peace Policy" for the last four decades. This approach has been supported by the US-Japan relationship. But whether the world will enjoy peace in the future depends upon how international and regional systems are constituted and how they function, not on the defense posture of one single country.

If Japan pursues its security within global and regional frameworks, it could reduce concerns among neighboring countries. What worries the neighboring countries is the nation of a Japan moving ahead alone without paying due attention to the possible impacts of its behavior on their security perceptions. These worries apply even to a Japanese role played under the auspices of the United Nations. Therefore, it will be extremely important for Japan to make a firm commitment to pursue its security through dialogues with the neighboring countries. Furthermore, through Japanese governmental joint efforts to enhance global and regional security, the Japanese people themselves could understand the importance of international cooperation. This is the way in which Japan can get support on its foreign and security policy from the rest of the world.

## US-Japan Relations and the Security Dialogues in the Asia-Pacific Region

As was pointed out, US-Japan relations are still the most important aspect of foreign and security policy for Japan. Economically, the United States provides the largest market for Japanese products. In security terms, the United States is the only country on which Japan can rely for its security.

In postwar Japan, disputes on security affairs have been mainly focused on the US-Japan bilateral security framework. Now in the post–Cold War era, Japan needs to pay more attention to the possible relations between Japan's security relations with the United States and the emerging regional framework in the region, as well as strengthening the US-Japan bilateral security relations. This means that the US-Japan security alliance will be placed in a broader regional security framework emerging in the Asia-Pacific region.

US-Japan relations will be of vital importance in terms of maintaining the free and open international economic system. In this context, it will be very important for the Asian region and American regions to be connected closely through the framework of Asia-Pacific cooperation. Japan should enhance Asia-Pacific regional economic cooperation through the Asia-Pacific Economic Cooperation Council (APEC) and the Pacific Economic Cooperation Council (PECC).

## Security Studies

The task for security studies in Japan in the coming decades is to broaden the intellectual community for security studies through promoting policy-related research activities and to present clear and fresh ideas of the region, as well as the world. There remain a large number of security-related issues in both regional and global scenes on which Japan has to present fresh ideas. One, for example, is how Japan should respond to the issues of reforming the United Nations, especially the Security Council. What kinds of reforms should be done to strengthen the security-related function of the United Nations? What roles should Japan play at a reformed United Nations? Japan has to present more clear views of itself. A further question would be how Japan should contribute to solving the Korean conflict. What concrete steps should be taken individually and collectively? At this moment, Northeast Asia has a serious problem in North Korea's nuclear development. In order to stop the authoritarian regime from having dangerous weapons, the countries and international organizations concerned have to cooperate. And the solution of North Korea's nuclear problem through multilateral diplomatic efforts may provide some foundation to develop subregional security arrangements in Northeast Asia which have been lacking in the region. Taking this possibility into consideration, Japan should show its own ideas and policies. Furthermore, what issues should be put into the agenda of the ASEAN Regional Forum and how should dialogue processes be organized? How and what working group should be organized to promote security dialogues at the regional forum? How should the Asia-Pacific region approach regional security issues? There still exists a serious territorial dispute between Japan and Russia, but how will Japan describe its desirable future relations with Russia? What steps should be taken to get mutually beneficial relations between Japan and Russia?

In addition, there are now emerging new security agenda such as environmental degradation and a population explosion. The relations between economy and security also should be addressed.

Japan has so far waited for someone else to take initiative and present ideas. However, if Japan wishes to share responsibilities for managing the international system, Japan has to present fresh and feasible ideas and policy-oriented recommendations to be elaborated and examined with other interested nations. New ideas and new initiatives taken by Japan may sometimes have severe criticisms from other countries. However, it will be inevitable for new ideas to be confronted with some criticisms. Japan has to overcome this through dialogues and mutual consultations if it determines to play more constructive roles in international affairs. And judging by its economic power, Japan will have no other option but to engage in international affairs more actively.

These efforts should be made in both government circles and academic ones. In particular, the academics should make more efforts to formulate new policy options based upon fresh ideas. And training process (programs) for security experts also have to be enhanced. In this context, of importance is that scholarships for young students specializing in security affairs should be promoted. In addition, various opportunities should be given to young scholars to attend international conferences and participate in joint research activities with experts of other countries on security affairs facing the region. Probably, through these efforts, security studies in Japan will be more institutionalized and a security community will have a more firm foundation in the Japanese society.

## Notes

1. Professors Masataka Kohsaka of Kyoto University, Yohnosuke Nagai of Aoyama-gakuin University, Seizaburo Sato of Keio University and Masashi Nishihara of the Defense Academy are among the most respected scholars in this school.

2. Professor Yoshikazu Sakamoto, then professor of international politics, Faculty of Law, Tokyo University, has played a leading role in this school. Professor Takehiko Kamo of Tokyo University is a leading figure in this group at this moment.

3. "Asia-Pacific" in security contexts refers to Western Pacific, including Northeast and Southeast Asia.

4. Mr. Yoichi Funabashi, Head of the Washington Bureau of Asahi Shinbun, presents articulated arguments on this matter. See, *Nihon No Taigai Koso (Japan's External Strategy)*, Iwanami-Shoten, 1993

5. See, Ichiro Ozawa, *Nihon Kaizo Keikaku (A Reform Plan for Japan)*, (Tokyo: Kohdansha, 1993). An English version will be published shortly.

6. Regarding debates over Japan's security policies after the end of the Cold War, including the Japanese debate on participation in UN peace/security activities, see Yoshinobu Yamamoto, "Japan's Security Policies in the Post–Cold War Era," *Australian Journal of International Affairs*, October 1993, vol. 47, no. 2, pp. 286–99.

7. Yamamoto, ibid.

8. On the developments of Japan's Asian policy, see Akio Watanabe, *Ajia-Taiheiyou No Kokusai Kankei To Nihon (International Relations in the Asia-Pacific and Japan)*, (Tokyo: University of Tokyo Press, 1992).

9. The Institute of Oriental Studies of the University of Tokyo, the Center for Southeast Asian Studies of Kyoto University, and the Institute of Developing Economies are among the major research institutes focusing on Asian studies.

   The following are some of the leading research institutes dealing with security issues: Japan Institute of International Affairs (JIIA), Research Institute of Peace and Security (RIPS), and Institute for International Policy Studies (IIPS).

   The National Institute of Defense Studies is the most important government-based research and training institute in security affairs.

   The National Institute for Research Advancement (NIRA) has provided for security-related dialogues, especially in the Asia-Pacific region.

10. JAIR has more than one thousand members. According to a survey on research interest among the members of JAIR conducted in 1988, 18.8 percent of the respondents expressed their interest in security studies.

11. Most of the members of the Japan Association of Defense Studies and the Japan Association of Peace Research have memberships in JAIR.

12. On this part of our article, we owe much to Professor Akio Watanabe's various works.

# Security Studies in Korea

YOUNG-KOO CHA[1]

## Perception of Security

Security or national security is a very ambiguous term and it means different things to different people at different times under different circumstances. Traditionally security or national security is defined as "protection from external threat."[2] Thus it can be interpreted primarily in terms of military defense against external military threats. However, this traditional definition of security is too narrow to encompass various aspects of security. Security means more than that. According to Arnold Wolfers, "security, in an objective sense, measures the absence of threats to acquired values; in a subjective sense, the absence of fear that such values will be attacked."[3] Thus we can say that security is a condition that allows a nation to maintain its value(s).

Then we have to ask what are the most cherished values which nations are desperate to defend. Those can be a nation's territorial integrity, national independence, national survival, and prosperity. There are various factors which can threaten or promote these values. As these factors change, the conditions for maintaining and enhancing those values change constantly. As the conditions and factors change, operationalization and measurement of security change. Security is not a static condition that exists in a vacuum. Rather it is determined in the context of both international and domestic environments, both of which are changing constantly. These characteristics of security are also reflected in security studies in Korea.

According to the *Defense White Paper of the Republic of Korea*, the national goals of South Korea are:

1. to assure permanent independence by safeguarding the existence of the nation under the ideal of free democracy, and for peaceful national unification;

2. to achieve social welfare by guaranteeing the freedom and constitutional rights of the people, and by fostering a balanced improvement in their living standards; and

3. to promote the country's international standing and contribute to the realization of a lasting peace throughout the world.[4]

At the surface, with the exception of national unification, the national goals of South Korea look similar to those of other democratic countries in the world. Thus security can be defined as the absence of threats and obstacles to the achievement of these national goals. And the perception of security seems very broad. However, in reality, security has been very narrowly defined and perceived by the South Koreans due to the given characteristics of the security environment of South Korea. As its security environment has begun to change since the late 1980s and early 1990s, perception of security has begun to change; that is, from a very narrowly defined concept of "military security" to that of "comprehensive security."

Up to the end of the 1980s, the primary security concern of South Korea was the ever-present North Korean *military threat* to the survival of South Korea. North Korea, who waged war against South Korea in 1950, has presented an enormous threat to South Korea and has left no room for the South Koreans to think other than about the military aspects of security. Nothing could possibly compare with North Korea's military threat due to North Korea's military superiority over South Korea, its past record of reckless and aggressive behavior, and its ultimate goal of national unification under its own terms. The confrontation between South and North Koreas since 1945 has led people to perceive and define security mainly in terms of the military dimension; that is, security means the defense of South Korea against North Korea's military attack and the denial of North Korea's ultimate goal of unification under its own terms by using its huge armed forces. Security itself has become defense of the homeland, and defense objectives tend to be translated exclusively into security objectives. Defense objectives of South Korea are "to defend the nation from armed aggression by potential adversaries, support the nation's effort for peaceful unification, and contribute to the security and peace of the region."[5] Such a conception of security has several characteristics and consequences. First of all, since security is defined as protection from external military attack, the establishment of reliable armed forces and the attainment of military superiority, or at least rough parity, for successful deterrence appear to be the most important and urgent requirements for ensuring and enhancing the security of South Korea. Thus, whenever there is a debate over "guns versus butter," the former has always won. Or, sometimes the debate itself has been inconceivable. Actually until recently very few had questioned the meaning of reliable armed forces and the adequate size and level of the armed forces. Whenever the government announced its defense budget, almost no one questioned the size of it, the rationale for determining its size, or how it was to be used and had been used, and how it was to be allocated between several services. Up to the mid-1980s, a quota system applied to the defense budget; that is, a certain percentage of the government budget was allocated to the defense budget. Between the mid-1980s and the early 1990s, the government guaranteed a certain increase rate of defense budget. In other words, there was a systematic guarantee and assurance through which the defense budget was guaranteed.

Second, in terms of game theory, security is perceived as a kind of zero-sum game where one player's gain always comes at the expense of other player. Security is a kind of all-or-northing game; that is, until one party wins the security game completely, there can be no security at all. This means that, although security is a relative condition, security tends to be perceived in absolute terms. Thus, we have been pursuing absolute security which cannot be achieved in reality, and we have not been concerned with what levels of insecurity are acceptable. One of the most important consequences of such a conception of security is the perception that peace and security through negotiation is inconceivable and infeasible, and that security can be achieved through intense competition. concepts such as mutual security or common security, which represent a non-zero-sum game situation, seem quite alien to the Koreans.

Third, a relatively narrow perception of security was also closely related to the Cold War confrontation between East and West. As children of the Cold War, the political character of the two Koreas was determined, from the outset, by the ideological rivalry between the United States and the Soviet Union. For political and military security reasons, South Korea (as well as North Korea), has been sensitive to any change in superpower relations and military balance between the two countries. The changes in superpower relations have greatly influenced each Korea's threat perception and, consequently, each one's respective foreign and security policies. For example, anything which seemed to benefit the former Soviet Union was considered to be a threat not only to the United States but also to the security of South Korea.

Fourth, and closely related to the third point, each Korea's security is dependent upon each one's security tie with its own allies. In the Korean War, each of the Koreas were saved by the involvement of its own security guarantor. Since then each one's security has been backed up by security commitment of its own respective allies. In terms of South Korea's security, in addition to the establishment of reliable armed forces of its own, the maintenance of strong and reliable military alliance with the United States has been the most important security measure. Anything which may undermine the ROK-US security alliance must be considered a threat to South Korea's national security.

Such a prevailing perception and definition of security in South Korea and the above-mentioned characteristics have created the the following characteristics for security studies in South Korea.

First of all, the scope of security studies in South Korea has been very narrowly defined: that is, it has only encompassed military affairs. Of course, while they do not necessarily disregard economic, social, and political security, relatively few scholars and policymakers have paid attention to these dimensions of security because of the importance of military security under the given security environment of Korea. This characteristic of the Korean security environment has led scholars and policymakers to isolate military dimension from other dimensions of security.

Second, a very small number of civilian scholars have been involved in security studies. Security studies seem to be the domain of the military or some scholars who have a military background. The restriction on the access to military information has also contributed to the lack of interest in security studies since information controls tended to impede any extensive research on security matters. These two factors have prevented the emergence of a security study group in South Korea. Major security studies which are relevant to policy formulation have been done by the government itself or government-funded research institutes. There has been no close cooperation between academic circles and the government. This has resulted in a lack of public debate regarding security matters.

Third, few scholars have paid attention to regional security affairs. Most scholars have been concerned with ROK-US relations and US foreign policy in

general. This might be a natural consequence of South Korea's security dependence on the US security commitment. Thus most scholars have been interested
in the study of US foreign policy vis-à-vis East Asia in general and in the ROK-US
security alliance in particular. There are a relatively small number of scholars in
security affairs who are specialized in the study of Japan, China, and the
former Soviet Union. But they recognize that the Korean peninsula is the point
where the vital interests of four major powers—the United States, the former
Soviet Union/Russia, China and Japan—intersect. Consequently, there are a
substantial number of country specialists but few regional specialist. Furthermore, there is no commonly shared definition of "region" among the scholars
and policymakers. Or sometimes when they say "region" they mean Northeast
Asia. The scope and definition of region have rarely gone beyond Northeast
Asia.

However, two important things have changed security studies in South
Korea. One is the successful democratization of South Korea. The other is the end
of the Cold War. These two events have broadened the scope of security studies
and have brought new issues under the academic scrutiny of security studies.
Democratization of domestic politics has encouraged public debate over security
and civilian participation in formulating and implementing security policies for
South Korea. At the same time, the end of the Cold War has allowed South Korea
to pursue a multidimensional approach toward security studies, and has generated a different set of security issues in addition to the military ones.

In the case regarding the effects of the end of the Cold War on Korea's security
studies, the scope of security has begun to change to encompass and reflect
various aspects of security. Security has begun to give way to a more balanced
definition of security which includes economic, social and domestic political security aspects. Among these, the economic aspect of security has gained more
importance than ever before. The South Korean government has begun to emphasize that without a sound and prospering economy, there can be no democracy, and
that economic competition in the international market has become intense as
other developing countries in East Asia have intensified their efforts to modernize
and develop their own economies. The benign world economic environment which
has contributed to the successful economic development of South Korea has begun
to disappear, and South Korea has begun to lose its economic edge. Consequently,
South Korea should pay more attention to economic security.

Second, as the security environment has begun to change, so has the concept
of security. Generally speaking, the security environment of South Korea has
improved since the end of the 1980s. The establishment of diplomatic relations
with the former Soviet Union and China has contributed to enhance the security
status of South Korea vis-à-vis North Korea which has not been able to establish
its diplomatic relations with either the United States or Japan. Consequently,
even though it is faced with North Korea's potential nuclear threat, South Korea
has begun to feel more confident and secured in coping with North Korea's
military threat. Security which was once described as a zero-sum game has
become a non-zero-sum game. Security in absolute terms has become security in
relative terms. This perception has led South Korea to be able to think of "peaceful
coexistence" and "security through negotiation."

Third, in the post–Cold War era, scholars and policymakers have begun to pay more attention to regional affairs and to widen the concept of "region." As I mentioned before, US foreign policy has been the dominant theme in security studies. However, since the end of the 1980s, while ROK-US security ties are still the dominant theme, we have witnessed an increase of interest in the study of other great powers' security policies. There was a tendency to isolate Northeast Asian affairs from Asia-Pacific regional affairs. But that tendency has begun to yield to a trend to integrate Northeast Asian affairs into those of the broader Asia-Pacific region.[6] The expansion of the geographical scope of study may imply an increasing economic interdependency between the countries in the Asia Pacific, and the importance of economic cooperation between these countries for their co-prosperity.

Finally, South Korea has become more concerned about its neighboring countries' security policies and their military capabilities than ever before. Given the reduced role of both the United States and Russia in the Asia-Pacific region, Japan and China are likely to wield greater influence in determining the strategic environment in East Asia. Japan, as the world's largest creditor nation, has emerged as the second largest economy next only to the United States. It has the world's third largest defense expenditure. China is the only genuine Asian nation with strategic nuclear forces, and it maintains the world's largest military of 3.2 million troops, thus standing in a position to effect a major change in the strategic environment in Asia. Recently these two great powers are modernizing their military capabilities.[7] The relative decline of US and Russian influence and an increase of Chinese and Japanese power in determining Asian affairs have complicated South Korea's strategic calculation and increased its uncertainty about the future strategic configuration in Northeast Asia. Now, in addition to North Korea's threat, South Korea is faced with another type of threat; the uncertainty about how and in what direction the regional balance of power will shift.

In sum, the relative simple and straightforward conception of security has become more complicated. The scope of security has widened. Consequently, security now means not the protection from external military threats but the very comprehensive security which includes economic, social, political and diplomatic security. And there is a new set of security issues South Korea should tackle.

## Intellectual Traditions

In the West, security or peace studies actively engages academics and government officials. Even in academic circles, we can easily identify some intellectual traditions and groups of thought. In contrast, in Korea, although it is possible to identify some leading scholars in security studies, it is difficult to distinguish intellectual traditions. This is worse in peace research which has gained little public recognition and support. In Korea, peace research tends to be associated with the antigovernment movement because the subject of peace research is closely related to issues such as human rights, antinuclear issues,[8] and the environment which are, to a certain degree, secondary issues for most Koreans because of imminent military threat from North Korea.

What is dominant in shaping the thought on Asia Pacific security studies is the government policy interests. At least in security studies, government policy interests tend to represent national security interests in themselves. Actually, the government itself has been the leading actor in defining and shaping the thought on national security and regional security and, at least in the security field, government policy interests tend toward being synonymous with national security interests. Few have challenged and questioned the security policy of the government.

It does not necessarily mean that there has been no involvement of scholars in formulating and implementing government policies. Some scholars have participated in policy formulation and implementation as consultants or advisers on personal bases. And the South Korean government have been providing research funds to individual scholars on selected research topics. And a select number of scholars have become government officials, and vice-versa. Thus, we can say that there has been a linkage between government and scholars in security studies, but that linkage has been relatively weak. Therefore, public debate over security has not been active.

These circumstances have also influenced research issues. The most dominant theme in the security field is international relations and diplomatic history. *The List of Materials on Unification and Security Affairs*, which was published by the National Unification Board in 1990 and covers materials published between 1987 and 1990, classifies books, reports, articles, and dissertations into ten categories: security and defense; unification; South-North Korean relations; North Korea in general; politics and administration in North Korea; economy, science, and technology of North Korea; diplomacy and military affairs of North Korea; society, culture, and education of North Korea; and international relations which include great powers' foreign policies between themselves and their polices toward the Korea peninsula. We can reclassify these materials into four groups: security and defense; South-North relations including the unification issue; North Korea; and international relations. The size of materials on international relations is the greatest.

### * Table 7.1
### Classification and Size of Literature on Security
### Between 1987 and 1990

| Subject | Number of Books, Articles, Reports |
| --- | --- |
| Security and Defense | 950 |
| South-North Relations | 1,200 |
| North Korea | 3,200 |
| International Relations | 3,500 |

* The numbers shown in this table are rough numbers.

The most dominant issue in security studies and international relations is US-ROK alliance politics, US foreign and security policy vis-à-vis the Korean peninsula, how it has evolved over the years, and what factors influence the US-ROK alliance. The second dominant research topic is foreign policies of the neighboring countries—China, the Soviet Union, and Japan. In other words, security studies in Korea have been mainly oriented toward the study of diplomatic history of each country.

As the security environment has changed fundamentally over the last few years, research topics in security studies have changed. Topics such as deterrence, nuclear arms and arms control, conventional weapons studies, and confidence building measures which were inconceivable during the Cold War period, have emerged as important research topics in Korean security studies.

However, these research topics are relatively new, and there are a relatively small number of scholars specialized in these fields. Consequently, research on these subjects has a relatively weak theoretical background, and is oriented mostly toward policy recommendations. What is required in the near future for Korean security studies is a comprehensive and complete theoretical survey of these new topics, and the accompanying theoretical debate among scholars, in addition to policy recommendations. Such activities will enhance and widen our understanding of security issues, and will improve the quality of security studies in Korea by providing a firm theoretical background.

Furthermore, we must expand our geographical scope to meet the security requirements of the Asia-Pacific era in which any single security issue cannot be solved in isolation by a specific country alone. It requires multilateral cooperation. In order to enhance such multilateral cooperation, we need regional specialists as well as country specialists. We have a substantial number of scholars specialized in country studies. However, these are scholars specialized in domestic politics of certain countries. Their specialty is not strategic issues, but comparative politics. The dominant theme in their research is "political development" and they have rarely paid attention to security issues either of certain countries or the region. This issue leads us to the third question—training regional specialists.

## Training Regional Experts

By the end of 1992, the "Korean Association of International Studies" included among its members 629 scholars of whom 300 hold doctoral degrees in international relations. Others specialize in comparative politics and political theory. Among these, there are a relatively small number of indigenous regional or security experts. Most of the regional experts working actively in this field have been educated abroad, mainly in the United States.

During the 1960s and 1970s many students of international relations studied extensively, mostly in the field of international relations and comparative politics. When these new doctoral scholars returned, they brought new theories, approaches, research techniques, and a new set of research agendas with them. They have formed the second generation of scholars in international relations.

Since the late 1970s the second generation scholars began to offer some courses in security fields as well as regional affairs. However, they were unable to

develop a systematic program in the national security field as a separate academic specialty. The course offerings were poorly organized, due mainly to a lack
of student interest in national security affairs, and to the prevailing perception
that security is a field for government officials and the military. Students did not
regard security studies as a separate academic field and they thought that
security issues were politically exploited. The only institute which has been
offering an MA degree in national security affairs is the National Defense College
since 1982. The National Defense College has produced approximately thirty to
forty masters per year in the security field.

During the 1980s, there was another surge of students who went abroad to
acquire doctoral degrees. Most of them took undergraduate or graduate-level
education at home. During this time, some students went to Europe. Most of them
have finished or are just about to finish their doctoral programs. These scholars
constitute the third generation.

There were several primary reasons that these people studied abroad during
this period. Few academic institutions in Korea offered courses in security studies. Information regarding the region or country in which they were interested
was limited and was hard to obtain. The government and private companies had
little interest in training regional or security specialists. And, among the first
generation of scholars in international relations who had their educational training during the Japanese occupation or shortly after the Korean War, there were
very few scholars who could teach the emergent third-generation scholars.

Because of these facts, there are today a very small number of indigenous
regional experts in security studies. But we expect that there will be more
indigenous experts as the general interest in security affairs increases and as
some institutions continue to produce indigenous scholars. Thus, it is premature
to expect that there is any difference in analysis and policy advice between
specialists primarily trained at home and others trained abroad. Rather we can
observe some differences among the scholars on a personal basis, not on group
basis, and even sometimes between the scholars trained abroad.

The government has been trying to expand its own research capabilities by
providing government officials the opportunities to study abroad. The Ministry of
Foreign Affairs and the Ministry of National Defense have been quite active in
their educational programs. Consequently, many government officials have
obtained some level of expertise in regional affairs or country studies. But it is
difficult to regard these government officials as regional experts since their
education is not extensive and they are not given sufficient time to become true
regional experts. The average stay abroad for their education is about two years.
Because of the time constraint on their stay abroad, most of them are unable to
obtain a doctoral degree and instead leave with a master's degrees. Thus it is
difficult to determine their level of expertise.

What we can say about the current stage in Korean security studies is that
we still don't have a sufficient number of *"true security specialists,"* those with
considerable technical understanding of specific strategic issues, to meet over
national security needs. However, as the security environment has begun to
change and people have begun to recognize the necessity of having a substantial
number of civilian security specialists to meet national security needs, many

civilian scholars and academic institutions such as Seoul National University, Yonsei University, and Korea University have begun to offer courses on security studies. It will take some time to achieve a sufficient number of security specialists. To make their training more adequate, training in foreign languages is required. While English is the most commonly used language in security studies and is the first foreign language required in PhD programs in the social science field, English alone is insufficient to make the training of regional experts adequate to meet national security needs. In order to enhance their first-hand research capability, additional languages—Chinese, Russian, and Japanese—will be useful.

# Participation

It is very difficult to determine the level of participation of security specialists in regional or global dialogue programs since it is almost impossible to keep track of each individual's participation in international forums or dialogue. Some scholars or security specialists have the opportunities to participate in research and dialogue through invitations and proposals from abroad on a personal basis. Thus it is difficult to say that the security specialists actively seek to participate in regional or global research. Some specialists are members of academic associations such as the American Political Science Association, the International Studies Association, and the International Institute of Strategic Studies. Thus they usually participate in the annual meetings or conferences of these organizations. And the Asia Foundation, which was established to promote the Asian studies, supports these scholars' participation.

Government-funded research institutes such as the Korea Institute for Defense Analyses, the Institute of Foreign Affairs and National Security, and the Research Institute of National Unification support and encourage their researchers' participation in regional or global dialogues. What is important regarding these government research institutes are their efforts to host international conferences and to support joint research projects with foreign research institutes.

Private or academic research institutes, which are usually affiliated with academic institutions, have the same kind of program. But, due to a lack of financial resources, the level of support these academic institutions provide to their researchers or professors is much lower than that of government research institutes.

There are at least two relatively recent but dominant changes in security specialists' participation in academic forums. First of all, until the late 1980s, their participation in regional or global research was a kind of one-way traffic: that is, Korean specialists tended to participate in research projects or dialogues hosted by foreign research institutes or organizations. However, since the late 1980s, the Korean specialists, research institutes, and academic institutions have begun to increase the number of their research projects and international dialogue programs proposed and hosted by themselves.

The second important change is the diversification of their participation. That is, the Korean specialists tended to participate in dialogue or research programs in the United States. Their foreign counterparts have usually been US research institutes or organizations. However, since the late 1980s, they began to diversify their foreign counterparts—mostly Russia, China, and Japan. While the number of joint research projects or seminars with research institutes in these countries is still small, I expect that will increase. I consider this to be the product of the normalization of diplomatic relations between South Korea and the former Soviet Union and between South Korea and China. Such diplomatic development has contributed to an increase in the exchange of scholars and specialists among the Northeast Asian countries.

# Institutions

We can identify three types of research institutes: government-supported research institutes, research institutes affiliated with academic institutions, and private research institutes.

As we already discussed, in Korea, the government is the leading actor in security studies. Three branches of the government—the National Unification Board, Ministry of Foreign Affairs, and Ministry of National Defense—have their own research institutes related to security studies. These research institutes are fully supported by the government, and are quite influential in formulating policies.

**Table 7.2**
**Government-funded Research Institutes in Security Studies**

| Name of Institute | Supporting Ministry | Number of Researchers |
|---|---|---|
| Research Institute of National Unification (RINU) | National Unification Board | 50* |
| Institute of Foreign Affairs and National Security (IFANS) | Ministry of ForeignAffairs | 25* |
| Korea Institute for Defense Analyses (KDA) | Ministry of National Defense | 164 |

* The number may become larger than this if we include visiting scholars and part-time and full-time consultants.

As you can see in Table 7.2, KIDA is the biggest research institute in the security field. KIDA is so large because it is devoted not only to research on security policy, national defense strategy, and arms control, but also force development, weapons systems studies, manpower management, and resource management. RINU is mostly devoted to unification policy studies and IFANS is mainly oriented toward the study of foreign affairs and international relations. Unlike KIDA, other institutes deal with more general issues of security, foreign affairs, and unification policies.

The level of influence of each institute cannot be determined at a general level because of each institute's affiliation with a particular government branch, and each one's distinctive research orientation, roles, concerns, and specialty. However, each institute's influence in determining and formulating policies in its own specialty area cannot be underestimated, since each one has direct communications channels with its government branch. Government officials often seek advice and recommendations from these institutes regarding some policies or issues. Some former government officials join these research institutes as researchers, advisers, or consultants. They provide another channel of communication and influence. For example, IFANS has a substantial number of ambassadors-at-large and KIDA utilizes former military officials as consultants.

The relationship between these government-funded research institutes is very cooperative. They often consult each other and try to share their knowledge and information. Unfortunately, we have not developed a systematic cooperative research network between these institutes and have not done any research jointly. We are working to establish such a cooperative research network. But there is no systematic barrier, such as security regulations or restrictions on joint researches with other institutes, to hinder research cooperation. On the other hand, we cannot rule out the possibility of conflict because of a researcher's personal orientation and preference, and because of bureaucratic organizational interests. From an attitudinal perspective, researchers in KIDA tend to be relatively conservative since they are affiliated with the Ministry of Natinal Defense which is the most conservative government branch, whereas researchers in IFANS and RINU are relatively liberal because of the subject they deal with. But the differences between the researchers in these institutes are much smaller than those between the researchers in these institutes and the researchers in private institutes or academic institutions. This leads us to the second and third type of research institute.

As we can see in Table 7.3, most major national universities have their own affiliated research institutes. And there are several private research institutes: Sejong Institute; Research Institute for International Affairs; Institute of Far Eastern Affairs; Institute of North Korean Studies; Korea Institute of International Relations; Daeryuk Institute; Academy of Social Science; and the Research Institute of Peace and Unification.

Compared to government research institutes, which we have already discussed, these research institutes have a relatively small number of full-time researchers. Their fund is very limited and their major concern is not security. As shown in the table, they are mostly oriented toward unification studies. These institutes have limited access to information regarding national security matters. It is very difficult to determine their influence over government policy. But some leading scholars in these institutes tend to exert substantial influence through their personal and institutional linkage with government and their reputation in the academic circle. While the scholars who are interested in security affairs are relatively conservative in their orientation, compared to that of researchers in government institutes, they tend to be more or less liberal.

## Table 7.3
### Research Institutes Affiliated with Academic Institutions

| Name of Research Institute | Academic Institution |
| --- | --- |
| Institute of International Affairs | Seoul National University |
| Institute of Unification Studies | Pusan National University |
| Institute of Unification Studies | Choongbook National University |
| Institute of Unification Studies | Choongnam National University |
| Institute of Unification and Security Studies | Jeojoo National University |
| Institute of Communist Studies | Jeonbook National University |
| Institute of Unification Studies | Jeonnam National University |
| Institute of International Affairs | Cheongjoo University |
| Institute of Regional Studies | Choongang University |
| Institute of Unification Studies | Choshun University |
| Institute of Security Studies | Dongkook University |
| Institute of Unification Studies | Dongyi University |
| Institute of Chinese and Russian Studies | Hanyang University |
| Institute for Peaceful Unification | Inchon University |
| Institute of International Relations | Inha University |
| Institute of Asian Studies | Korea University |
| Institute of Peace Studies | Korea University |
| Wharangdea Institute | Korea Military Academy |
| Institute for Peace Studies | Kyungbook University |
| Institute of East Asian Affairs | Kyungnam University |
| Institute for International Peace | Kyunghee University |
| Institute of Northeast Asian Studies | Kyunghee University |
| Research Institute of National Security Affairs | National Defense University |
| Institute of East Asian Affairs | Seokang University |
| Institute for Peace and Unification | Taegu University |
| Institute of East and West Studies | Yonsei University |
| Institute of Unification Studies | Youngnam University |
| Institute of Unification Studies | Wonkwang University |
| Institute of Unification Studies | Sookmyung Woman's University |

It is very difficult to determine the level of influence and reputation of these institutions. However, some major research institutes publish journals and books regularly. So we can say that we can determine the level of influence and reputation of each institute based on the fact of whether it publishes journals or books regularly or not. Among these research institutes, the Institute of Chinese and Russian Studies (Hanyang University), the Institute of Asian Studies (Korea University), the Institute of East Asian Affairs (Kyungnam University), the Research Institute of National Security Affairs (National Defense University), the Institute of East Asian Affairs (Seokang University), and the Institute of East and West Studies (Yonsei University) publish journals and books which are quite influential in security studies in Korea.

The biggest problem in security studies is information. Until recently the South Korean government has been very reluctant to share information in security matters. But such an attitude has begun to change. The South Korea government has recognized that information sharing is not detrimental to national security. Rather, it can contribute to a better understanding of security issues among the general public and it is necessary to create a consensus and strong support regarding security policies. Research institutes affiliated with academic institutions and private institutes can play a significant role in this aspect.

## Consumers

The biggest consumer of security analysis are government agencies. Since government agencies are busy with their regular duties, they don't have time to do deep and detailed analysis on security matters. Thus they tend to rely on the analyses done by their own research institutes and academics. There are two kinds of research done by the government research institutes: research topics raised by the government agencies and those raised by researchers themselves. And sometimes the government provides research grants to private institutes and scholars on selected topics. These three types of research provide very valuable analyses and policy recommendations. The results of their research can be produced in several different formats: classified reports; unclassified reports; articles in major journals; edited books; and a series of articles in newspapers. The determination of format usually depends on the sensitivity and nature of the research topic, and the affiliation of research institutes. For example, there are a substantial number of classified reports which are not available to the general public. Reports classified as "confidential" can be distributed to government agencies, researchers in other government research institutes, and the civilian participant who are authorized or involved in designated research. For reports of higher classification, usually, distribution restriction policy applies, and these reports cannot be distributed even to other government agencies or research institutes.

On the other hand, on the civilian side, there are approximately twenty to thirty journals related to security studies. There are eight journals published in English and others are published in Korean. These journals can be considered a channel of communications among scholars and policymakers. And sometimes they carry valuable information and analyses. Journals written in Korean are dominant.

**Table 7.4**
**Major Journals of Security Studies Published in English**

| Name of Journal | Publisher |
| --- | --- |
| *Asian Perspective* | Institute of East Asian Studies, Kyungnam University |
| *Journal of East and West Studies* | Institute of East and West Studies |
| *Pacific Focus* | Institute of International Relations, Inha University |
| *Journal of East Asian Affairs* | Research Institute of International Affairs |
| *Korea and World Affairs* | Institute of Peace and Unification |
| *Sejong Review* | Sejong Institute |
| *Korean Journal of Defense Analysis* | KIDA |
| *Korea Observer* | Hankook Haksool Jaedan (Korea Foundation of Academic Studies) |

While these journals are available to the general public, the main readers of these journals are scholars and students of security studies. And the circulation of each journal is relatively small: approximately 1,500 to 2,000. Until recently, major themes of articles shown in these journals include unification, North Korean studies, and international relations in general. Very few articles have been directly related to security issues. However, as the security environment continues to change and the South Korean government becomes more flexible regarding discussion of security matters, these journals will continue to carry articles which are more directly related to security issues.

In terms of authorship, English journals carry articles of foreign authors as well as Korean scholars. Some Korean journals publish translated articles of foreign authors.

## Future Needs

As the security environment has changed fundamentally over the last few years, security studies in Korea have gained wider recognition and support. What I can say at the current stage is that security studies in Korea have entered a new era. The subject of security studies has also become wide and comprehensive. However, there are several things we must do in order to make security studies in Korea a real security study.

First of all, we need more security specialists. Up to now, as a matter of fact, the so-called security specialists are not really specialized in security studies. Their background tends to be either international politics in general or comparative politics. Of course, they have very good analytic skills and excellent insight. However, their analyses tend to stop just short of details of security matters and military affairs. They should become more familiar with details.

## Table 7.5
## Journals of Security Studies Published in Korean

| Name of Journal | Publisher |
| --- | --- |
| *Hankookkwa Kookje Jeongchi* (*Korea and World Affairs*) | Institute of East Asian Studies, Kyungnam University |
| *Pyoungwha Yeonkoo* (*Peace Studies*) | Institute of International Peace Studies |
| *Asea Yeonkoo* (*Asiatic Studies*) | Institute of Asian Studies, Korea University |
| *Tongil Nonchong* (*Unification Forum*) | Institute of Unification Studies, Pusan National University |
| *Kookje Moonje Yeonkooso Nonmoon Jip* (*Journal of International Affairs*) | Institute of International Affairs, Seoul National University |
| *Tongil Nonjip* (*Journal of Unification Studies*) | Institute of Unification Studies, Sookmyung Woman's University |
| *Kongsankwon Yeonkoo* (*Journal of Communist Studies*) | Institute of Far Eastern Affairs |
| *Bookhan* (*North Korea*) | Institute of North Korean Studies |
| *Bookhan Nonchong* (*North Korean Forum*) | Association of North Korean Studies |
| *Kookje Moonje* (*International Affairs*) | Korea Institute of International Affairs |
| *Kyekan Sasang* (*Ideology Quarterly*) | Institute of Social Science |
| *Oekyo* (*Foreign Affairs*) | Korean Council on Foreign Relations |
| *Kookbang Nonjip* (*Defense Journal*) | KIDA |
| *Jukan Kookbang Nondan* (*Defense Weekly Forum*) | KIDA |
| *Jeonmang* (*Perspective*) | Daeryuk Institute |
| *Kookbang* (*National Defense*) | Ministry of National Defense |
| *Bookhan Yeonkoo* (*North Korean Studies*) | Daeryuk Institute |

Second, the relationship between the government and academics should become much closer. As I have said before, there is no systematic linkage between scholars and policymakers. Up to now the linkage has been based on personal connection. As we know, personal connection may be more influential but it is limited in scope. Thus, it is necessary to establish a good and active communications channel between the government and academic circle.

Third, more information sharing is required. The government has been reluctant to share some, not all, information regarding security matters not because of the sensitive nature of information but because of the fear of backlash of sharing information. If some information is released or shared, it might become a domestic political issue between the government and the opposition party or antigovernment groups. However, without sufficient information on security matters, security studies cannot become true security studies. There should be a kind of information pool system through which scholars and policymakers can share their knowledge and information. Of course, it is necessary and understandable to have restrictions on the access to information. But those restrictions should become more realistic.

Fourth, the cooperative and professional relationship between domestic research institutes and between local institutes and foreign research institutes should be developed further. The relationship between research institutes has been based on personal linkage. Personal linkage is insufficient to develop cooperative research relationships. Based on personal linkage, we should try to nurture long-lasting relationships between institutions.

In sum, in the post–Cold War era, security studies in Korea have grown in scope and public recognition. The concept of security has become more comprehensive. The government has become more relaxed and flexible in dealing with security matters. And people have become active in discussing security matters. Taking advantages of a supportive atmosphere, scholars and policymakers should continue to expand them even further so that security studies in Korea can continue to meet the demands of an increasingly complex and challenging world.

## Notes

1. I'd like to express my sincere thanks to Dr. Kang Choi, Mr. Doohyun Cha and Mr. Myungchul Lee for their devoted and dedicated support in preparation for this paper. Their efforts significantly and directly contributed to a professional paper on "Security Studies in Korea" presented at the conference on "The Future of Asia Pacific Security Studies and Exchange Activities" held in Bali, Indonesia, December 12–15, 1993.

2. Donald M. Snow, *National Security: Enduring Problems in a Changing Defense Environment,* 2nd ed. (New York: St. Martin's Press, 1991), pp. 4–6.

3. James E. Dougherty and Robert L. Pfaltzgraff, Jr., *Contending Theories of International Relations: A Comprehensive Survey,* 2nd ed. (New York: Harper & Row, Publisher, 1981), p. 109.

4. The Ministry of National Defense of ROK, *Defense White Paper, 1992–1993* (Seoul: The Ministry of National Defense), pp. 19–20.

5. Ibid., pp. 21–23.

6. By Asia-Pacific region, the author means one that includes Northeast Asia, Southeast Asia, and North America. In Korea, rarely are Australia and New Zealand included in the security realm. However, these two countries are included in the economic field.

7. For details, see Gerald Segal, "Managing New Arms Races in the Asia-Pacific," *Washington Quarterly,* Summer 1992, pp. 83–101 and "New Arms Races in Asia," *Jane's Intelligence Review,* June 1992, pp. 269–71; Robert Karniol, "Asian Buildup: Regional Powers Strengthen Their hand"; and Young-koo Cha, "The Changing Security Climate in Northeast Asia," *International Defense Review,* June 1991.

8. Antinuclear movement was closely related to anti-American movement and, indirectly, related to antigovernment movement in South Korea.

# Security Issues and Security Studies in Mongolia

TSEDENDAMBYN BATBAYAR

## New Environment and New Challenges

### Mongolia's Changing Role in Sino-Russian Relations

Since Mongolia launched its policy of *Perestroika* in the late 1980s, the contours of a new foreign policy, free from ideological dogma and a one-sided orientation towards its northern neighbor, emerged more and more clearly. However, recent developments in both the internal and external environment—such as the painful institution building process of a parliamentary democracy, an economic uncertainty connected with the transition to a market-driven economy, the dissolution of Mongolia's sole security protector the Soviet Union, and more access to the world community in terms of political cooperation—lead us to question how Mongolia should reevaluate its security policy to adjust to an emerging new situation in the aftermath of the Cold War.

The changes that may directly affect Mongolia's security policy are the dissolution of the Soviet Union, Russia's improving and expanding relations with the People's Republic of China (PRC), and Mongolia's own political and economic open-door policy. What effect would these changes have on the security of Mongolia? If any change has been brought about, how should Mongolia best adjust itself to such changes?

Sino-Soviet relations, due to geography and geopolitics, have a profound influence on Mongolia during the last several decades. There is hardly any necessity to explain why this is so. Now Sino-Russian relations (SRR) still influence, rather less so than in the past, the atmosphere of the immediate international environment of Mongolia

Following the USSR's disintegration in 1991, Russia's orientation towards developing a democracy and a free-market economy (US-European version) produced an "Atlantist" tendency in its foreign policy. It took shape wholly by Yeltsin's internal political considerations. Russia's ideological antipode—China—then could not have a priority in Russian policy. The romantic revolutionary enthusiasm in the country and the attempt to disassociate Russia's image as a backward Asian country and reaffirm it as a European nation with a tradition of enlightenment and certain political culture put Asia (including China) into the background. Naturally, this direction was criticized at once on the part of those who saw Russia's future solely as a Euro-Asian power. They criticized "Atlantist" adherents for underestimating the role of the Pacific for the country's future, and for underestimating the Muslim factor and the growing influence of China. Two years later after the "Atlantist" victory, there can be observed a shift in Russian foreign policy towards a "Euro-Asian" direction. Yeltsin's visits to South Korea, India and China, greater attention to Japan, Russian statements about foreign policy independence and its own priorities in Euro-Asia are examples. The strengthening of this "Euro-Asian" direction can be explained, in my opinion, by deepening social chaos in the country, the West's slowness in terms of rendering substantial aid to Russia, an anticipated tough struggle with Muslim countries and their fundamentalist political institutions for influence in Central Asia, the growth of centrifugal trends in Siberia and the Russian Far East, and by the attractiveness of an Eastern Asian model for economic growth under conditions of an administratively guided society. Complementarities between the economies of Russia and the fast-developing countries of East Asia and the perception of the vital importance of the development of resources in Siberia and the Far East have determined Russia's new turn towards the Orient, including China.

What are the major factors which lay a more stable foundation for a Sino-Russian relationship in the 1990s? Each country is attracted to the other for numerous reasons, two of the most important of which are singled out. First, is their solidarity as multinational states opposing disintegration. Centrifugal trends in the Russian Federation at the level of the populated districts and regions represents probably the most dangerous tendency for Russia as a state. Regionalism is materializing both economically and politically. Likewise jeopardized is the Russian influence in Central Asia. If Russia leaves that region it would seem that a greater Turkestan would emerge, which is the worst example for China. The Muslim factor and growing regionalism make China one of a few countries positively interested in retaining Russia intact as a single centralized state.

Mutual economic interest is yet another factor laying a stable foundation for Sino-Russian relations. It includes a substantial volume of Chinese purchase of Russian military equipment. For the purpose of modernizing its armed forces, China has recently purchased twenty-six SU 27 military aircraft and is interested in acquiring long-range interceptors, and building its own aircraft carriers and modern submarines. Russia needs hard currency and its people at work in the factories of its military industrial complex, while China needs equipment to make its army a fighting force capable of engagement far away from Chinese borders. In addition to military-related trade, both sides are interested in joint development of Siberia, the Russian Far East and Northeastern China.

How long will the current stability in SRR last? History gives evidence of the recurrence of cooperation and rivalry in Sino-Russian relations. But for both countries, constant geopolitical interests to expand their limits (not only territorial) will gradually wash away the very foundation of that stability. China will, as ever, latently seek to restore its influence in the Russian Maritime Province and the Far East as a whole as it aims at affirming its leadership in the South China Sea. But this rivalry is not likely to grow into a similar type of antagonism as that of the 1960s–1970s. For the successful development of reforms, both countries ought to be closely linked to world economic and political relations. Such an integration will induce them to reckon with the principles of international relations in an interdependent world.

What is the Mongolian role in Sino-Russian relations? Under conditions of antagonism and confrontation Mongolia could influence, to a certain extent, the balance of power within the triangle, but always at the expense of restricting its sovereignty. In the 1950s and the beginning of the 1960s during the short period of Sino-Russian cooperation both nations attempted to win over Mongolia. It was then that a policy of carefully deriving benefit from "friendly rivalry" would have brought success to Mongolia. But the development of a political and geopolitical situation depended upon Mongolia.

At the present stage, when both countries are preoccupied with their internal problems, Mongolia has a chance to get out of the Sino-Russian relations framework, to secure the basis of a historic breakthrough into a truly real international environment, and to finally abandon the role of a "pawn" and a hostage of Russia. However, it should be remembered that Russia and China are the only countries which, due to their geopolitical interests, will try to take root and consolidate their positions in Mongolia irrespective of economic dividends. China, being on the rise, now has more possibilities to actively invest in Mongolia.

On a wide range of political-strategic issues in history, Mongolia has viewed both neighbors' policies with hope and apprehension. Regarding these issues, there are different opinions within Mongolian society. Certainly, historical lessons have to be taken into account. Meanwhile, we should avoid both an ideology-oriented approach and an emotional approach based on historical experience in reevaluating our security policy.

## Mongolia's Security Options

As stated above, Mongolia's unique geostrategic location between the two powers has, in the main, dictated its foreign policy behavior. In order to survive as a nation-state Mongolia has been forced, from time to time, to choose the "lesser of the two evils." The collapse of the former Soviet Union, improved relations between China and Russia, and the withdrawal of Russian troops from Mongolia created a completely new situation in the strategic environment of Mongolia. In these new circumstances, Mongolia has to develop equal, mutually beneficial and good neighborly relations with both Russia and China. Such a relationship offers opportunities and challenges for Mongolia, which will benefit from improved relations with each, especially economical relations with China. But Mongolia will face a challenge of how its security (political and economic) will be provided in the future.

Our first concern with Russia was whether it was ready to accept a new reality and to conclude a new bilateral agreement. The Treaty of Friendship, Cooperation and Mutual Assistance between the Mongolian People's Republic and the USSR, especially the obligation stipulated under article 5, was concluded in 1966 under the shadow of Sino-Soviet confrontation. Given the fact that there never was a joint command or combined forces based on a legal framework, it should be pointed out that Mongolia and the former Soviet Union were never equal security allies. They were only defense allies within the narrow sense of Sino-Soviet confrontation.

The new bilateral treaty between Mongolia and the Russian Federation, concluded in January 1993, not only deleted the mutual military assistance related article of the 1966 treaty, but stipulated the important obligation under article 4 by which the two countries refused to take part in any alliance directed against the other or at a third country and not to use their territory for aggressive purposes. It should be pointed out a similar obligation was stipulated earlier in the Joint Declaration on the relationship between the Russian Federation and China, signed in December 1992.

A number of possible security options have been discussed among the Mongolian security and defense circles for the last two to three years. Neutral status for Mongolia was the first one. That option enjoys some support because of its attractiveness. Our security planners have been studying the experience of countries such as Finland, Switzerland and Nepal to see what clues they might offer in Mongolia's search for a credible neutral policy. However, Mongolia's lack of essential requirements for a neutral country, such as sufficient economic and military power, makes that choice almost impossible.

The second option is based on the notion that after the Russian (Soviet) withdrawal from Mongolia, developed countries (the United States, Japan and EC countries) should be invited to come to Mongolia as a counterbalance against any single-country domination in the country. In other words, the power vacuum created in the wake of the disintegration of the Soviet Union would be filled by developed countries. However, it is not very reliable for the time being because of the minimal economic and security interest of the developed countries in Mongolia, at least, for the near future.

A more widely shared option is multisided diplomacy based on the concept of a flexible nonalignment. It is dictated by the objective assessment of the proper place of Mongolia in the world and the Asia-Pacific region. Realistically appraising its development level, Mongolia has announced that it is a developing country. It also wants to be identified as a member of the Asia-Pacific community. Mongolia became a full-fledged member of the Non-Aligned Movement in 1991. By doing so it can theoretically get the support of more than 100 countries, which is an important psychological factor during the crucial transition period.

Due to its unfavorable geographical position and heavy dependence on a foreign source of arms supply, Mongolia should seek a combination of political and military policy means, putting more emphasis on diplomacy in security policy. By opening more channels of international communication and promoting multilateral cooperation in Northeast Asia, Mongolia can diminish the country's heavy reliance on its neighbors. Therefore, Mongolia should focus more efforts on diplomatic solutions to ensure its security.

## The Changing Attitude Towards National and Regional Security

### "National Security" Concept

In 1993 during an interview with the newspaper *UG*, Secretary Enhsaihan of the NSC stated that a draft of the national security concept was finalized. By the end of that year, it was submitted to parliament. The final draft defines national security more broadly than before. Not only does it contain issues such as

Mongolia's subsistence as a nation, social and state order and safety as formulated by the constitution, a guarantee of citizens rights and freedoms, and the survival of Mongolia's nomadic civilization, but it also includes economic, national scientific and technological, national information and ecological aspects of security.

## The Research Institutions and International Contacts

The research institutions of Mongolia, involved in national and regional security studies, can be divided into two types: academic and government-affiliated. In Mongolia the academic institutions have a longer history than the government ones and have shaped thinking on Asian security studies until very recently.

### The Institute of Oriental and International Studies

The Institute of Oriental and International Studies was founded in 1968 as a research institute of the Mongolian Academy of Sciences. The name and the structure of the institute were borrowed from the similar institute of the Academy of Sciences in the former Soviet Union. During the 1970s and 1980s the institute conducted mostly Contemporary Chinese studies and produced several publications. It was also active in elaborating and propagating Asian peace and security initiatives that were formulated by the subsequent congresses of the ruling party, the Mongolian People's Revolutionary Party.

In June 1991, the institute was reorganized into the Institute of Oriental and International Studies. The institute now has about thirty staff in-house, one-third of them having a social science degree such as history or economics. Historians and economists trained in Mongolia constitute one-third of all staff. China, Japan and Korea specialists trained in the USSR comprise the next third. The final third are the former diplomats and government employees. As at other institutes, the staff have been trained mostly at home or in the former USSR. Just recently a few young people were sent to China, Korea and Germany for language training or a postgraduate education. Besides the native Mongolian language, most of the researchers speak Russian. Spoken English is still rare although most can use special literature in English.

The institute's primary research focus is on the developments in Mongolia's two neighboring powers: Russia and the PRC, and their interactions and the implications of those for Mongolia. The institute is conducting research on the history, evolution and the present situation and prospects of Mongolian-Russian and Mongolian-Chinese relations.

The second area of interest is the PRC's domestic reform and foreign policy issues. The PRC's political and economic reform, foreign policy directions, special economic zones, and national minority problems are the main topics of Chinese studies. China's traditional doctrine and foreign policy behavior towards neighbors are also an essential part of the program.

In recent years, priority has also been given to research on security and economic cooperation issues of the Asia-Pacific region, especially Northeast Asia. For example, the institute was involved in a Canadian multilateral project on "North Pacific Cooperative Security Dialogue," which was conducted from 1991 to 1993. Since April 1993, the institute started to take part in the multilateral project on "Northeast Asian

Economic Cooperation Issues" sponsored by the Sasakawa Peace Foundation in Japan. In January 1994, the institute was invited to a multilateral dialogue on "Prospects for International Cooperation in Northeast Asia" sponsored by the Asia Society and Japan Institute of International Affairs.

The institute has made exchange arrangements with overseas institutions such as the Institute of Far Eastern Studies, and the Institute of Oriental Studies (both belong to the Russian Academy of Sciences); the Institute of East Asian Studies, University of California (Berkeley); the Seijong Institute for East Asian Studies (Seoul, Korea) and the Asia Foundation of the United States. It should be pointed out that our contacts were strictly within the Soviet bloc until 1985. Professor Robert A. Scalapino and his colleagues were the first to visit Ulaanbaatar in 1985 and established direct contacts with Mongolian scholars. Consequently, in 1986, 1988 and 1990, the Mongolian Institute of Oriental and International Studies and the Institute of East Asian Studies (UC, Berkeley) held three Mongolia-US bilateral conferences on a wide range of issues covering the Asia-Pacific region. Mongol-American contacts were followed by Mongol-Korean ones. Consequently, the institute and the Seijong Institute for East Asian Studies (Seoul, Korea) held bilateral conferences in 1991 and 1993.

The institute has been publishing a biannual journal, *Questions of Oriental Studies*, since 1978. In 1991 it was renamed *East and West* and is now issued as a quarterly which covers studies on Mongolia's historical and contemporary foreign relations as well as broad discussions on major current international issues. It is published in Mongolian with an English summary of important articles, mostly written by the researchers at the same institute.

**The Government Institute of State Policy and Social Issue Studies**
The institute was established in July 1990 in order to supply the government with up-to-date analysis of the major domestic and foreign policy issues. The main focus is on the domestic issues such as the medium-term program of economic development, public opinion monitoring on important government decisions, economic inequality and national minority issues. Regarding external policy, the institute is watching the latest developments in CIS nations and in China. It is asked periodically to make analytical presentations to the government on the situations in neighboring countries. The institute has sixteen in-house staff, most of them former government employees.

**The Institute for Strategic Studies**
The institute, which is affiliated with the Ministry of Defense, was founded in early 1990. It has six to eight in-house staff, some of them former generals or high-ranking officers of the Mongolian army. The first director was a former general staff chief of the Mongolian armed forces. The main research focus is on defense-related issues of national security, Sino-Russian defense relations, UN peacekeeping forces and Mongolia's possible role in it, etc. The result of the institute's work are disseminated in the form of studies and position papers. From 1992 the institute started to publish a quarterly, *Soyombo* (from 1994 the title will be *Strategic Studies*), which covers international and domestic defense issues.

The institute is active in arranging contacts with similar institutions abroad. It has held bilateral conferences with the Research Institute for Peace and Security (Japan) three times since 1991. It also established contacts with the China Institute for International Strategic Studies and held the first bilateral conference in July 1993.

## *The Future Needs in the Security Studies*

Security studies in Mongolia is in the process of transition from an over-centralized, ideologically-motivated endeavour to a decentralized, practice-oriented one. It can be said that security studies in the Western sense is something new for Mongolia, for the well-known reason that Mongolia did not have to take care of its own security until recently. Mongolian security planners had to reevaluate its past experience and build a new structure or mechanism by which its national security could be secured at a reasonable level. The new constitution of 1992 introduced the concept of national security and newly created the National Security Council headed by the president. Such a change at the top should be followed by the restructuring and strengthening of security studies itself in order to address a whole set of new issues in the security field.

The first immediate task is how to train national security experts. Mongolia now has a great shortage of such experts and the few available ones are all trained in the former USSR. Two possible ways can be suggested to ease this problem. One is to establish a special school or university department in the country. For that purpose the School of Foreign Service was established within the foreign language department of the Mongolian National University in 1991. However, it is far from achieving the standard which is required from such a school. The second and more effective way is to choose a few able persons from people who have already finished undergraduate courses and to send them to foreign countries to take postgraduate education in required fields. The concentration in study abroad for Mongolian students in security studies should be at the master's level. Areas of interest include general international relations and security studies.

The second problem is how to use effectively the available, yet limited, human resources and how to strengthen security studies institutionally. The experience of other Asian countries, in my opinion, is quite useful for us. The study tour of Asian think tanks—the first of such kinds of experience for us—was arranged by the Asia Foundation in April 1992. The participants visited five Southeast Asian nations, plus Taipei and Seoul. We found the Indonesian and Malaysian experiences very attractive, in their integrated approach to national security issues and close contact between security experts and decision makers. Based on that and other experiences, it seems to me that it is important to have an institute for comprehensive studies of security issues in Mongolia, like CSIS in Indonesia or the ISIS in Malaysia.

# New Zealand Peace and Security Studies

## KEVIN P. CLEMENTS

New Zealand's security dilemmas have always been characterized by preoccupations with the challenges posed by size and remoteness. Since 1942 when New Zealand assumed independent responsibility for its foreign policy, the problems of smallness and isolation have been resolved principally by the pursuit of collective security in military alliances with larger powers. In the first place New Zealand's major protector was the United Kingdom (which assumed direct responsibility for New Zealand's defense and security from European settlement until the fall of Singapore) and more recently both the United Kingdom and the United States until the rupture with Washington over New Zealand's antinuclear policy in 1985.[1]

While the relationships with the United Kingdom and the United States were vital to New Zealand's defense thinking until the mid-1980s, New Zealand's most durable and significant defense and security relationship has been its Trans Tasman relationship with Australia. This was formalized in 1944 in the Canberra Pact and given additional reinforcement in the 1951 ANZUS Treaty. It has been reinforced over the years in a series of bilateral exchanges of staff, policies, equipment sharing and joint exercising, etc.

New Zealand's current defense policy (as reiterated in a variety of defense white papers, the most recent being 1991) has the following key objectives:

1. The direct defense of New Zealand territory. This includes its 200-mile maritime economic zone (which is one of the largest in the world) and the defense of Niue, the Cook islands and the Tokelaus for which New Zealand has direct constitutional responsibilities.[2]

2. The preservation of security (defined in terms of safety, law and order) within New Zealand's area of direct strategic concern. This area includes Australia and the Pacific island states.

3. Defense cooperation with Australia (and prior to the ANZUS break, with the United States and the United Kingdom).

The 1987 *New Zealand Defence Review* notes "[there] is a basic identity of strategic concern which New Zealand shares with Australia... and [a] shared common strategic interest in the South Pacific."[3]

Since the breakdown in relations with the United States the Australian connection has become even more important to New Zealand with strong support for the United Nations, especially Peacekeeping Operations, and an ongoing commitment to the Five Power Defense Arrangement (covering the defense of Malaysia and Singapore).

In the 1991 review these were added to with a desire to restore closer defense ties with the United States and the United Kingdom while maintaining New Zealand's antinuclear policies.[4]

Collective security is the overarching concept that has guided New Zealand's "official" national security thinkers over the past forty-five years. While there has been a strong acknowledgment from both major political parties (but particularly within the Labour Party) of the benefits of common security this has manifested itself primarily in support for the arms control, disarmament and peacekeeping work of the United Nations rather than in terms of a particularly innovative or proactive foreign policy promoting preventive diplomacy and early intervention in disputes before they cross the armed threshold.

There has been some (largely academic) awareness of the value and importance of concepts of comprehensive and cooperative security but no effort to work through the political implications of these concepts for New Zealand.[5]

The general awareness of the terms "common," "comprehensive" and "cooperative security" has not resulted in any fundamental displacement of "collective security" as the best description of New Zealand's diverse defense relationships with the UK, the United States and Australia, even if this position is one that sits a little uneasily with New Zealand public opinion which has some bias in favor of nonnuclear, nonoffensive and neutral defense postures.

## New Zealand Security Studies

New Zealand security studies have changed considerably in the last ten years. Prior to 1984, academic and official orthodoxy accepted nuclear deterrence, the necessity to maintain alliance solidarity and a conceptualization of defense and security issues in very narrow military terms. The unilateral antinuclear stance of the fourth Labour government placed a question mark over many of these assumptions, however, and resulted in some fundamental questioning of other taken-for-granted ideas about defense and security issues. After the United States withdrew its security guarantees from New Zealand in punishment for its antinuclear policies, New Zealand security studies took a different turn as public opinion started questioning the costs and benefits of unilateral antinuclearism and how to defend New Zealand in a truncated alliance relationship with Australia.

New Zealand's antinuclear policies and the security studies these generated, preceded the end of the Cold War by five years. These policies were profoundly conditioned by what was seen by many as slow progress on arms control and disarmament and heightened confrontation between the superpowers in the early 1980s.

The specific conflict with the United States was precipitated by a refusal to admit nuclear-powered and nuclear-armed warships to New Zealand ports but underlying it was a deeper debate about nonaligned and neutral defense options and the development of alternative means of guaranteeing security.

As this debate took place (focused by a nationwide inquiry into how New Zealanders wished to be defended)[6] considerable disquiet was expressed by many of the most influential opinion leaders at the time at the narrowness of the military concept of security. This resulted in a number of studies aimed at underlining its economic, political and social dimensions as well.[7] There was also a deepening acknowledgment of the central importance of ecological security because of the ways in which environmental degradation threatened all other forms of security and the specific challenges posed by global warming to the physical integrity of some of the microstates in the South Pacific, e.g., Kiribati and Tuvalu.

Thus while official rhetoric continues to reinforce the centrality of collective security as the guiding security concept for New Zealand, academic researchers and nongovernmental organizations have found comprehensive and cooperative security more congenial concepts to help them understand the particular and probable threats facing New Zealand and the Southwest Pacific. These concepts have been easily grafted into New Zealand security studies because of the absence of direct physical threat facing New Zealand. In fact, the incorporation of these ideas in other parts of the world has also been easier in areas of stable peace as well.

Different groups and individuals tend to embrace different concepts of defense. The department of defense and the armed services, for example, continue to adhere to a very narrow military view of security. (Although this is broadening somewhat in response to changed external circumstances).The Ministry of External Relations and Trade, the Labour Party, the Alliance Party and certain sections of the governing National Party, however, all tend to adopt a more inclusive conception of security. Most academics and peace movement analysts also tend to opt for a more inclusive view of security.

In relation to the South Pacific, for example, the South Pacific Policy Review Group after extensive discussions with South Pacific business leaders, etc., discovered that "the security issues of most concern to Pacific Island governments relate not to conventional military threats but to internal stability, protecting maritime resources, providing relief following natural disasters and maintaining control over their own resources and environment."[8]

This view also tends to apply to New Zealand security thinking as well. Given the absence of any external military threat to the region, most security concerns have to do with low level challenges such as terrorism, poaching of fishing resources, hijacking and external interference in New Zealand's domestic affairs.

# The Asia Pacific Region

New Zealand, along with Australia and Canada is engaged in a process of working out an appropriate relationship with the Asia Pacific region. While acknowledging cultural roots to Britain and Europe, most politicians and opinion leaders also acknowledge geopolitical realities and the necessity to engage the Asian region across a broad spectrum of policy areas—economic, political, military, social and cultural. This has involved some consideration of which countries should be included or excluded from the Asia Pacific region. For most official purposes the boundaries of the Asia Pacific region means all those Asian countries bordering the Pacific rim plus Mongolia, and Laos as well as all the microstates of the Southwest Pacific. It normally includes North America but excludes South America and it normally excludes South Asia which is considered *sui generis*. The primary focus of New Zealand's strategic thinking is the Southwest Pacific— which is the arc stretching from Australia through Papua New Guinea to Kiribati in the north and across to the Cook Islands in the east. The Southern ocean to 60 degrees south is also considered within New Zealand's area of direct strategic interest as well.

Aside from national security needs, the other factors that have contributed to the development and direction of New Zealand security studies over the past ten years have been:

1. The breakdown in relations with the United States. As mentioned above this rupture changed many of the taken-for-granted assumptions about the nature of New Zealand's strategic relationships and stimulated a reevaluation of a wide variety of nuclear issues, defense and security options, foreign policy directions and military alliances.

2. New Zealand's expanded awareness of its own bicultural identity. This growth in bicultural awareness has resulted in an affirmation of the shared Polynesian-European character of New Zealand. This has had a series of important internal effects in terms of the settlement of indigenous claims under the Treaty of Waitangi and important external consequences as well in terms of New Zealand's official orientation towards the South Pacific. Successive New Zealand governments have asserted that New Zealand's bicultural identity enables a closer identification of interest with the island communities of the South Pacific than is available to countries such as Australia. This was an important element in the 1975 discussions about the establishment of the South Pacific Nuclear Weapon Free Zone, for example, although it is also clear that this shared identity of interest has been challenged by a number of island states in recent years ( e.g., by Fiji since the coup, and Tonga).

Government policy interests have tended to drive most of the thinking about security in the Asia Pacific region. This official thinking has been supplemented and critiqued by analyses done under the auspices of the New Zealand Institute of International Affairs and by individual studies done by international relations specialists within university Departments of Political Science and History. Most of this past work has been empirically grounded and descriptive rather than theoretically motivated and has often been driven by specific foreign policy dilemmas confronting different governments, e.g. anxiety over British entry to the EEC, Forward Defense in Southeast Asia, the Vietnam War, nuclear and conventional arms debates, bilateral and multilateral foreign policy concerns.

In addition to these sources:

- The New Zealand Foundation for Peace Studies was developed as an independent source of peace research and peace education in 1975.

- The Centre for Peace Studies was established as a research center at Auckland University in 1988.

- The Interdepartmental Course on Peace Studies at Canterbury University started offering courses and providing research information from 1988.
- The Department of Defence and Strategic Studies was opened at the University of Waikato in 1992, and
- The Centre for Strategic Studies, in the Institute of Policy Studies at Victoria University was established in September 1993.

These different institutional locales have been supplemented by increased academic and official attendances at conferences within the Southwest Pacific and the Asia Pacific region. These have both been important means of raising popular awareness of Asian issues among New Zealand academics and decision makers.

New Zealand's incorporation in the Malaysian ISIS Roundtable discussions, for example, provided important academic and official contacts for New Zealand scholars and officials and certainly influenced thinking about the importance of regional confidence and security building measures, etc., and introduced New Zealanders to the new security architecture emerging in the region.

By and large, however, most of New Zealand's thinking about the Asia Pacific and security studies has been done within university Departments of International Relations, History and Asian Studies. It is only relatively recently that there has been an expansion of more precisely targeted peace research and strategic studies centers within New Zealand.

# Training Programs

Asia Pacific regional experts are initially trained in New Zealand universities. Most students normally complete their undergraduate and first graduate degrees in New Zealand before venturing overseas. While there is a long tradition of overseas postgraduate research at the PhD level (e.g., Asian studies specialists have been trained at the School of Oriental and African Studies, London, the Harvard Yenching Institute, etc.) this too is changing as more students opt to do postgraduate work in New Zealand. Japanese experts are increasingly being given language training in Japan under bilateral New Zealand-Japan Foundation arrangements. Similarly Chinese specialists study in China under bilateral New Zealand-China scholarships. Both MERT and the Ministry of Defence assign their best trainees to overseas universities for further training. There is no tradition of in-house diplomatic or defense training in New Zealand.

The primary destinations for New Zealand postgraduate students in international relations, strategic studies and Asian studies are the United Kingdom, the United States, Canada, and Australia. There is some diversification now to Asian institutions (particularly within Japan) but first preferences remain with the English-speaking countries mentioned above.

There is little debate about where such experts should be trained. The major divide is over the pursuit of postgraduate research within New Zealand or overseas. The arguments for staying in New Zealand revolve around the development of a body of postgraduate research grounded in local conditions. The arguments for overseas are normally couched in terms of broadening horizons, seeing the familiar world from unfamiliar surroundings. There is little actual difference in the analyses of those trained within New Zealand and those trained overseas.

Asian languages (principally Japanese and Chinese) are now challenging European languages as the preferred foreign language in New Zealand secondary schools and at university.

There is a widespread recognition of the importance of becoming proficient in at least one Asian language in terms of doing business in Asia and understanding Asian defense and security interests.

There is very little specific involvement in regional or global research programs. Most scholars pursue their own individual research interests and connect with others only when they need to. The major constraint is distance and not being connected to international research teams or programs. The tyranny of distance is being overcome somewhat by electronic communication systems and by relatively inexpensive travel within the region but many North American scholars, for example, would not think of connecting with New Zealanders working on the South Pacific or Southeast Asia.

The principal institutions engaged in Asia Pacific security work are as follows:

1. New Zealand's six universities. The four institutions with designated peace research or strategic studies centers are as follows:
   University of Canterbury, Peace Studies Program
   University of Auckland, Centre for Peace Studies
   University of Waikato , Defence and Strategic Studies
   Victoria University of Wellington, Centre for Strategic Studies.
   (The last two were established in 1992 and 1993 respectively.)

   In Dunedin, the University of Otago produces a very important foreign policy school each May. This has been in existence for the last twenty-five years and brings together local foreign policy analysts with key invited experts from overseas. This annual school has built up an important reputation as a source of authoritative, in-depth papers and publications on most of the major defense, security and foreign policy dilemmas confronting New Zealand since 1968 .

2. The External Intelligence Unit of the Prime Minister's Department and the diverse intelligence units in the Ministry of External Relations and Trade and the Department of Defence.

3. The New Zealand Institute of International Affairs (Wellington) which has branches in most of the major metropolitan areas and in a variety of country towns as well.

4. The New Zealand Foundation for Peace Studies, Auckland.

5. Greenpeace and Peace Movement Aotearoa, which both have small research capabilities in relation to their own issue areas.

   Probably the most influential organization—because of age and proximity to government—has been the New Zealand Institute for International Affairs. Certainly, *New Zealand International Review,* the bimonthly journal of the institute has provided consistently reliable analyses of international events confronting New Zealand policymakers. Their influence will undoubtedly be contested by the new peace and strategic studies centers once these bodies start producing their own publications but in the meantime the institute remains the most important constant source of foreign policy information and analysis.

Because of the limited number of international relations, strategic studies and peace research experts there is considerable interaction between the few individuals concerned about these issues. There is room for more interinstitutional cooperation, particularly between government and nongovernmental organizations. There is no tradition in New Zealand, for example, of "think tanks" like the Peace Research Centre at the Australian National University, providing foreign policy, defense and security advice to government except in a very ad hoc and personal fashion. The former New Zealand Planning Council and the current Institute of Policy Studies provide economic advice to government but (until the formation of the Centre for Strategic Studies at Victoria) there was nothing equivalent to these institutions on defense and security issues. Hopefully the new center will become an important source of independent policy advice for government on defense and security issues generally and the Asia Pacific in particular.

The principal consumers of "security studies" have tended to be students, academics, business organizations and government in that order. The literature on security studies is not enormous in New Zealand but it covers the spectrum of books, single-authored books, and journal articles. This literature is almost exclusively produced in English.

The principle journals are as follows:

1. *Foreign Affairs Review*—Quarterly publication of the Ministry of External Relations and Trade.

2. *New Zealand International Review*—Bimonthly publication of the Institute of International Affairs

3. The Ministry of External Relations and Trade, *Information Bulletins* are a regular source of information on such things as disarmament and arms control, the United Nations, etc.

4. *Political Science* publishes articles on international relations and security issues in almost every issue.

5. The Public Advisory Committee on Arms Control and Disarmament also publishes intermittent monographs on issues confronting the international disarmament community.

6. *The New Zealand Listener* is a popular radio/TV weekly which always has at least one article on defense, security, or foreign policy.

With the exception of the first two which are clearly oriented towards both a domestic and an international audience, the other journals are mainly oriented towards domestic markets. There are many classified reports on Asia Pacific security interests, which are not normally available in the public domain for thirty years and then only if they do not contain sensitive information. More of these reports could be "sanitized" and published to provide official input into the

New Zealand security debate. New Zealand official analysts have very widespread access to regional security specialists (these were attenuated after the United States withdrew its security guarantee to New Zealand). Those that have bothered to attend conferences within the region normally have had no trouble making and maintaining these contacts through time. Language does not seem to pose any particular problem since most of the regional scholars working on these issues do so with an excellent command of English. New Zealand has trained many of its defense security specialists at the Strategic and Defence Studies Centre at the ANU. Since 1992 the New Zealand government has funded PACDAC Fellowships to the Peace Research Centre at the ANU also. These are specifically oriented towards encouraging New Zealanders to study regional and global arms control and disarmament issues in Australia and to do high level work on confidence and security building in the Asia Pacific region. Until the Centre for Strategic Studies at Victoria University generates its own research and training opportunities, these two Australian institutions will continue to provide the most important training opportunities for those New Zealanders wishing to specialize in peace and security studies.

New Zealand academics with specific expertise in the defense and security areas have quite a lot of individual access to political decision makers and the bureaucracy. Their work is read and acknowledged by desk officers in the Departments of Foreign Affairs and Defence. The overall relationship, between the private and the public spheres on defense and security matters is not as close, however, as that which exists between academics in the Strategic and Defence Studies Centre, or the Peace Research Centre at the ANU and officials in the Australian Departments of Defence or Foreign Affairs and Trade. The current director of the Centre for Strategic Studies in Wellington wishes to develop something equivalent to the Canberra model in relationships between his center and appropriate departments in Wellington.

The principal obstacles to expanding security expertise in New Zealand is the limited job market for such experts. They can be employed in academic institutions and appropriate government departments and within different branches of the mass media but there is no tradition in New Zealand of "independent" security think tanks or research centers. Thus the first and overriding problem for an expansion of peace and security studies is a buoyant job market for graduates in this area. The second obstacle, until recently, has been the absence of suitable institutions for training and research in this area. Hopefully, the new research institutes that have evolved in the past few years will rectify this imbalance.

It would help those few academic experts with an interest in this area to be incorporated more directly and fully into regional research programs, dialogues and debates. While the New Zealand voice will be a small one on bodies such as CSCAP, for example, it is an important one especially in relation to the security problems of the Southwest Pacific where New Zealand seems to have a comparative advantage over Australia. More collaborative research programs, would, therefore, be highly desirable. This kind of collaboration could be advanced without the development of new institutions as long as some effort was made to include New Zealanders more fully into the emerging academic and governmental networks developing in the region.

New Zealand defense and security experts like their counterparts in other parts of the region acknowledge that the Asia Pacific enjoys its most favorable strategic environment in nearly 150 years. The business of strategic studies is to adjust to this environment. While continuity is important, traditional (great power) concepts need reappraisal and Asia Pacific peace and security studies must now assert an authentic perspective from within the region itself. This requires a willingness on the part of Australian and New Zealand academics, for example, to listen sensitively to the specific concerns of their Asian colleagues and think carefully about appropriate responses. While the return of military threat is possible in the Asia Pacific region, it seems clear that economic competition will be the more important and immediate regional preoccupation. This and concern about the new challenges to security are forcing a reevaluation of the concept of security, to take account of nontraditional threats such as those from environmental degradation, drugs, refugee problems, resource protection, human rights violations, AIDS, technology and global communications systems.

Although New Zealand is a relative newcomer to many of these debates it has a number of advantages over some other countries in the region. In the first place those scholars and research institutes working on these areas are not as constrained politically as some of their counterparts in other parts of Asia. They can take a short- and long-term view of the region and offer a variety of different perspectives on probable future scenarios without worrying about "political correctness." Second, peace and security studies in New Zealand are not dominated by narrow military perspectives and there is a willingness to think inclusively about problems. Third, since New Zealand sits in a very safe and privileged position geographically New Zealand academics and policymakers can think about many of these issues in a calmer and more reflective fashion than those who feel directly challenged by internal or external threats. This privileged position means that New Zealand experts working in this area can reflect in more detail about what is needed to avoid conflicts and to enhance mechanisms that advance preventive diplomacy. This orientation stresses peacebuilding and peacemaking processes rather than processes based on worst case threat assessments which is an important counterpoint to the more strategically oriented assessments that characterize most studies in the Asia Pacific region.

## Conclusion

An increased concentration on regional multilateral security arrangements in the Asia Pacific region will result in an increased demand for multilateral security studies as well. New Zealand perspectives on these issues are important since multilateralism is not an optional extra for small powers but an absolute imperative. Thus New Zealand academics and policymakers working in these areas should be able to provide some insights into the particular security dilemmas facing states and peoples with modest economic, political and military resources. New Zealand like Australia sees its future as inextricably linked to the Asia Pacific and wishes to be a part of whatever security community evolves in this region. The shape of this security community and what new conceptual and theoretical frameworks are required to help understand it will determine the agenda for New Zealand strategists and peace researchers over the next five to ten years.

## Notes

1. There are some current moves to heal this rift. On February 18, 1994, for example, the United States reopened access for New Zealand diplomats to its top officials in Washington, thus signaling an easing to the diplomatic sanctions that have been in place since the mid-1980s. Although there is no indication that this move will result in a thawing of the military relationship between both countries, it does represent an acknowledgment of long-held, shared political and military interests between the United States and New Zealand.

2. The fact that New Zealand has no direct enemy and faces no major threat to its sovereignty has given much security thinking in New Zealand a slightly hypothetical quality. This was resolved during the Cold War by New Zealand assuming that the enemies of its allies were also enemies of New Zealand but this position seems less tenable in the post–Cold War era. Despite this there has been a strong focus in recent reviews on defense self-reliance and on the South Pacific as New Zealand's area of direct strategic concern.

3. New Zealand Government, *Defence of New Zealand* (Wellington: Government Printer, 1987), p. 34.

4. A somewhat problematic objective given the continuing adherence to the "neither confirm nor deny" policy on the part of the United States although the recent announcement from Washington restoring top level access indicates that this objective is being partially realized politically.

5. There has certainly been nothing comparable to the Australian Foreign Minister's "Blue book" in the New Zealand context—see G. Evans, *Cooperating for Peace: The Global Agenda for the 1990s and Beyond* (Sydney: Allen and Unwin, 1993).

6. See report of the Defence Committee of Enquiry. *Defence and Security: What New Zealanders Want*, 1996, New Zealand Government Printer.

7. Many of these new ideas were reflected in the 1990 report *Towards a Pacific Island Community*, Wellington Government Printer, which adopted an inclusive and multi-dimensional view of security in its assessments of the major threats and challenges facing the Southwest Pacific.

8. See *Towards a Pacific Island Community*, Report of the South Pacific Policy Review Group, 1990, p. 191.

# Security Studies in Non-ASEAN Southeast Asia

## HENG HIANG KHNG

S ecurity studies during the Cold War was dominated by strategic problems arising from the ideological conflict between the Communist bloc and the Western democracies; more specifically, these were problems of military balance and alignment in international relations. That has changed fundamentally in a post–Cold War situation, thus requiring a review of what should be considered within the realm of security studies nowadays. When politicians, bureaucrats, scholars and other interested parties meet to discuss security, the current trend is to add more items to the security agenda, so much so that security studies is beginning to span a range of issues as diverse as environmental protection, unfair trade practices and AIDS. Under the circumstances, it is unlikely that there would be a definition of security that would satisfy everybody.[1] A more practical approach would be to identify the issues that are generally accepted as *de rigueur* in security studies. A quick scan of topics in a major security studies journal, *Adelphi Papers,* for the past twenty years would show that whatever strategic changes there have been in the world, there is a perennial core of security concerns comprising the following: national sovereignty, unchallenged territorial possession, safety of citizens, regime maintenance (regardless of whether the regime is considered good or bad by international opinion or public opinion within the country), nonhostile geographical neighbors, military capability and a strategic environment supportive of that particular country's development goals. Anything that undermines one or all of these would be perceived as a security threat and threat perception is a major component of security studies.

Are these core security issues sufficient to capture the post–Cold War security environment in the Asia Pacific region? To answer this question requires clarification of what is regarded as belonging to such an Asia Pacific region. It would include:

1. Countries that can claim geographical affiliation to both Asia and the Pacific Ocean, that is, all those states on the Asia mainland down to archipelagic Southeast Asia and countries that fringe the Pacific Ocean. Those would include Russia, China, the two Korea's, Japan, Vietnam, Cambodia, Thailand, Malaysia, Singapore, Indonesia and Papua New Guinea. Taiwan and Hong Kong should also be included even though they are not strictly speaking independent states. Some countries on this list can also claim membership to

other geopolitical regions, e.g., Russia in Europe and Papua New Guinea in the South Pacific.

2. Myanmar, Laos and Mongolia which do not fit into 1 above; geographical proximity and historical connections to the latter make it convenient to include these three states also.

3. Pacific rim countries which are not of the Asian continent but have the interest and capability significantly to engage some of the countries of 1 and 2 in terms of politics, economics and security. That would justify bringing in the United States and Canada but not Mexico and other Latin American countries fringing the Pacific; also Australia and New Zealand would be included but not the small island states of the South Pacific.

The above description is really a combination of subjective preference and common sense. In other words, there is an element of arbitrariness which is open to challenge and that is to be expected in matters such as this. If Asia Pacific is demarcated in such a manner, then are the core security issues identified in the first paragraph sufficient to study the post–Cold War strategic situation that obtains in this vast region?

Basically yes, but stated as broad categories they do not quite capture the scope and some of the details of the changes that have taken place, and their profound impact on security. The starting point of this idea called the Asia Pacific region or community is dynamic economic growth and linkages through free market practices, and this produces the following implications for security for both the individual state and the region as a whole (some of these changes actually began before the end of the Cold War but the ending of worldwide ideological conflict in the 1990s increased their impact and momentum):

1. Within individual nations, good economic performance is recognized as a basis for stability and takes precedence over hitherto ideological verities. Vietnam and Laos and their bid to reform their Marxist-oriented centrally planned economies are good examples.

2. Also within individual nations, economic development can and has unleashed forces requiring significant political readjustments. For the newly industrializing economies (NIEs) like South Korea and Taiwan, fast economic growth has created a sizeable middle class which demands more political participation.[2] For the transitional economies like that of Vietnam, market reforms have also made it necessary for totalitarian leadership to relinquish control in many areas of everyday life.[3] In both these groups of countries, such economic-led political changes have posed challenges for regime maintenance, one of the core security issues identified above. This is posed in questions such as would the Chinese Communist Party maintain its monopoly of power and how destabilizing it would be for China if it does not.

3. International relations are conducted with the promotion of economic development as the dominant preoccupation. This has helped create a new mood whereby states are moving beyond the old habit of managing their security in terms of perceiving a threat and then countering it, to one of setting up

regionwide mechanisms to explore security cooperation in peacetime, e.g., ASEAN Regional Forum and the Council for Security Cooperation in Asia Pacific (CSCAP). However this does not altogether obviate the possibility of military conflagration breaking out in the Asia Pacific region. Two such possibilities which are drawing the most media and political attention are the nuclear power program of North Korea and the Spratly islands territorial dispute. The impact of economic prioritization on classical security concerns such as territorial disputes is possibly a tempering effect on the urge to use military force; witness the willingness to let the dispute over the Spratlys just simmer without damaging growing economic ties among its claimants.

4. The increasing stress on economic priorities has created new security challenges or highlighted growing ones. For instance, economic prowess has enhanced military procurement sparking concerns about an arms race. It has also enhanced Japan's de facto superpower status strictly based on economic might. Similarly, there is also growing sensitivity to China's expanding influence not just in military but also in economic terms. Together with the United States, another superpower belonging to the Asia Pacific region, the situation portends the region as an arena in which a new strategic balance is being worked out, a classic concern of security studies.

5. The predominance of economic concerns highlights a paucity of shared political values, begging the question is the latter necessary to hold together Asia Pacific as a collective entity. Yet another consideration is the emerging contest between nations or groups of nations over the political values each should live by. Presently, in its most vocal form, it is the discourse on Asian democracy versus Western democracy.[4] Basically it means some Asian countries like Singapore, Malaysia, Indonesia, Vietnam, China and Myanmar which are by no means similar in ideology, resent the political encroachment posed by the values of human rights and democracy advocated by the West in general and the US, in particular. In the case of the Vietnamese, Cold War terminology has been resurrected to articulate the official perception of this challenge as a security threat. They have chosen to call it a continuation of John Foster Dulles' 1953 policy of "Peaceful Evolution"—a policy aimed at converting Marxist states not through direct military confrontation but through a long-term process of gradually introducing ideas into those closed societies by means of nonmilitary engagements.[5]

Given these emerging trends in the Asia Pacific region, the question now is how do security studies in the four non-ASEAN countries tackle them, which is the main theme of this paper. These four countries are Myanmar, Cambodia, Laos and Vietnam, and the rationale for grouping them for a discussion such as this is largely one of technical convenience, i.e., banding those who are not of ASEAN together. This does not preclude security studies in all four places actually having similar features although any commonality is likely to be coincidental rather than deliberate (with the exception of Vietnam and Laos whose ruling Communist parties still maintain close ties).

# Myanmar

Given the present situation within Myanmar where a military junta SLORC (State Law and Order Restoration Council) refuses to accept the results of its own organized election, security preoccupation is primarily that of regime maintenance. This would involve overcoming domestic challenges as well as getting a critical level of international support. Basically, regime maintenance is about regaining legitimacy to govern, a legitimacy lost through disastrous performance on the economic front. This in turn has prompted economic reforms which would bring Myanmar in line with the overall shift to economic priorities in the Asia Pacific region. The redefinition of the old balance of power in this region involving the US, Japan and China also has profound implications for Myanmar since both Japan and China do not quite share the US ideological antagonism against Myanmar's political system. In addition, an economically expanding China is seeking new avenues across its land border into Myanmar and beyond which may lay the foundation for a new form of Sinocentric continental influence.[6] Yet another key factor in Myanmar's attempt to break out of international isolation would be its relations with the ASEAN countries. The latter has not offered membership because of the current political situation in Myanmar while Yangon's public position is that it has no formal plans to join ASEAN but it regards itself as a Southeast Asian country.[7] Meanwhile as substantive diplomacy, ASEAN countries temper the human rights sanctions of the West against Yangon by practising a "constructive engagement" policy which keep lines to Myanmar open. It is an arrangement which the Myanmar regime appreciates and terms as "meaningful ties."[8]

Clearly an external environment like this requires adjustment in Myanmar's neutral foreign policy. Beginning with its independence in 1948, its architect was the country's first prime minister, U Nu, who saw neutrality as comprising five basic principles: nonalignment with any power bloc; friendly relations with all countries and enemy of none; acceptance of no economic aid with strings attached; impartial examination of every foreign policy issue on its merits; and willingness to contribute to building world peace, and to help any national that might need help.[9] This amounted to a security doctrine for the country in a world made dangerous by superpower conflicts and has been maintained up until now although it has undergone various modifications.

In its original form, it was a positive neutralism which saw Myanmar leaders active in international forums mediating between different ideological factions. This lasted until the 1962 Ne Win coup which saw the country adopting an ideology of the Burmese Way to Socialism. It also meant the elimination of foreign economic and cultural influence and, in terms of foreign policy, what was practiced was a negative neutralism where Myanmar reduced contact with the foreign world to a minimum. This lasted until 1972 when US rapprochement with China reshaped the international balance of power and Myanmar relaxed its isolationist posture.[10] However, neutrality as it has come to be associated with Myanmar is not generally regarded as having played a useful role in promoting regional security in Southeast Asia, certainly not in the sense that the neutral countries of Europe have played their role during the Cold War. Even in terms of the policy's contribution to Myanmar's own welfare, the conclusion is a doubtful one. Neutrality has become more like a formula for oblivion, marginalizing the country in international affairs. Neutrality is also partly responsible for the country's economic backwardness, political instability and national disunity.[11]

This key concept of Myanmar security has not engaged much scholarly attention within the country and is a reflection of the deficiency of security studies in the country. Generally, matters related to security are left to be announced by officialdom. Going by the paucity of official pronouncements on the subject, there is no apparent interest within the Myanmar foreign policy establishment to relook at and redefine the concept of neutrality in a post–Cold War situation. This could mean an incapability to tackle this question because as a doctrine, it never had much intellectual depth, and was carried out more by the whims of a dictatorial military leadership (not known for its thoughtfulness) than anything else. It could also mean the regime just wants to quietly bury the policy. If isolation was self-imposed in the past by a neutral foreign policy, now isolation is imposed by others and Myanmar wants to get out of it. Therefore, clinging to a neutral policy does not make tactical sense.

Furthermore, the focus of security concerns is presently on political opposition to the regime and ethnic insurgency. Where these sensitive security questions are concerned, it is unrealistic to expect that research can be done by anybody in Myanmar except the internal security apparatus. Sampling official statements by Myanmar's leaders and reports on Myanmar in the Southeast Asian press,[12] the following security issues are probably of major interest to the country's bureaucratic elite:

1. Relations with ASEAN with the eventual possibility of membership;

2. the growing influence of China in the region;

3. the policy of the West to promote human rights and democracy;

4. and cross-border ethnic and religious affiliations.

The last refers to a host of complex problems which Myanmar has with its Southeast Asian neighbors, some of which are old (Karen insurgents seeking refuge in Thailand) and some new. An example of the latter is the problem with Rohingya Muslims seeking refuge in neighboring Bangladesh and how this has provoked protest from Malaysia, Singapore and Indonesia (countries with majority or sizeable Muslim communities).[13]

A few institutions which are doing work related to security studies are:[14]

1. International Relations Department of Yangon University;

2. International Relations Department of Mandalay University;

3. Research department of the War Office in the Ministry of Defense; the Ministry also has a National Defense College and a Command and General Staff College which are largely training institutions;

4. Foreign Ministry;

5. Office of SLORC Chairperson has a research department; its predecessor was the National Defense Committee which was made up of civilian and military officials and used to lay down guidelines for national policies;

6. National Intelligence Bureau in the Prime Minister's Office.

Essentially, these institutions can be divided into two broad groups: there is academia made up of students and teachers with hardly any research capacity or motivation; and there is officialdom which comprises the bureaucrats in the foreign policy and intelligence establishments whose professional duty it is to assess security issues. Academics are sometimes asked to be advisers in government departments but the bureaucrats are not known to be involved in any teaching function at the universities.

The two International Relations Departments at the universities each has about 400 students spread over a four-year course. Another year is required for honours students. Each annual intake by either of the departments is about 100 and admission is highly competitive because many students want to get into this discipline as it offers the possibility of a job in the Foreign Service and thence a posting overseas. The courses are taught by Myanmar lecturers, some of whom have been trained overseas. It teaches the basics required of an International Relations course: the theoretical background as well as contemporary issues. Myanmar foreign policy is also part of the curriculum and where international issues are concerned, there is very little which is taboo. The collapse of Communism in Eastern Europe can be taught and so can reforms in China and the Indo-Chinese countries. There is a specialization at the end of the four years but this tends to look at regions, e.g., Middle East or Southeast Asia rather than any specific country. What is significant to note is that despite the country's isolation and tight political control, the intellectual tradition has remained relatively akin to that of the outside world. This contrasts with the training situation in the Marxist countries where students of social sciences (which includes security studies) have to analyze things according to a doctrinaire framework.

But while it is all right to teach facts and to keep informed, academics deem it prudent not to be too probing or to set down opinions which are too independent, particularly where they pertain to Myanmar's foreign policy. As a result, research and university publications tend to be centered on the less sensitive disciplines, such as history and archaeology. Works for publication have to be sent for clearance and that further deters scholastic participation in discourse. Then there is the problem of poor library facilities. Academics are also inadequately paid and spare time outside working hours has to be spent moonlighting to make ends meet. Doing research on one's own time is a luxury few can afford. So these and a lack of resources to pay for publication explain why there is no academic journal dealing with security studies. Nor are the works of Myanmar scholars easily available in international journals, also for the reasons of control just stated.

The one publication that dealt with security issues used to be the *International Bulletin*, a Myanmar-language published monthly by the Burma Socialist Program Party Central Organizing Committee. This was not an academic journal but a news magazine aimed at informing the public on a broad range of serious subjects from international relations to science. Sold on the market, it was popular, although given its content, its readers tend to be from the intelligentsia who appreciated it as the only source of translated reports from the international media. With the political changes in Myanmar in 1988, the monthly has been replaced by a fortnightly which deals with both domestic and international issues.

It is less substantive and nowhere as popular and its publisher, SLORC, seems to want to keep it at a low profile too. Official perception of strategic issues is occasionally carried in the official daily *New Light of Myanmar* which replaces the *Workers People's Daily*.

Apart from providing information, essentially the media or whatever local publications, in as far as they touch on security issues, are vehicles for SLORC-endorsed views. They are not yet a forum for discourse on security issues. Foreign publications such as *Times*, *Newsweek* or *Far Eastern Economic Review* are not banned, except for the odd issue which the military regime cannot suffer. Restriction is not so much by official control of distribution as by the pricing mechanism. Not many Myanmar people can afford these magazines which are sold on the ubiquitous black market. One popular source of free information is the American Center run by the US Embassy where books, journals and magazines are available (not for loan) and can be photostatted. In such a system, it is unrealistic to think about the availability of classified and other privileged material to academic/independent researchers.

Myanmar's bureaucrats, having access to a much wider range of information than their counterparts in academia, are better informed. However the research output from the bureaucracy is not easily available, and any understanding of its security concerns and perspectives has to be derived from official pronouncements and the odd conference papers as and when Myanmar is represented. In the final analysis, whether it is the work of Myanmar academics or bureaucrats, an overall impression is that Myanmar is not disposed to be vocal on the major security concerns of Southeast Asia. Contact with Myanmar academics is still difficult given the present political isolation faced by the country. Except in a few cases, it is still not possible to invite Myanmar scholars to international conferences as individuals. Invitation has to be issued to institutions. In allowing scholars to go overseas, the regime is likely to be better disposed towards countries where governments are less likely to promote any potential anti-SLORC viewpoints.

# Cambodia

Cambodia was itself a major security question for the Asia Pacific region and now that a negotiated peace has returned a rather complex and fragile polity to the country, there is much scope for security studies. However, any discussion of security studies within Cambodia must start by recognizing that the country has many more priorities to attend to first.

Cambodia has few tertiary institutions and before the 1991 peace agreement, they were offering rudimentary forms of technical education and teacher training. There is also Phnom Penh University with a history department which is said to be interested in expanding its curriculum to include an understanding of politics in the region. All these institutes are in a perilous state owing to the unstable political and economic situation. The newly formed coalition government inherits this system but is unlikely to be focused on the problem of tertiary education, let alone the particular subject of security studies. Any emerging bureaucracy that deals with questions of strategic interests would have functionaries from the previous regime whose perspectives would have been instructed according to the

Marxist tradition. However of all the three Indo-Chinese countries, Cambodia would have the least need to hew closely to any such ideological dictates. In addition, there would be expertise brought in by returned Cambodian expatriates, the supporters of the non-Communist FUNCINPEC or KPNLF.

In August 1993, a Khmer International Relations Institute (KIRI) was set up by a returned PhD graduate, Thach Bunreoun from the East-West Center of the University of Hawaii, with an aim of promoting both research and training on current problems related to Khmer society and its relations with the world. Security studies would come within the purview of KIRI. This institute comes under the umbrella group of the Preah Sihanouk Raj Academy (PSRA). Altogether PSRA plans to have seven institutes covering international relations, economics and trade, educational research and development, social development, natural resources management, industrialization and urban life, and culture. Besides KIRI, one more institute, the Khmer Institute of Culture and Vipassana has been set up as of January 1994.

KIRI has the endorsement of Prince Sihanouk and various levels of the Cambodian political elite but given the paucity of financial and human resources, it is premature to be certain about the long-term viability of this fledgling institution. Given manpower constraints, quality and quantity of research output is likely to be a problem in the foreseeable future. So far, KIRI has an active program of organizing conferences/seminars. In November 1993, it hosted its first international conference on post-UNTAC Cambodia, looking at politics, economics, culture and religion, education and foreign affairs. Looking at the seminar and training workshops planned for 1994, these are some of the topics KIRI is seeking to cover: economic planning and public accountability.[15]

Other research institutes have also sprouted in Phnom Penh. There are the Cambodian Institute of Human Rights and Khmer Institute of Democracy, but beyond their names nothing is known about them. There could well be more and the list will grow as nongovernment organizations and foreign funding agencies increase their operations in Cambodia. How well such nongovernmental efforts to promote security studies or work related to it will do is difficult to say. Will they exist in synergy with the emerging bureaucracy and policy-making elites? If the bureaucracy is inept, will they provide for a more informed perspective on security issues in Cambodia? This is a problem probably more germane to Cambodia than any other states in Southeast Asia; a situation where the state is extremely weak and also has no effective policy of managing NGOs (say unlike in Myanmar) which therefore encourages a tendency of NGOs to replace the state in many ways.[16]

Cambodian institutes/researchers or civil servants working on security or security-related issues will need to bear in mind the delicate balance of diverse ideological interests represented by the country's four major political factions. Such sensitivities will obtain particularly in questions about internal threats to security. Where external security issues are concerned, a natural priority would be to understand Cambodia's position in the larger regional strategic order. A perspective which derives from Cambodia's history would be how to balance its relations with its neighbors, Thailand and Vietnam. There is also the question of whether Cambodia should look towards membership in ASEAN, a trend which is more or less accepted by the other two Indo-Chinese countries, Laos and Vietnam.

# Laos

Laos has to readjust in major ways to strategic changes brought about by the end of the Cold War: close alignment with a Soviet-backed Vietnam had lead to tension-ridden relations with two other neighbors, China and Thailand, and that must now be readjusted to make for more balanced relations with all three. But from most accounts, the concern is more with internal security than with external threats. Examples of domestic security concerns would include the guerilla threat organized by ethnic minority groups, and, on a broader front, the typical political challenges that come with a measure of pluralism and openess which the Marxist regime has permitted as part of economic reforms.

Research activities in Laos suffer from the inadequate tertiary education facilities within the country. Given its sparse population and lack of resources, there are only basic postsecondary training institutions (the equivalent of a polytechnic) for medicine, teachers training and the civil service. Within the bureaucracy, individual ministries would have their own policy-oriented research capability. There is no research institute or think tank operating separately from the government ministries, although some years ago a National Center for Social Sciences was set up. However the latter's status is now indeterminate. No academic journal of any sort is available.

Those within the bureaucracy with an interest in security studies would be from the Communist Party, the internal security apparatus, the Defense Ministry and the Foreign Ministry. But given the paucity of the educated elite and the nature of their education (in the erstwhile Soviet bloc and Vietnam), the bureaucrats in these institutions are probably not too familiar with security studies cast in a Western political science tradition.

# Vietnam[17]

## *Post–Cold War Security Perceptions*

The end of Cold War has required significant strategic readjustments on the part of Vietnam. Some clear indicators would include; recognizing the loss of the Soviet option, coming to terms with China, disengaging from Cambodia and altering its attitude towards ASEAN. It is a near total revision of strategic vision and security interests. Essentially, it means Vietnam's leaders have moved from viewing their strategic environment in terms of a struggle between imperialism and world revolution to one of recognizing the interdependence of states and economic constraints on conflict.[18] This offers much scope for research and reflection. At a practical level, Vietnam had to turn around its entire foreign policy and, during that process, much debate was involved within the country. It is still going on although many major battles have already been won by those wanting to open up the country to more international influence.[19]

All these strategic changes coincided with and helped hasten Vietnam's attempt to introduce economic and political reforms. Popularly known as *doi moi,* it was officially endorsed in 1986 and has given intellectual activities more scope as well as opportunities for contacts with the outside world. Indeed if *doi moi* has come about, it is due as much to intellectual ferment inside the country as to external events. This is heartening for researchers but they still face many serious problems such as limited resources for research and, where security studies is concerned, there are still political constraints.

To identify what are some of the major security issues which engage Vietnam's attention, a survey was done of topics covered by regular publications since the beginning of 1991 from the Vietnam Communist Party (VCP), Ministry of Foreign Affairs, Ministry of Defense, and the Institute of Southeast Asian Studies representing academia.[20] This was supplemented by interviews with scholars or professionals working in areas related to security studies, international relations and regional issues. The security concerns which can be identified (not in any order of importance and in many cases interrelated) are:

1. the China threat;

2. Peaceful Evolution;

3. the role of external powers in the region: China, US and Japan;

4. how to develop closer economic, political and strategic ties with ASEAN;

5. and the high military spending within Southeast Asia and the security forum needed to lower the risk of military conflicts.

## Impact on Security Studies

Three broad conclusions can be drawn from the above survey of journal articles:

1. Published works on security issues/international relations are using far less ideological jargon.

2. There is a paucity of assessments besides stating highly evident conclusions.

3. There is a high degree of convergence between Vietnam's new security perceptions and those of its ASEAN neighbors with which it used to disagree over the regional and global security order. However, there is a lack of expertise on and interest in specific issues in ASEAN countries, e.g., issue of leadership transition, and ethnic and religious problems.

Revolutionary jargon is rather more muted in Vietnamese publications nowadays compared to those written in the period after 1975 till the early 1980s. That was a period when the VCP was flushed with its victory over the US in the southern half of Vietnam. Just to refresh memory, during that period, Vietnam was pushing an international strategic vision of Three Revolutionary Currents (Ba Dong Thac Cach Mang) which would change the world. These currents referred to the socialist countries, the liberation movements in the Third World fighting imperialism and progressive forces in the developed capitalist countries, all three of which were supportive of each other. It was such revolutionary ethos which set Vietnam on a collision course with ASEAN at the 1976 Colombo Non-Aligned

Conference rather than accept ASEAN's prescription of a zone of peace, freedom and neutrality for Southeast Asia. Today, ideological rhetoric is retained, albeit in a milder form, only when celebrating ties with a handful of remaining socialist allies like Laos or Cuba. It is naturally used most to discuss ideological matters such as the leadership of the party, its continued commitment to socialism and the need to guard against the enemies of socialism.

Although the study of security issues has become relatively free of doctrinaire language, political concerns of the leadership still color what is studied and how it is said. This is also partly why research articles are usually highly narrative, collating masses of facts (already published and therefore safe) and sparse on assessments. An illustrative example would be an article, "Vietnam and Mekong Cooperation," by Hoang Nguyen in *Nghien Cuu Dong Nam A* (*Southeast Asia Review*) vol. 3, 1991. The article was a record of the physical and human geography of the four riparian states of the Mekong. Contrary to expectations of an article like this, it says nothing of the problems between Thailand and Vietnam in the project nor anything about the issue of Cambodian membership. The closest it got to an assessment of problems of cooperation was to point out in the last three sentences that there was a huge discrepancy in per capita income between Thailand and the three Indo-Chinese states and to ask a cryptic question about the relevance of Mekong development schemes to the people at the lower course. Weak research products are also partly the result of difficult access to information (to be discussed later).

But there are signs of things improving based on a comparison of content in the journal *Nghien Cuu Quoc Te* (*International Studies*) and its predecessor *Thong Tin Quan He Quoc Te* (*International Relations Bulletin*), published by the Foreign Ministry's research institute Vien Quan He Quoc Te (Institute of International Relations or IIR). This comparison is made between the two journals' maiden issues both relaunched after a lull in publication and promising readers assessment articles. The *International Studies* just out in September 1993 carried articles on China's internal and external problems after its 14th Party Congress, the first 150 days of the Clinton administration, Japan's strategic interests in the South China Sea, and agricultural products in the GATT negotiations. All addressed contemporary issues and had proper reference and footnotes. They were not ground-breaking research but they were precise and to the point. This is in great contrast to the content of the June 1991 issue of its predecessor, *International Relations Bulletin*. The latter had a long piece by the then Foreign Minister Nguyen Co Thach on the continuing necessity of Marxist theory for some foreign policy issues and even that was an old speech made three years earlier. Other articles were equally polemical dealing with the strategy for developing external economic ties, and the question of international unity. One actual research article looked at the history of China from the Warring States to the Republican Revolution early this century. None of them had proper references or footnotes. It is not surprising to see such a transformation in an organ of the Foreign Ministry, for within the policy-making elite, this ministry is considered the most reform-minded, the reason being its cadres have the most opportunities to live in the outside world. Academia is also equally outward looking but the Party and the army are more cautious although they are also starting to interact with foreign institutions outside those in the old Socialist bloc. The Ministry of Interior is believed to be the most cloistered of this group of state bodies that have a role in security policy.

The trend in Vietnam may point towards more independent and stimulating research in security issues/international relations but as of now, many scholars still feel some need to err on the side of caution especially when writing or speaking publicly. Naturally those who are more senior or have powerful backers can be more forthright. Generally, economic issues are more readily discussed than politics and the most evident manifestation of this is in the numerous articles written about the newly industrialising economies as economic models but nobody is as yet disposed to address the question of political models. Another example of a sensitive research issue is that of the China threat, something Vietnamese understand instinctively. However China after the Cold War is no longer simply the enemy. Given the great decline in the number of Communist states, China and Vietnam now have a common strategic interest and that is to combat "peaceful evolution." Indeed it has been said that there are sections of the Vietnamese leadership who would like to put more stress on this aspect of foreign relations than concentrate so much on expanding ties with the West and ASEAN. To what extent this is true is difficult to verify, but as these are rumors doing their rounds among Vietnamese researchers, it makes people careful when writing about Sino-Vietnamese issues.

It is also necessary to make a distinction between research writings meant for publication and those which are assigned within state-funded research projects. In the latter, the finished product is meant primarily for the information of policymakers with some papers occasionally released for publications. In this realm of assigned research, sensitive topics may be tackled. It has not been possible to get a full listing of these national research projects (chuong trinh cap nha nuoc), but two that have been undertaken within the five-year planning period 1991–95 (the five-year plan is a a basic feature of Vietnamese bureaucracy) deal with interesting security topics: KX-05 looks at the political system in the country's transition to socialism with a brief that includes studying ways of renovating the substance and mode of leadership in the party;[21] and KX-09 entitled Scientific Discourse in the new phase of defense and security strategy. The first, comprising twelve subtopics, is supervised by the party school, the Ho Chi Minh National Academy of Politics and the second with fifteen subtopics is supervised by the Ministry of Defense.[22] It is also evident from the selection of national research projects that have been been made public that many are focused on the challenges of political and economic transition.

## Research Institutes and Training

Vietnam has a large intellectual community based primarily in Hanoi and Ho Chi Minh City. The major research capability in security studies and other related activities are in Hanoi where the relevant institutes can be divided into five broad categories: those in the Ministry of Foreign Affairs, Ministry of Defense, Ministry of the Interior, the Vietnam Communist Party and academia in the form of the National Center for Social Sciences and Humanities (NCSSH). Each has its own orientation or professional emphasis although there are overlapping areas of research interests. A common structure among them is also evident. The ministries and the Party would have research departments and/or affiliate institutes, as well as information departments (ban thong tin) to collate information and disseminate it to their staff. Library facilities would usually come under the information department. Quite often, a research institute within a ministry would have its own information department as well. Most institutes would publish a regular journal. The details are as follows:

1. The Ministry of Foreign Affairs like that of any country has separate departments focusing on different parts of the world (e.g., Southeast Asia and Pacific Department) or different aspects on international relations (e.g., Department of International Organizations). Ministry officials would tend to the day-to-day needs of foreign policy, keep track of events, draft briefing reports and put up policy papers. The ministry has the IIR (Hoc Vien Quan He Quoc Te) mentioned above which engages in research of a more academic nature as well as runs the College of Foreign Affairs. The research staff of about fifty is divided into six departments looking separately at North America, Japan, China, Europe (including Russia), Southeast Asia (including Laos and Cambodia) and Vietnam's foreign policy. The college with another fifty or so teaching staff trains foreign service officers, although some of its graduates may work in other ministries or institutes. Members of research staff also do some teaching.

2. The Ministry of Defense and its research institutes would have the most expertise on the pure military aspects of strategic issues, e.g., balance of forces, arms procurement and weapons technology. The Defense Ministry has always been less accessible to foreigners than the Foreign Ministry or the academic institutes although the situation is gradually changing. Exchanges with countries outside the socialist bloc are beginning. Still, little is known about the research capability or organization within the ministry itself but it does have two known research institutes: the Institute of Military History (Vien Lich Su Quan Su) and Institute of Military Strategy (Vien Chien Luoc Quan Su). The names of the two institutes define their major research focus. Of the two, the Institute of Military History has a higher public profile partly because it has a quarterly review Military History from 1987. Its focus on history is also less sensitive an area of research than that of the Institute of Military Strategy which has the function of submitting proposals on strategic issues to the ministry. The ministry also publishes a monthly journal *The All People's Defense Journal (Tap Chi Quoc Phong Toan Dan)* together with the Department of Military Theory and Politics (Co Quan Ly Luan Quan Su va Chinh Tri) of the Military Affairs Commission of the Party Central Committee (Dang Uy Quan Su Trung Uong). The predecessor of this journal was *Tap Chi Quan Doi Nhan Dan* or *People's Army Journal*, a major publication on military and strategic questions. The coverage of the *All People's Defense Journal* would include ideology, doctrine, developments within Vietnam down to the provincial level and looking at world military and political events.

3. Research units of the Interior Ministry look at national security questions and they include the country's intelligence community. If the Defense Ministry is only just beginning to open up, this ministry is still very much a closed community. There is no public research institute or journal.

4. The Party has extensive research capability on all areas of national policy; just to name two, there are the Committee for Strategic Estimates (Tieu Ban Nghien Cuu Du Bao Chien Luoc) which serves the Party Secretariat and the Central Committee Commission for Ideology and Culture (Ban Tu Tuong Van Hoa). But the two public research institutions are the Institute of Marxism-Leninism (Vien Mac Lenin) and the Ho Chi Minh National Academy of Politics (Hoc Vien Chinh Tri Quoc Gia Ho Chi Minh); the latter incorporates the Party cadre training school which used to be called the Nguyen Ai Quoc Academy. Both are large institutions because they are the intellectual custodians of the country's central ideology. The focus of their work is to look at the ideological challenges faced by the Party in a world where Communism has collapsed in many places and, in the context of Vietnam, this is a central component of security. The Institute of Marxism-Leninism publishes three journals: *Journal of Theoretical Information* (*Thong Tin Ly Luan*), *Journal of Party History* (*Lich Su Dang*) and *Information on Theoretical Issues* (*Thong Tin Van De Ly Luan*). The other institute publishes *Theoretical Studies* (*Nghien Cuu Ly Luan*). These party journals mainly deal with theoretical issues of ideology but would, from time to time, also publish articles on international relations and strategic issues. But what is best known to scholars of Vietnamese studies is *Communist Review* (*Tap Chi Cong San*), the monthly journal published by the Central Committee.

5. Academia is represented by the NCSSH (Trung Tam Khoa Hoc Xa Hoi Va Nhan Van Quoc Gia). It has sixteen research institutes of which two are involved in research related to international relations/security. They are the Institute of Southeast Asia (Vien Dong Nam A) and up until recently the Institute of Asia Pacific Studies (Vien Chau A Thai Binh Duong). Hanoi's Institute of Southeast Asian Studies has about fifty researchers looking at almost every country in the region but its strength has traditionally been in areas of history and culture. It is now attempting a more comprehensive issue-oriented approach to research which will mean looking at politics, economics and security issues. It publishes a quarterly journal, *South East Asian Review* (*Nghien Cuu Dong Nam A*). The other institute, the Institute of Asia Pacific Studies, is in the process of being reorganized into four centers looking individually at China, Russia, Japan and North America.

If those looking at international economic issues and questions of political economy are included, then the list of institutes related to security studies will be much longer. For instance, there are the Institute of World Economy (Vien Kinh Te The Gioi) and Institute of Economics (Vien Kinh Te Hoc), both in the NCSSH. In the government, the State Planning Committee has the Central Institute of Economic Management (Vien Quan Ly Kinh Te Trung Uong), and the various ministries that deal with economic issues has would also have research departments or institutes. Little has been heard of security studies being done in Ho Chi

Minh City but at least three institutes in this southern city have a research interest in Southeast Asia. They are the Center for Vietnamese and Southeast Asian Studies in the Ho Chi Minh City University, the Asia Pacific Research Center of Ho Chi Minh City University of Education, and the Institute of Social Sciences which is the southern branch of the NCSSH.

Such a huge research community has both its assets and liabilities. First, it is evidence of the country's respect for education and knowledge and, therefore, intellectual discourse has a place in such a culture. Numbers also help maintain a lively intellectual climate. Finally there is a wide spread of linguistic skills which, if properly organized, can be a valuable resource for good research. For instance, within Hanoi's Institute of Southeast Asian Studies are staff members fluent in Thai/Lao, Khmer, Indonesia/Malay, Burmese, Hindi, Chinese, English, French and Russian. This is a capability which possibly no other research institute in the Southeast Asian region can match.

Quantity usually raises the question of quality and that is related to training. Courses on contemporary Southeast Asia are taught in two universities in Hanoi: University of Hanoi's History Department and the Southeast Asian Center in the Teachers Training College but the level at which the subject is taught is very basic. For instance, at the Teachers Training College, the trainees are really being given some rudimentary knowledge on Southeast Asia to teach in the schools. After a few years of discussing and soliciting assistance from foreign universities as well as getting approval within the country, Hanoi University intends to start its first course on political science in September 1994. This will first come under the rector's office until it is ready to be a full department.[23]

Within the security-related professions, different ministries such as Defense, Interior and Foreign Affairs will run their own training courses. Of the three, the IIR belonging to the Foreign Ministry has the most public profile. The institute's College of Foreign Affairs offers a five-year degree course which is really geared at producing cadres for the Foreign Service and so the curriculum would also include intensive training in either English or French, protocol and international law, besides imparting an understanding of international relations and strategic issues. The course content needs to be revamped but even as the college administration is doing this, it is uncertain how far they are allowed to stray away from core units on the curriculum which derive from the Marxist intellectual tradition, e.g., Party history. The graduates of this institute are usually highly competent in English or another foreign language which has enabled many of them to get scholarships or training attachments with institutions in the West. This is producing in socialist Vietnam a first generation of scholars and civil servants trained in a non-Marxist tradition and, in the long run, they will make their impact. As for now, any difference between an older elite of Marxist-trained cadres (some in the old Soviet Union, Eastern Europe and Cuba) and the Western-trained returnee is not evident as the latter are mostly too junior to want to exert themselves within the system yet. However the example cited above of the IIR's new journal being more professional is an indication of how research has benefitted from experience gained in the non-Marxist countries.

To discount training in the Marxist intellectual tradition is not to say that such an education is intellectually feeble or that the Vietnamese made bad students. It is just that Marxist analysis of international events and its revolutionary ethos are no longer appropriate for the new definition of security interests in Vietnam. Officially, Vietnam cannot say this too clearly. Furthermore, it still has inadequate resources to correct this situation quickly because the present generation of lecturers and senior researchers schooled in the old way are not able, with a few exceptions, to teach the new intellectual discipline required. This problem of training is not insurmountable. Vietnamese institutes are keen to promote foreign exchange and political obstacles to such activities are fast being removed. Foreign teaching expertise can be and are starting to be brought in. As mentioned above, students and officials have also gone to Western universities to read international relations and political science.

Then there is the matter of poor working conditions which affect all professionals and academics, and not just people working on security studies. These difficulties fall into two broad categories: physical working conditions in terms of pay and support facilities for research; and political environment permitting objective independent research (described earlier). The average monthly wage of professionals and academics is between US$30 to US$50 which is insufficient. The state however cannot afford to pay more because there are too many research institutes and within each institute too many staff. This is a bureaucratic legacy from the days of socialist planning when everybody was guaranteed a job and now the numbers are just too large to manage. So, on the one hand, the pay is too meagre for scholars to devote their time entirely to research, having to supplement their income by doing second or third jobs which can be totally unconnected with their profession (e.g., teaching English or translating documents for foreign companies). On the other, there is wastage because there are large numbers being paid to do very little or nothing for the institutes which employ them.

At the moment, research projects are funded at three levels: national, ministry and institute. The national budget is managed by the Ministry of Science, Technology and the Environment. Ministries and institutes are also expected to use their own resources to fund small-scale research projects. Most ministries and institutes, however, claim they have little excess resources to do this and have to rely on foreign funding. National-level funding by the Ministry of Science, Technology and Environment is the only source of large-scale financing although this would again be modest by international standards. Based on conversations with people who have worked on such projects, the amounts of money made available for a national research project in the social sciences can range from US$3,000 to US$10,000, depending on the size of the project. However, given the large numbers of research institutes in Vietnam, the national research budget is just not enough to keep most researchers fully engaged and has also led to charges that these funds are disbursed according to personal ties and influence rather than actual merit or need. There is also wastage because the end products of some of these projects are just verbiage.

### Access to Information

For good research to be done, there must be easy access to sufficient information. Vietnam's ministries or research institutions have a complex system for collating and disseminating information. Depending on how sophisticated the institute is, or how important is its work, the information can be packaged on a daily, weekly or monthly basis by its Information Center. Essentially, this would be foreign publications, news-agencies and broadcast material translated into Vietnamese. Each ministry would of course focus on its own professional needs. For example, the Defense Ministry would collect information on the military and the Interior Ministry would focus on the craft of intelligence. The Institute of International Relations, for instance, would do chronologies of major political events of interest to Vietnam.

But over and above the efforts of individual institutes are the products of Vietnam News Agency (VNA) (Thong Tin Xa Vietnam). Twice daily, VNA sends to all government departments *Tin Nhanh* (*Quick News*) which are short summaries of important news carried by Reuters, AFP and the major international broadcasting service. It also does an overall daily edition *Tin Tham Khao* (*Reference News*) which provides the news in a more complete form. Then there is *Tai Lieu Tham Khao Dac Biet* (*Special Reference Material*) which carries commentaries (as distinct from news) and this is marked for restricted circulation only. As and when there is a topical issue, VNA would also issue special collections of articles called *Tai Lieu Tham Khao* (*Reference Material*). Examples of special topics would include US-Vietnam Relations and Conflict in the South China Sea. Collected reference materials done by the ministries are usually given a restricted classification but in actual fact, they are not repositories of state secrets. They merely contain information from foreign sources which used to be controlled more tightly in the past. Vietnamese do not take these classifications seriously now and some have quipped that a classification is sometimes used as a gimmick to boost circulation. Classification is also used as a means of publishing without clearing the contents with the custodial Ministry of Culture. An illustrative example of the loose implementation of classification is *Cong Tac Tu Tuong* (*Ideological Work*), a monthly published by the Party's Committee on Ideology which is placed on the open shelves in the National Library reading room. It is marked for internal circulation only and to be treated as secret material. Official publications like this are likely to be gradually declassified.

So on a regular basis, there is information for researchers. The problem is are these publications readily retrievable when necessary. That really depends on the library: its size and organization. Some libraries have no catalogue to keep track of these regular publications. Others do not have the space. There are three specialists libraries which are likely to be used by students of security studies: that of the Institute of Southeast Asia Studies, the Institute of International Relations and the Army Library. They are small by international standards with ISEAS having 8,000 books and IIR having 10,000. Owing to lack of funds, many libraries do not have money to acquire books or publications regularly, particularly foreign publications. Most are totally reliant on exchange programs or foreign funding agencies. But in general, the libraries would have regular subscription of *Times*, *Newsweek*, *Far Eastern Economic Review* and *Asiaweek*. Regional dailies available are the *Bangkok Post* or *The Nation of Thailand*. The ISEAS library actually has 100 different titles of magazines and journals.

The Army Library is the best equipped and best organized of the three. A new wing is being constructed and there will be computerized catalogue. But generally speaking, catalogue systems in Vietnam when it applies to security studies are inadequate. Due to the small number of books on these subjects, they are usually classed broadly as politics/social issues. Reflecting the Marxist tradition of scholarship, books on Marxism, the Party and the late President Ho Chi Minh have very detailed subcategories. Books are also catalogued according to countries but once again, depending on the number of books on a particular country, the titles may not be further divided into subcategories. And if they are, there would at best be three broad categories: economics, politics and miscellaneous. These three are not the only specialized libraries in Hanoi but they are the most accessible. There is, for instance, the library belonging to the Institute of Military History which will admit some researchers from outside. It has 10,000 books and another 25,000 titles for restricted use. The availability of restricted material is discretionary. You tell the librarians your research needs and they release what they think is useful material for you.

Generally speaking, researchers in Vietnam have a hard time when sourcing information but it is not an entirely impossible task. A fair amount of information is available but badly organized. A researcher will have to be tenacious by doing his round of the libraries. More so than researchers anywhere else, he will also need to collect material on his own as he goes along. But given the poor pay conditions, it is difficult to expect such devotion in the average scholar.

## Exchange Activities

Exchange activities between Vietnam and countries of the Asia Pacific and Europe are increasing steadily. They cover a range of activities including participation in international or bilateral conferences, exchange of publications, grants for books, scholarship, familiarization trips and visiting lecturers. Increasingly, many research institutes have one project or another receiving foreign funding because there is interest in promoting scholastic activities in Vietnam.

Vietnam is also plugged into the Southeast Asian conference circuit and its representatives are regularly invited to various meetings. In addition many delegations are sent out or invited to study the experience of neighboring countries although these are mostly economic delegations or civil servants looking to share bureaucratic experience. But participation in larger Asia Pacific forums is still rather limited. Paul Evans of the Joint Centre for Asia Pacific Studies in Toronto, has identified at least nineteen such regional conferences/workshops.[24] Of these, Vietnam only participated in three: Asia-Pacific Roundtable organized by ASEAN ISIS; Pacific Security After the Cold War organized by the Institute on Global Conflict and Cooperation, and the series of meetings on the South China Sea sponsored by the Indonesian government.

But the Vietnamese presence at regional security forums (both for Southeast Asia and the wider Asia Pacific region) will grow. Currently, the problem, given Vietnam's large research establishment, is who are the most suitable participants to invite. It is hard to say which institute is the most influential, for in all likelihood none is, of its own, very influential. But this is a system where expertise on and the prerogative to address an issue have been very compartmentalized by the bureaucracy. And so on issues of international relations, the Institute of International Relations or Foreign Ministry officials would have an edge over other research bodies. When proceedings at international forums are in English, it also limits the choice of Vietnamese participants. Academia and the Foreign Ministry are known to most foreigners. Increasingly, there should be more exchanges with the military research institutes for they are the best informed on issues like strategic balance of forces and should also be exposed more to foreign perspectives on international issues. For the same reasons, it would also be useful to engage departments or institutes within the Party in scholarly exchanges.

# Conclusion

Viewed together, the situations facing security studies in all four non-ASEAN Southeast Asian countries have some basic similarities. All are faced with fundamental challenges to their old political systems requiring a reevaluation of national ideology which in turn makes it necessary to carry out reforms in many major areas of public life: how the economy is run and the form and substance of governance. These come at a time when larger changes in the surrounding Asia Pacific region also require major readjustments. It is a situation which poses big challenges for security studies.

However, the facilities for security studies in all four countries are commonly hampered by lack of resources. This can be relieved to a certain extent by external assistance in terms of training or financial aid. But another aspect of this problem is structural and has no easy solution. For instance, in the case of Vietnam, the research establishment is just too large and has to be reduced by retrenching or redeploying manpower.

Apart from inadequate resources, another problem is that of political constraints. For Myanmar, Laos and Vietnam, it is authoritarian governments suspicious of any research on sensitive security matters other than those done by state appointees. However in the case of the two Marxist states, Laos and Vietnam, the ideological reservation is more profound than just regimes fearing challenges to their authority. It is also intellectual baggage from a Marxist intellectual tradition which conditions the educated elite to look at things in a doctrinaire way. Myanmar's brand of socialism never had such intellectual depth.

Cambodia for the moment is free of authoritarian control, but its government of many factions and subfactions while making security studies more exciting does not make it any easier, particularly for those working for the state and not sure whose instructions they should take. But on balance, now more so than at anytime in their recent history, the prospects for improvement in security studies are promising. All four regimes are set on a course of forming links with the world outside rather than abjuring these ties. Even if these contacts are motivated mainly by commercial motives, their very expansion would encourage more openness within the polity and allow more space for research activities and intellectual exchange.

Of the four, Vietnam would seem to be most promising case. It has the largest research infrastructure even if it is a highly flawed system. Myanmar can probably muster such manpower resources as well but presently, Myanmar is not as well placed as Vietnam is to engage in any exchange activities to promote security studies. This is largely because the Hanoi government compared to the Myanmar regime, is far more welcoming of intellectual contacts with foreigners either by the foreigner visiting or allowing its own people to travel abroad. In addition, the international community is currently more attracted to Vietnam than to Myanmar because of the latter's pariah political status. Vietnam is also popularly perceived as being a very important country strategically, certainly more so than Myanmar. These are reasons that have accounted for the disproportionately large amount of attention given to Vietnam in this paper. Of course, the writer's greater familiarity with Vietnam has also been a factor.

## Notes

1. See Joseph S. Nye Jr., "The Contribution of Strategic Studies: Future Challenges," in *Adelphi Paper* 235, Spring 1989: pp. 20–25; and Stephen Walt, "The Renaissance of Security Studies," in *International Studies Quarterly*, vol. 35, no. 2, June 1991, pp. 212–13.

2. Tun-jen Cheng, "Is the dog barking? The middle class and democratic movements in the East Asian NICs" (research paper), Graduate School of International Relations and Pacific Studies, University of California, San Diego, 1990.

3. Carlyle A. Thayer, "Renovation and Vietnamese Society: The Changing Roles of Government and Administration" in Dean K. Forbes et al., eds., *Doi Moi—Vietnam's Renovation Policy and Performance* (Australia National University: Panther Publishing and Press, 1991), pp. 21–33.

4. Senior Minister Lee Kuan Yew of Singapore is one of the most vocal proponents of Asian democracy. For a detailed account of the Singapore position, see Kishore Mahbubani, "The West and the Rest," *The National Interest*, no. 28, Summer 1992, Washington, pp. 3–12.

5. Le Xuan Luu, "Dien Bien Hoa Binh—tu mot tu tuong chi dao trong chinh sach doi ngoai den mot chien luoc" (Peaceful Evolution—from a foreign policy guideline to a strategy), *Tap Chi Quoc Phong Toan Dan*, no. 4, 1993, Hanoi, pp. 60–64.

6. Mya Than, "Striking it rich in the Golden Quadrangle," *ISEAS TRENDS*, No. 39, in *Business Times* 27–28, November 1993, Singapore.

7. Statement by Myanmar Foreign Minister in Indonesia reported in "Myanmar seeks meaningful ties with Asean," *Straits Times*, December 24, 1993, Singapore.

8. Ibid.

9. Chi-sha Liang, *Burma's Foreign Relations—Neutralism in Theory and Practice* (New York: Praeger, 1990) pp. 62–63.

10. Ibid., pp. 221–32.

11. Ibid., p. 234.

12. Papers sampled are English-language dailies: *Straits Times* of Singapore and the *Bangkok Post* and *The Nation of Thailand*.

13. See article "Anxious neighbours—ASEAN members break silence on refugee issue," *Far Eastern Economic Review*, March 26, 1992, pp. 27–28.

14. Information on the research institutions in Myanmar and the environment within which they have to work was provided by Myanmar émigrés working in the West and who do not want to be identified.

15. Based on a conversation with KIRI's Acting Director Thach Bunreoun in January 1994 and promotional literature from the institute.

16. This is an assessment of five people: two businessmen with investment in Phnom Penh, one NGO worker who has worked there, a Khmer émigré and Professor David Wurfel after a visit.

17. Information for this part of the paper was gathered in Hanoi in October 1993.

18. Gareth Porter, "The Transformation of Vietnam's World View: From Two Camps to Interdependence," *Contemporary Southeast Asia*, no. 12, June 1990, pp. 1–19.

19. For a more detailed account of debate leading to changes in Vietnam's foreign policy, see chapter 7, "Vietnamese Foreign Policy: Ideology and Constraints," in Gareth Porter, *Vietnam—The Politics of Bureaucratic Socialism* (Ithaca: Cornell University Press, 1993), pp. 185–215.

20. Reference materials used are as follows: *Tap Chi Cong San* (*Communist Review*), a monthly VCP Central Committee journal; *Thong Tin Ly Luan* (*Theoretical Information*), a monthly journal of the Institute of Marxism-Leninism and Ho Chi Minh Thoughts; *Tap Chi Quoc Phong Toan Dan* (*All People's Defense Journal*), a monthly journal published by the Ministry of Defense and the VCP Central Military Affairs Commission; *Nghien Cuu Quoc Te* (*International Studies*), a quarterly published by the Ministry of Foreign Affairs' Institute of International Relations; *Nghien Cuu Dong Nam A* (*Southeast Asian Review*), a quarterly published by the Institute of Southeast Asian Studies within the National Center for Social Sciences and the Humanities.

21. Leaders view plan to modernize political system, Hanoi Vietnam Television in Vietnamese 1200 GMT October 31, 1992, in FBIS–EAS–92–217, November 9, 1992, p. 59.

22. Nguyen Dinh Tu, Cac chuong trinh cap nha nuoc ve khoa hoc xa hoi voi nghi quyet 01 cua Bo Chinh Tri, a chapter in Cong Tac Ly Luan Trong Giai Doan Hien Nay, Nha Xuat Ban Su That, Hanoi. 1992: pp. 113–15.

23. Senior staff members including the rector of Hanoi University announced this to Professor David Wurfel when he visited in January 1994.

24. Paul M. Evans, "The Dialogue Process on Asia Pacific Securties Issues" (see chapter 15 of this volume).

# Country and Area Studies: Asia Pacific Region, Soviet/Russian Angle

ALEXEI G. ARBATOV[1]

One Russian novel about the Far East of the early twentieth century was called *In the Backyard of the Great Empire*.[2] The quality of the novel aside, its title was very precise as to the role, priority and perceptions of the Far East and the whole Asia Pacific Region (APR) in Russia's domestic and foreign policies, and in its academic studies as well.

Extreme centralization of the tzarist administrative system and economic management, designed to sustain the huge and backward expansionist and super-militarized empire did not leave much hope for Russia's areas as seemingly far-flung from Moscow or St. Petersburg as Bangkok or Zanzibar. During the Soviet decades communications became somewhat better, but the level of central-ization was enhanced even more to support totalitarian, expansionist and still further militarized superpower. The collapse of the Communist empire in August 1991 and the ensuing disintegration of administration, economy, science and culture under the rule of President Yeltsin's democrats made the Far East and Russia's Asia Pacific economy, policy and academic studies even more of a "back-yard," than ever before in this century.

A short-lived "golden age" of the Soviet/Russia APR policy and studies came under Gorbachev-Shevardnade's "new political thinking" in the late 1980s when an attempt was made to achieve in this region the same monumental break-throughs that were attained in Europe and in US-Soviet relations. However, this attempt largely failed, for the political environment in APR was very different from that in Europe. Besides, there were neither diplomatic cadres nor an aca-demic community in Moscow to understand the difference and provide practical advice to policymakers. Their colleagues in European and American fields, by the nature of their subjects, received two decades of training in modern political and strategic studies and were prepared for the big change that came after 1985. That was not the case with experts on APR.

During the Cold War years after the early 1960s, the Asia Pacific security environment evolved in a very different way from other regions of the world and was overshadowed by bipolar confrontation. Hence, the end of the Cold War in the late 1980s did not affect it as deeply as Europe or other arenas of US-Soviet "mortal rivalry." Likewise, during the rest of 1990s, the politics of ARP will be shaped by quite different factors than those in Europe and South Asia, where the decisive issue will be Russia's relations with other former Soviet republics (the so-called "near-abroad") and its effect on Moscow's relations with the West and the Muslim world. In the 1990s, the prospects of Russia's successfully adapting to the new environment in APR and choosing the best security strategy in relation to it are not very bright. At present, apart from the general effects of economic and political crisis, deficiencies of foreign policy-making and mounting impact of nationalist and neo-imperialist moods, there is one specific problem. As a result of the "shock therapy" of 1992–93 Asia Pacific studies in the Russian academic community, as modest as they were, were hit even harder than other areas of global and regional political research or other areas of humanitarian sciences.

The fragile intellectual foundation of modern foreign policy that was emerging in the Soviet Union in the late 1980s may completely disintegrate in the near future, with no prospect of revival for many decades and with serious consequences for Russia's foreign policy. To prevent this, an urgent salvage operation must be initiated quickly, first of all by the Russian government, the Academy of Sciences, and private charity foundations, and secondly by those foreign partners of Russian scholars who do care about preserving a common intellectual language and framework with Russia on APR security issues in the years to come.

## The Evolution of Soviet Asia Pacific Studies in the 1980s and 1990s

From their very beginning, Asia Pacific studies in the USSR were directed at assisting Moscow's grand foreign and security policy designs to achieve success in a global confrontation with the world capitalist system led by the United States. That meant that the studies themselves were an element and, to a certain extent, an instrument of the governmental foreign security policy as well as of the Communist ideology.

In the former USSR, Asia Pacific studies—as regional studies—were commenced in the late 1970s and early 1980s. They were pioneered by two institutes of the Soviet Academy of Sciences—the Institute for Oriental Studies (IVAN), then directed by Yevgeniy Primakov, and the Institute for USA and Canada Studies (ISKAN), directed by Georgi Arbatov. Large-scale, although not properly coordinated, research on the regional problems and the problems of its particular countries was conducted at IMEMO, then directed by Nicolai Inozemtsev.

During the Cold War, the Soviet attitude to specific regions, including the Asia Pacific, was customarily subordinated to interests of global confrontation with the United States. In the context of bipolar geopolitics, the military balance in Europe, which was characterized by direct interaction of huge military forces of the two leading blocks along inter-German borders, played a much greater role than the potential Far Eastern theater of military operations. In the Asia Pacific Region, SEATO remained intact along with ANZUS until it was paralyzed by New Zealand's antinuclear policy at the beginning of the 1990s. But their role was largely symbolic. Of greater importance were the bilateral alliances of the United States with Japan, South Korea, the Philippines, Australia and Thailand. The USSR had developed close military cooperation with Vietnam and also North

Korea. Russia and China in fact waged war by proxy in Cambodia, with Moscow rendering full support for Vietnam, while China (together with Thailand, the United States and other states) assisted anti-Vietnamese forces in Cambodia.

By 1975 the most acute problems of European security were partially solved by the Helsinki process, which codified a *modus vivendi* for the USSR's Western strategic direction. That permitted a diversion of attention to other regions. The end of the self-isolation of China (the second biggest Soviet potential adversary) was becoming more and more evident in the course of 1970s. Beijing's slow but steady rapprochement with the United States and Japan, emerging in contours of a grand anti-Soviet coalition, were fraught with the prospect of turning the Sino-Soviet border into the permanent conflict zone, the second global frontline.

Fast economic growth in Japan and other "capitalist" Asia Pacific countries, as well as the US withdrawal from Indo-China, increased political autonomy of local states. From objects of bipolar confrontation, they were becoming independent subjects of regional and world politics. Besides, by the end of decade, the United States not only halted its plans to continue withdrawals from the region but also decided to improve capabilities enabling it to conduct "the second war" in the Western Pacific. At the same time Soviet leaders and strategists, who had provoked to a large extent such a shift in Washington's policy, overreacted to the newly emerging threats. They frightened themselves with the perspective of the Pacific NATO (NATO-2) on the eastern borders of the USSR. Researchers were "mobilized" to study such a critical situation and to find ways to neutralize new threats.

But the process of scientific research had its own inner logic, leading to the conclusions and appraisals not fully coinciding with the views and expectations of those at the top who ordered or requested the analysis. Many high-ranking officials preferred not to express clearly their position but instead "shared the opinion" of certain scientists. The Soviet academic community in some cases proved to be capable of modifying the initial position of the Central Committee for the CPSU. One vivid example is with the Pacific Community Project which looked very menacing at the outset for the Kremlin, but later was presented by a group of academic scholars not as a direct threat for the Soviet state but rather an objective manifestation of an integration process in the Pacific rim which did not exclude Soviet participation at later stages. Of course many academic publications also had to pay tribute to ideological incantations.

Like international studies in general, the big portion of Asia Pacific research was designed to fulfill propagandistic needs of the state. In the late 1970s, the Institute for Far Eastern Studies (IDV) of the Academy of Sciences was established. According to most Russian Asia Pacific experts, its original and main mission was to provide propagandistic support for Soviet policy in the region, especially policy on China. The institute maintained close contacts with the Department for International Information of the Communist Party Central Committee. Other academic Asia Pacific research centers in IVAN, ISKAN, Institute for World Economy and International Relations (IMEMO) were functioning in a similar vein, although to a lesser extent.

A considerable numbr of half-propagandistic and quasi-scientific books glorified "the struggle of the Soviet diplomacy for peace and security in Asia," the foreign policy of Vietnam (as the "vanguard of socialism" in Southeast Asia), and exposed "sinister designs" of Maoist China, etc. (For I. Kovalenko, M. Kapitsa, M. Isaev and others, that was the principle area of activity.)

It should be mentioned, however, that wise use of academic experts in counterpropagandistic missions created feedback for the regime. It had to expand access of intellectuals to foreign publications and trips abroad. Some of them, voluntarily, or by inadvertantly delivering facts and arguments hitherto unknown by the larger public, transformed their "counterpropagandistic activities" into the opposite—an interpretation of the positive elements of the "capitalist" experience. For example, in the early 1980s, writings on Chinese economic reforms and successes inevitably raised readers' questions about the necessity of market reforms on Soviet soil. The same applied to the analysis of Vietnamese economic reforms, which surpassed in their scope and boldness everything undertaken in the USSR. A series of publications on that subject (by E. Bogatova, N. Makarov) appeared in the academic magazines and also in "Communist" (in that period, a vehicle for reformers within the CPSU). Such articles not only enlightened the readers but "revolutionized" the attitudes of many Party members, preparing the ground for deep and irreversible reforms in the Soviet Union and Russia.

Hence, inadvertently in late 1970s and early 1980s, Soviet Asia Pacific studies had already outgrown their function as a support of the regime's propaganda by scientific means. Research centers and individual researchers, especially from ISKAN, IVAN and IMEMO, conducted purely academic studies, and propaganda findings were usually their secondary by-product. Before *perestroika*, progress in Asia Pacific studies was seriously limited by barriers, endemic for the Communist regime: domestic military and economic statistics were unavailable, severe censorship (and a self-censorship) laid impediments for dissent and innovative views, writings were overburdened by ideological clichés and it was impossible to directly criticize the official position.

By the mid-1980s, studies at IMEMO were concentrated on economic and political developments in Japan,[3] while individual researchers analyzed several problems related to China and economic situations in other individual Asia Pacific nonsocialist states. In 1985, on the initiative of A.Yakovlev (at that time, the director of the institute), the Department of Pacific and Japanese studies was established within IMEMO, later transformed into the Center of Japanese and Pacific Studies. Thus, Asia Pacific studies have acquired a more comprehensive and systematic character. Although in IVAN the region received more attention, the research work there was mainly directed at economic, cultural, historic, and, to a lesser extent, political subjects. No military or serious political studies were attempted. In 1983 experts from IVAN and ISKAN issued a book titled *Pacific Regionalism: Concepts and Reality*, which represented, in fact, the first regional study (including some security aspects). However, in this book, the authors addressed international and security relations in the region from positions of the global US-Soviet confrontation.[4]

China studies were concentrated in IDV and IVAN; Vietnamese studies—in IVAN and IEWSS. The latter title—Institute for Economy of World Socialist System—was misleading and served mainly as political camouflage because it did not exclude research on acute political and social problems of Asian countries.

The views of a number of IDV researchers proved to be quite conservative and even dogmatic, reflecting not only sceptical but highly critical attitudes toward economic reforms in China at their initial stages. But later on, some scholars at IDV considered Chinese reforms as a very good example for Russia and as a manifestation of the "creative possibilities" of a socialist system. Lately Taiwanese studies have been on the rise. The Taiwanese authorities have been generously supplying different Russian scientific centers with Taiwanese newspapers and magazines.

Contrary to the viewpoint of their colleagues in IVAN and IMEMO, leading Japanologists of IDV were substantiating the position of "no territorial concessions to Japan." But there were also some dissidents within IDV. B. Plavinsky (deputy editor of *Problems of the Far East*) published at his own expense in 1993 the book *Soviet Occupation of Kurile Islands* (in Russian). Also, despite enormous financial shortages, IDV has regularly held conferences under the title "China, Chinese Civilization and the World" (October of 1992 and 1993) with all reports being published.

By the mid-1980s, Soviet Asia Pacific studies did not represent an integrated system of research centers which specialized on the region. Although a Soviet scientific school of Asia Pacific studies had not fully taken shape, a number of prominent scholars (Sarkisov, Chufrin, Delyusin, Petrov, Pevzner) had prepared the way for it. And in their path, bright researchers emerged (Lukin, Kuzmenko, P. Ivanov, V. Ivanov, Kunadze, Goncharov, Aliev, Stolyarov). What helped that process enormously were contacts, exchanges and discussions with Western colleages, and expanding access to the literature published abroad. As for the position within the Soviet decision-making mechanism, academic Asia Pacific studies, like the security studies in general, had a very limited influence.

Since the proclamation of *perestroika* in early 1985 by Mikhail Gorbachev, Asia Pacific studies have undergone important changes. They were determined by a number of factors, both positive and negative. Dramatic changes in Moscow's security interests in the region, as well as profound domestic transformation seriously affected research. Since 1985 the following factors played the most important roles in Soviet/Russian Asia Pacific studies:

First, the role of the Asia Pacific region in Moscow's security perceptions was changing in different directions. In 1985–89, the gradually softening Cold War confrontation provided more room for maneuvering in relations with the third-party countries, including those in the Asia Pacific. Since 1989 the disintegration of the Soviet alliance system, and the USSR itself, has diverted the Kremlin's attention to the post–Cold War settlement in Europe and the former Soviet Union.

In 1985–89, deep but gradual changes in the domestic and international environments required elaboration of the new Soviet strategy towards the Asia Pacific area—a region of priority interest for the top decision makers. The precipitous retreat from Eastern Europe stimulated the efforts of Moscow's diplomacy to compensate (at least partially) for the losses in the West by gains in the East through rapprochement with China, Japan, and the newly industrialized countries of East Asia.

After the disintegration of the USSR, the place of the Asia Pacific in the hierarchy of Russian international priorities was occupied by new Central Asian states—all former Soviet republics. Intense discussion of this subject by Russian Asia Pacific hands in the most authoritative newspapers (*Izvestia, Nezavisimaya*) and magazines (*World Economy* and *International Relations*, with headlines such as "Problems of the Asia Pacific Region," "International Life," "USA," "New Times" and others) were very helpful in defining the major issues in Russian Asia Pacific policy. Some of these publications even provoked official replies from the Foreign Ministry (with regard to Cambodian settlement and its financial cost to Russia and the demarcation of the Russian-Chinese border, to cite only two examples). Still, there has been no consistent Russian policy in Asia Pacific and, correspondingly, there has been consistent absence of official interest in the academic research on the region for the last twenty years.

A greater role for China in Russia's security perceptions would theoretically suggest potential government interest in Asia Pacific developments and studies. However, Chinese studies promote different approaches to Beijing. Russian scholars of China view that country from different angles, though a broad consensus is reached in the country in favor of good-neighborly and peaceful relations with PRC. But there is a small minority which tends to look at China like a security risk and argues against "excessive concessions" to Beijing. There is also another extreme view which qualifies China as in fact a valuable anti-American partner—erratic Russian policy-making has not been conducive to organizing a comprehensive discussion and to consistently assessing the alternatives.

Aside from the fundamental geopolitical factors, domestic trends also had controversial effects. Positive factors, like achievements of *glasnost* policy and removal of ideological restrictions, were by 1989 neutralized by a progressive lack of financial resources. Severe financial constraints placed the Asia Pacific studies, like Russian academic science in general, in a situation where its very survival was at stake and forced the reduction of a number of conferences, meetings and exchange visits.

In the period from 1985 to 1989, Soviet Asia Pacific studies rapidly developed. Higher demands from the decision makers, especially after the trip of Mikhail Gorbachev to Vladivostok in 1986, increased the role of academic experts in decision making as well as enhancing their prestige. It led to the expansion of studies. In IVAN, Konstantin, Saskisov and Gennady Chufrin came to the forefront of academic and consultative activities. At IMEMO, research on the region was consolidated in the Center for Asia Pacific Studies, specially established (in 1986). It was strengthened by experts for IVAN (Vladimir Ivanov, Georgy Kunadze). New names emerged (Alexei Zagorsky, Viktor Rosin). In ISKAN studies were also maintained, although at smaller scale than at IMEMO. This was partially explained by the fact that Vladimir Lukin left ISCAN for the Foreign Ministry. But at the same time experts such as Konstantin Pleshakov and Alexei Bagaturov were trying to fill the gap. The general orientation of IDV was also beginning to change,[5] especially after Dmitrii Petrov was recruited there from IMEMO. IDV's several pragmatically minded experts (e.g., Dr. Goncharov) received promotions.

The consolidation and upgrading of the Asia Pacific studies were evident during the first years of Gorbachev's reign. Some observers believe that the year 1987 represents the true beginning of the comprehensive regional studies in the

USSR. As for IEWSS, it did not drop Asia Pacific studies, although it was much more preoccupied with developments in Eastern Europe. As a result of *glasnost* the researchers more openly expressed their views, initially in semiclassified meetings with governmental officials, and later, in international conferences and seminars, and, finally, in their open publications. By 1990 the censorship was lifted, foreign publications were transferred to common branches of libraries and direct access to copy machines had been legalized. More domestic statistics, including economic and military, became available. Ties with foreign research centers were expanded dramatically. In 1988 an unprecedented number of the Soviet Asia Pacific scholars took part in international conferences and seminars. Since 1986 the number of foreign visitors to the Soviet Asia Pacific centers has been also considerably increased.

Still in 1989–91, the propagandistic function of the studies played a role.[6] Academic experts were found by the Party propagandists to be very useful in their efforts to demonstrate the new, more open image of the Soviet Union under *glasnost* and *perestroika*. They were more frequently recruited for preparing materials for the propaganda machine (for example, Novosti Press Agency).

In the late 1980s, academic institutions fulfilled a new function. The Asia Pacific academic community was used for establishing initial ties between South Korea and the USSR. IMEMO in a competition with other research centers won the status of an "umbrella organization," and in this capacity organized a visit to Moscow of then South Korean opposition leader Kim Young Sam. That was the first semiofficial trip of a high-ranking politician from Seoul to the Soviet Union. That visit represented a milestone in the Soviet-South Korean relations, opening the way to the establishment of diplomatic relations between the two countries.

Since 1989 lower priority has been given to foreign policy, and together with the relative decline in the interest in the Asia Pacific has accounted for lack of attention from decision makers to the region's studies. Disintegration of the USSR, a deteriorating economic situation, as well as a general degradation of the Academy of Sciences' position within Moscow's establishment, led to drastic decrease in budgetary support of academic research on the whole, and Asia Pacific studies in particular.

The rapid formation of a Russian Asia Pacific research school, which took place in the 1980s, has been halted. The best representatives of the middle generation of researchers, who flourished under *perestroika*, now work mostly for the Western centers and companies, getting foreign grants or consultative jobs. Some have left Russia permanently. The breed of late-1980s postgraduates either emigrated or changed their jobs for much better paid commercial activities. For example, at the Center for Asia Pacific Studies in IMEMO, there is only one researcher below the age of thirty-five. In other institutions the situation is similar. The supply of postgraduate schools by new graduates has been also halted. According to some assessments, if such developments continue for a few more years, the disintegration of Russian Asia Pacific studies might be unadvoidable.

# The Evolution of Definitions of Security and Region

The direction of Asia Pacific security studies in the Soviet era was seriously affected by the desire of the Soviet military and intelligence institutions to monopolize the subject and prevent any competition from civilian experts. Monopolization of research findings in the sphere of the security-related questions permitted them to establish themselves as the only source of data and analysis for the Soviet leadership. Hence, they enjoyed a comfortable position for manipulating the decision-making mechanism in order to obtain more budgetary allocations. Even in the absence of the direct embargo, the results of any autonomous security study could be easily ignored and simply couldn't find the way to decision-making centers.

By the mid-1980s this led to two consequences. First, the majority of Asia Pacific experts avoided defining their research as "security studies" and were not addressing military matters at all. Asia Pacific studies were mainly devoted to general evaluations of economic and political developments in the region, very often made in a descriptive manner. Despite the fact that all the studies might be considered as supporting the state security interests in the area, the term "security studies" was defined very narrowly and referred to military threats and contingencies. For instance, an authoritative academic publication defined Asian security as "an absence of wars and military dangers in Asia."[7]

The second consequence was that the number of researchers involved in military-political studies was relatively small. Asia Pacific civilian experts were concentrated mainly in ISKAN, where they were protected from possible "organizational sanctions," which could be inspired by the military and intelligence by access of the institute leadership to the Party corridors of power. Still the studies were seriously unbalanced. They had to deal only with security policy of foreign capitalist countries, while any unbiased analysis of the Soviet policy and posture was not possible. Also, the ISKAN experts were not permitted to study security policy of regional "socialist" countries. Furthermore, being an Institute for USA and Canada studies, it could consider the developments in the area mostly through the prism of relations of the Asian countries with the United States.

The Yearbook, *Disarmament and Security* published by IMEMO (ed. by A. Arbatov) since 1986, paid considerable attention in recent years to the military problems of APR, thus filling the vacuum in that field. The breakthrough was achieved by applying the expertise and analytical methods of START and European strategic studies to the APR environment. In this sense, Russian studies come close to matching the US and Canadian strategic studies of the Asia Pacific Region. In the Yearbook's 1986, 1987, 1988–89 and 1992 editions, the strategic environment in APR for the first time in Soviet literature was analyzed on a professional level and as an alternative view to a traditional assessment of the Soviet military and intelligence community. That was done by the experts, who were basically trained to research European or Soviet-American security problems and trying to apply their methods to APR.

They immediately noticed that the military situation in the Asia Pacific region was distinctly different from the situation on the European continent, and this had to be taken into account in the search for approaches to problems of disarmament in this region of the world. In Europe the confrontation had a distinct bilateral nature, the watershed (between the Warsaw Treaty and NATO) lying in the longitudinal, north-to-south direction; the confrontation was mostly between the deployed land and air forces opposing one another in Central Europe. In this context the confrontation of naval groups in the north Atlantic and in the Mediterranean had basically been of an auxiliary, or flank character.

In the Asia Pacific region, on the other hand, the basic military confrontation had acquired in the 1970s and 1980s a trilateral structure and a T-type configuration. One of its watersheds was situated in the latitudinal direction between the land and air forces of the Soviet Union and China, deployed from west to east along the border between the two powers and that between China and Mongolia. The other axis ran north to south, perpendicular to the first one, and divided, on the one hand, the Soviet Union and China (plus North Korea), and on the other, the United States and Japan (plus South Korea and Taiwan). The center of gravity of this element of confrontation was lying with the air and naval forces in the Western Pacific. Interestingly enough, the intersection of this T-type confrontation was located exactly on the Korean peninsula, by far the most dangerous and complicated strategic trigger in the Western Pacific.

Logically, the military détente in the Western Pacific among the USSR, China, the United States and Japan hinged largely on the alleviation of political tensions, reduction and limitation of the armed forces, and confidence building measures on the Korean peninsula. This led to the conclusion that the reduction and limitation of the armed forces and activities in the Western Pacific could not follow the European model and would demand innovative ideas and nontraditional approaches.[8] Some promising options were proposed, reflected in IMEMO Yearbooks but were never integrated into Soviet practical security policies due to the tough resistance by the military and security establishment. Evidently Gorbachev and Shevardnadze, having twisted the arms of this influential group on European and US-Soviet breakthroughs, lacked the stamina to go even further and do the same in Asia.

In line with the universal concept of international security adopted by the 27th Party Congress in 1986, Asia Pacific studies also shifted to a broader definition of "security."[9] Thereafter they interpreted the security positions of the USSR in the region as a combination of military, political, economic, and humanitarian factors. It seems, however, that the new definition did not reflect a deep philosophical breakthrough, but provided an ideological background for a very practical need: to justify reductions of overstretched military capabilities, including those deployed in the Asia Pacific area.

The experts obtained an opportunity to argue that the Soviet security positions in the area were unbalanced. Strong military presence was not supported by adequate political, and, even less by economic influence. Moreover, they said that the military presence there was the main barrier to the promotion of political and economic cooperation with local states which were concerned with potential Soviet military threat. By that logic, reduction of military forces in the Asia Pacific would not have undermined, but rather strengthened the USSR's real security in the Far East.[10] This explains why after the end of the Cold War, when the US reductions were implemented, Russian Asia Pacific experts returned to a more traditional and narrow interpretation of "security" as an evaluation of external security challenges of a military nature[11] (with inclusions of certain political and economic considerations). However, since 1985 the security dimension of the studies has been expanded. In the late 1980s they occupied an important position in research of IMEMO's Center for Asia Pacific Studies. Although later general decline of the region's research in both IMEMO and ISKAN also affected the security studies, they nevertheless maintained stronger positions than in the early 1980s.

The term "Asia Pacific region" appeared in the Soviet academic research as early as in the late 1970s, soon after the emergence of the term in the United States. Until the early 1980s, it was used only sporadically but by the mid-1980s it became a generally approved term within the Soviet political science. During Gorbachev's years it also entered the official lexicon. Present definitions of the region made by academic studies are similar to that of American political science. The Asia Pacific region includes Russia, the United States, all Asian countries of the Pacific Basin, Myanma (formerly Burma) and land-locked Mongolia, plus Australia and Oceania. All other states of the American Pacific coast (including Canada) have been traditionally excluded from the area. The Asia Pacific region is usually divided into three subregions: (1) Southeast Asia (ASEAN, Indo-China and Myanmar), (2) Australia and Oceania, and (3) Northeast Asia (Russia, China, Japan, North Korea, South Korea, and Mongolia). There are also different division lines: Confucian and non-Confucian Asia; mainland and maritime countries; northern and southern ones.

However, geographical limits of the region were subject to change and different interpretations. The Gorbachev leadership understood the Asia Pacific region in a very broad sense: as a part of Asia east of Afghanistan (including South Asia), plus Australia and Oceania (a definition accepted by the UN). North America was considered as a part of the proposed system of Asia Pacific security, and, unlike Latin America, was also included within the region's boundaries.

On the other hand, the official structure of the MID has never corresponded with an academic definition of the region. Until the late 1980s, relations with the regional countries were supervised by three MID departments. The First Far Eastern Department dealt with the socialist countries (China, Mongolia, North Korea, Vietnam, and, later, Laos and Campuchea). The Second Far Eastern Department was responsible for ties with other regional capitalist and developing states, and, since 1975, with Australia and Oceania. Relations with Burma were managed by the South Asian Department.

Reorganization of the MID in 1992 removed the artificial ideological separation, but the region is still the responsibility of several departments. Moreover, Myanmar remains under the "jurisdiction" of the "non-Asia Pacific" South Asian Department. All the departments were directed by the Deputy Minister of Foreign Affairs, Kunadze, who was responsible for relations with the whole continent, including Middle-East, Central and South Asia. (In 1994 he was removed from this post and sent as ambassador to Seoul.)

Despite some achievements in the Soviet/Russian Asia Pacific academic studies, and their influence on Russia's decision making, the region is still bureaucratically understood not as a separate entity, but as a "part of Asia" with some Pacific attachments.

# Intellectual Traditions and Asia Pacific Studies

The intellectual traditions, which shaped Soviet/Russian thinking on Asia Pacific security studies, might be aggregated into five groups: traditional Orientalist studies of individual region's countries (economic, cultural, historic, and, later, political); modern academic studies on international relations and economy; recent academic peace research with strong propaganda flavor; new professional academic security studies; and government policy interests.

Russia's traditional Orientalist school is rooted in as early as in the nineteenth century, when it rapidly developed along with the geopolitical advance of the Russian Empire to Central Asia, China and the Middle East. Historically, there were two main centers of prerevolutionary Orientalist research—Moscow and St. Petersburg universities. Until the late 1970s they maintained their roles mainly in the educational field, while the Institute for Oriental Studies (IVAN) occupied the position of the leading Orientalist academic research center.

The Soviet Orientalist studies traditionally were tied to individual countries. The studies were devoted to a broad range of aspects: cultural, linguistic, geographic, historic, economic, and political. Among them, studies on the Middle East and Japan were considered the most advanced. Surprisingly much attention was always paid to Chinese and Indian studies. Some studies dealt with the problems of Southeast Asia. The monographs written by Soviet and Russian authors on ASEAN (and representing different viewpoints) possibly outnumber the books on that subject published in the United States and Japan. But the quality and level of Soviet "scientific production" were usually poor, a number of books printed by the "Nauka" publishing house were a result of hard work, and the insights were based on original sources and contained innovative ideas. Deserving mention is A. Popov's *Small Business of Indonesia*, published in 1991. A growing number of articles and books by Russian academic authors examined the phenomenon of East Asian NICS—newly industrialized countries. That is a relatively new subdivision of Orientalist research, which arouses great interest in governmental departments.

The Orientalist research provided a breed of experts who initiated Asia Pacific studies in the late 1970s. It was not coincidence that the leading Orientalist research center, IVAN, pioneered regional research. Academic studies on international relations can be considered as the second source. They started in the 1950s at IMEMO, and by the 1970s they were significantly expanded and were held in several institutions of the Academy of Sciences, including ISKAN. Those studies were close to Western-type political science. Experts on international relations enjoyed easier access to the contemporary Western scientific literature. On Asia Pacific problems, it reached Soviet scholars specializing in the United States, mainly from ISKAN. Availability of pragmatic experts on international relations, who could constantly follow foreign scientific innovations, provided to the institute an opportunity to initiate, together with IVAN, Asia Pacific studies in the Soviet Union. Academic peace studies, and, especially security studies, did not directly initiate Asia Pacific research, but played an important role in shaping its development. Security studies, by the mid-1980s especially strong in ISKAN and, partially, in IMEMO,[12] positively affected the Asia Pacific research in IVAN and IDV.

East Asian studies were also carried out in a framework of so-called "Third World studies," which have a long-standing tradition and some academic achievements. One example is the Center of Developing Countries in IMEMO headed by Dr. N.Simoniya. The major stress is on developmental strategies and socioeconomic problems typical for the majority of the countries of that group.

It should be mentioned that Asia Pacific studies in IMEMO during *perestroika* absorbed the best characteristics of all schools and emerged from several sources. They were led by researchers from IVAN (Vladimir Ivanov, Georgi Kunadze), who followed Yevgeniy Primakov when he got the post of IMEMO director in 1985. In the then newly formed Center for Asia Pacific Studies, the newcomers's were enriched by a relatively strong IMEMO school of research of the region's countries, first of all, Japan (Rafik Aliyev,[13] Pevzner, Vadim Ramzes, Vladimir Khlynov, Yelena Leontieva) and Australia (Igor Lebedev). The center was also strengthened by younger generation researchers (such as Andrei Kuzmenko), who specialized on Chinese policy and absorbed ideas of academic security studies, which were on the rise in the institute in the mid-1980s. Also, quite strong were IMEMO strategic and security studies, applying the most sophisticated Western analytical tools to military problems and arms control in the Department on Disarmament and Security, run by Alexei Arbatov, and helping to bring the APR studies to a higher level in military, as well as political, aspects.

Government policy interests provided a crucial incentive for the beginning of these new studies in the USSR. It is not completely clear whether the initiative was born somewhere in the Party apparatus, or it just sanctioned an idea that came form Yevgeniy Primakov or Georgi Arbatov. But without such a sanction no new research could commence.

Still, a strong influence of traditional Orientalist studies, as well as specific governmental demands, prevented Soviet Asia Pacific studies from paying too close attention to such problems as nuclear arms and arms control, or conventional weapons balance. When necessary, those problems were addressed by scholars, who specialized in the fields of general security studies,[14] but were relatively inexperienced in the regional details. The Asia Pacific studies mainly addressed more traditional topics, like international relations and diplomacy. A lack of experts also did not permit the writing of any fundamental, theoretical monographs. Instead, scholars had to concentrate on supporting the current political needs of decisions makers. The fruitful cooperation between strategic and regional experts was started but did not have enough time to mature before the collapse of the USSR and the economic/financial crisis of 1992–93 in Russia.

## Training of Asia Pacific Regional Experts

The Soviet/Russian education system relies on a strong tradition of the university education of experts on individual regional countries (mainly China and Japan) as well as on traditional Orientalism. Undoubtedly, an impressive part of the education is that the overwhelming majority of students learn local languages, and receive deep knowledge on the country's history, culture, and socioeconomic developments. The fact is that almost all of the Asia Pacific experts also speak English fluently and this is an important achievement of the Russian education system. Knowledge of English is a necessary precondition for successful research. About 90 percent speak one of the region's languages, primarily Chinese and Japanese.

Traditions of classical Orientalism are alive in the Oriental Faculty of the St. Petersburg State University. The Historic-Philological Faculty of the Institute for Countries of Asia and Africa (ISAA), which was formally subordinated to Moscow State University, keeps similar traditions. The complex education with special attention to economic and political topics is provided by ISAA's Socioeconomic Faculty and the Moscow State Institute for International Relations, which belongs to the Ministry of Foreign Affairs (MGIMO). While education in the former is considered to be of a higher quality, the latter institute is the principal source of new cadres for the Foreign Ministry. Besides these three main educational centers, small groups of students might be found in the foreign Faculties of Geography, Economics and History at the Moscow University.

The deficiency of education is that it has mainly dealt with individual countries but not with the region as a whole. There is also a great deficiency of disciplines on foreign and security policy of the countries, as well as the strategic environment of the region. Only since 1990 have the first small courses on security and arms control issues appeared in MGIMO.

Each of the above educational centers possesses its own postgraduate school. Academic institutions also have the right to grant PhD degrees, so they have their own postgraduate classes. This is true as well for all institutes that participate in Asia Pacific studies (IMEMO, ISKAN, IVAN, IDV, IEMSS). Classes for postgraduates in academic research centers usually provide more knowledge on the region than those in universities, and are of a more advanced nature and more liberal political orientation.

There is no special system for training future officials. Decision-making agencies engaged in Asia Pacific affairs recruit employees from MGIMO and ISAA, and only in very modest numbers, from the Moscow University. The graduates, as a rule, possess an adequate language proficiency as well as a basic knowledge of the main regional states. Lack of security and arms control education is the main problem that cannot be alleviated during the routine office work. Some of the young officials from the ministries prefer to receive their doctoral degrees in academic institutions, while those feeling scientifically insecure usually apply to MGIMO and universities where the criteria have been traditionally "friendlier."

Elements of the Soviet education system, like MGIMO and ISAA, were established to fulfill the needs of governmental agencies in training new employees. Their educational programs used to be oriented primarily on demands of those agencies. By 1985, due to bureaucratic inefficiency, the quality of education was becoming less and less adequate to the requirements of the changing domestic and international environment. The other problem was that the education was too indoctrinated and handicapped the nurturing of students for academic research.

Until recently, not a single expert in Russian Asia Pacific studies received education abroad. Since 1985, the growing number of under- and postgraduate students passed their terms (from several weeks to several months) in foreign universities. But there are still no cases of completed education abroad. The majority of students traveled to the United States. The second place is occupied by Japan; other countries are much less important (China, Vietnam, Indonesia, South Korea). Usually, the regional states (other than Japan) represent an interest from the viewpoint of a language practice, while the United States provides opportunities for advancing education in regional academic studies.

Due to the short term spent abroad, the trips were hardly sufficient to seriously affect attitudes and quality of the students. Nevertheless, they seemed to be marginally useful for improving experience and knowledge, as well as for establishing contacts that could be academically or politically valuable in future. Prospects of the travels also give to the brightest students an incentive to continue education instead of leaving for well-paying commercial enterprises.

## Participation in International Research Activities, Principal Institutions and Their Influence

A high level of participation in international research and dialogue activities, achieved by the Asia Pacific experts in the late 1980s, is still generally maintained. The absence of institutional money for travel expenses was partially neutralized by a decrease in numbers of academic experts, as well as by the increase in funds from foreign sources. Russian experts mainly cooperate with their colleagues from the United States. The United States is followed by Japan, and then, with a big gap, by South Korea and Australia. Ties with the centers from less affluent states (China, ASEAN) have been radically reduced.

The forms of the participation largely vary from taking part in conferences and seminars abroad and their organization in Russia, to fellowships and scholarships in research centers abroad and writing articles and chapters together with foreign researchers. The majority of international contacts has been recently made on an individual base. Large academic institutions, without budgetary support, proved to be too inflexible for keeping even a limited amount of the institutional cooperation with foreign research centers gained in the late 1980s.

There are a few reported cases of cooperation between Soviet/Russian and foreign Asia Pacific research centers. Since 1986 IDV has participated in a joint project with the Center for International Security and Arms Control at Stanford University. This is perhaps the only project which is still operational.[15] In the late 1980s ISKAN promoted a project with Brown University. IMEMO established regular ties with Japanese, South Korean and Australian and Vietnamese counterparts. But they have gradually come to a standstill for lack of funding and the Russian inability to render reciprocity in exchange programs and conference organization.

The main roles in the Asia Pacific studies are played by institutes at the Academy of Sciences: IMEMO, ISKAN, IVAN, IDV, and to a lesser extent, IEWSS and Institute of Universal History (IVI). Due to financial difficulties and poor leadership, the Vladivostok-based Institute for World Ocean Problems was disbanded; some researchers found new jobs. The last director of that institute was Dr. R. Aliyev. It seems there has been difficulty in discovering new spheres of activity and new sources of income for the staff of the institute. At the same time,

Khabarovsk's Institute of Economic Research headed by P. Minaker, is still functioning and demonstrating its usefulness in exploring ways to expand external economic relations of the region and its participations in the Pan-Pacific cooperation.

Novosibirsk scientists, in their own turn, contribute to the development of various projects of Siberian and Russian participation in schemes of Pacific cooperation. The Russian National Committee for Pacific Economic Cooperation draws its analytical support from the Center of Japanese and Pacific Studies where a special unit for that purpose was formed. The Director of IMEMO, Professor V. Martynov, is the deputy of the Academic and A. Granberg is the chairman of the above committee.

Outside the academic institutions some research takes place in universities: Institute for Asian and African Countries (ISAA), Faculties of Geography, Economy, and History at Moscow State University, Oriental Faculty of St. Petersburg State University, Foreign Ministry's Moscow State Institute for International Relations (MGIMO). The research there is mainly done by teachers and postgraduates, who usually have to address superficially a wide range of topics and are preoccupied by their classes. Individual experts on the region also might be found in institutes and organizations, subordinated to the Defense Ministry. The most doing nonclassified work is the Institute of Military History (at one time, directed by General P. Volkogonov). Among the governmental organizations interested in dialogue activity are ministries (first of all, Ministry of Foreign Affairs, Defense Ministry, and Ministry of Foreign Economic Relations).

The present transitional period is characterized by the appearance of numerous nongovernmental organizations (NGOs), which are potentially interested in dialogue with foreign counterparts. One of the examples is the Russian Agency on International Cooperation (RAMSIR). The latter was created on the basis of the Union of Soviet Friendship Societies, once a powerful "public" organization which coordinated semiofficial ties with foreign countries and organizations. Traditionally, academic institutions have played some role in the Soviet decision-making process. Since the 1950s, all directors of IMEMO occupied positions on the Party Central Committee (Arzumanyan, Inozemtsev, Yakovlev, Primakov, Martynov). The same was true of G. Arbatov, the head of ISKAN. Except in some special cases, that role had been secondary to official agencies.

During *perestroika,* the political situation became much more conducive to increasing the role of the Asia Pacific academic studies in decision making. Greater influence of the Ministry of Foreign Affairs (MID) under Eduard Shevardnadze, and specifically, his authorizing closer ties between academic institutions and MID, together with other decision-making bodies (the reformist wing of the Communist Party Central Committee), considerably strengthened the impact of Asia Pacific academic experts. Some of them entered MID and other governmental agencies (like Vladimir Lukin). The others received direct access to key official figures appointed by Gorbachev, like Alexander Yakovlev and Yevgeniy Primakov, who, in their turn, had also come from the academic community.

In the post–Cold War period, Russian Asia Pacific studies found themselves in a position somewhere between their peak during the Gorbachev era and the difficult years prior to *perestroika.* The generally erratic and disorganized manner of Russia's decision-making process, as well as uncertain and constantly changing positions of various bodies dealing with foreign policy, eroded the influence of academic Asia Pacific experts on the practical formulation of foreign policy. Nevertheless, academic research centers still keep some influence. This influence is primarily based on personal relations with officials, who, before entering decision-making bodies, had their jobs in academic organizations. The Center for Pacific Studies at IMEMO (now directed by Viktor Rosin) maintains its leading and most influential role among other academic institutions. Several of its former researchers are working in MID and managing a relationship with the Asia Pacific area (Andrei Kuzmenko, Georgy Kunadze, who was Deputy Minister of Foreign Affairs, responsible for the relations with Asian countries). A certain access to decision makers is enjoyed by IDV's experts on China: Dr.Goncharov directs the MID's department supervising Russian-Chinese relations. Still, personal ties have been too weak a basis for a regular relationship between governmental agencies and academic centers.

Relations between organizations involved in Asia Pacific research and dialogue activities were determined by both practical and personal factors. All the centers are struggling to receive a bigger share of relations with the academy, governmental contractors and foreign partners, who have been recently providing contributions to the funds of individual experts and a number of research centers.

Political and personal disagreements and differences in views account for the lack of contacts between the more liberal IMEMO, ISKAN, and IVAN, on the one side, and the conservative IDV, on the other. In the late 1980s both sides made a de facto attempt to define and divide the spheres of their research interests. IDV concentrated on Northeast Asia, while IMEMO and ISKAN concentrated on other areas. They still confronted each other on studies of Chinese security policy and of South Korean problems. Differences between modern- and security-oriented scholars from IMEMO and ISKAN, and traditionalists from IVAN, also have been an obstacle to closer cooperation among those institutions.

## Principal Consumers of Academic Security Analysis

Until the end of the 1980s governmental agencies were considered as principal "consumers" of Asia Pacific security analysis. There was nothing strange in that. Within the old Soviet system the state was the single employer for security experts and the primary consumer of their research. On the other hand, the analysis of academic experts in some cases was relatively more attractive for top decision makers, especially in the years of *perestroika*, than the assessments of state analytic agencies. The academics usually provided more honest and innovative reports: they were financed by the state indirectly through channels of the semiautonomous Academy of Sciences. Unlike analysts from classified institutions of the Ministry of Defense and KGB, they enjoyed much freedom in contacting their foreign colleagues, had access to the press, and were free from institutional discipline and vested interests.

Academic advice to the decision makers was delivered by two principal channels. Under one of them, a top scholar (director or deputy director) asked his subordinates to prepare an analysis on a given subject (an important event, political assessment of a situation prior to the visit of a Soviet or foreign official, the necessity to make an urgent correction of policy of propaganda, etc.). A staff, responsible for data support collected necessary information. Senior researchers (head of departments or sections) then processed the obtained data and prepared an analytic report. It was delivered to the top scholar, who made corrections and then sent it to the decision makers. The volume of the report could not exceed several typed pages (sometimes with a fifteen to twenty page addendum). The reports were invariably classified.

Under the other method, the analysis was implemented at secluded or semi-secluded meetings and seminars with governmental officials. In close and informal meetings, advice was given in an oral form; sometimes, a written memo, which was prepared earlier, was handed to an official. Results of larger, semiprivate seminars (*sitanaliz*—seminar on the situation analysis) were reviewed by academic participants and were also sent to decision makers in written form. Nonattribution was one of the principles to encourage greater freedom of views at the seminar, although self-censorship, cautiousness and desire for ideological and political safety prevailed even at closed discussions.

Since 1991 the demands of decision makers for Asia Pacific expertise had drastically decreased. This fact has mostly affected the method of informal meetings and seminars, while written reports, although in a much less regular mode, are still being prepared. In 1992–93, the Foreign Ministry was disorganized and plagued by numerous mishaps. Contrary to expectations and precisely in the crucial founding phase of the new policy of allegedly democratic leadership of Russia, there was a complete lack of interest (especially in contrast to Shevardnadze times) in comprehensive, consistent analysis of major policy issues involving experts from the Academy of Sciences and new independent think tanks and foundations. In MID and the government in general, the decision-making pattern was highly irregular and secluded, and for a long time no serious efforts were made to bring on board parliament, the mass media, or the academic community to forge a solid domestic political basis for Russia's foreign policy.

One interesting episode took place in the summer of 1992, while the visit of President Yeltsin to Japan was in preparation. The problem of the Kurile Islands was naturally at the center of attention, and there was some bitter infighting, reminiscent of the times of *perestroika*. That was the moment when the deficiencies of the security studies on APR became especially clear. The military and security community (supported by conservatives in the Supreme Soviet and political parties) claimed that the islands historically belonged to Russia and were indispensable for its security in the Far East. Liberal MID and academic experts argued that the islands belonged to Japan and were not needed for Russia's security since war was inconceivable. Besides, they promised that substantive loans and investment from Japan would be crucial for Russia's economy.

For obvious reasons, the position of the military and nationalists looked much stronger on political and security grounds, and eventually it overcame the others, leading to a scandalous cancellation of the summit only several days in advance (and after the president had claimed that he had fourteen options for resolving the territorial dispute).

Only one group of experts (from IMEMO's Department on Disarmament and Security) addressed the issue from a completely different point of view, and made their case at closed sessions, and publicly, after the cancellation of the summit.[16] They did not try to dismiss the arguments or data of the military but analyzed them head-on and came out with conclusions that caught them by surprise. In particular, they pointed out that the Sea of Okhotsk (where Russian strategic missile submarines were patrolling) was not Russia's inland water area and was accessible from the Japanese island of Hokkaido where, according to Russia's General Staff data, Japan's strong Northern Army and US units were deployed). Regardless of the control over the Southern Kurile straights, US and Japan forces were capable of ensuring, from shore, the naval breakthrough into the Sea of Okhotsk, by way of the straits south of Sakhalin and Kunashir. Moreover, they argued that in view of the preponderance of US naval task forces and marine forces and because of Russia's poor reinforcement capabilities, Russia's units on the Southern Kuriles had only a symbolic role. By a concentrated effort of its aircraft carriers and amphibious forces, the enemy could break through into the Sea of Okhotsk via any other navigable strait between the Kuriles with nothing but border guards and radar posts stationed on them. At the same time, they pointed out that the danger of surprise attacks from the sea and of US and Japanese landing operations against Russia's Maritime Territory were greatly exaggerated. Still, as was further pointed out, Russia's present position in the Asia Pacific region was weak economically, unfavorable politically and vulnerable strategically, even if it kept the Southern Kuriles and built up its military presence there.

Experts suggested that Russia could strengthen its position in the region by radically restructuring relations with other countries. It was proposed that the islands be given to Japan (not "back" to Japan) by analogy with the 1979 Camp David accord, when Israel exchanged territory (Sinai) for important gains in security. It was recommended to give the two small and later the two big islands to Japan in a phased, long-term schedule (ten to fifteen years). Parelleling the settling of bilateral political relations and recognition of Japan's sovereignty over the islands, Russian special military rights (use of radar and communications installations) and economic interests (fishing, tourism) would be given legal guarantees. Both sides were to make commitments on eventual demilitarization of the islands, nondeployment of troops, weapons, military installations, foreign military bases, etc. That would have facilitated joint economic development of the islands and the surrounding zone.

It was further recommended to expand the scope of the security settlement geographically and from a bilateral to trilateral format (including the United States). Specifically, political commitments were to be combined with measures to cut the armed forces of Japan, the United States and Russia and the Far East, agreements on curtailing the activity and exercises of air and naval forces (particularly of antisubmarine, amphibious and airborne forces) and on confidence building measures. Application of these limitations to only the four islands was strategically senseless and easily reversible. Hence, it was proposed that to be militarily and politically substantive during the ten to fifteen years, not only the four islands, but the entire Kurile archipelago, Hokkaido and Sakhalin islands

should have been demilitarized. To remove the threat to Russian strategic submarines in the Okhotsk sea, it was prosed to eventually redeploy them completely
from the Far East to the Arctic basing and patrol areas covered under the
START-2 Treaty.

This was a radical revision of the accepted ways of addressing the issue: from
historic and legal arguments to a political and security framework; from "islands-
for-credits" mode to a comprehensive strategic package; from two-to-four islands
scope to a much broader geographic zone; from bilateral to trilateral format of
security agreements. Although this position was appealing, and endorsed by some
military experts, the disorganized decision-making mechanism was unable to
digest it and transform it into practical diplomacy—the Foreign Ministry was
neither interested in nor able to promote it in the government. The rising nationalist mood in Russia (to a great extent a reaction to a subservient pro-Western
policy of MID), excluded any rational solution. After cancellation of the summit,
the leadership immediately lost interest in the issue.

Besides classified writings for decision makers, the experts fulfilled traditional academic jobs: writing books, articles, and papers. Books and articles were
directed mainly at academic audiences. The overwhelming majority of them were
published in Russian and, thus, were addressed to the domestic public. Some of
them, especially the most interesting articles, were translated on a regular basis
by other Soviet states. As was mentioned above, books and articles written for
propagandistic purposes were translated into foreign languages by the Soviet
agencies (in particular, Agency Press News). This created a distorted picture of
Soviet literature in the foreign academic community, which for linguistic reasons
had access mostly to the worst books and articles from an analytical point of view.

Difficulties related to the publishing process (censorship, bureaucracy, obsolete technology, a long lead-time), severely limited the number of published books.
Many of them became obsolete even before publication. Usually, every research
center was able to publish no more than one edited book every three to five years.
Writings of single-authored books were motivated by career considerations. Normally, a researcher might receive a promotion into the rank of senior researcher
only after publishing a book of his own. Sometimes, such books could be put
forward as a dissertation for receiving a second doctoral degree. More typical was
for the first and second doctoral dissertations to be published later as books.

Publication of classified monographs was frequently used as a way of avoiding excessive censorship restrictions. Such books could not be sold in open book-
stores, but they were distributed free of charge among interested academics and
decision makers. These publications were less propagandistic, more analytically
objective, and published faster. This is why by the late 1980s the volume of such
literature exceeded that of openly published books. By the end of the 1980s, due to
the lifting of censorship, publication of classified books was stopped altogether.

Since 1991 lack of financial support has completely halted the publication of
books on Asia Pacific studies in Russia. A few published books had a symbolic
circulation usually at the personal expense of the author. For instance, the recent
fundamental book by S. Verbitsky, *Japan Searching New Role in World Policy* had
a print run of only 400 copies.[17] Since the second half of the 1980s, along with the
progress in *glasnost*, the Asia Pacific experts included extracts from classified

reports and books in their open publications (articles for the Soviet/Russian and foreign journals, papers for conferences and seminars). Thus, open publications presented an adequate and almost entire picture of writing on Asia Pacific studies in the 1980s.

Recently, articles in journals have represented the main type of Russian scientific publications. Asia Pacific writings might be found in various academic journals. However, only one of them is specially devoted to the region: *Problemy Dal'nego Vostoka* (*Problems of the Far East*). Paradoxically, the journal, which is published by IDV, was not considered to be the leading periodical on the area by a majority of the regional experts. The best articles on the region appear on pages of two academic journals: *MEiMO* (*World Economy and International Relations*), published by IMEMO, and *SShA-Ekonomika, Politika Ideologiia* (*The USA: Economy, Policy and Ideology*), published by ISKAN. *MEiMO* with some modest financial support from private banks managed to be published on a regular basis and without reducing the distribution (as was the case with most other academic magazines). Until recently *MEiMo* had its own correspondent in Tokyo. Every issue of that monthly journal contains articles devoted to the Asia Pacific region.

The monthly *Asia and Africa Today* presents both popular and scientific articles. In 1993 its circulation was increased and the quality of production was improved. The founders of the journal are IVAN and the Institute of Africa. For more than a year a new monthly journal has been printed in Russia: *Japan Today* (in Russian). In mid-1993 another publication was launched: *News of Asia Pacific Region*. But the Russian Information Agency (RIA) managed to publish only one pilot issue and had to start searching for a suitable partner to print that paper. Two other magazines, *International Life* and *New Times*, are translated into other European languages, including English. Until the late 1980s the former was published by MID and mainly contained views of governmental officials. Recently it separated from the Foreign Ministry and provided serious competition to other academic journals. *New Times* is a magazine for the elite and is not oriented to a broader public. They both are devoted to the international situation in general, and the pieces on Asia Pacific problems appear on an irregular basis.

Among other periodicals a bimonthly journal, *Narody Azil i Afriki* (*Peoples of Asia an Africa*), should be mentioned. It has a pronounced academic character and covers a broad range of problems on the two continents. Another magazine, *Znakom'tes' s Yaponiyey* (*Get Acquainted with Japan*), is a popular periodical for broad public.

Since 1991 there has been a radical shift in the writings of the Russian Asia Pacific experts. While previously their primary orientation was on publications in Russian, recently the majority of their writings have been devoted to foreign journals and books. A predominant part of these have been published in the United States, followed by Japan in the second position, which is followed (with a big gap) by South Korea. Part of the reason is economic. Another point is that when they do publish in Russia, they do not count on economic returns, but rather aim at political effect. Hence, they prefer weekly journals (*New Times*) and academic magazines that have long lead-time (two to six months) and narrow distribution.

One can note that at present some prominent Soviet/Russian Orientalists undergo not only a financial but also a prolonged creative crisis. Former functionaries of CPSU Central Committee, which supervised the Asia Pacific region and relevant activities of academic institutions with different degrees of liberalism, have lost comfortable and privileged positions. Earlier they easily got valuable materials, information from a wide range of sources (including classified papers from academic quarters) and had easy access to periodicals and publishing houses. Foreign trips presented no problem. But now, put on equal footing with the "ordinary" scientific colleagues, many of them are unable to reaffirm their competence and ability to work in new conditions. However, some experts from the former Central Committee have successfully reintegrated into the Foreign Ministry or taken up important positions in the mass media.

The quality of Russian Asia Pacific security studies is significantly undermined by inadequate access to foreign publications. Due to the lack of financial support, libraries can no longer acquire a large variety of foreign publications. The situation is also aggravated by the collapse of a relatively well-developed system of interlibrary exchange, in which foreign books and journals were received in exchange for Russian periodicals and monographs. This is partially explained by the policy of journals, including *MEiMO* and *SShA*, which, seeking higher incomes from sales abroad, refrain from further participation in the exchange. As a result, Russian libraries most often do not receive foreign periodicals, and the journals are no longer delivered to academic consumers abroad.

## Principal Needs for the Future

Future developments in Asia Pacific studies will be largely determined by an ability to solve two main problems: the overcoming of the recent lack of financial resources and the reviving and improving of access to decision makers. The solution to both problems would not be possible without changes in the governmental policy towards academic research in general.

An inadequate number of trained specialists in postgraduate schools as well as difficulties in recruiting university graduates to research centers leads inevitably to the aging of the Russian Asia Pacific studies community. However, the continuing influx of young people to universities, which provide the basic training of regional specialists, together with availability of middle generation experts, leaves some hope that the APR studies many survive another three to five years without irreversible consequences.

The training system also faces significant problems. This is why the goal of keeping the already achieved level seems to universities more practical than plans for raising it further. Nevertheless, the system needs serious improvement. Education in the field of modern political and security studies is still at an initial stage. Lack of professors on the subjects could not be corrected immediately: unattractiveness of work in universities severely handicaps recruiting academic security experts for teaching.

New opportunities for training abroad have already become an important factor in the Russian training system. But until recently it had a very limited practical effect on the stability of Asia Pacific studies. Existing short-term exchange programs for university students and postgraduates, as well as fellowships for younger experts, with all their undoubted importance, would hardly solve the main problem: highly insufficient salaries in academic science against much higher and more easily gained incomes in business (particularly against the background of prices and inflation). The severe environment for academic studies in Russia gives few illusions that the best students and postgraduates, wanting to receive their diploma abroad, would ever return back.

Increasingly, domestic instability might further remove the decision makers' attention from competent academic analysis in the security field. If democratic development is halted, or even diverted, and the power of the executive branch is extended, the role and prerogatives of the security ministries (defense, security) would certainly increase. Past experience demonstrates that it may lead to a policy of squeezing out or downplaying the role of academic competitors in the area of security analysis. Conversely, if the domestic situation develops toward the establishment of viable democratic, and in particular, parliamentary institutions, one should expect a higher demand for academic expertise.

In the coming years it would be unrealistic to foresee any expansion in Asia Pacific security studies. A more realistic aim is to secure the survival of existing research centers with the best scholars by preventing the emigration of middle-aged and younger experts, and through keeping sufficient opportunities for international contacts, publications, and access to decision makers, thus establishing a more attractive environment for recruiting graduates and postgraduates. In this respect, it would be useful to create an international network, which might be able to provide support for Russian (and other states') Asia Pacific experts. Its activities might be aimed at the creation of a more favorable moral and financial environment for experts working in Russia. This may be done by sponsoring individual research projects undertaken by Russian and foreign experts. Another direction could be in providing sufficient support for Russian libraries and research centers to subscribe to foreign periodicals and academic literature, covering expenses for participation in conferences and seminars, and promotion of the educational activity of academic security experts by individual stipends, or by helping with the acquisition of computers, fax machines, copiers, and e-mail equipment, which are now too expensive for Russian scholars to purchase on their own. This help could also be shown in the form of grants.

Special attention should be given to postgraduates and younger experts. They do not enjoy sufficient scientific contacts to permit them to earn money through publications abroad or to participate in joint research projects. This means more active efforts in promoting publishing activities of young scholars, sponsoring their conferences and seminars and financing trips abroad for collecting research materials for their dissertations.

## Notes

1. The author is deeply grateful for information, advice and valuable comments to G. Chufrin, S. Chugrov, E. Grebenshikov, V. Lukin, A. Nagornyi and M. Nosov. This paper was also greatly facilitated by the research and technical assistance of K. Alexandrov, S. Goriacheva, A. Pikaev, V. Vladimirov and Zh. Shatilova.

2. V. Pikul, *In the Backyard of the Great Empire* (Moscow: Khudozhestvennaya Literature, 1978).

3. V.G. Leshke, *Japanese-American Alliance: Results of Three Decades* (Moscow: Nauka, 1983) (in Russian).

4. V.I. Ivanov and K.V. Malakhovsky, eds., *Pacific Regionalism: Concepts and Reality* (Moscow: Nauka, 1983) (in Russian).

5. For example, see T.N. Kaul, "Problems of Asian Security", *Problemy Dal'nego Vostoka*, 1987, no. 4, pp.14–21. Also see V. Vorontsov and A. Muradyan, "Security in the Asia Pacific Region—Concepts and Reality," *Problemy Dal'nego Vostoka*, 1989, no. 6, pp.15–27 (in Russian).

6. For a modernized version of *perestroika* propaganda see *Pacific Security, International Council for Peace and Disarmament* (Moscow: Main Editorial office for Foreign Countries, Nauka, 1987), in cooperation with the Soviet Peace Fund (in Russian, English, Spanish, German, French).

7. "Asian Security," Ye. Primakov, ed., and A. Vlasov, project manager, *What Is What in the World Policy? Directory* (Moscow: Progress Publishing House, 1987), pp. 20–22 (in Russian).

8. See Ye. Primakov, ed., and A. Vlasov, project manager, "Disarmament and Security," IMEMO Yearbook, 1986, part 4, Moscow, APN, 1987; Yearbook 1987, part 8, Moscow, APN, 1988; Yearbook 1988–1989, part 7, Moscow, APN, 1990.

9. See V. Petrovsky, "Soviet Concept of Universal Security," *MEiMO*, June 1986, no. 6, pp. 19–34 (in Russian).

10. As an early example see V. Lukin, "Pacific Direction of International Policy," *MEiMO*, November 1986, no.11, pp. 65–75 (in Russian). Also see G. Apalin "Asia Pacific Region—Peace and Security, New Approach," *International Life*, May 1986, pp. 30–35 (cit. from Russian version).

11. Some illustrations to that can be found in *From the Cold War to Trilateral Cooperation in Asia Pacific Region* (Moscow: Nauka, 1993). See also N. Simoniya, "On Definition of National State Security," *Problemy Dal'nego Vostoka*, Moscow, 1993, no. 2, pp. 3–14 (in Russian).

12. For example, see I.D. Ivanov, I.A. Lebedev, N.V. Shaskolsky et al., *Pacific Community, Plans and Prospects* ( Moscow: Nauka, 1987 ) (in Russian—and [short version] English).

13. In 1986 his book received much publicity. See R.-Sh. A. Aliyev. *Foreign policy of Japan in 1970s–Early 1980s: Theory and Practice.* (Moscow: Nauka, 1986) (in Russian).

14. See "Disarmament and Security," IMEMO Yearbooks 1986, 1987, 1988–1989, 1992.

15. See M. Titarenko and L. Kulik, "Russia's Foreign Policy: Far Eastern Vector," *Problemy Dal'nego Vostoka*, 1993, no. 1, pp. 14–28 (in Russian).

16. For the unclassified digest version of the report, see A. Arbatov and B. Makeev, "The Kurile Barrier," *New Times*, no. 43, October 1992, pp. 24–25 (in English).

17. S.I. Verbitsky *Japan: Searching a New Role in World Policy* (Moscow: Nauka, 1992) (in Russian).

# Asia Pacific Security Studies in Taiwan

LEE LAI TO[1]

## Introduction

After its debacle in the mainland, the KMT government in Taipei has been constantly reminded of the Communist threat from the other side. The seige mentality and the ensuing Cold War in the Asia Pacific no doubt had governed for a long time the study of security issues in the island. For one thing, security studies and concerns were mainly the purview of the KMT government, particularly the military. For another, the focus of analysis was mainly national security. Under martial law and Temporary Provisions Effective During the Period of Communist Rebellion, the KMT government had to take stock of the security situation in Taiwan as well as in the mainland in order not to incur more setbacks and military upsets. Uppermost in the minds of the security specialists in the KMT government were Beijing's troop movements, military strength and related defense and intelligence issues. In that connection, Taipei's defense aids from the United States, the Mutual Defense Treaty with the United States and politics in Washington, especially issues on US policy towards Asia, were of great concerns and had been given due attention in Taiwan.

As expected, most of the studies done by the KMT government, particularly those from the defense establishment, were kept confidential. And for works on security studies published openly, they were obviously influenced by the concerns of the government. Thus, the Asia Pacific security studies were firstly narrow in scope in that the major concern was mainland China or the Communist threat. Secondly, the anti-Communist stand quite naturally gave rise to publications tainted heavily by Cold War rhetoric. Thirdly, the works demonstrated very little interest in theoretical analysis and the practical value of the studies was heavily emphasized. By and large, they surveyed international, regional and Chinese affairs and special attention was directed at military-security and particularly Communist issues of the day.

While the concern with the Communist threat from the mainland remains constant even today, Taiwan's security strategy underwent dramatic changes starting from the 1970s. The reliance on and alliance with the United States were visibly shaken by Nixon's visit to Beijing in 1972, the normalization of Sino-American relations and the termination of the 1954 Mutual Defense Treaty in the Carter administration. In spite of the assurance from Washington, the legislation of the Taiwan Relations Act and the desire of Taipei to continue considering the United States as an ally, the KMT government began to explore other security options by diversifying its sources of arms supplies and pursuing what is dubbed as "substantive" or flexible diplomacy with as many countries as possible after the derecognition shock from Washington.[2] With remarkable growth starting from the 1970s, there was also a rise of Taipei's "dollar" diplomacy to win more friends. Taiwan's growing prominence as one of the major newly industrialized economies and its dependence on international trade and foreign investments also drove home the message that it had to pay relatively more attention to other parts of the world besides East Asia. The rise of the Pacific Basin as the future growth area and the participation of Taipei in regional forums like the Pacific Trade and Development Conference (PAFTAD), Pacific Basin Economic Council (PBEC), Pacific Economic Cooperation Council (PECC), the Asia Pacific Economic Cooperation (APEC) forum, highlighted the importance of paying due attention to the Asia Pacific.[3] This is especially true in the post–Cold War era when economic interdependence in the Asia Pacific will be more pronounced. In view of the moves to promote political and security dialogues and the importance of maintaining peace and stability for development in the region, Taiwan also joined the chorus of suggestions for confidence building measures. Notably, it had made known that it favored a collective security system in the Asia Pacific and would use its economic muscle to support such an arrangement.[4] In fact, President Lee Teng-hui suggested establishing a collective security protection fund with donations from countries concerned, presumably including Taipei, in order to maintain collective security and reduce the arms race in the region.[5] The suggestion was mooted probably by the diminished economic resources of the United States to play a leading role in Asia Pacific security and Taipei's desire to help keep American military presence in Asia in the post–Cold War era.[6]

Domestically, winds of change also seem to have swept Taiwan notably from the late 1980s. Its economic successes in the 1970s and 1980s witnessed the concomitant demands for political participation and liberalization which naturally questioned various governmental restrictions. Under Chiang Kai-shek and especially Chiang Ching-kuo, a process of localization or Taiwanization was put in place. The diminished international support and fear of not getting enough support domestically to stay in power probably forced the KMT government to adjust its policies at home. The growing desire for democratization and the rise of the opposition, especially the Democratic Progressive Party (DPP), would question the propriety of the government, particularly the military, in monopolizing and keeping a firm grip on security matters. After the lifting of martial law in 1987 and with more opposition members voted into various elected bodies, there is added pressure for the government, notably the Ministry of National Defense, to be more accountable for their activities. Probably, the civilianization of the Ministry of National Defense in recent years, i.e., the appointment of two civilians, Chen Li-an and Sun Chen as Defense Ministers, has also contributed to the opening up of opportunities to study and debate on security issues. In view of the changing international, regional and domestic scenes, there is also growing realization of the need to solicit more help and do more in security because of the complexities and comprehensiveness of the issues involved. The concerns and interests in security issues and studies were demonstrated vividly by the publications of defense reviews or white papers written by individuals and most important of all, the Ministry of National Defense.[7] For the latter, the publication of *1992 National Defense Report* served as a landmark in the study of security issues, including Asia Pacific security studies.

The changing political scenes have also affected relations between the two sides of the Taiwan Strait. While it is beyond the scope of this study to examine PRC-Taiwan relations per se, it remains to be emphasized that such relations no doubt have been and will be shaping security studies, including Asia Pacific studies, in the island.[8] While clinging onto what was termed by Soong Chang-chi, the defense minister then, as the doctrine of "strategic defense" in the early 1980s,[9] it was clear that starting from the later years of Chiang Chiang-kuo, Taiwan has been readjusting its policy towards the mainland. As analyzed by the author elsewhere, the adjustment to condone indirect and unofficial interactions between the two sides of the Taiwan Strait were not so much a response to the "peaceful offensive" mapped out by Beijing to reunify China, but more of a need to introduce political reforms to consolidate the power of the KMT in Taipei in view of the increasingly diversified and pluralistic society in Taiwan.[10] The adjustment, notably the sanctioning of visits to the mainland, indirect sociocultural exchanges and economic interactions between the two sides of the Taiwan Strait, has by and large made the "three-no policy" meaningless. The change was made on the principle that the security of Taiwan and the power of the KMT government, including its ability to conduct its de facto "one country, two governments" policy, would not be affected. Nevertheless, the "China fever," as exemplified by the increasing interactions between the two sides since the lifting of the ban to visit the mainland in late 1987 has not only increased the importance and convenience of conducting research on contemporary China by the KMT government, but has also aroused the interests of the public and academic institutions to branch into "China watching." The abolition of the 43-year-old Temporary Provisions Effective During the Period of Communist Rebellion and thereby the termination of the National Mobilization Period in May 1991 further fueled and emboldened the desire to pay much more attention to the other side of the Taiwan Strait. Judging from the plethora of articles on China in popular and professional publications and budding programs on China in some of the universities in Taiwan, it seems that Contemporary Chinese studies have been given added importance and that there is certainly a demand for people familiar with China for political, economic and other reasons.

With the dawning of the post–Cold War era, the dramatic changes towards a more democratic government in Taiwan, and the relaxation towards interactions between Beijing and Taipei, it seems that there is now a gradual recognition in Taiwan, whether in the official or private circle, that the concept of security should be given a much broader definition. It follows that a more comprehensive understanding of security by looking into not only political, military and strategic issues but also socioeconomic and cultural factors will become more and more acceptable. It could be anticipated that there would be more broad-based security research in Taiwan. While Taipei continues to be occupied with the China threat and spend disproportionate manpower and resources on Contemporary Chinese studies, its involvement in regional economic organizations and its battle to fight for a place in the international community and the United Nations no doubt will force it to be outward looking. This would probably broaden its research interests on subregional, regional and international developments. This is particularly true in studies on political economy, be they on the Greater Chinese Economic Circle, regional economic organizations and cooperation in the Asia Pacific or other issues.

## The Major Research Institutions

While the KMT government, particularly the Party, the Ministry of National Defense and National Security Council and National Security Bureau, has research organizations on security, including Asia Pacific security, its activities are, as usual, cloaked by a veil of secrecy. The sensitivity and confidentiality of many of the works, particularly those related to intelligence and the operational side of security studies are still off-limits to most researchers. Nevertheless, the educational arm of these security-related organizations, notably the College of Political Warfare and institutions under some ministries, notably the Ministry of National Defense, do publish periodicals or even books for public consumption. In addition, there are more academic bodies in the government dealing with Asia Pacific security research. Ostensibly, some institutes of Academia Sinica, which is under the President's Office, have occasionally done works on the area. The institutes, like the Institute of European and American Studies, formerly the Institute of American Culture, have done some work on, inter alia, Sino-American Studies. In fact, the Institute of European and American Studies has its own conference, library and computer facilities for its research staff. It should be emphasized that no institutes in Academia Sinica are conducting specific research on security studies and that the academy as a whole excels more in scholarship and academic attainment in a wide range of subjects. For institutes which are seriously concerned with Asia Pacific security studies, the most established organization is the Institute of International Relations (IIR) which has been formally affiliated with the National Chengchi University since 1975. The research staff of the IIR are divided into four groups, namely, international affairs, Chinese Communist affairs, international Communist affairs and economic affairs. With the dissolution of the Soviet Union and changes in Eastern Europe and the research done elsewhere by other institutes on economic issues in Taiwan, the two groups on international Communist affairs and economic affairs at the IIR are quite small and by comparison, the two groups on international affairs and Chinese Communist affairs are much bigger in size. Quite naturally, the latter two groups are the backbone of the research staff of the institute and are most relevant to Asia Pacific security studies. Most of the IIR research staff have advanced degrees notably from Taiwan, the United States, Japan, Korea and Europe. And a majority of the new staff have received their PhDs.[11] Besides conference facilities, the institute has a library which is well stocked with materials on mainland China and Taiwan. These materials include newspaper clippings and a lot of primary sources on the study of Contemporary China. The institute is one of the best research centers in the study of Chinese Communism and the largest research center for international relations in Taiwan. Its research findings are partly released in books, monographs, occasional papers and periodicals in English and Chinese. It also prepares background papers for the various ministries, notably the Ministry of Foreign Affairs. In their individual capacities, selected members of the institute serve as advisers of various committees in the government. Another research organization which could be considered to be interested in Asia Pacific security studies is the Society for Strategic Studies. Founded and headed by General Chiang Wego since 1979, the society has branches in major cities in Taiwan and even a branch in the United States. Of its more than one thousand members, 30 percent comes from the academic community, the private sector and the military respectively. The remaining 10 percent are from the press, the police and other professionals. The society has extensive links with other like-minded institutes in other parts of the world. Its research interests can be divided into political, economic, psychological and military affairs. The results of these research efforts can be found in the quarterly and monographs published by the society. One more research institute which is related to Asia Pacific security studies is the Asia and World Institute (AWI) started by Han Li-wu in 1976 and presently headed by John Kuan. The research interests of the AWI are Asian and international affairs, Chinese history and politics and Taiwan's developmental experience. It also had some interests in the security of the sea lanes in the Asia Pacific. Its publications include the AWI Monographic Series, AWI Lectures and Essays Series, and a periodical that is entitled *Asia and World Digest*.[12]

With the advent of the 1980s, at least two more up-and-coming research organizations began to make their presence felt in the area of Asia Pacific security studies. The first was the Sun Yat-sen Center for Policy Studies (SCPS) located at the National Sun Yat-sen University and founded by the former University President Lee Huan in November 1984. In addition to the study of the modernization of China according to the thought of Sun Yat-sen, the SCPS was interested in studying the economic cooperation, regional stability and security of the Asia Pacific.[13] A majority of the researchers at the SCPS held PhD degrees from American, European and Japanese universities. Their research was facilitated by the computerized information and facilities at the center. The center has organized a number of workshops related to Asia Pacific security and the most important one since its inception has been the Workshop on People's Liberation Army (PLA) Affairs. Out of this successful workshop, the SCPS decided to publish the papers in a *Yearbook on PLA Affairs*. As the academic activities of the center began to grow rapidly, there was a decision to reorganize SCPS into the Chinese Council of Advanced Policy Studies (CAPS) in 1992. To facilitate its work and coordination with scholars at home and abroad, CAPS set up an office in a well-located building in Taipei in 1992.[14] Another think tank which has sprung into prominence recently is the Institute for National Policy Research (INPR). Established in 1989 and funded by the Chang Yung-fa Foundation, the INPR is a major research organization in the private sector. Although the leadership of the institute is known to have links with the government, including President Lee Teng-hui, the institute considers itself to be reformist but not radical in orientation. As a result, its views could be considered both by the KMT as well as the opposition.[15] It must be added that the bulk of the resources of the INPR is spent more on the analysis of domestic issues. This is reflected by its publications which include, among other things, a biweekly called *National Policy Dynamic Analysis*. More related to Asia Pacific security studies is the Committee on Asia Pacific Studies in the INPR. Established in 1989, the committee is interested specifically in the political and economic developments in the Asia Pacific and security of the region. The committee had a small research team of eleven members by late 1993 and is guided by Professors Hsu Chieh-lin and Shiau Chyuan-jenq from the Department of Political Science of National Taiwan University.[16] Two of its members are doing research on defense with special reference to the situation in mainland China. However, from the publications of the committee, it seems that it has tried to take a much broader view of Asia Pacific security as analyzed in the next section.

Because of the significance of economics in security, the relevance of political economy or international political economy to the study of security issues and the need to have a more comprehensive understanding of security, some of the think tanks on economic research are most relevant to Asia Pacific security studies in Taiwan. The vibrance of the economy and the need to use economic links to further its diplomatic interests in view of its lack of official ties with many countries in the Asia Pacific would also propel Taiwan to pay more attention to economic diplomacy and spend more resources on research organizations to help Taiwan find a niche in the region. In this regard, at least two economic research organizations should be noted. The first one is the Taiwan Institute of Economic Research (TIER). Established in 1976 as a private and independent economic research organization, the institute is interested in conducting research on finance, taxation, trade, investment, and various economic issues.[17] It is also in charge of the secretariat activities of the Chinese Member Committee of the Pacific Basin Economic Council in Taipei and the Chinese Taipei Pacific Economic Cooperation Committee. This feature undoubtedly increases the relevance of its work to Asia Pacific studies, including the studies on security issues. Quite obviously, the TIER collaborates closely with the committees mentioned earlier in its research and activities on the Asia Pacific.

Another major think tank on economic research is the Chung-hua Institution for Economic Research (CIER). Established in 1981 and funded partly by the government and the private sector initially, the institution carries out research on Taiwan, mainland China and international economics.[18] Its research findings are highly respected, especially those on contemporary China. The institution is known to have been commissioned to undertake various projects on economics. Between 1981 to 1991, it completed eighty such projects which yielded a total of 247 reports.[19]

In addition to the above major research organizations which work on Asia Pacific security studies in Taiwan, there are a number of other institutes, associations, and university centers, programs or institutes notably at Tamkang University, National Chengchi University, Chinese Culture University and National Taiwan University, which are interested in promoting Asia Pacific studies. Some of their publications do bear relevance to security issues and will be analyzed in the following section.

For the major institutes in Taiwan, especially those mentioned earlier, there are regular and irregular activities to build up links with like-minded research organizations and individual scholars elsewhere. These could include the sponsoring of international conferences, lectures, workshops, seminars, symposiums and the like. In fact, some institutes have institutionalized these functions by having such meetings held alternately in Taiwan and research organizations in the collaborating countries. A good example are the ones organized by the IIR. These include regular conferences with selected research organizations in the United States, Japan, Korea and Europe. On top of these, some of the institutes may be affiliated with research institutions elsewhere. They may also have exchange programs or visits with like-minded institutes in other places. While these may promote scholarship and deepen mutual understanding of international, regional, national and security issues, it is quite obvious that the activities are related to academic diplomacy and that they could be used to promote Taiwan's friendship and relations with the outside world in view of its diplomatic isolation. Moreover, with economic success, there is a blossoming of a number of foundations to support the activities. These foundations include the Chiang Ching-kuo Foundation for International Scholarly Exchange, Chang Yung-fa Foundation, Foundation for Scholarly Exchange, Pacific Cultural Foundation, 21st Century Foundation, Taiwan Research Fund, United Daily News Cultural Foundation, China Times Cultural Foundation, to name just a few. Chances are, funding for worthwhile projects and activities will be available, thus helping, among other things, the promotion of Asia Pacific security studies.

## The Literature

As a Chinese territory, it is natural that the bulk of the publications on Asia Pacific security studies, or for that matter, area studies, in Taiwan, are in Chinese. Nevertheless, from the publications kept in the National Central Library and libraries of major research institutes, there are a few publications of some importance in English.[20] Notably, the list of periodicals on Asia Pacific studies and/or area studies related to the region includes English journals like *Issues and Studies* (monthly) published by the IIR, *Sino-American Relations* (quarterly) published by The Chinese Culture University in cooperation with the China Academy, *Tamkang Journal of American Studies* (quarterly) and *Area Studies* (quarterly) published by Tamkang University and others. A more recent but up-and-coming periodical in English is *China's Military: The People's Liberation Army (PLA)*, initially published by the Sun Yat-sen Center for Policy Studies (SCPS) of National Sun Yat-sen University in 1991 and later on Chinese Council of Advanced Policy Studies (CAPS) when SCPS was expanded to form the CAPS in 1992. It should also be noted that there are always bilingual publications in Taiwan. A notable example as far as journals are concerned is the *American Studies* (renamed *Euramerica* since 1991) published by the Institute of American Culture (renamed Institute of European and American Studies since 1991) of Academia Sinica, the premiere research institution under the President's Office in Taiwan. It should be emphasized that for these English periodicals, the contributors are not necessarily from Taiwan. In fact, a majority of the contributors are foreign scholars and that for most security specialists in Taiwan, they prefer to write in Chinese. As a result, it is the literature in Chinese that best reflects the state of Asia Pacific security studies in Taiwan.

A survey of the publications, especially periodicals in Chinese, would reveal first that there were not many works on Asia Pacific security studies in the early years. Nonetheless, special agencies in the KMT and its government, notably those in the Ministry of National Defense, have been monitoring the developments by conducting intelligence-gathering activities with special emphasis on the mainland since the establishment of the KMT government in Taipei. The concern with subversions and armed attacks by the communists would suggest that there must be many reports and analyses on various aspects of mainland China based on the intelligence gathered. The studies could also make use of other sources like mainland Chinese newspapers, magazines, radio broadcasts, interviews with refugees and defectors and others. Efforts were also made to translate selected works on security into Chinese. Quitely obviously, these sources, especially the primary sources from China and first-hand intelligence information gathered by Taipei are rarely made available to the public.[21] Nevertheless, there were a few publications available for public consumption. Notably there were works on the study of security and strategic thinking of Sun Yat-sen and Chiang Kai-shek. In addition, a respectable journal, *Wen-ti Yu Yen-chiu* (*Issues and Studies*) published monthly by the Institue of International Relations of National Chengchi University since October 1961, has a disproportionate amount of articles on area studies, including security studies of the Asia Pacific. Other think tanks or organizations with official links and interests on defense and strategic matters could also have publications on security studies of the regoin. These could include, among other things, *Chung-hua Chan-lueh Hsueh-kan* (*Journal of Chinese Strategic Studies*, quarterly) of the Society for Strategic Studies, publications of the College of Political Warfare and others.

Second, and as expected, there is a disproportionate number of publications on contemporary China. In fact, there are quite a number of periodicals devoted mainly to that subject. These include *Chung-kung Yen-chiu* (*Studies on Chinese Communism*) and its *Chung-kung Nien-pao* (*Yearbook on Chinese Communism*) , *Mainland China Studies* (formerly known as *Fei-ching Yueh-pao*), *Mainland China Monthly*, *Kung-tang Wen-ti Yen-chiu* (*Studies of Communist Problems*) and others. In addition, there are many other publications, both popular and professional ones, which have a disproportionate emphasis on contemporary Chinese affairs. While it is difficult to generalize the articles on mainland China, there was a tendency for these studies to be tainted by Cold War rhetoric. Notably, the articles in *Wen-ti Yu Yen-chiu* referred to Peking as "Peiping," the PRC as "bandit area" and Mao and other Communist leaders in derogatory terms. Such rhetoric persisted in the publication well beyond the Sino-American détente until at least the late 1970s. As noted by a study of mainland China studies in Taiwan and the United States, there was also a tendency for the specialists in Taiwan to emphasize the dominance of leading personalities like Mao in China, factional struggles, destruction of Chinese values and traditions by the Communists and the totalitarian and authoritarian nature of the Communist regime.[22] With the passage of time and the emergence of new generations of China watchers in Taipei, a more balanced and realistic coverage and assessment of the mainland is emerging. This is especially true after the lifting of martial law and the ban on visits to the mainland in the late 1980s. The familiarity of the specialists with the Chinese language, culture, history, ideology and their training in social sciences, could upgrade mainland Chinese studies in Taiwan.

While the Chinese literature on Asia Pacific security studies remains to be dominated by the national security concerns, particularly the Communist threat from the other side of the Taiwan Strait, it does show some interest in examining developments elsewhere in the region. This is reflected by the scholarship in Soviet, American, Japanese and Korean studies. For Soviet studies in Taiwan, its beginning probably had to do with Peking's close relations with Moscow in the early years. Specialists on Chinese Communism also found it necessary and convenient to watch developments in the former Soviet Union in order to understand Peking's moves. Even after the Sino-Soviet split, interests in Soviet studies seemed unabated as evidenced by the publication of quite a number of these articles in publications like *Wen-ti Yu Yen-chiu* and specialized journals like *Soo-er Wen-ti Yen-chiu* (*The Study of Soviet Russian Problems*). The meticulous analysis in some of these articles demonstrated that Taiwan has a respectable collection of materials on Soviet studies. With the disintegration of the Soviet Union, the specialists will probably have to adjust their research interests to new developments. As for American studies, the close US-Taiwan strategic and economic relations no doubt have paved the way for its development in the island. In addition to the English publications mentioned earlier, the Chinese literature in this area include books, monographs, and more importantly perhaps, articles in specialized Chinese journals like *Mei-kuo Yueh-kan* (*American Monthly*), *Euramerica* (partly in Chinese) and *Chung-mei Yueh-kan* (*Sino-American Monthly*). Articles on the United States are also readily published in a wide range of professional and popular journals and magazines. Scholars and other professionals also seem to have a special interest in Japan. In fact, quite a number of Taiwan residents of the older generations could understand and speak Japanese because of the colonial rule of Tokyo before the end of the Second World War. The political and especially economic significance of Japan for Taiwan naturally would have promoted Japanese studies at least to a certain extent. On top of the many articles in political, economic and security journals and other periodicals, there are specialized journals on Japan like the *Jih-pen Yen-chiu* (*Japan Studies*), a monthly published by the Chung-jih Kuan-hsi Yen-chiu Hui (Society for the Research on Sino-Japanese Relations), *Japanese Journal*, an annual publication of the Japanese Studies Association in Taiwan, *China and Japan*, a quarterly published by the Japan Research Office of the Sino-Japanese Cultural and Economic Association and others.[23] Besides, there are occasional publications from Japanese studies centers at major academic institutions like the Graduate Institute of Japanese Studies of Tamkang University and Japanese Research Center of National Taiwan University. As for Korean studies, the common concern with the Communist threat, especially in the Cold War period, Sinicism in both areas and economic interactions between Seoul and Taipei could have sparked some interests in developments in the Korean peninsula and Sino-Korean relations in Taiwan. Notably, there are institutes, like the Institute of Korean Studies of the

Chinese Culture University, Graduate Institute of Korean Studies of Tamkang University and associations like the Chinese Association for Korean Studies and Sino-Korean Economic Cooperation Association, which specialize and publish on various aspects of Korea. The regular publications include, among other things, *Han-kuo Yen-chiu (Korean Studies)* and *Han-wen Hui-kan, (A Compilation of Korean Studies)* published annually by the Institute of Korean Studies of the Chinese Culture University, *Korean Studies*, published annually by the Chinese Association of Korean Studies and *The Sino-Korean Report* published by the Sino-Korean Cooperation Association.

It should be emphasized firstly that the above area studies cover not only security studies but also other aspects related to the area. Secondly, the security-related studies are, as a rule, not really that interested in theoretical analysis. Thirdly, while there may be publications and associations on Southeast Asia and other parts of the Asia Pacific, it is clear that the security studies in Taiwan pay by far much more attention to Northeast Asia (China, Japan and Korea), especially mainland China, the former Soviet Union, and members of the Commonwealth of Independent States (CIS), especially Russia, and the United States. While the publications may touch upon the Asia Pacific in a general way, the attention of the area studies is naturally concerned with one country, or at the most, a subregion in the Asia Pacific. And even if they touch upon the Asia Pacific, it seems that the thinking of quite a number of authors was, and still is, that Northeast Asia, meaning Japan, Korea and two sides of the Taiwan Strait and Southeast Asia should be considered the Asia Pacific. As noted before, of the two subregions, there is much more emphasis on Northeast Asia, particularly China. Countries like the United States, the former Soviet Union (later on Russia), the CIS and India are treated separately in Asia Pacific security. These may not be looked upon as part of the Asia Pacific, but as crucial and/or relevant factors in the analysis of Asia Pacific security.[24]

With the changed domestic, regional and international environment, especially starting from the 1980s as noted earlier, the literature on security studies began to grow, albeit gradually at the very beginning. More books, including translated ones, on military and defense studies began to be available in book stores and libraries. The scope in Asia Pacific security studies also began to be widened. Notably, economic issues began to take more prominence in these analyses than before. This was probably due to the impact of Taipei's participation in regional economic organizations like PBEC, PECC, APEC and others. In fact, as far as Asia Pacific studies were concerned, there was a rise of some prominent institutes specializing in economic research. As noted before, these include the Taiwan Institute of Economic Research (TIER) which houses Taipei's committees for the PECC and PBEC. The TIER, together with Taipei's committees of PECC and PBEC, has published a lot of works not only on Taiwan itself, but also on many other aspects related to the economic cooperation in the Asia Pacific.[25] Likewise, the Chung-Hua Institution for Economic Research (CIER) has produced many works on economic issues, especially those related to Taiwan and mainland China.[26]

The growing consciousness to broaden the analysis in Asia Pacific studies, including security studies was probably best exemplified by the works of the

Committee on Asia-Pacific Studies of the Institute for National Policy Research (INPR) set up in 1989. The research emphases of the committee are political and economic developments in the Asia Pacific countries and security of the Asia Pacific region. It has published policy papers and monographs on various aspects of the region.[27] Among these, it has compiled all the materials related to the Asia Pacific economic and political developments and published them in a book entitled *Ya-tai Tzu-liao Chi (A Collection of Materials on the Asia Pacific)*.[28] More interestingly, selected members of the committee have published a book on *Tai-wan te Ya-tai Chan-lueh (Taiwan's Asian-Pacific Strategy)* emphasizing, among other things, the salience of economics in security.[29] The work shows its marked difference with those dealing with just defense and military issues and demonstrates vividly the broadening of the concept of security.

The increasing literature on Asia Pacific security studies was also augmented by works produced by some think tanks like those published by the Asia and World Institute whose research interests include Asian and international affairs, Chinese history and politics and Taiwan's own developmental experience.[30] The large number of law journals, university journals (general journals for the whole university) or studies of San-min Chu-yi (The Three Principles of Sun Yat-sen) could also have studies on aspects of Asia Pacific security.

## Concluding Observations

In surveying the state of Asia Pacific security studies in Taiwan, one cannot help but notice the lack of conceptual clarity with regard to the definition of the field and some of the terms. Notably, while there may be indications showing that there is a broadening of the definition of the term "Asia Pacific," there is still a tendency for many to confine the term to Northeast Asia and Southeast Asia. And for the field of strategic studies or security studies, there are different emphases in their analyses, ranging from those which are mainly concerned with military or defense-related issues to those which are much more willing to dabble at political, diplomatic, economic, social and other issues related to strategic or security studies. The lack of conceptual clarity could be attributed partially to the fact that Asia Pacific security studies in Taiwan have not so far demonstrated much interest in theoretical and conceptual analysis. By and large, the studies are more on empirical research and policy studies.

For the empirical and policy studies, it is clear that the most important area of concern is mainland China as noted before. Taiwan's strength in the area, that is, in terms of research facilities, financial support both from the public and private sectors, plus the language training programs for foreigners interested in contemporary China, would make it one of the best places to study China. After years of mutual suspicion and hostility, it seems that the ice is beginning to break with recent exchanges between the two sides of the Taiwan Strait, albeit on an indirect and unofficial level as insisted officially by the KMT government. It must be emphasized that although initial steps have been taken by Taiwan to invite mainlanders from think tanks and academic institutions to visit the island and that many more Taiwanese have been to the PRC, it remains to be seen if security specialists from both sides of the Taiwan Strait will meet either within China (mainland China and Taiwan) or in third countries formally or informally. At the moment, both sides have great reservations in doing so and seem to be extremely cautious in having such encounters, at least officially.

The strength of Taiwan in Contemporary Chinese studies is in a way exactly the weakness of its present state of Asia Pacific security studies. Because of its concern with its national security and the threat from the other side of the Taiwan Strait, there is a tendency to pay relatively less attention to other parts of the Asia Pacific. Even if one confines security studies to Northeast Asia and Southeast Asia, it is quite obvious that there is room for improvement in the study of security issues of Southeast Asia, not to say that of countries like Australia, New Zealand, the South Pacific which may not fall within the definition of the term Asia Pacific in the minds of some security specialists in Taiwan. At a time when Southeast Asia, particularly the countries of the Association of Southeast Asian Nations (ASEAN), are getting more interested and active in security dialogues, it would only be prudent for Taipei to spend relatively more resources and manpower on Southeast Asian studies and promote its links with the subregion.

With the democratization of the Taiwanese polity and the changed international and regional environment in the 1990s, it seems that Asia Pacific security studies in Taiwan will be given relatively more emphasis. The personal interests of President Lee Teng-hui in the Asia Pacific, judging from some of his recent views on the region, could also be a boost to the promotion of such studies.[31] At a time when various suggestions for a security dialogue or framework have been mooted or tested, it could also fire the imagination of security specialists in Taiwan to join the exercise. Probably, more coordination among the major research organizations in Taiwan would be necessary to make better use of its talent and resources and to buttress its expertise on various issues related to Asia Pacific security. In concert with its flexible diplomacy and desire to be more engaged in regional and international affairs, Taiwan will be keen to build up more links with like-minded think tanks or research organizations elsewhere and join various informal or formal security forums , dialogues or organizations.

## Notes

1. I would like to thank Professor Lin Bih-jaw for the extensive help rendered during my two trips to Taipei. This paper has benefited not only from discussions conducted with specialists at the Institute of International Relations but also with leading experts at the Institute for National Policy Research, Institute of European and American Studies, Academia Sinica, Chinese Council of Advanced Policy Studies, Graduate Institute of International Affairs and Strategic Studies, Tamkang University, Armed Forces University, Society for Strategic Studies, Chung-hua Institution for Economic Research, Taiwan Institute of Economic Research and other organizations and individuals. As usual, I alone am responsible for the views expressed here.

2. For details, see Michael Y.M. Kau's section on "Security and Defense Capabilities" in James Hsiung et al., eds., *The Taiwan Experience 1950–1980*, (New York: Praeger Publishers, 1981), pp. 421–94.

3. For an analysis of Taiwan's role in the Asia Pacific economy, see, for example, *Issues and Studies* (Chinese edition), no. 11, vol. 28, August 1989, pp. 1–16; and no. 1, vol. 31, January 1992, pp. 14–30; no. 3, vol. 31, March 1992, pp. 1–9 and pp. 11–24.

4. *Strait Times*, July 11, 1993

5. See Lee Teng-hui, "Asia-Pacific and America," in *Sino-American Relations*, Autumn 1993, pp. 13–14.

6. Ibid., pp. 12–13.

7. For the studies on defense issues, see, for example, the Defense Research Group of the Taiwan Research Fund, *The Defense White Paper* (Taipei: Chien-wei Chu-pan She, 1992). For the government's defense white paper, see *1992 National Defense Report, Rupublic of China* (Taipei: Li Ming Cultural Enterprise Co. Ltd., 1992).

8. For a detailed study of PRC-Taiwan relations, see Lee Lai To, *The Reunification of China — PRC-Taiwan Relations in Flux* (New York: Praeger Publishers, 1991).

9. The Defense Research Group, *1992 National Defense Report*, p. 92.

10. Lee Lai To, *The Reunification of China*, pp. 35–58.

11. The following is based on a conversation with Professor Lin Bih-jaw, director of the Institute of International Relations, National Chengchi University on September 7, 1993.

12. Chyuan-jenq Shiau, Hsu Chieh-lin et al., eds., *Ya-tai Tzu-liao Chi (A Compilation of Materials on the Asia Pacific)*, (Taipei: Institute for National Policy Research, 1991), p. 333.

13. *SCPS Newsletter*, vol. 1, no. 1, July 1988, p. 1.

14. See CAPS, *China's Military, The PLA in 1992/1993* (Taipei: Chinese CAPS, 1993), p. v.

15. That was emphasized to the author in a meeting with the Committee on Asia-Pacific Studies of INPR on September 8, 1993.

16. This is based on a discussion between the author and the Committee on Asia-Pacific Studies of INPR on September 8, 1993.

17. Chyuan-jenq Shiau et al., eds., *Ya-tai Tzu-liao Chi*, pp. 340–41.

18. Ibid., pp. 334–35.

19. For the abstracts of the reports, see Yu Chung-hsien, ed., *Shou-t'o Yen-chiu Pao-kao Chai-yao 1981–1991 (Concise Reports on Commissioned Research Projects, 1981–1991)*, (Taipei: Chung-hua Institution for Economic Research, 1991).

20. This excludes the specialists who come from Taiwan originally but work in the United States presently.

21. Selected intelligence reports are, however, available in institutes closely related to the government, notably the Institute of International Relations.

22. For details, see Tai-chun Kuo and Ramon H. Myers, *Understanding Communist China, Communist China Studies in the United States and the Republic of China, 1949–1978* (Stanford: Hoover Institution Press, 1986), pp. 40–63.

23. Chyuan-jenq Shiau et al., eds., *Ya-tai Tsu-liao Chi*, p. 338.

24. See, for example, the colloquium on "Changes in the Power Relations of the Asia Pacific in the Post–Cold War Era" as published in *Wen-ti Yu Yen-chiu*, vol. 31, no. 7, July 1992, pp. 11–23.

25. For the list of recent publications, see Chyuan-jenq Shiau et al., eds., *Ya-tai Tzu-liao Chi*, pp. 340–41.

26. For details of recent publications of the Institute, see ibid., pp. 334–35.

27. Ibid., pp. 335–36.

28. Ibid.

29. See Hsu Chien-lin, Lee Wen-chi, Shiau Chyuan-jenq, *Tai-wan te Ya-tai Chan-lueh (Taiwan's Asia Pacific Strategy)*, (Taipei: Institute of National Policy Research, 1991).

30. Chyuan-jenq Shiau et al., eds. *Ya-tai Tzu-liao Chi,* p. 333.

31. See, for example, Lee Teng-hui, "Asia-Pacific and America."

# Asia-Pacific Security Studies in the United States

## CHARLES E. MORRISON[1]

The United States, for reasons relating to its Cold War involvement, has been a leading center for research and analysis of Asia-Pacific security issues. These issues have never had the salience of the security issues in Europe nor the closely related discourses on strategic bargaining, nuclear deterrents, or arms control. This is natural in view of the relative absence of traditional close cultural bonds with Asia or a strong perception of linked security (as in Latin America). But since the Korean War, Asia has been regarded as an arena of Cold War conflict that required considerable attention and expertise from Americans. Thus throughout the Cold War, there has been a relatively large apparatus within the US government devoted to the political and military analysis of Asian and Asia-Pacific security issues as well as extensive government funding for developing expertise in these areas outside the public sector.[2] Foundation priorities often mirrored those in the government; most security work was devoted to issues associated with the central balance between the United States and the Soviet Union, but considerable funding was also available for issues relating to the military balance in Northeast Asia and to the security and economic development of developing Asia, these seen as part and parcel of Cold War ideological and superpower competition.

This paper reviews the state of Asia-Pacific security studies in the United States from four principal vantage points. First, what issues have motivated US analyses of security issues? How have these issues been changed and with what implications for the field? Second, what has been the background of the Americans working on Asian security issues? Third, the paper describes the main institutional actors, and finally, it discusses needs in the field and ends in a series of questions concerning the future of Asia-Pacific security studies.

## The Issues — Old and New

For our purposes "security studies" relate to violence or its potential among states in the Asia-Pacific region or internal violence that may affect government survival or vital national interests. Thus our discussion is not confined to "international security." Nor it is limited to such matters as weapons acquisition and strategic doctrine; rather "security" may involve any development, including economic deprivation, environmental degradation, and ethnic nationalism where a clear connection to internal and international violence affecting governmental survival or vital national interests can be drawn.

## Cold War Security Issues

For much of the Cold War period, the motivating interest of much US governmental and nongovernmental security studies in the developing world in general lay in the perceived vulnerability of these societies to Communism. For Asia, this led to several principal research interests: the interest of the Soviet Union and China in projecting their ideologies in the region and their capabilities to do so, the potential for revolution in Asian countries, the factors that affected these countries' strategic alignments with respect to the central Cold War rivalries, and local conflict situations that were being or could be exploited by outsiders. In much of this literature there was an emphasis on prescription—what policies should be taken by the United States or by the non-Communist states themselves to maintain stability and prevent the spread of Communism?

This agenda of issues tended to favor research rooted in "area studies." With some exceptions (by country and period), outright military aggression was not perceived as the main threat to US interests. Particularly in Southeast Asia, the threat was regarded as more internal in nature and this meant that close examination of these societies—their domestic politics, ethnic composition, level of economic dissatisfaction and/or progress—was required. For this kind of research, individuals with area training and, where feasible, language skills were needed. This will be discussed at greater length below.

With some modifications, a similar statement could be made of analysis of the perceived major external threats to the non-Communist Asian countries. Soviet and Chinese weapons capabilities were important, but so were the perceptions of Russians and Chinese toward the region, their connections with and rivalries over the Communist movements in these countries, and the role of overseas Chinese in much of Southeast Asia, all subjects that again directed the discourse on Soviet and Chinese policies in Asia into the realm of area studies.[3]

The concerns with Communism and prescription also encouraged a large literature on economic development. We will not deal with that literature per se since very little of it is directed explicitly toward the problem of prevention or suppression of violence, but it should be noted that the US interest in and funding for economic development analysis and aid programs in East and Southeast Asia was rooted not only in humanitarian concerns, but also in its security interests.

## Asian Security Issues in the 1990s and Twenty-First Century

It is difficult to write with great confidence about how the end of the Cold War will affect US studies of Asia-Pacific security issues, but some preliminary observations can be hazarded. Clearly American perceptions of both the saliency and the nature of the security dilemma in the Asia-Pacific region is changing.

In terms of saliency, there appear to be contradictory trends. With the end of a global threat from Communism, US society as a whole has been much less concerned about security issues in general, including those arising in Asia. On the other hand, the end of the Cold War division in Europe appears to have had the effect of increasing the relative weight of Asia in the US analyses of global security issues. The rapid economic growth of Asia has also increased its strategic importance in American eyes.

A review of the articles in the professional journal, *International Security*, may be instructive. Between 1983 and 1989, this journal gave very limited coverage to Asian security issues—two on Japanese defense strategy in the Winter 1983/84 issues (one of these by a Japanese), and historical pieces on US policy in the Korean War, the Taiwan Straits crisis of 1954–55, and army strategy during the Vietnam War. But between 1990 and 1993, the same journal carried two articles on Chinese arms sales as well as articles on US-Japan relations, Japanese national security policy, the Japanese culture of antimilitarism, and the Chinese ballistic missile programs. Although not an Asian area journal, all but one of these articles were authored by area specialists suggesting the continued dominance of such specialists in the analysis of security issues of the post–Cold War period.

In terms of the nature of the security issues in Asia-Pacific, a review of the public literature suggests the following changes:

1. Many of the perceived threats of the Cold War era have faded. These include the Soviet threat, the Vietnamese threat, the implications of Sino-Soviet rivalry, and insurgency movements in Southeast Asia. And, of course, with their fading, so too has the literature on these subjects. Whereas these and other Asian security issues formerly were usually implicitly or explicitly seen as theaters in a global struggle centered on Europe, there is a growing ability to see the Asian security issues of today in a more detached manner and address them on their own terms.

2. "Threat-based" modes of thinking remain, but with some exceptions, the threats to security are perceived of as jeopardizing the overall tenor of international relations within the region as well as outside it, rather than the national security of specific Asia-Pacific states. Such security concerns include a competitive arms race (China's rapidly increasing defense expenditure and weapons and arms technology acquisitions are frequently cited as a possible triggering cause, particularly if there is a more substantial drawdown of US forces),[4] nuclear proliferation (largely associated with the concern about North Korea's nuclear potential),[5] possible Sino-Japanese competition for influence in third areas,[6] Japanese defense policies and relations with Asia,[7] and arms exports (especially to South Asia and the Middle East).[8] Southeast Asian security problems are in a distinctly secondary category and the South Pacific (a matter of some concern in the mid-1980s when the Russians concluded a couple of fishing agreements with island nations) have dropped out of sight.[9]

3. Following the example of the Soviet Union and several states in Eastern Europe, US security concerns relating to China and North Korea have become more ambivalent. These countries constitute the exceptions, to some degree, to the observation that territorial threats to neighbors have become of less concern. North Korea continues to be perceived as a conventional and

possible future nuclear threat to the South, and there remains concerns that in an extreme case China might use force to assert its claims to territory in the South China Sea or reunify its country. On the other hand, there is also a concern about the potential for disorder in these countries and its possible consequences. The scenario of a contested future succession to the Kim dynasty in North Korea brings fear of widespread disorder, large refugee movements into South Korea or China, appeals for intervention by South Korea, and/or a reemergence of rivalries among outside powers for position in North Korea. Similarly any contestation for leadership in China in the post–Deng era or substantial further weakening of the central authority could lead to considerable instability in China with important ramifications for neighboring countries.

4. There appears to be growing interest in nonconventional security threats, such as economic conflict, population movements, narcotics, transnational environmental problems, and religious and ethnic nationalism contributors to social instability.[10] However, there is relatively little in-depth research systematically and explicitly connnecting such issues to security as defined here.[11]

5. The prescriptive literature has shifted from how to support vulnerable states to questions relating to building a "new regional order," or to use other terminology, from an emphasis on collective security to one on cooperative security. There are several main lines of inquiry: new institutional arrangements and their implications for US policy, modes of dealing bilaterally and multilaterally with the countries that seem least integrated into the regional security dialogues (China, North Korea, Vietnam), and means of addressing problems of arms races and exports.[12]

Many Americans working in the security field see US security commitment and presence as of continuing vital importance to Asia-Pacific stability and security. Indeed, a common concern in much of the prescriptive literature on US policy is how to maintain that commitment. This leads in several different directions— redefinition of the rationale for US presence in terms of more general order maintenance, discussion of possibilities for increased burden sharing of US forces in Asia by allied governments, enhanced Asian contributions to international peacekeeping and the sharing of other "global responsibilities," and accommodation of US economic concerns in order to improve the environment for continued security cooperation and rectify an inequitable division of labor.[13] The implications of the new era for the US military presence in Asia remains a central concern for government policymakers and analysts.[14]

## The Analysts

As suggested earlier, most of the research on Asia-Pacific security issues, especially in the academic sector, has been rooted in the "area studies" tradition rather than that of strategic studies. From the 1950s to 1970s, a large share of those going into Asian area studies had had some formative experience in the region. They were the sons and daughters of missionaries, US diplomats, and US military personnel. Others were Asian-Americans, whose parents or grandparents had lived in the region. Still others were first generation Asianists, with no previous interaction in the region until serving there in the US military, traveling on an exchange program, or (after the 1960s) undertaking a Peace Corps assignment there.

These specialists were generally trained at the major US area centers or international studies programs with considerable area expertise, the centers themselves created under legislation designed to strengthen US knowledge of foreign areas and languages as part of the war against Communism. Because of the investments involved in language learning, area studies programs tended to encourage country specialization rather than broad international relations training. Those specialists who did develop an interest in international relations tended to focus on an aspect of foreign policy of a particular country. In general, area training was not heavily conceptual.

Aside from regional specialists, because of the saliency of Asian wars and policy issues at certain periods during the Cold War, the region did attract the interests of generalists on US foreign policy. Such prominent figures as Henry Kissinger, George Kennan, George Ball and Robert Osgood felt compelled to deal with issues in US relations with China, Korea, or Indo-China as part of more general works on foreign policy.[15] There was a great deal of writing on US policy toward Vietnam by individuals who knew virtually nothing about Vietnam itself. On the other hand, in recent years when Asian security issues have not had the same salience in American foreign policy, much of the writing on US policy in Asia has been done by US scholars of Asia, whose grounding in American society, economics, and political institutions can be questioned.

Despite the Korean and Vietnamese wars, there was relatively little interest in Asia on the part of US international relations theorists and experts in arms control until very recently. One fairly extensive bibliography covering major books and articles during the 1950s through the 1980s on the theoretical viability of arms control, theoretical material on regional arms control agreements, nuclear proliferation, and empirical studies of arms control during the Cold War period shows virtually no literature by Americans devoted exclusively to East and Southeast Asian arms control issues, in contrast to a number of entries on Europe, the Middle East, and South Asia (where there has been substantial interest in proliferation problems). The few articles that did appear in American journals were authored principally by non-Americans from the region and largely dealt with possible nuclear-free zones.[16]

This lack of interest may be accounted for in several ways: the greater perceived importance of the central strategic issues in Europe (especially nuclear deterrents); the difficulties in applying many of the theories developed around models of conventional or nuclear war to the more complex Asian security situation; the greater ease of doing case studies in Europe and facile assumption that these were generalizable; and, as mentioned above, the theorists' lack of a comparative advantage vis-à-vis Asian area specialists in addressing regional security issues. For the last reason especially, the decline of East-West security studies seems unlikely to be accompanied by a large migration of theorists toward Asian security issues.

A few Asian security issues (the conventional standoff in the Korean peninsula, aspects of Sino-American and Sino-Soviet relations) were more amenable theoretical constructs in the international relations literature, but even in these areas, country or regional experts tended to dominate US analysis. Several individuals with strong interests in general strategic and arms control issues did leave a mark on thinking about Asia. Examples include Herman Kahn, who wrote a farsighted book on the rise of Japan,[17] and Michael Armacost, who left an early academic career for an Asia-oriented career in diplomacy, becoming ambassador to the Philippines and Japan.

In recent years several trends have been evident within the community of Asia-Pacific analysts. First, there has been a heavy intrusion of first generation Asian scholars in regional security studies, usually with graduate training in the United States and frequently staying for several years or more, although sometimes retaining their Asian citizenship. Such individuals include Muthiah Alagappa at the East-West Center, Masaru Tamamoto at the American University, Xue LiTai at Stanford, and Guocang Huan, affiliated with the Atlantic Council. Moreover, much of the best writing in English on Asian security issues that appears in American journals or in journals that Americans read currently comes from Asians. These phenomena blur the distinction between the US security specialists on Asia and mostly US-trained Asian security specialists who use basically the same modes of analysis and language as the Americans and thus, from an American viewpoint, are colleagues in the same field.

Second, former government officials play an increasingly important role in institutions dealing with Asian security issues. Former ambassadors, for example, head a number of the institutions and organizations prominent in research or public education activities relating to Asian security issues including the Asia Society, the Carnegie Endowment for Peace, the US Institute of Peace, and the US-Japan Foundation.[18] Other former government officials are active in think tanks and university institutions including the many Washington-based institutions, the Council on Foreign Relations, and the Vanderbilt Institute for Public Policy.[19] Other former officials, such as Richard Armitage, a former assistant secretary of defense, and Douglas Paal, an Asian specialist on the National Security Council staff, have created their own institutions. Such individuals play an enormously positive role in bringing their practical experience and knowledge of policy issues and processes to the consideration of Asian security issues and US foreign and security policy. Understandably, some may have difficulty in adapting frameworks of thinking and analysis adopted during the Cold War period.

Third, the growth of interest in the "Pacific Basin" as a concept, the increased integration of Asia, and the development of regional institutions has helped draw the attention of country experts in a more concerted way to broader regional issues. It has become increasingly necessary to view China or Japan within their regional contexts, not just in terms of their own societies or bilateral relations with the United States. This has been reflected in the efforts of several distinguished country specialists to increasingly shift part of their attention to broader regional political and security issues. Examples of such individuals include Gerald Curtis (Japan), Harry Harding (China), Michael Mochizuki (Japan), Daniel Okimoto (Japan), and Michel Oksenberg (China). They follow a tradition established years earlier by Robert Scalapino.

Fourth, the opportunities for short-term travel to the region for senior American scholars have tended to increase over the years, with large numbers of invitations from Asian organizations. Many US scholars travel several times a year to Asia, and some seem to be virtually constantly on the road. Such travel opportunities provide frequent first-hand exposure and certainly contribute to "network building." However, the opportunities for and ease of international travel may also substitute for longer, more concentrated periods of time in the region, with attendant implications for the quality and depth of understanding. Moreover, such travel is often associated with the production of conference papers that reiterate established positions rather than break new ground.

It should be noted that although this paper has highlighted the role of Asian area specialists as prominent contributors to the literature on Asia-Pacific security in both the public and private sectors, area specialists do not have the same degree of influence in the setting of actual policy. Although they serve as resource persons and help shape governmental and public views of issues, key higher level decision making is usually the province of politicians and bureaucrats with relatively little background on the region.

## Institutional Actors

The major centers of US security studies of Asia can be broken down into several categories.

First, there are the government agencies. Within the Executive Branch those with considerable research capacity include the Defense Department and military services, the Central Intelligence Agency, and the State Department's Intelligence and Research Division (INR). The personnel of these agencies generally produce both classified and unclassified reports. US government analysts have frequent contact with academic researchers through meetings of professional associations (such as the annual meetings of the Association of Asian Studies conference and International Studies Association) and meetings sponsored by government agencies (such as the National Defense University or the Center for Naval Analyses) and universities and think tanks.

Aside from the Executive branch agencies, the Congressional Research Service (CRS) has a small core of analysts dealing with Asia-Pacific political and security issues. In contrast to the Executive agencies, the CRS work is virtually all unclassified.[20] It should be noted that the Congress itself through its hearings and oversight functions is a very significant contributor to public debate in the United States, including security issues. It was a congressional action ("the Nunn-Warner amendment") that led to a comprehensive review of the US security posture in East Asia in 1990. Other issues of interest to the Congress have been North Korea, Japanese and Chinese defense policies, burden-sharing issues, Cambodia and Vietnam.[21]

Several public institutions lying outside the government structure proper but deriving the majority of their support from federal funding are also active in the field of Asia-Pacific security. The East-West Center was explicitly established to promote US-Asia-Pacific understanding, but only in recent years has developed a program relating to security issues. The US Institute for Peace, now under the leadership of Richard Solomon, former assistant secretary of state for Asia and the Pacific, has a major interest in Asian security issues. The Asia Foundation, including its Center for Asia Pacific Affairs, is active in funding and sponsoring research activities, some of which relate to security issues.

A second set of actors are nongovernmental think tanks. Some of these, such as the American Enterprise Institute, the Brookings Institution, the Carnegie Endowment for Peace, the Center for Strategic and International Studies, the Heritage Foundation, the Hudson Institute, Pacific Forum-CSIS, and the RAND Corporation are independent, dependent upon foundation grants, government contracts, or private donations for support. Other institutions including the Center for International Affairs and Center for Science and International Affairs, both at Harvard, and the Hoover Institution and the Center for International Security and Arms Control, both at Stanford, are associated with universities. University institutes focused exclusively on the Asia-Pacific region include the East Asia Institute at the University of California-Berkeley; the Graduate School of International Relations and Pacific Studies at the University of California-San Diego, the East Asia Institute at Columbia University; the Reichauer Center at the Johns Hopkins School of Advanced International Studies University; the School of Asia, Pacific and Hawaiian Affairs and the Spark Matsunaga Institute for Peace, both at the University of Hawaii; the National Bureau of Asian Research (with many links to the University of Washington); and the Gaston Sigur Center for East Asian Studies at George Washington University. Asia Society and Japan Society, both based in New York, have active public affairs programs.

These institutions vary greatly on such dimensions as their size, degree of interest in Asia-Pacific as opposed to other regions, attention paid to security as opposed to other issues, their emphasis on original research as opposed to public education, and the extent to which they have developed integrated programs. Some, like the Heritage Foundation and the Asia Society, are largely devoted to providing public education and influencing public policy. Others, like the Hudson Institute and the RAND Corporation, are primarily supported by government contracts. The more academic work is usually associated with the university centers; the agendas of such centers is usually defined by the individual research interests of those associated with these centers.

One can make some general observations about the nongovernmental sector. First, there is no concentration of Asia-Pacific security expertise in any single institution. The largest centers have only three or four senior specialists working full-time on Asian security-related topics, although often supplemented by visiting fellows (many non-Americans) and less senior persons. Second, and partly related to size, none aspires to provide a comprehensive view of security issues in the region. Because their agendas usually are the composite of individual research interests, this is particularly true of university centers. Finally, the agendas of such organizations has been heavily affected by the key policy interests. Funding, whether from government or foundation sources tend to revolve around such issues.

The foundation community comprises yet another set of actors. In American foundations, there is a very small number of individuals with knowledge of and responsibility for funding and evaluation of projects on Asia-Pacific security issues. However, because of the limited amounts of programmatic and research funding available for nongovernmental security analysis, their views of the critical issues and quality individuals and institutions have enormous influence. In recent years, the American institutions supporting Asia-Pacific security research (Ford, Rockefeller Brothers Fund, Olin, Pew Charitable Trusts, MacArthur come most readily to mind), have been supplemented by several funds derived from Japanese sources (these include the US-Japan Foundation, the Center for Global Partnership, and the Sasakawa Peace Foundation). Korean and Taiwan foundations also support some American activities related to Asian security problems.

# Needs in the Field

At one level the needs in the field are quite simple: to develop a research agenda appropriate to the twenty-first century, train the human resources needed to address this agenda, and secure adequate financial resources to implement the research program. In fact, questions relating to agenda and human and financial resources are very complex and involve highly subjective judgments. Despite some overlap with the preceding discussion of new direction in the field, some comments may be in order about possible future research directions and questions that should be debated by those in the Asia-Pacific security field.

## *Research Issues*

The author's list of key research questions include the following:

1. The interaction between the domestic sphere and the international sphere should continue to be a high priority in future research on regional security issues. With a looser and less competitive post–Cold War international system, domestic politics have probably become even more important in the shaping of foreign and national security policies. In developing US security policies and efforts to control arms buildups and the diffusion of sophisticated defense technologies, Americans will need to understand the domestic pressures and forces that lie behind the policies of Asian governments. Since Asian societies are undergoing processes of rapid economic, political and social change, these processes of change and the pressures they place on often relatively new and underdeveloped institutional frameworks have great relevance for stability. Such matters as population pressures, income inequalities, and transborder pollution will become security issues, if at all, through the medium of domestic politics. The United States, of course, also needs to understand how its own policies reverberate in the domestic politics of other countries with consequences that may be counterproductive to those intended. Such analyses may draw both upon Asian cultures and traditions as well as more abstract work developed from comparative historical examples on such topics as the role of the military and nationalism in rapidly industrializing societies.

   While much of the effort in the study of domestic forces will be focused on the larger actors, the domestic politics of smaller countries should not be ignored. Traditionally, the sparks of conflict have been most easily ignited in smaller countries, and there is every indication from recent crises in other regions that this will continue to be true in the rest of the 1990s and the early twenty-first century.

2. Closely related is the study of decision-making processes and the practice and instruments of "statescraft" at the national and international levels. If countries are to truly "share responsibility" for international order keeping in Asia as well as elsewhere, the decision-making processes become incredibly complex, operating at many different levels. Such decision making is increasingly affected by cultural conditioning and (mis)perceptions.

3. The relationship between economic and security issues is frequently discussed and a number of implicit assumptions are made in much of the Asian security analyses about the impact of economic growth (that higher growth increases national security, that the higher growth rates of Asian allies of the United States as compared to the United States itself has undermined public support for US presence, that increased interdependence including that within "growth triangle" strengthens political cooperation and reduces the chance of military conflict), but there is relatively little systematic work on the subject. Moreover, despite the extensive work now being done in the United States in the "political economies" of the Asia-Pacific region, little effort has been made in this literature to connect it explicitly with security issues.

4. The study of institutions (meaning established patterns of international behavior, international agreements and regimes, and organizational structures) continues to be important. Most security specialists, in the United States and elsewhere, give emphasis to the basic principle of self-help. The decline of alliance systems and the uncertainties of alignments on one hand make self-help even more relevant, but institutions can moderate the self-help need and, hopefully, help control the tendency of self-help strategies to spiral into competitive arms acquisitions.

5. There can be considerable value in examining historical international relations as well as the historical literature in Asia on national security. On one hand, there is a reemergence of historical local patterns of interaction that were less visible when overlain by the Cold War superpower rivalry. Similarly traditional notions of security and other concepts relating to governance, rebellion, and international relations continue to be relevant. Clearly, such patterns and perceptions, however, need to be evaluated in light of new factors such as economic and technological interdependence, vastly changed weapons technologies, new international institutions, and the telecommunications revolution.

In all the above areas, the integration of area studies and more conceptually based analytical and theoretical work could be valuable.

## Some Questions

We close with several questions that should be of concern to the US Asia-Pacific security studies community.

1. Who sets the agenda? In the past much of the agenda was established by an overriding common sense of societal priorities in the Cold War era. The government policy agenda played a very strong role. As government and public interest in many of the local aspects of Asian security issues wains, how will the agenda be set? It has been noted earlier that a number of Asian-based foundations have become active in supporting US work relating to Asian security issues. These foundations, where they have supported US institutions as the principal partners, have generally not sought to push any particular research area. But if this funding is not matched by US funding, over time it is likely to have a subtle but definite influence on the research agenda.

2. What should be the standards for relevance? Few would dispute that research efforts should be grounded in relevance for real world problems. Encouraged by the openness of the US government to ideas from the outside, many of the US efforts on Asia-Pacific security issues seek to address issues of immediate policy significance, but this has put a premium on such writing at the expense of more in-depth studies seeking to place such policy issues in a broader and more conceptual frame. But such research is also highly relevant.

3. Toward what kind of activities should limited financial resources be directed? Most financial support goes into four kinds of activities: research, publication, dialogues, and public education, with most projects combining two or more of these functions. However, the literature on Asia-Pacific security issues appears to reflect the large number of dialogue activities with little substantial research components.

4. Related to the above question, is there sufficient funding for individual research as opposed to institutional programs in this as well as other fields? There is a scarcity of solid, single-authored books on Asian security issues in comparison with conference collections. This may reflect funding priorities or the choices being made by individual scholars as to how they choose to allocate their time. Nevertheless, it appears that the opportunities for serious individual scholars to find funding for in-depth research are very limited as opposed to grants to institutions. This may reflect to some extent the extreme burdens on foundation personnel, and in this context, the cheaper burdens of administering larger institutional grants.

5. Another related question is whether the United States can and will continue to support as many Asian affairs institutions and activities in the post–Cold War era as in prior years. In many ways, these institutions have been fortunate; a decline of US public and political interest in some of the security issues of the region has been matched by the increased salience of issues of economic competitiveness. Thus programmatic activities have been shifted within institutions away from security issues and toward economics issues, but so far there has not been an outright loss of institutions.

6. Related to the above question is that of how efficiently are the available resources being used. Since no research is definitive, some duplication of efforts is desirable. However, it often appears that there is considerable

overlap in research activities that reflect different institutional or foundation sponsors rather than significantly different research. There may be a couple of explanations for this: that because of past investments and current connections some institutions are being supported despite the lack of innovative activities, or that funders do not sufficiently coordinate their funding activities to eliminate duplication.

7. To what extent does the United States need to train a core of its own Asian specialists in political, foreign policy, and national security issues given the broad Asian talent available in the larger Asia-Pacific security community? There is evidence of a decline in the number of younger Americans working in these areas as compared to the heyday of area studies, particularly in the area of Southeast Asia. An offsetting trend is the increased numbers of Asian nationals working in degree programs in US universities or on postdoctoral fellowships and in jobs in the United States. While such individuals are an enormously valuable resource and, along with their cohorts in Asia, will provide the bulk of expertise on country-specific security issues, the United States may need to have a small core of US specialists with a strong sense of US national interests, if only because such individuals will have stronger credibility in US political debate on Asia-Pacific security issues.

## Notes

1. The author appreciates the suggestions and support of several of his colleagues at the East-West Center, particularly Muthiah Alagappa, Yaacov Vertzberger and David Wolff.

2. "Asia-Pacific" generally encompasses the North Pacific including its North America and Asian maritime states, Southeast Asia, and the Southwest Pacific. Claims are made for the inclusion of other areas such as South Asia and the Latin American Pacific states, but this broader definition is not in common use. In the 1950s–1970s, Americans writing on security issues in this part of the world, generally referred to "Asian" security; it is only in the past decade that the term "Asia-Pacific" looking at Asia and North America in a more integral fashion has become common. Earlier works reflecting the earlier view of the United States as an extraregional actor include Ralph N. Clough, *East Asia and U.S. Security* (Washington: The Brookings Institution, 1975); Fred Greene, *U.S. Policy and the Security of Asia* (New York: McGraw-Hill Book Company, 1968); D.E. Kennedy, *The Security of Southern Asia* (New York: Frederick A. Praeger, 1965); and Richard H. Solomon, ed., *Asian Security in the 1980s: Problems and Policies for a Time of Transition* (Cambridge, Mass.: Oelgeschlager, Gunn & Hain, 1979). On the changes in the US perceptions of whether it is a part or not of "the region," see the author's "The United States and Cooperation in Asia-Pacific," *Australian Journal of International Affairs*, forthcoming.

3. Some of the more prominent area American analysts of Russian and Chinese foreign policy behavior toward the region included A. Doak Barnett, Ralph Clough, Melvin Gurtov, Harold C. Hinton, Arnold L. Horelick, Paul L. Langer, Charles B. McLane, Thomas Robinson, Robert Scalapino, Richard Solomon, Jay Taylor, and Donald S. Zagoria.

4. See, for example, Michael T. Klare, "The Next Great Arms Race," *Foreign Affairs*, Summer 1993; Nicholas D. Kristof, "The Rise of China," *Foreign Affairs*, Novem-

ber/December 1993; Bonnie S. Glaser, "China's Security Perceptions: Interests and Ambitions," *Asian Survey*, 1993; Mel Gurtou, "Swords into Market Shares: China's Conversion of Military Industry into Civilian Products," *The China Quarterly*, June 1993; *United States and China: Relations at a Crossroads*, Policy paper of the Atlantic Council, February 1993; Barber B. Conable Jr. and David M. Lampton, "China: The Coming Power," *Foreign Affairs*, Winter 1992–93; John W. Lewis and Hua Di, "China's Ballistic Missile Programs: Technologies, Strategies, Goals," *International Security*, Fall 1992; Michel Oksenberg, "The China Problem," *Foreign Affairs*, Summer 1991; and Lucian Pye, "China: Erratic State, Frustrated Society," *Foreign Affairs*, Fall 1990.

5. See Amos A. Jordan, "Coping with the North Korea Nuclear Weapons Problem," Pacific Forum/CSIS, November 1993; William J. Taylor and Michael J. Mazarr, "North Korea and the Nuclear Issue: US Perspective," *The Journal of East Asian Affairs*, Summer/Fall 1993; Young Whan Kihl, "North Korea's Foreign Relations: Diplomacy of Promotive Adaptation," *Journal of Northeast Asian Studies*, Fall 1991; Selig Harrison, "A Chance for Détente in Korea," *World Policy Journal*, Fall 1991; Nicholas Eberstadt and Judith Banister, "Military Buildup in the DPRK: Some New Indications from North Korea Data," *Asian Survey*, November 1991; "Issues and Opportunities in U.S.-Korean Relations: A Report of the Committee on U.S.-ROK Relations, February 1991; and James Goodby, "Operational Arms Control in Europe: Implications for Security Negotiations in Korea," *Korean Journal of Defense Analysis*, Summer 1990.

6. Jonathan D. Pollack, "The Sino-Japanese Relations and East Asian Security: Patterns and Implications," *The China Quarterly*, December 1990; Allen S. Whiting and Xin Jianfei, "Sino-Japanese Relations: Pragmatism and Passion," *World Policy Journal*, Winter 1990–91. See also John W. Garver, "China and the New World Order," in William A. Joseph, ed., *China Briefing, 1992* (Boulder: Westview Press, 1993), pp. 55–80. Akira Iriye, *China and Japan in the Global Setting*, (Cambridge, Mass.: Harvard University Press, 1992), provides a more historical treatment with contemporary relevance.

7. See Francis Fukuyama and Kongdan Oh, *The U.S.-Japan Security Relationship after the Cold War* (Santa Monica: RAND National Defense Research Institute, 1993); Peter J. Katzenstein and Nobuo Okawara, "Japan's National Security: Structures, Norms, and Policies," *International Security*, Spring 1993; Chalmers Johnson, "Japan in Search of a 'Normal' Role, *Daedalus*, Fall 1992; Louis D. Hayes, "Japan and the Security of Asia: PostCold War Relations," *Current Politics and Economics of Japan*, vol.2, no. 3/4, 1992; Tsuneo Akaha, "Japan's Comprehensive Security Policy: A New East Asian Environment," *Asian Survey*, April 1991; Eugene Brown, "Contending Paradigms of Japan's International Role: Elite Views of the Persian Gulf Crisis," *Journal of Northeast Asian Studies*, Spring 1991; and Fred Charles Ikle and Terumasa Nakanishi, "Japan's Grant Strategy," *Foreign Affairs*, Summer 1990.

8. R. Bates Gill, *The Challenge of Chinese Arms Proliferation: U.S. Policy for the 1990s*, Strategic Studies Institute, US Army War College, 1993; Richard A. Bitzinger, "Arms To Go: Chinese Arms Sales to the Third World," *International Security*, Fall 1992; "Chinese-Indian Rivalry in Nepal: The Clash over Chinese Arms Sales," *Asian Survey*, October 1991; John W. Lewis and Xue LiTai, "Beijing's Defense Establishment: Solving the Arms-Export Enigma," *International Security*, Fall 1991; R. Bates Gill, "China Looks to Thailand: Exporting Arms, Exporting Influence," *Asian Survey*, June 1991.

9. It should be noted that although beyond the scope of this paper, there is a considerable US interest in security issues in South Asia including Indo-Pakistan rivalry, the Indian perceptions of its regional role, ethnic conflict, and Afghanistan. For recent studies of Southeast Asian security issues by American or US-based analysts, see Donald K. Emmerson and Sheldon W. Simon, "Regional Issues in Southeast Asian Security: Scenarios and Regimes," *NBR Analysis*, July 1993; Muthiah Alagappa, "The Dynamics of International Security in Southeast Asia: Change and Continuity," *Australian Journal of International Affairs*, vol. 45, no. 1, May 1991; and Muthiah Alagappa, "Regional Arrangements and International Security in Southeast Asia: Going beyond ZOPFAN," *Contemporary Southeast Asia*, vol. 12, no. 4, March 1991. The Spratlys have received considerable attention, principally for the questions they raise about China's policies toward the region. On this subject, see Mark J. Valencia, " Spratly Solution Still at Sea," *Pacific Review*, vol. 6, no. 2, 1993, and "The South China Sea: Potential Conflict and Cooperation," in Rohana Mahmood and Rustam A. Sani, eds., *Confidence Building and Conflict Reduction in the Pacific* (Kuala Lumpur: Institute of Strategic and International Studies, 1993).

10. Some articles in this vein, although not necessarily focusing on the Asia-Pacific region, are Matheo Falco, "Foreign Drugs, Foreign Wars," *Daedalus*, Summer 1992; H. Richard Friman, "The United States, Japan, and the International Drug Trade," *Asian Survey*, September 1991; David S. Painter, "International Oil and National Security," *Daedalus*, Fall 1991; Theodore H. Moran, "International Economics and Security," *Foreign Affairs*, Winter 1990/91; Gareth Porter, "Post-Cold War Global Environment and Security," *The Fletcher Forum of World Affairs*, Summer 1990.

11. One effort that examines the security-economic linkage in the context of US policy is David Denoon, *Real Reciprocity: Balancing U.S. Economic and Security Policy in the Pacific Basin*, (New York: Council on Foreign Relations, 1993).

12. For example, Stephen J. Blank, *Helsinki in Asia?*, Strategic Studies Institute, US Army War College, 1993; David B.H. Denoon, "Alterative Directions for U.S. Strategy in the Changing Pacific Basin," in James C. Hsiung, ed., *Asia-Pacific in the New World Politics* (Boulder: Lynne Rienner, 1993); Don Oberdorfer, "Clinton and Asia: Issues for the New Administration," Asia Society, 1993; Charles E. Morrison, "The United States in Post–Cold War Asia," in Rohana Mahmood and Rustam A. Sani, ed., *Confidence Building and Conflict Reduction in the Pacific*, Kuala Lumpur, Institute of Strategic and International Studies, 1993; Patrick M. Cronin, "Pacific Rim Security: Beyond Bilateralism?" *Pacific Review*, vol. 5, no. 3, 1992; Norman D. Palmer, *The New Regionalism in Asia and the Pacific* (Lexington: Lexington Books, 1991).

13. See Denoon, "Alternative Directions"; Alan Romberg, "The U.S. and Asia in 1991," *Asian Survey*, January 1992; Stephen W. Bosworth, "The United States and Asia," *America and the World 1991 /92*; James A. Baker III, "America in Asia," *Foreign Affairs, Winter 1991/92;* and Robert A. Scalapino, "The United States and Asia: Future Prospects," *Foreign Affairs*, Winter 1991/92. Ralph A. Cossa, ed., *The New Pacific Security Environment* (Washington: National Defense University, 1993), contains a number of thoughtful essays by Americans on US security policies in the region and on regional issues including the security policies of Japan, South Korea, Vietnam, nuclear proliferation, the Spratlys.

14. For US government statements, see in particular, Bill Clinton, "Remarks in an Address to the National Assembly of the Republic of Korea, White House press release, July 10, 1993; Winston Lord, "A New Pacific Community: Ten Goals for American Policy," opening statement at confirmation hearings, March 31, 1993; Admiral Charles R. Larson, "United States Pacific Command, Posture Statement

1993"; Department of Defense, "A Strategic Framework for the Asian Pacific Rim: Report to Congress 1992"; and Department of Defense, "A Strategic Framework for the Asian Pacific Rim: Looking toward the 21st Century," April 1990. These statements as well as the Defense Department's 1993 "bottom-up review" point in the direction of a gradually phased and relatively modest reduction of US military forward-based forces in the region.

15. See, for example, George F. Kennan, *The Cloud of Danger: Current Realities of American Foreign Policy* (Boston: Little, Brown & Co., 1977); Robert E. Osgood et al., *America and the World from the Truman Doctrine to Vietnam* (Baltimore: Johns Hopkins Press, 1970).

16. For example, Alexei Arbatov, "Arms Limitation and the Situation in the Asian-Pacific and Indian Ocean Regions," *Asian Survey*, November 1984.

17. Herman Kahn, *The Emerging Japanese Superstate: Challenge and Response* (Englewood Cliffs: N.J., Prentice-Hall, 1970).

18. These are respectively Nicholas Platt, Mort Abramowitz, Richard Solomon, and Stephen Bosworth.

19. For example, Paul Wolfowitz, a former ambassador to Indonesia and assistant secretary of state of Asia-Pacific, became the dean of the Johns Hopkins School of Advanced International Studies; Dick Clark, another former assistant secretary of state for Asia-Pacific and ambassador to India, joined the Center for Strategic and International Studies; and James Auer, a former Defense Department official, is at the Vanderbilt. Winston Lord served for several years at the Council of Foreign Relations, and other former State Department personnel associated with the council staff include Paul Kreisberg and Alan Romberg.

20. For example, Shirley A. Kan, "Chinese Missile and Nuclear Proliferation: Issues for the Congress," *CRS Issue Brief*, 1992; Robert G. Sutter, "Japan-U.S. Relations: Issues for Congress in the 1990s," *CRS Issue Brief*, 1993; and Richard P. Cronin, "Japan-U.S. Relations in a Post–Cold War Environment: Emerging Trends and Issues for U.S. Policy," *CRS Report for Congress*, March 1992.

21. It should be noted, however, that the Asian expertise within the Congress and its staff is very limited. Probably only about ten congressional staff members have significant Asian expertise, including Richard Bush of the House Foreign Affairs Committee staff, a China specialist, and Richard Kessler of the Senate Foreign Relations Committee staff, known best for his work on the Philippines.

# PART II

## Multilateral Dialogues

# Call Girls in the Old World: Of Multilateral Think Tanks, Dialogue Programs and Other Promiscuous Activities In and Around Europe

HANNS W. MAULL

The idea of think tanks as a way to improve the way governments discharge their tasks goes back at least as far as Francis Bacon (compare "Solomon's House" in his *New Atlantis*[1]), if not to Plato's philosopher-king[2] in "The Republic" which, in today's parlance, proposes to hand over political power to the experts. Even those precursor ideas could at least implicitly be "multilateralized" (to use today's jargon again) in the sense of a body of advisers and experts, not necessarily philosophers and rulers, and perhaps even deliberately not, coming from one "Republic." After all, Plato's own rather disastrous flirtation with the role of political adviser to the tyrant of Syracuse (he was packed off and sold as a slave when his suggestions met with the disapproval of his political master) suggests that he saw himself as a "transnational" political asset.

The other notion of importance to the subject at hand is that of the multilateral dialogue in conferences and networks involving experts, practitioners and aficionados—those who simply cannot resist the temptation, or sense of obligation, to give a positive response to the proverbial phone call in Arthur Koestler's famous novel *The Call Girls*. Off they go to their conference, workshop, or dialogue forum—presumably vaguely in search of an ideal of times past when the reins of governments in Europe were held by representatives of a thoroughly internationalized elite. The perceived need for networks and dialogue programs harks back to the days of absolutism when the ruling families of Europe essentially shared one culture (baroque) and one language (French).[3] Or perhaps it extends even further to those of the Holy Roman Empire, with the common religion of Christianity and the common language of Latin, or the Roman Empire itself, in which the title of *civis Romanus* was conferred, as in the famous case of Paulus, to members of other communities, as well as to Romans. In those different times, mutual understanding between members of different elites was easy, both linguistically and culturally. But we ought to remember that this did not necessarily preclude aggression, violence and war between or within states.

## Defining the Subject

The purpose of this paper is to look at today's manifestations of those ancient notions in Europe. One of the major differences between "then" and "now" (a difference which in my view even adds up to a major discontinuity in the history of mankind[4]) is, of course, the intensity of interdependence between societies. Not only issues and interests, but also power and political processes, today are transnationalized to a degree which still has not been fully digested analytically, let alone politically.[5] Nongovernmental dialogue activities have expanded commensurably, and no doubt also have grown in importance for the system of international relations as a whole. They thus warrant greater attention.

However, to make the subject manageable within the confines of this paper, some restrictions on the scope of analysis will be needed. After all, the number of transnational organizations has literally exploded in recent years: in 1960, the United States was represented in 671 international organizations (governmental and nongovernmental), Germany in 911 and Japan in 454; by 1976, those figures were up to 1,190, 1,480 and 949, respectively.[6] I therefore shall narrow the focus of my discussion by making the following specifications:

1. The organizations to be considered are all multilateral in the sense that membership and leadership are drawn from several countries, and that the organizations see themselves as multilateral. This excludes all exclusively or primarily national activities and institutions, even though many of them, such as the Atlantic Council of the United States, may organize activities with participants from a multitude of countries.

2. The discussion will be defined to the realm of security issues.

3. Only "track two" organizations will be considered, leaving aside governmental or quasi-governmental bodies. GOs and NGOs, of course, are in reality not always sharply discrete;[7] there is a grey area into which we might sometimes stray. I have excluded, however, the activities in and around parliamentary assemblies (such as the North Atlantic Assembly).

4. Emphasis will be more on dialogue activities and organizations, rather than on research institutes. But since the think tank dimension is integral to some of the dialogue organizations I will discuss, it cannot be totally left aside.[8]

5. I will also ignore the salient and important segment of transnational corporate interest groups in the defense sector. Given the long history of efforts in, and the more modest but substantial results from, multinational defense industry cooperation within the Atlantic Alliance and the Euro-Group of NATO, this is quite an omission—but one which I feel justified to make for two reasons: one, this area of multilateral nongovernmental activities is commercial and/or quasi-governmental and follows a very different logic; and two, I don't know much about defense industries.[9]

6. Geographically, I have been asked to discuss the "European experience." But what is this experience? What is Europe? My favorite answer to this question was given by the late Andrew Shonfield, who entitled his Reith Lectures for the BBC "Europe: Journey to an Unknown Destination."[10] Europe, in other words, is a process, not a cleary definable geographical entity. This problem immediately comes up in our context as well: dealing with European multilateral security dialogues can mean at least five things (four of which will be considered in this paper):

a)  activities within, and confined to, Western Europe

b)  activities across the old East-West divide in Europe

c)  activities involving (Western) Europe and North America (the transatlantic framework), in which the European element is co-equal[11]

d)  activities involving (Western) Europe, North America and Japan (the trilateral framework), in which the European element is co-equal, and

e)  activities involving Western Europe and other regions, such as the Middle East. This last geographic dimension will be excluded from consideration in this paper.

7. Finally, I will have to confess to a subjective element of selectivity. Even with all this effort to reduce and define more narrowly the scope of this paper, the number of organizations is substantial. I will therefore develop arguments, bringing in organizations which I know better, often from personal experience, and probably unduly neglect others. In that, as well as in any other sense, this paper therefore is still preliminary, and its author welcomes and gratefully accepts suggestions.

# What Roles for Multilateral Dialogue Organizations?

It stands to reason that multilateral dialogues and dialogue organizations in the realm of security policy satisfy needs and meet demands other than those of the "call girls" themselves for status recognition, self-aggrandizement, intellectual stimulus and frequent physical displacment. Otherwise, sensible people and sensible organizations (such as foundations) would not put up money for those purposes.

But what are those needs and demands? It may be useful to approach this question from the angle of official security policies, assuming that "track two" activities will to some extent mirror, or at least relate to, official preoccupations. Western security policy[12] has centered around four different tasks, whose delineation and pursuit reflected processes of social learning in all major regions involved (that is, North America, Western Europe and Japan). Those tasks have been:

1. *War prevention.* This objective reflected the experiences in Europe and Japan with the horrors of World War II, but also American recognition of the new realities of the "delicate balance of terror" in the nuclear age. Major war was no longer deemed an acceptable option; the task thus became to prevent it from happening.[13]

2. *Collective defense.* This involved social learning primarily in American, but also in British foreign policy—both countries after 1945 eventually came round to the conclusion that an effective balance of power, and an effective defense of respective interests, required their permanent military presence on the European continent (as well as in East Asia). Old notions of isolation as a splendid way to defend American or British interests were thus discarded—once and for all, one likes to hope.

3. The *building of security communities.*[14] The crucial advance on the curve of social learning in this context probably took place in Europe. There, a generation of postwar political leaders, urged on first by a wave of public enthusiasm, and then, behind the scenes, by that quintessentially influential "track two" one-man operation, Jean Monnet and his "Action Committee for the United States of Europe," decided to develop a new, fundamentally different approach to dealing with the threat of war: economic, social and political integration. Although after the failure of the "European Defence Community" in 1954 the focus of European integration shifted away from security to economics, leaving the security realm essentially to NATO, without the European Community the Atlantic security community could not have succeeded.

4. *Stabilizing market-oriented democracies.* This reflected the assumption that democratic states do not wage war against each other,[15] an assumption which now has been backed up by very substantial empirical evidence. The lessons drawn from the experience of the 1930s were to try to strengthen democracy in Germany and Japan, as well as in other emerging democracies (Spain, Portugal, Greece, Turkey, etc.), as an end in itself, but also as a way to prevent war.

The nongovernmental dialogue and exchange programs in which we are interested here took their cues from the tasks Western governmental security policies set out to achieve. Their purposes were thus, in brief, to develop and strengthen the fabric of the Western security community, and to enhance cooperation and reduce tensions with countries outside. In this context, dialogue activities and organizations assumed the following five functions:

1. networking

2. facilitating intergovernmental relations

3. training

4. developing new policy analysis and policy ideas through joint research

5. exercising influence in decision-making.

The most basic and ubiquitous objective of multilateral dialogue programs and organizations is *networking*—developing personal contacts leading to close working relationships. The simple idea here is to enable participants in such progams to call on, and be called by, people in other countries for ready advice, help and mutual effort. And the ideal is that of an "epistemic community" of experts,[16] which already exists in many areas of both natural and social sciences and other fields of transnational activities. The principal means to build such networks are conferences, workshops and regular meetings, although the advances in information and communication technology have opened up new avenues to develop such networks. Most of the organizations and institutions I have considered for this paper (see appendix) include this objective among their activities, and therefore organize conferences, albeit to a varying degree: some do *only* conferences and seminars (e.g., Ditchley; the Salzburg Seminar; the annual "Wehrkunde" conferences organized by a leading German security policy and defense journal; the NATO Review conferences, organized by the Foundation for Science and Policy in Ebenhausen in Germany; or the series of European-Japanese Hakone conferences). Others combine conferences with cooperative research efforts (e.g., the Trilateral Commission or the Pugwash conferences; but also the European Strategy Group (ESG, a network of major European research institutes); the Center for European Policy Studies (CEPS) in Brussels; the International Institute for Strategic Studies (IISS) in London; or the Institute for Security Studies of the Western European Union in Paris). Institutes by and large tend to give less emphasis to large conferences, preferring smaller groups of experts over larger gatherings (though the annual conferences of the IISS number several hundred participants). Even activities which at first glance do not try to fulfill this role—those which are very specifically geared towards research projects, such as the reports produced and written in collaborative efforts by a variable geometry of Western or European research institutes[17]—in fact contain an element of "networking": in this case, developing cooperative ties between the institutes involved through joint-project work.

Beyond networking, multilateral dialogue programs and organizations may *facilitate relations between governments*. Here, it may be useful to distinguish between different types of wider political relationships within which the dialogues are located, namely adversarial relations (i.e., dialogue and exchange programs across the old East-West divide), security community relations (i.e., within Western Europe, across the Atlantic, and within the trilateral world), and arm's-length relations (essentially, other relations such as, say, between Western Europe and the Maghreb/Mashrek area), which remain outside the scope of this paper.

The idea of facilitating official relations involves at its simplest an informal, congenial environment for discussion, with a more or less structured intellectual framework (agenda, introductory papers written by experts, etc.) to help focus on critical issues. Government officials are usually invited to participate together with outside experts, but the informality and confidentiality of the setting (discussions are usually off the record) mean that they need not feel obliged to assume formal negotiating postures.

Among allies and friends, such a context can provide a safety valve to let off steam, a means to assess the importance of an issue for another government, and a way to get a better mutual understanding of perceptions, stakes and involvement. In that sense, "track two" multilateral dialogues among partners may assume functions of "early warning" and "damage limitation" within alliances. They may also help to develop better understanding of positions and mutual adjustment, and to hammer out new ideas for resolving conflicts (using the most important time component of conferences, the coffee break and the evening sessions in the salons and bars). And they may try to go one step beyond this:

actively to help bring about solutions to political conflicts by providing their own input to the process.

The role of facilitator in its more modest forms is something to which again most of the organizations and activities under consideration subscribe. For the security-community dialogue activities within Europe,[18] CEPS, the ESG, and the WEU Institute all try to achieve this role; in the Atlantic/Trilateral[19] context, it is Ditchley; the IISS, the defunct Atlantic Institute for International Affairs, Bilderberg, the Ebenhausen NATO Review and the Wehrkunde conferences; and in the trilateral framework proper it is the Trilateral Commission; and, for European-Japanese relations, the Hakone conferences. For the adversarial context, it used to be the Stockholm International Peace Research Institute (SIPRI), the International Institute for Applied Systems Analysis (IIASA), the International Institute for Peace and the Pugwash conferences. The most exclusive, and perhaps most ambitious activity of this type in a global context is the Interaction Council, which regularly unites famous elder statespeople from around the globe.

The objective of helping to mediate conflicts may sometimes shade into that of influencing policies (the line between mediating as a "honest broker" and exercising influence, perhaps on both parties, can be a fine one). Generally, however, mediation will be done not so much on the basis of specific proposals but by offering a framework for discussions within a context in which the commitment to communality is very strong. The ability to offer effective mediation will depend on the prestige and influence of the organization involved and its credibility with the governments concerned. In West-West relations, the Bilderberg meetings and the Trilateral Commission have at times apparently played this role.

Turning now to adversarial relations, dialogue activities geared towards a real political role in East-West relations inevitably pursued more ambitious objectives—namely, the mitigation and eventual transformation of East-West tensions. Or, more precisely, the functions of damage limitation, early warning and safety valve merged with those of nudging along conflict management, reduction of tensions, and conflict resolution. In the sample under consideration here, this objective was perhaps most evident in the Pugwash meetings, marginally also at the IIASA (which tried to focus research on long-term issues of common concern to East and West).

The third role to be considered is that of *training*—involving the training of future security experts with a broad outlook, by giving promising young scholars experience in a multilateral context, but also, more vaguely, the socialization of the "successor generation." Here, there is some overlap with the first role we discussed, that of networking. Although most dialogue institutions try to keep participation up to date in line with changes in societies and elites (often not all too effectively: Europeans could take a leaf out of the American book here) by renewing their membership and "regulars," it is mostly the institutes which have developed specific training programs. Thus, the IISS, the WEU Institute and the ESG have all undertaken special efforts to recruit young and upcoming people— as research fellows or as participants in "young leaders" conferences. The practice of ESG and WEU of rotating young research fellows between institutes is perhaps the most interesting progam among those geared towards training of future security experts.

In terms of *joint research,* to varying degrees a number of the institutions under consideration have tried to assume the role of a multilateral think tank: all the institutes and the ESG (really a network of institutes) have done so, as well as the Trilateral Commission. Moreover, there have been a number of joint reports on security issues produced by research institutes in the Euro-Atlantic region, starting with the report by Karl Kaiser et al. in 1980.[20] The ESG represents an effort to put such cooperative work on a more systematic and enduring basis.

This role of providing policy analysis and guidelines is no doubt more ambitious than networking, training or even facilitating: it aims at influencing policy processes by providing independent input. Following on the work by Dror on national think tanks,[21] this set of functions could involve, in the context of multilateral security relations: policy paradigm reconsideration; diagnostics of fundamental problems and their causes; development of broad and long-term perspectives; providing bases for consensus; grand-policy innovation; and evaluation of multilateral governance.

In this role, organizations can choose between reliance on a more traditional approach orientated towards individual research (which may, of course, then be assembled into multi-author studies) or genuinely integrated research efforts aimed at producing a joint document. The latter path not only confronts some of the systemic problems think tanks face in getting their message across effectively. It also has to deal with particular difficulties of carrying joint research through to joint conclusions (which, inevitably, will involve not only the practical problems of organization and substantive differences over policy issues, but also "soft" differences of outlook, perception and culture).

The most ambitious multilateral research efforts have probably been those of the Trilateral Commission, of the various combinations of institutes (primarily the four-institute study on Western security of 1980 and the seven-institute study on European security of 1992–93), the European Strategy Group, a network of European institutes, and the transatlantic Nuclear History Program. Originally concerned primarily with what has been termed "interdependence issues,"[22] the Trilateral Comission turned to security issues only with some hesitation. In its relatively few reports on such issues, the Trilateral Commission has usually relied on its normal format of three authors, one from each region (although in a report on East Asian security, this format was changed in favor of one principal author, Masashi Nishihara[23]). The first effort by the Trilateral Commission at producing analysis and policy recommendations on East-West relations was undertaken in the mid-1970s and resulted in two reports, one concentrating on the adversarial aspects of East-West relations, the other on the cooperative dimensions.[24] It is interesting to note that these reports predate the formal establishment of the notion of common security interests of trilateral countries by several years,[25] and that the commission at the time undertook extensive (although somewhat frustrating) efforts to consult with Soviet scholars and officials. These first reports took the commission down a road which made security issues a regular, and sometimes even a dominant, concern in the research work and the discussions of the organization.[26]

To enhance the weight and influence of its policy recommendations, the Trilateral Commission has relied on the prestige of its co-authors and on a semiendorsement of the reports by the organization itself with its prestigious membership (they are officially reports to the commission which do not commit the organization or the members, but they are distributed by the commission and published under its name).

The efforts at joint research on security issues by major Western institutes have followed a similar pattern: they have relied on the prestige of the authors and the institutions they represent, and (just as the task force reports of the Trilateral Commission) they have primarily been highly focused, relatively short-term projects. A different approach towards genuinely multilateral research has been adopted by the European Study Group, a joint effort by a number of Western European institutes including the French Institute of International Relations (IFRI), the two German institutes in Bonn and Ebenhausen (the Research Institute of the German Society for Foreign Affairs (DGAP) and the Foundation for Science and Policy (SWP), the Italian Institute for International Affairs (IAI), the Norwegian Institute of International Affairs (NUPI), and the Royal Institute of International Affairs (RIIA, Chatham House).[27] In its research work, the EGS aims at analysis and policy prescriptions from a genuinely multilateral perspective. This is to be developed through rotation of researchers and integrated multilateral study groups.

Last to be covered is *exercising influence on policy*. This aim is, of course, implicit in most policy-oriented research—certainly in the task force reports of the Trilateral Commission, in the joint reports by institutes who consider themselves national think tanks, but also in the work of SIPRI, the IIP, and the ESG. Ultimately, their work is targeted at governments—directly, through feeding it into governmental decision-making processes, or indirectly, via the media and the public. But policy-making is mainly driven by interests, not by ideas; and even where it does turn around analysis and policy ideas, the needs and demands of governmental decision makers may not easily correspond to the supply from the think tanks. For outsiders, including multinational dialogue activities and organizations, to have an impact on policy, thus involves two different tracks with a common set of hurdles. The two tracks are "interests" and "ideas," the hurdles are represented by the difficulties of access to the decision-making processes.

Interests and ideas need to be articulated and communicated to be effective. There is no clear distinction, but a continuum between "interests" and "ideas." Think tanks produce ideas, but they also promote interests. In the United States, and to a lesser degree even in Western Europe, national think tanks have tended to drift towards partisan coalitions with interest groups.[28] And in Japan, national think tanks have traditionally been lined up with particular interests, anyway.

The "interests" under discussion here are those of "internationalism," orientated towards the development, consolidation and gradual enlargement of security communities, albeit in varying geographical frameworks (West European, Atlantic, trilateral, pan-European, etc.). Basically, they represent a perspective, a specific approach towards security policy, which emphasizes communality of national interests and the need for mutual accomodation. Those interests are real in a sociological sense; they are anchored in the rapidly growing webs of economic, sociocultural and political interdependence between societies. The transnational articulation and insertion of multilateral interests and perspectives into policy-making is therefore necessary and important, but it is also impeded by the logic of policy processes which continue to be profoundly national. This is particularly so in the case of foreign policy and security issues.[29] Moreover, the type of transnational interests with which we are dealing here may have a sociological base, but not one which gives the organizations under consideration effective leverage: interests pushing for enhanced and widened security communities do not have sanctions at their disposal. They are consequently better seen as activities of persuasion and influence (the French call this *groupe de persuasion*) than traditional interest groups, who rely on power based on their ability to mobilize supporters and implement sanctions.

Most of the multilateral dialogue activities and organizations under consideration here harbor ambitions to influence policy. They do so by inviting and involving influential people from different countries and different walks of life (in hommage to Michael Curtiz' movie *Casablanca*, they are also known as "the usual suspects"); by publishing analysis and policy reports which are presented as "authoritative," thanks to the prestige of the institution and/or its members and participants; by trying to persuade officials and political leaders directly; and by communicating with and through the media.

## A Brief Note on Financial Support for Multilateral Dialogues in Europe

A systematic analysis of sources of financial support for the activities discussed here goes beyond the scope of this paper. A few remarks, however, may be appropriate. First, and most obviously, substantial amounts of money have flowed into those activities. Since they involve much travel, often across long distances, dialogue activities are expensive. Secondly, the money has come from a broad variety of sources, and the patterns of financial support differ widely. Thus, while some activities have relied almost exclusively on government support (e.g., SIPRI, IIASA), others have been supported entirely by foundations. Apart from those two sources of support (which probably represent the two major elements of overall financial assistance), international organizations such as NATO or the EC Commission, wealthy individuals, corporations, and other social organizations also played a role.

Third, foundation support overall has probably been the single most important element of financial support—not only through its overall magnitude but through its ability to help launch valuable new initiatives and programs. Unfortunately, funding for multilateral activities has traditionally been confined almost exclusively to foundations from two countries: the United States and Germany.[30] Their willingness to support activities involving nationals from several other countries has been tremendously important in helping many of the programs and activities discussed here to take off—among them CEPS (Ford Foundation), ESG (Volkswagen), Hakone conferences (Thyssen), the IISS, and the Trilateral Commission (with both receiving support from probably all major US and German foundations). Foundation support of this kind in my view has fulfilled a unique role which neither government nor corporate money could have assumed alone.

## Multilateral Dialogues: Successes and Shortcomings

In the widest sense, multilateral dialogue activities and organizations are part of complex processes of social learning. To assess their success or failure is thus quite difficult: the achievements of social learning are always tenuous and threatened by "unlearning" and regression. But even a less permanent assessment often poses difficulties precisely because those dialogue activities are part of a broader process of transnational interaction. Moreover, "success" in the security realm often will be the absence of certain developments whose independent probability may be extremely hard to assess. To take one example: if the threat of war between Western European countries has been removed from the realm of the politically plausible, has this been the result of a few fundamental policy decisions in Washington and Moscow, combined with the realities of a bipolar international system under conditions of the nuclear age—or has it been the result of an ever-closer web of economic, social and political interaction between societies and states in Europe itself? And if the latter factors are accorded some significance, then what percentage of this should be credited to the kind of activities under discussion here?

If those measures of success and failure are too ambitious, others, which may be easy to evalute, do not tell us much about the really interesting questions. It is relatively easy, of course, to evaluate—even quantitatively—the success of organizations in terms of networking or training. But those are not ends in themselves.

On the following pages, I shall try to assess the successes and shortcomings of multinational dialogue activities against the ambitious tasks of "facilitation" and "influence" in the qualitative (and possibly quite subjective) terms of an observer who participated in some of those activities. Before doing so, however, it may be useful to reflect briefly on the difficulties and impediments to success by the kind of activities under consideration here. These difficulties, it seems to me, are fourfold:

1. *Competition for attention.* To have a positive impact on intergovernmental relations either as facilitators or in terms of influence, multilateral dialogue activities need to get attention. In this, each program competes not only with other multilateral activities of similar or different bents (and the number of conferences, workshops, symposiums, etc., seems to be growing relentlessly), but also, and more importantly, with similar national activities. Successful multilateral dialogue programs will thus have to build on competitive advantages.

2. *Competition for access.* Public and/or elite attention is an important step towards access to decision makers but this access, again, constitutes a fiercely contested bottleneck. One way to gain competitive advantage here may be the association with particular political tendencies, i.e., going "partisan." But this may have a price: access may be lost, or at least drastically reduced, under changed political circumstances, and the independence and identity of an organization may be compromised.

3. *Openness of decision making for outside influence.* Governments will be open to being "helped" and "influenced" to different degrees. Thus, the American decision-making system with its large number of political appointees is more permeable than those in Western Europe or Japan, where bureaucracies have much more entrenched positions. And there will also be different political cultures shaping the interaction between outsiders and insiders in decision making in each country.

4. *Reverse influence* (instrumentalisation). In Marxist-Leninist and many authoritarian systems, governments will try to develop their own transnational channels of informal diplomacy, rather than open up to outside influence. But in pluralist political systems, this problem exists, too, if in different forms: dialogue activities and organizations may be manipulated by governments, they may become battlegrounds for, rather than carriers of, influence. One example for this was the struggle within the IISS in the early 1980s between the transatlantic "hawks" backed by the Reagan administration, and the primarily Continental European "doves." Within limits, this extension of government influence into multilateral dialogue activities may not even be a bad thing: the real flows of influence may be more intricate than intended by governments, and the balancing act between access and independent identity may well be successful. But instrumentalisation becomes a problem if and when organizations no longer are what they pretend to be.

Let me now finally turn to the question of success and failure. I will do so by returning to the geographical distinction made earlier, and discuss the issues first in the old East-West context, then along the West-West dimension.

*a) The East-West Conflict.* The "New Thinking"[31] in Soviet foreign and security policy, which actually began to take shape since the early 1980s but made its breakthough under Mikhail Gorbachev, clearly played a very important role in ending the East-West conflict. "New Thinking" originated in the Soviet Academy of Social Sciences, among the very institutes and professionals who had been involved in the various East-West exchange and dialogue activities. Many of those academicians later on assumed highly influential political positions, such as Alexandr Yakovlev, one of Gorbachev's key advisers, or Andrei Kokoshin, presently Russian Minister of Defense under President Yeltsin.

The thoroughgoing reevaluation of the premises, interests and objectives of Soviet foreign policy under "New Thinking" was driven primarily by the realities of Soviet decline—but it was also clearly shaped by discussions in the West. The conclusions, which the "New Thinking" drew from its sober analysis of international realities, in fact remarkably resembled conclusions arrived at in the parallel Western debate between "realists" and "functionalists." In the realm of security policy, the term "security partnership," which replaced the old notion of "adversary" and played an important role in "New Thinking," was originally coined by Egon Bahr, the Germn Social Democrat who had been the architect of Ostpolitik in the 1960s and 1970s. I was once told by a well-placed source that Gorbachev's foreign policy advisers had carefully studied the collected reports of the Trilateral Commission, and had produced a summary which greatly contributed to the reorientation of Soviet foreign and security policy under Gorbachev. This may be true or not—but it is certainly plausible: the reports of the Trilateral Commission

provide a summary of Western "new thinking," a *mixtum compositum* of pragmatic internationalist reformism; and many of its elements can be found again in
the rhetoric and in the actions of Soviet foreign policy under Mikhail Gorbachev.

May we then conclude that the West "persuaded" the Soviet Union on how to
end the East-West conflict? It seems to me that this conclusion is quite plausible.
But what was the contribution of multilateral dialogue activities to this outcome?
I would not hang too much evidence on the assertion about Trilateral Commission
influence on Soviet foreign policy under Gorbachev—and in any case, the Trilateral Commission's work on security issues was not primarily geared towards a
direct dialogue with the East (though a number of ccommissioners did meet with
the Chinese leadership in 1981, and a Trilateral Commission task force composed
of Giscard d'Estaign, Yasuhiro Nakasone and Henry Kissinger met with
Gorbachev in Moscow in the course of preparing its report[32]). Rather, the role of
the Trilateral Commission was to serve as a framework of analysis and policy
discussions for Western policies towards the East.

Among the activities under consideration here, only a few were genuinely
multilateral dialogue activities across the East-West divide in Europe. The oldest
of these is the series of Pugwash conferences, which developed into a veritable
industry; others are the International Institute for Peace in Vienna and the
International Institute for Applied Systems Analysis (IIASA), also in Austria
(which, however, dealt with security issues only at the margin of its activities). All
these institutions were to a considerable extent compromised by their willingness
to accomodate Marxist-Leninist governments.[33] Still, in the early stages of
détente in the 1960s, Pugwash did have some influence on political processes
related to arms control (for instance, on the nuclear test ban or on the Nonproliferation Treaty).

Some of these multilateral East-West activities may have contributed to the
changing assessment among social scientists and experts in Moscow. But none of
them, in my view, played a major role in crystallizing "New Thinking." The real
conveyor belts of change were only implicitly multilateral—they consisted of a
dense web of multilateral conferences organized by national institutions,[34] and
bilateral exchange and dialogue programs such as the regular meetings between
the major Western research institutes and IMEMO in Moscow. Within the West,
however, there was also a constant dialogue with and about those dialogues—for
example, but certainly not exclusively, in organizations such as the IISS or the
Trilateral Commission. This provided extensive opportunities for consensus
building, feedback, and interlinkage. It was this web of bilateral channels of
dialogue embedded in a wider, multilateral framework of security discussions
within the Western security community which helped to influence changes in the
former Soviet Union.

This remarkable success was made possible by a number of circumstances.
First and foremost, the Soviet system was broke; it could no longer sustain the
competition with the West. In this situation, segments of the elite were very
receptive to radically different approaches, and hence naturally attracted by the
alternatives provided by an apparently highly successful West. This secured
attention where it mattered. Nor was "access" too difficult once the "reformers"
came into power: competition for access was not a major problem since there was

a sufficient supply of "institutniks" not only willing and eager to travel, but also cleared to do so—and they did not mind going to Washington *and* London, to Paris *and* Vienna. Once the walls of the citadel of decision making had been breached in this transitional phase, neither attention nor access were major obstacles: the policy process did not yet have the complexity associated with a highly differentiated interest group structure. The new Soviet leadership was open to this type of outside influence because it needed an alternative body of experts and expertise. And since it was itself groping for new policies, it was niether interested nor even able to manipulate its advisers.

*b) Intra-Western Relations.* International dialogue and exchange activities have thus possibly been quite influential in overcoming the East-West conflict—if not primarily through explicitly mutilateral channels, then through an implicitly multilateral web of interaction. How, then, to evaluate their importance in West-West relations?

It is certainly plausible to assume that multilateral dialogue activities have contributed to strengthening the fabric of the Western security community and democratic stability in countries such as my own. Again, the really effective multilateralism was probably that implicit in a crisscrossing web of ties linking societies and countries with each other. The bilateral elements were the oldest and strongest—the annual Anglo-German Koenigswinter Conference (so called after its first venue, now alternating between Koenigswinter and Cambridge) is always cited as the benchmark of a successful nongovernmental dialogue program—but the European Movement from the beginnings in 1945 added a genuine and powerful multilateral dimension.

The implicit and explicit contributions of nongovernmental dialogue activities to Western security in strengthening the sense of "community" within Western Europe, across the Atlantic, and (somewhat more tenuously) also within the trilateral framework are thus probably by no means trivial, though impossible to evaluate precisely. In this sense, those activities have no doubt also facilitated the management of intergovernmental relations within the Western alliance system. The facilitation may have been most important in its more modest forms of providing early warning, safety valves for tensions, and an agreeable battleground to slug it out without too serious a risk. Among the multilateral institutions under consideration here, the most influential specifically in terms of security policies were probably the IISS, the Wehrkunde conferences, and more recently the NATO Review conferences organized by SWP; more generally, the Trilateral Commission and, to a lesser extent, Ditchley have also been of some importance.

In the pursuit of this relatively modest but useful objective, the difficulties and obstacles outlined above do not weigh too heavily. In the competition for attention and access, multilateral dialogue activities have the advantage of their international flair; "access" here primarily means active participation of officials, but not access to decision making itself. Since governments generally recognize the usefulness of good "facilitators," they will in principle be open to participation. Efforts at reverse influence are also no major problem since the simpler forms of facilitation do not need a distinct identity and sense of misson (other than "internationalism" itself).

These impediments, however, become more serious as we shift our attention from "facilitation" to "policy influence." As we have seen, only a handful of the organizations under consideration here aspire to exerting influence on security policy—primarily the think tanks and their joint research projects, and the Trilateral Commission. In this field, the obstacles outlined above begin to weigh heavily. The principal problems would appear to be the competition for attention and access with domestic concerns, and the incompatibility between think tank and governmental policy-making approaches. In his brilliant analysis of national think tanks, Yehezkel Dror concludes that think tanks must create new ideas so as not to waste money or effort. He goes on to say:

> If they come up with new ideas contradicting established policies, it is much worse, because it endangers and attacks what the organisations have done. ... Only if think tanks come up with new ideas after politicians and bureaucrats are in a state of despair ... is this accepted as a pure blessing.[35]

Multilateral think tank exercises face similar but possibly worse problems. First, if they are to result in genuinely integrated policy analysis, they have to agree among themselves, and negotiate common language. This will tend to diminish the chances for innovative thinking, and enhance those for conventional wisdom. Second, competition for attention and access with domestic concerns and national think tanks will push multilateral activities into relying on name recognition. This may enhance the chances for attention and access but will probably again compromise originality and independence. The most likely result is either a circular process of conventional wisdom, in which the differences between actually espoused and recommended policies become relatively small and mutually supportive, or a purified version of established policies, minus the blemishes owed to the messy realities of politics, such as the need to accomodate particular interests, bureaucratic infighting, and the like. In both instances, the analysis and recommendations still may have served useful purposes for both the think tank organization involved and governments. But this is different from policy influence.

The attempt to forge an influential private multilateral organization able to develop specific policy recommendations has probably been taken furthest by the Trilateral Commission. Yet while the commission is undoubtedly important and enjoys high attention and access, its actual influence is much less clear. It did have influence in the United States under the administration of Jimmy Carter, in particular, who had been a member himself, and had recruited his whole foreign policy team from fellow trilateralists. Among other things, the Trilateral Commission in the mid-1970s was a vehicle for the Democratic foreign policy establishment to design and project a "nonrealist" American foreign policy as an alternative to the Nixon/Ford/Kissinger policies. It was influential when the Democrats gained power because many of those who had participated in designing the new policy were now involved in implementing it.[36] But had they used the Trilateral Commission to gain influence, or had the Trilateral Commission gained influence through them? The realities of influence were clearly circular, and hard to pin down to any part of the circle.

When the Republicans returned to power under Ronald Reagan, the Trilateral Commission "lost influence," never fully to recover it in the old sense. Partly perhaps mirroring more complex international realities, and partly because of the very visibility and success of the Trilateral Commission, policy recommendations tended to become less specific and less original, more negotiated consensus and conventional wisdom. This does not make them bad or useless; many of the reports contain superb analysis and sensible recommendations. But few, if any, of the specific policy recommendations had a visible impact on government policies. Yet the commission remained important—in its more modest but probably more important function as a facilitator of consensus building and conflict management within the Western alliance system.

Have integrated multilateral research projects been more successful in influencing government policies? Probably not. Again, this does not suggest that those reports were useless or bad. But their value lay mostly in articulating a consensus view on urgent international security issues and policy recommendations which took conventional wisdom one step further.

The difficulties in organizing an effective transnational "epistemic community" on security issues are probably deeply structural. After all, it would have to assert itself against powerful national bureaucratic and military constituencies with lots of expertise of their own *and* gain dominance in a domain which during the last twenty years has become highly politicized: the most influential transnational security force in the Atlantic area has probably been the international peace movement.

How about the more modest objective of organizing multilateral research, without the ambitions of a think tank? Again, the difficulties seem to be substantial. The IISS represents a successful example, SIPRI offers a mixed picture, the Atlantic Institute for International Affairs a clear failure (it was closed in the early 1980s). The ESG brought a fresh approach to this issue, emphasising networking between institutes—but it also aimed in the direction of policy influence, and may have overreached itself in the process. The ESG has certainly not been particularly successful in coping intellectually and analytically with the dramatic changes in the European security landscape.

## Implications for the Asia Pacific Region

As Paul Evans has documented,[37] the Asia Pacific region has recently witnessed a veritable explosion of bi- and multilateral dialogue activities of a "track two" nature, and a significant shift towards offical multilateral activities. If one compares what has been happening in Asia Pacific with the European experience, several differences are striking. First, the number of "track two" activities seems to grow much more rapidly than in the case of Europe—a difference which probably reflects advances in communications and transport technology, but also the existence of institutional infrastructures and ready models in the Atlantic context. Secondly, multilateral dialogue activities in the Asia Pacific region started in the economic realm, with security-related activities following, with a delay of several years, a strikingly similar pattern. This contrasts sharply with the European experience, in which efforts at multilateral security dialogue paralleled, or indeed preceeded, similar activities with regard to economic issues. This is particularly true about the intra-European and transatlantic activities and reflects the (today often neglected) fact that in the immediate postwar period, economic and security considerations were closely intertwined. But it also holds in the context of East-West relations, as the example of Pugwash shows. And thirdly, and perhaps more controversially, it seems to me that multilateral "track two" dialogues in the Asia Pacific are more dependent on official preoccupations and less inclined to attempt to exercise independent influence than in the European case. Thus, the European Movement, Jean Monnet's Action Committee and the Trilateral Commission all tried to influence official policy at early stages of the relevant political developments (European integration, trilateral relations) as facilitators or with policy suggestions from an essentially independent position. The Asia Pacific dialogue activities by comparison seem to prefer a more oblique approach to policy, in which controversial issues and actual or potential conflicts are put aside in the hope that closer communications and cooperation will dilute conflicts and prevent tensions from arising. This may be in line with "the Asian way" of doing things, and prove quite successful. But from a European perspective, one wonders whether this attitude of resolutely pushing the tricky issues under the carpet will really work. Perhaps this has to do with the more openly conflictual European (and American) approach to political differences—but simply agreeing to disagree on basic security and foreign policy concerns has not really worked in Europe.

What conclusions can be drawn for multilateral dialogue activities in the Asia Pacific region from the analysis offered about Europe? First, nongovernmental dialogue activities and organizations in Europe have probably played an important role in defusing the potentially most dangerous conflict in the history of mankind so far. But multilateral activities did not play a particularly conspicuous role in this context. The influence resulted from a dense web of bilateral and multilateral activities. Taken together, they acquired a new quality, which if have called "implicit multilateralism." Transposed onto the Asia Pacific theater, this clearly argues for efforts to intensify dialogue programs across the divides of intergovernmental rivalry, balance of power politics and open tension.

Second, within the Western alliance system, multilateral dialogue activities have been useful and important, but in ways which are less easy to demonstrate and assess. These activities have helped to develop and strengthen security communities by focusing on communality, but also by providing safety valves and informal mechanisms to facilitate the day-to-day management of relations. Still, these achievements may be more precarious than we like to think—if one considers the recent rapid deterioration in public attitudes and perceptions in the US-Japan or, perhaps even more surprisingly, in the Anglo-German relationship. And it is as yet unclear from the European experience how effective such nongovernmental dialogue activities in the security realm can be in extending security communities geographically. Still, it will remain worthwhile and important to continue to try and expand the realm of those security communities, to "deepen" and "widen" them through informal as well as formal channels. And this also goes for the Asia Pacific region.

Third, some skepticism seems appropriate about the more ambitious objectives of nongovernmental security dialogue activities. Neither influence on policy nor innovative policy suggestions can easily be expected from such activities. Transposed onto Asia Pacific, the implication seems to me not to aim too high. What matters is not so much the glamorous feats of influence but the development of communality and the ability to absorb shocks and cope with trouble.

Fourth, I tend to be less bullish than Gerald Segal about the institute approach. To create a truly multilateral institute will not be easy—even the IISS has not quite succeeded yet. In the Asia Pacific context, the problems and sensitivities may be even greater. The way of the Asia Pacific region—informal webs and networks crisscrossing the area—may have its advantages in our context, too.

Fifth, there is no particular mystique to multilateralism. In one sense, it simply represents a natural stage in the evolution of bilateral ties of interdependence. There is thus no point in trying to be "multilateral" for the sake of it, just as there is no point in trying to avoid multilateral frameworks once conditions are ripe.

Sixth and last: the purpose of informal dialogue activities is social learning. Openness and variety is essential for this purpose. Those activities should thus deliberately follow variable geometry approaches, creating dialogue and exchange cascades. Given the challenges to our ability to learn as a species, no region—not even the Asia Pacific region—can afford the luxury to be exclusive.

## Notes

1. Francis Bacon, "Nova Atlantis," London 1627, in Klaus Heinisch, ed., *Der utopische Staat* (Reinbek b.Hamburg: RoRoRo 1960), pp. 171–215 (esp.Part IV). I owe this insight to Yehezkel Dror, "Required Breakthroughs in Think Tanks," *Policy Sciences* no. 16, 1984, S. 199–225 (219).

2. Plato, "Politeia" in *Plato, Sämtliche Werke Bd. 3* (Reinbek b.Hamburg: RoRoRo 1958), pp. 67–310.

3. Thus Frederick the Great of Prussia spoke only broken German; his language of daily intercourse was French, and he conducted a famous correspondence with the French philosopher Voltaire.

4. This is, of course, one of the most important questions faced by any social scientist interested in the future: to what extent is the present time fundamentally different from the past, to what degree is it similar to the past? This is not the place to pursue this question. But it is interesting that the two major recent works of historian Paul Kennedy—*The Rise and Fall of the Great Powers: Economic Change and Military Power from 1500 to 2000* (London: Fontana, 1988) and *Preparing for the Twenty-First Century* (New York: Random House, 1992)—are written from radically different perspectives. The former extrapolates the past struggle for power into the future, while the latter, by analyzing today's and tomorrow's challenges, totally departs from the traditional "realist" or "balance of power" perspective, presumably because Kennedy has become convinced that the challenges of the coming years are qualitatively different from those of the past, giving past experiences and models but limited value.

5. For my own efforts in this direction, see Hanns W. Maull, "Europe and the Changing Global Agenda," in Jonathan Story, ed., *The New Europe, Politics, Government and Economy Since 1945* (Oxford: Blackwell, 1993), pp. 140–59.

6. Anthony Judge, "International Institutions: Diversity, Borderline Cases, Functional Substitutes, and Possible Alternatives," in P. Taylor and J. Groom, eds., *International Organizations: A Conceptual Approach* (London: Frances Pinter 1978), quoted in James N. Rosenau, *Turbulence in World Politics, A Theory of Change and Continuity* (New York: Harvester Wheatsheaf, 1989), p. 410.

7. This is particularly obvious when dealing with authoritarian or Communist systems: witness terms such as "people's diplomacy through unofficial channels." While participation of representatives from such states may be formally nongovernmental, the reality is different. But even in democratic states, the realities of participation may be more complicated than the appearances; the problem thus exists independent of the character of the political system in the country in question.

8. For a more detailed discussion of the think tank issue, cf. the contribution of Gerald Segal in this volume.

9. For readers interested in this aspect, cf. William Wallace and Philip Gummett, *Nationalism, Internationalism, and the European Defence Market* (Paris: Institute for Security Studies, 1993, Chaillot Papers, no. 9).

10. Andrew Shonfield, *Europe: Journey to an Unknown Destination*, An Expanded Version of the BBC Reith Lectures 1972 (Harmondsworth: Penguin, 1973).

11. In other words, the paper does not include organizations which are basically American, such as the Center for East-West Security Studies (now East-West Studies) in New York or the Aspen Institute, which has conference centers in Berlin, Paris and Rome.

12. I define "Western" here not in a geographic sense, but as a term describing the US-centered alliance system with its Atlantic (NATO) and its Pacific components (the various security agreements between America and Asia-Pacific countries, the cornerstone of which is the US-Japan Security Treaty).

13. Cf. John Mueller, *The Retreat from Doomsday, The Obsolescence of Major War* (New York: Basic Books, 1991).

14. The term derives from the famous study by Karl W. Deutsch et al., *Political Community and the North Atlantic Area* (Princeton, N.J.: Princeton UP, 1957).

15. This was, of course, first argued by Immanuel Kant in his "Zum Ewigen Frieden." His thesis was corroborated over the last few decades by extensive empirical research. Cf. Andrew Hurrell, "Kant and the Kantian Paradigm in International Relations," *Review of International Studies*, no. 3, 1990, pp. 183–207; Michael W. Doyle, "Kant, Liberal Legacies and Foreign Affairs," *Philosophy and Public Affairs*, no. 3, 1983, pp. 205–35.

16. Cf. Ernst B. Haas, *When Knowledge is Power: Three Models of Change in International Organizations* (Berkeley: Univ. of California Press, 1989); and, for the example of a successful exercise of influence by one such community, Peter M. Haas, "Do Regimes Matter? Epistemic Communities and Mediterranean Pollution Control," *International Organization*, Summer 1989, pp. 377–403.

17. The first such report appeared in 1980—Karl Kaiser, Winston Lord, Thierry de Montbrial, David Watt, *Die Sicherheit des Westens, Neue Dimensionen und Aufgaben* (Bonn: DGAP, 1981). The first report produced wholly by European Institutes was written by Karl Kaiser, Cesare Merlini, Dominique Moisi, and John Roper under the title *The European Community: Progress or Decline?* (London: RIIA,

1983). More recently, there have been two reports on East-West relations in Europe by six resp. seven West European institutes, including the Netherlands Institute for International Affairs in Clingendael, The Hague, the Institut Français des Relations Internationales in Paris, the Istituto Affari Internazionali in Rome, the Research Institute of the German Society for Foreign Affairs in Bonn, the Foundation for Science and Policy in Ebenhausen and the Royal Institute for International Affairs in London. The first report—*The Community and the Emerging European Democracies* (London: RIIA, 1991)—focused primarily on the issues of association of Central Eastern European countries to the EC. Those institutes were joined for the second study—*Confronting Insecurity in Eastern Europe: Challenges for the European Community* (London: RIIA, 1992) by the Institute for Security Studies of the WEU in Paris.

18. All these activities and institutions are, of course, concerned about "widening" the circle of participation to include participants from Central European countries.

19. Many of these activities and institutions have included or added on a "Japan" dimension in recent years. Thus, the IISS has had Japanese membership and research fellows for many years; the Atlantic Institute had broadened its membership to include Japan (but got stuck with its name); and Japanese experts and officials have participated for years in the Wehrkunde and NATO Review conferences.

20. Cf. Kaiser et al., *Die Sicherheit des Westens.*

21. Cf. Dror, "Required Breakthroughs in Think Tanks" (see note 1); idem, "Think Tanks: A New Idea in Government," in Carol H. Weiss and Allen H. Barton, eds., *Making Bureaucracies Work* (Beverly Hills/London: Sage, 1980), pp. 139–52.

22. Cf. Stephen Gill, *American Hegemony and the Trilateral Commission* (Cambridge: Cambridge UP, 1990), p. 174, Cambridge Studies in International Relations: 5).

23. Cf. Masashi Nishihara, *East Asian Security and the Trilateral Countries* (New York: The Trilateral Commission, 1985, Triangle Papers, no. 30).

24. Cf. Chihiro Hosoya, Henry Owen, Andrew Shonfield, *Collaborating with Communist Countries in Managing Global Problems: An Examination of the Options* (New York: The Trilateral Commission, 1977, Triangle Papers, no. 13); Jeremy P.Azrael, Richard Löwenthal, Tohru Nakagawa, *An Overview of East-West Relations* (New York: The Trilateral Commission, 1978, Triangle Papers, no. 15).

25. This formal enshrinement of security issues as a common concern happened, of course, at the Williamsburg Summit in 1983.

26. Cf. Gill, "American Hegemony," pp. 179 ff. Further task force reports on East-West relations included Robert V. Roosa, Armin Gutowski, Michiya Matsukawa, *East-West Trade at the Crossroads* (New York: The Trilateral Commission, 1983, Triangle Papers, no. 24); Gerard C. Smith, Paolo Vittorelli, Kiichi Saeki, *Trilateral Security: Defense and Arms Control Policies in the 1980s* (New York: The Trilateral Commission, 1983, Triangle Papers, no. 26); William G. Hyland, Karl Kaiser, Hiroshi Kimura, *Prospects for East-West Relations* (New York: The Trilateral Commission, 1986, Triangle Papers, no. 31); Valery Giscard d'Estaign, Henry Kissinger, Yasuhiro Nakasone, *East-West Relations* (New York: The Trilateral Commission, 1989, Triangle Papers, no. 36).

27. The Steering Committee of ESG includes, in addition to the directors of the institutes, a number of additional well-known individual members representing other organizations and countries. Thus, the network in fact covers most of Western Europe.

28. Cf. Winand Gellner, "Politikberatung durch nichtstaatliche Akteure—Typen, Funktionen, Strategien" in Axel Murswieck, ed., *Regieren und Politikberatung* (Opladen: Leske & Budrich, 1993).

29. It is interesting to learn, though, that the transnational integration of military forces, which has taken place to a considerable degree within NATO and in the US-Japan security relationship, has opened up to channels of influence on national security policy decision making. See, e.g., Peter Katzenstein and Nobuo Okawara, "Japan's National Security, Structures, Norms and Policies," *International Security* Spring 1993, pp. 84–118 (97). In the realm of foreign policy, the process of European political cooperation (which so far is, strictly speaking, purely intergovernmental) has also shifted the modes and patterns of decision making in the direction of communality. See Elfriede Regelsberger, "European Political Co-operation," in Story, ed., *The New Europe* (see note 5), pp. 270–91. The case of Yugoslavia demonstrated, of course, how far the Community still has to go on this.

30. The Ditchley Foundation represents one exception—but I am not aware of any other major foundation outside the United States or Germany.

31. Cf. Mikhail Gorbachev, *Perestroika, New Thinking for Our Country and the World* (London: Collins, 1987); Hannes Adomeit, "Gorbachev and German Unification," *Problems of Communism* July–August 1990, pp. 1–23.

32. See Giscard d'Estaign, Kissinger, and Nakasone, *East-West Relations* (see note 26), Preface.

33. For a viciously critical analysis of Pugwash, exuding the spirit of McCarthyism, cf. *The Pugwash Conferences, A Staff Analysis prepared for the Subcommittee to Investigate the Administration of the Internal Security Act and Other Internal Security Laws*, Committee on the Judiciary, US Senate 87th Congress (Washington, D.C.: GPO, 1961).

34. Germany may have played a particularly important role in this regard with its political academies, Protestant academies, and Party foundations all of which heavily engaged in bringing experts from East and West together.

35. Dror, "Required Breakthroughs in Think Tanks," (see note 1), p. 147.

36. This has given rise to persistent conspiracy myths which portray the Trilateral Commission as the real rulers of the world. This view was salient on the extreme Right as much as on the Left, with Le Monde Diplomatique singing a similar song to Lyndon LaRouche's US Labor Party. For a book-length exposé of this myth, see Holly Sklar, ed., *Trilateralism: Elite Planning for World Management* (Boston, Mass.: South End Press, 1980).

37. Paul M. Evans, "The Dialogue Process on Asia Pacific Security Issues" (see chapter 15 of this volume).

# Appendix:
# Multilateral Security-Related Exchange
# and Dialogue Activities in Europe

1. *Atlantic Institute for International Affairs* (AI): Founded in 1961 in Paris as a "public arm of NATO." Principal activities: research (including policy research), networking, facilitation. Principal instruments: publications, conferences. Membership orginally transatlantic, later opened to include Japan. Research priorities in the realm of economics, but with substantial security dimension. Closed in 1981, in part because of competition from Trilateral Commission.

2. *Bilderberg*: Founded in 1952, over concerns of a possible withdrawal of the United States from Europe. Principal activities: networking, facilitation. Topics of discussion wide-ranging, but including substantial security dimension. Principal instruments: annual conferences. Membership transatlantic. Chaired by Prince Bernhard of the Netherlands, then Lord Home of UK, Bilderberg was long considered the quintessential international elite gathering with great influence.

3. *Center for European Policy Studies*(CEPS): Founded in 1982, originally conceived of as the "European Brookings." Principal activities: research (including policy research), networking, mostly in the economic/political realm but some work on seucrity issues. Principal instruments: publications, conferences. Membership/participation primarily from European Community countries (or transnational companies located there).

4. *The Ditchley Foundation*: Founded in 1958, first meeting in 1962. Foundation itself is Anglo-American but participation more broadly transatlantic/trilateral or global. Principal activities: networking, facilitation. Principal instruments: conferences. Topics wide-ranging, but substantial security dimension. The quintessential British dialogue retreat, occasionally also used by political leaders.

5. *European Strategy Group* (ESG): Founded in 1985 as a network of major European research institutes. Principal activities: integrated multilateral research (including policy research), training in the realm of European security broadly conceived. Principal instruments: publications, conferences.

6. *Hakone European-Japanese conferences*: First meeting took place in 1976; participation from Western European countries and Japan. Principal activities: networking, facilitating. Principal instruments: conferences. Security issues regularly form part of the agenda.

7. *Institute for Security Studies* of the Western European Union: Founded in 1989, the ISS became operational in Paris in 1990 as both an intergovernmental body and an autonomous research institute. Principal activities: networking (particularly with Eastern Europe), research, training. Principal instruments: publications, workshops, fellowships. Membership is drawn from the Western European Union countries.

8. *Interaction Council*: Founded in 1983, the Interaction Council regularly brings together more than thirty former heads of state or government. Membership "Western" in a global sense (though Gorbachev and a former president of Yugoslavia are members). Principal objectives: influence/policy recommendations, facilitation. Principal instruments: conferences, policy recommendations to governments. Security issues form one of three major areas of concern. The

ultimate "old boys network" but influence may be limited by tendency of political leaders to disregard their predecessors.

9. *International Institute for Applied Systems Analysis*(IIASA): Founded in 1972, with membership from East and West, including Japan. Principal activities: multilateral research (systems analysis), networking. Principal instruments: publications, conferences. Topics mostly long-term challenges, with security issues only of marginal importance. Subject to instrumentalisation from the East in the past.

10. *International Institute for Peace*(IIP): Founded in 1974, located in Vienna. Principal activities: research (including policy research), networking. Principal instruments: publications, conferences. With membership from Eastern and Western Europe, North America, Japan. Part of the international peace movement; as such, also subject to efforts at instrumentalisation during the Cold War by the East.

11. *International Institute for Strategic Studies*(IISS): Founded in 1958. The first, and most successful, multilateral research institute on security issues, with international council and staff. Membership originally transatlantic, now "Western" in a global sense (i.e., still excluding members from Socialist countries), though Anglo-American element still dominant . Principal activities: research, networking. Principal instruments: publications, annual conference, workshops and smaller conferences.

12. *NATO Review conferences*: First convened in 1988 by a German think tank, the *Stiftung Wissenschaft und Politik*, in Ebenhausen. Participants from transatlantic area and Japan. Principal purpose: facilitating, networking. Instruments: annual conference.

13. *The Salzburg Seminar*: Founded in 1947 as a place for in-depth seminars for decision makers and opinion leaders. Board of directors now has wide-ranging composition, including members from Asia/Pacific and former Soviet bloc. Interest in security issues marginal.

14. *The Trilateral Commission*: Founded in 1972, first meeting in 1973. Membership of about 350 from North America, (Western) Europe and Japan. Principal objectives: influence/policy research, networking, facilitating; principal instruments: task force reports, conferences (plenary, regional, national, executive committee, task force), publications. Security issues only one of several major areas of concern. Most-structured effort at exercising internationalist influence, generally considered among the most successful of such activities. A major achievement has been its role in integrating Japan into the Western alliance system.

15. *Wehrkunde conferences*: First assembled in 1963 by the editor-in-chief of the leading security and defense journal in Germany. Participation of about 180 people (both old-timers and newcomers) from transatlantic area and, more recently, Japan. Western security is central concern. Principal functions: newtorking, facilitating. Instruments: annual conference.

# The Dialogue Process on
# Asia Pacific Security Issues:
# Inventory and Analysis[1]

PAUL M. EVANS ·

> "To travel hopefully is a better thing than to arrive."
>
> Robert Louis Stevenson, *El Dorado*

## Introduction

The multiplication of channels for exchange on Pacific security issues has been a striking feature of the 1990s. A dominant image of the contemporary international relations of the region surely must be the banding together of various experts around tables of varying size, usually in the form of the familiar hollow square, sincerely (and normally politely) discussing regional matters. For at least the moment there exists a creative opportunity for individuals and governments of differing outlook, philosophy and interests to sit at the same table. It was not always so.

It is generally convenient to refer to these activities as "dialogues," something of a misnomer because there are almost always more than two parties and more than two points of view involved in the discussion. But the active part of the Greek word, *legomai*, means to converse and it is in the broader sense of an ongoing "conversation" that I think we can accurately capture the dialogue process.

Trans-Pacific dialogue on regional security issues is not a new invention. The first heyday might well have been the 1920s, another era in which the framework for security relations was in flux. The Institute of Pacific Relations established in 1925 was an ambitious and energetic effort to build an infrastructure for multilateral discussion, research, and institutional networks.[2] And during the Cold War period there were various efforts to create channels for exchange and discussion. Some of the broader, and less successful, included the Bandung forum of 1955 and various "intra-alliance" exchanges of the 1950s and 1960s linking several private US institutions with Asian counterparts.

The dialogue activities of the past three or four years are different in scope, quantity and character than their predecessors. They are being initiated by many different countries and institutes rather than an alliance leader or hegemonic power. Perhaps the most interesting intellectual challenge in examining the dialogue process is to place it in the context of changes in the regional security order or, a phrase preferred by some, security architecture.

At risk of oversimplifying what is still an evolving and inchoate situation, a consensus appears to be developing around the value and presence of something variously called a "multiplex," "multilayered," or "multifaceted" structure for Asia Pacific.[3] One level is bilateral, both in the sense of bilateral diplomatic contacts between states and bilateral security arrangements, especially between the United States and several partners around the Pacific. These include formal treaties in the case of Japan, South Korea, Thailand, Canada, and Australia, and understandings in the case of Taiwan and several other countries.

A second is the situation-specific instruments for multilateral cooperation that have grown up around specific disputes and areas of potential conflict. The multilateral activity focusing on Cambodia through the UN and regional efforts is one example. Another is the set of activities attempting to resolve potential disputes in the South China Sea.

A third level is the effort to establish channels for dialogue and consultation on a regional (e.g., the ASEAN Regional Forum) and subregional (e.g., ASEAN itself) basis. Many of the dialogues that I will discuss below fit into this category.

A fourth is the connection between regional processes and global ones, especially in areas such as nonproliferation and preventive diplomacy, usually involving institutions like the United Nations.

Dialogues, in addition to direct diplomatic action, can play a useful role at all four levels as an instrument for reducing uncertainty and anxiety in situations of instability. Tokyo and Washington, resistant to official or semiofficial multilateral dialogue on regional security issues until very recently, now see the process as reinforcing regional stability and mutual reassurance rather than undermining the bilateral foundations of the regional security order.

The dialogue channels can also be conceived as the harbinger of an order in the making and a method for reconfiguring the diplomatic and security architecture of the region. The Western domination of Asia for more than two hundred years meant that the modern nation-state was born outside of what Gerald Segal has described in his paper for this conference as "an indigenous pattern of international relations."[4] The Pacific, and especially Northeast Asia, has never attempted cooperative or collective security arrangements. And its specific experience with multilateral approaches and instruments has been brief, and not particularly positive. Any kind of collective security or concert system in future will depend upon the creation of new channels for action as well as shared attitudes and perspectives that cannot be rediscovered in Asia's recent past, but need to be invented.

My principal objective here is to inventory the specifically Asia Pacific dialogue channels that have arisen since the late 1980s or that are currently being considered. They are listed in an appendix to the paper. I should emphasize at the outset that I am aiming at a moving target and that the inventory is not exhaustive, though I believe it does cover most of the principal channels. After considering the origins and pattern of the dialogues, I will turn to some of the challenges and choices that need to be faced in the months ahead.

# The Dialogue Enterprise

At the end of 1993, the dialogue business could be judged a growth industry even by the legendary standards of Asia's "economic miracles." The number of meetings, as compiled in a recent listing by the Department of Foreign Affairs in Canberra identified more than three per month in 1994. A rough count suggests that upwards of one thousand different persons from some eighteen countries have participated in at least one of the meetings in the past year, not including the strictly military gatherings such as the Pacific Armies Management Seminar or the Asia Pacific Roundtable in Kuala Lumpur which itself attracted almost four hundred participants to the June meeting in 1993.

It is tempting to speculate that the proliferation of proposals and programs reflects some combination of (*a*) the fit between the academic's desire to talk and the politician's desire to launch "initiatives"; (*b*) the need for overworked foreign ministries to employ lower paid academics to keep an interesting topic simmering; (*c*) the inevitable attempt by Western-trained or Western-based intellectuals to employ European-inspired instruments (like the CSCA) for solving Asian problems.

Put somewhat differently, track two discussions are a response to a deep uncertainty about viable instruments and frameworks for managing a more complex security agenda into the coming century. In this situation of uncertainty, intellectual curiosity coincides in creative ways with low-risk and low-cost experimentation by governments.

Since 1986 several governments have issued concrete proposals advocating new multilateral processes, institutions and structures for addressing security matters.[5] The most important development at the formal governmental level has been the inclusion of security issues as part of the ASEAN PMC, now in the form of the ASEAN Regional Forum which includes the dialogue partners as well as China and Russia.

At the nongovernmental level, security issues, both narrowly and broadly defined, have been the subject of a significant outpouring of academic writing, research and conference activity, especially since 1990. In 1989 there were only three or four channels for trans-Pacific discussion of political and security matters in a multilateral setting. As the final section of this paper indicates, there are now close to thirty. The number is considerably larger if we include exclusively "subregional" dialogues within, for example, ASEAN or Southeast Asia.

This "nongovernmental" activity has at least three distinguishing features. First, though both bilateral and multilateral channels have grown considerably, the most dramatic growth has been of a multilateral nature involving simultaneous participation from several Asia Pacific countries. Second, while some of the channels of discussion are restricted to so-called "like-minded," the majority involve participants spanning previous ideological and national divides. The tendency is towards inclusiveness. Third, most of the channels have been of a "blended" or "track two" nature. They involve meetings of academics, journalists, and occasionally politicians and also tend to include government officials (usually from ministries of foreign affairs though also sometimes from defense ministries) attending in "unofficial," "private" capacities.

While having some features in common, the various nongovernmental channels differ along at least ten dimensions.

1. Definition of the region. There has been an approximate balance between those which conceive of the "region" as the broad Asia Pacific and those which focus on "smaller" regions such as South China Seas, ASEAN, Southeast Asia, Northeast Asia, or the North Pacific. Curiously, very few if any now take an exclusively Asian approach which includes South Asia and Central Asia and excludes the "Pacific" players, especially the United States. Considering the serious consideration of possible Asian futures, seen for example in the EAEC concept, an intracontinental channel seems almost inevitable in the near future.

2. Degree of policy relevance. Some of the channels have focused on direct policy questions framed in terms of current state agendas (e.g., arms control proposals, conflict-specific issues such as the South China seas or Korean peninsula) and others have taken a longer-term view focusing on such topics as strategies of reassurance, changing threat perceptions, alternative security frameworks, etc.

3. Inclusiveness of membership. In addition to the definition of the region, there are differing approaches to what countries should be represented. Most of the channels are tending to bring in participants from across ideological divides, though some are restricted to the like-minded.

4. Breadth of the definition of security. Most have focused on security narrowly conceived in terms of military issues and state agendas. Others are taking a broader cut to include such issues as environment, demography, transnational economic flows, good governance and human rights as part of the security agenda.

5. Backgrounds of participants. Most tend to be generalists on regional international affairs or regional security matters with occasional specialists on technical issues in arms control, proliferation, etc. Government officials have tended to come from foreign ministries though the number from military establishments has begun to grow noticeably in the past two years. Some dialogue participants have gone on to positions in government. The most notable example is probably Han Sung-Joo, formerly a professor at Korea University who was appointed the Korean foreign minister in early 1993. It appears that most of the dialogues make a conscious effort to balance generational representation, though this is less evident with respect to gender.

6. Degree of government direction and funding. Some channels have been primarily or exclusively funded by governments, others by private foundations. Most have received funding from a single source, though some have involved joint sponsorship from more than one country. In some channels government officials play a major role in determining the agenda of discussion; in others they do not.

7. Extent of original research and conceptualization. Though the normal formula is for papers to be commissioned in advance of meetings and then presented, few of these papers are produced as integral parts of ongoing, collaborative research programs.

8. Kind of gathering. Some have been small, focused workshops. Others have been large conference-like gatherings ranging from forty or fifty participants to as many as three hundred and fifty.

9. Role of institutes. Most but not all of the nongovernmental and track two dialogue channels appear to be organized by a single institute, usually working in cooperation with partners in other countries. There is a trend toward multilateralizing agenda setting, meaning that instruments like multinational "planning committees" create or at least approve conference topics and authors. For example, the ISIS Malaysia "Asia-Pacific Roundtable" has now become the ASEAN ISIS "Asia-Pacific Roundtable."

10. Locations. Unlike the situation in Europe with established programs at Bilderberg, Ditchley Park, Salzburg, Bologna, Wilton Park, and other choice locations for "country house diplomacy,"[6] the Asia Pacific dialogue process is unfolding in multiple venues, a decidedly movable feast at "no name" locations. With the exception of the Shimoda Conference hosted by the JCIE, almost none of the dialogues are named for the place in which they meet or, alternatively, for an inspiring individual or event. Probably the single most active city is Kuala Lumpur, though it perhaps has not yet achieved a "Helsinki-like" status.

The most ambitious proposal in the nongovernmental area has been the call for the creation of the Council for Security Cooperation in Asia Pacific (CSCAP). The idea of CSCAP was enunciated at a meeting in Seoul in November 1992 and restated in slightly modified form in Kuala Lumpur in June 1993. Its main thrust is to create a more structured regional process of a nongovernmental nature that is open to all countries and territories in the region. The council is to be guided by a steering committee consisting of representatives of nongovernmental institutions in the region. Broad-based member committees are to be formed in participating countries composed of academics and other individuals as well as government officials acting in their private capacities. CSCAP will establish working groups to undertake policy-oriented studies on specific regional political-security problems. Some of the topics being considered for the working groups include maritime cooperation in Southeast Asian waters, enhancing security cooperation in the North Pacific, alternative conceptions of security in Asia Pacific, and CSBM and transparency measures.[7]

## Accomplishments

Considering that the dialogue process is at such an early stage, it is difficult to draw any firm conclusions about its actual achievements. The interim results need to be considered from two perspectives: that of security policy and international relations; and that of research and academic achievement. Separating the two is difficult.

Using the criteria developed in Hanns Maull's thoughtful paper for this conference, there is no doubt that the dialogues have produced new networks linking several of the key institutes in the region. They probably have also increased the visibility and importance of regional security issues in elite discussion around the Pacific. The process has created a great deal of experience in blending academic and political cultures and, in some circumstances, like Canada's, expanding interaction between the academic and policy-making communities in matters of international security.

The prospective policy relevance of the track two and nongovernmental processes are relatively obvious. At the most basic level, they have laid some of the ground work for the current round of formal governmental consultations. The NGO-inspired activities of the late 1980s and early 1990s did a great deal to legitimate multilateral discussion at a time when several governments (the American and Japanese among them) ranged from sceptical to hostile about the process.

Beyond legitimating discussion (and discussion about discussion), have there been any direct contributions to policy development? Jaw-jaw might be better than war-war, but have any ideas been developed in the track two process which affect state action? Academics might be free to rush in where (and when) governments fear to tread. But what can they offer?

Using these more stringent criteria of policy relevance, several positive contributions should be noted. The dialogues have prepared the ground for formal diplomatic activity by increasing the comfort level for the frank exchange of views on issues previously considered too sensitive for open discussion. Viewed from another perspective they have played a useful role in shaping the vocabulary (e.g., preventive diplomacy, cooperative security, confidence and security building measures, transparency) that has recently entered into official forums.

The nongovernmental process has probably been reassuring to several governments not accustomed to this kind of public discussion (e.g., China, Vietnam) and to those which had been fearful that multilateral discussions could erode commitment to existing bilateral security ties (Japan and the United States). And it is worth emphasizing that the level of discussion has increased not just across the boundaries of previous ideological, cultural and alliance divides, but equally importantly among "the like-minded." For instance, both Japan and South Korea maintain close security ties with the United States but until recently the two countries have had comparatively little exchange on regional security issues and concerns. The multilateralization of the dialogue agenda has been one of the factors promoting Japanese-Korean discussion.

Viewed from the second perspective, academic and intellectual contribution, my impression is that most of the achievements lie in the future. Probably more than half of the dialogues have no interest in an academic or scholarly product, even though it is academics who manage many of them. Only a very few of the papers presented in these meetings are published in major journals or books which reach beyond the community already interested in specific technical questions or regional developments. By the standards of the best of international scholarship, the thinking and writing produced by the dialogues has not left any important theoretical footprint. The great books remain to be written.

Here again it might be wise to wait a year or two longer before coming to any final conclusions. Several projects now under way or being considered by such organizations as the East-West Center, the Australian National University, the Social Science Research Council (New York) and others are taking aim at the deeper questions of social science theory and method which the recent Asia Pacific experience raises. The next stage of activity could very well focus on international research teams, collaborative problem definition and problem solving which have a better chance of making a visible and durable academic mark.[8]

## Institution Building Asia Pacific Style

The soft and informal process by which multilateral security dialogues are taking form in the Asia Pacific context poses some interesting problems for observers of international institutions. One possible view is that the process is embryonic and as it matures will follow the pattern seen in Europe and North America. Another view is that it is emerging from unique historical circumstances and will likely involve in its own particular way.

At this point the second view is more compelling. Rather than understand Asia Pacific multilateralism based on historical experience of elsewhere, a more useful approach might be to theorize from the "inside out," that is to trace the features of the institution building process in the Asia Pacific context before formulating a precise definition of what institutions and processes should look like or how they compare to the institutions and processes developed elsewhere. While awaiting this insightful text on sociology of Asia Pacific diplomacy, let me offer several observations and questions.

The most important examples of multilateral institution building in the Pacific have been economic. A fundamental point to be made is that it is economics that defines the very concept of Asia Pacific. It has been economic problems and cooperation that have elicited the most active responses. The networks established through the Pacific Basin Economic Council, the Pacific Economic Cooperation Council, the Pacific Forum for Trade and Development, the Asia Pacific Economic Cooperation Forum have been the strongest institutional sinews pulling the Pacific together. They deserve more study as distinctive forms of regional cooperation which have potential applicability to what is emerging in the realm of political and security affairs.[9] What has been the style of institution building? What role have cultural differences played in shaping the kind of instruments and processes that have emerged? One of the distinguishing features of economic integration in Eastern Asia has been that it has been achieved without a complex set of intergovernmental arrangements and instead through a series of unilateral and interactive policy adjustments by national governments in such areas as investment regulations and taxation. Does this habit of informal policy adjustments have any meaning for the management of regional security relations?

A second observation is that many of the key participants in the security dialogues from both sides of the Pacific, but especially in Asia, have also been involved in a decade of activity in the economic cooperation enterprise, especially PAFTAD, PECC and APEC. It would be a splendid study in "epistemic communities," to trace the origins of the transnational intellectual community which produced the concept of "open regionalism" as a way of squaring global trade objectives with the peculiarities of intensified economic interaction in specific geographic regions. Translated into security matters, this is less a matter of creating new words than of borrowing them from elsewhere and giving them a specific meaning that is widely accepted within the region. Percolated through several levels of meetings and discussions, a variety of terms in the security area are currently being indigenized, among them "preventive diplomacy," "cooperative security," "transparency," and "security forum."

Gerald Segal's paper for this conference thoughtfully raises the issue of regional sensitivities to European involvement in the management of Asia Pacific security issues and the dialogue process. There are certainly deep historical reasons for these sensitivities, particularly among the Asian countries. His case for an "open multilateralism"—in which dialogues are constructed without fixed geographical definitions of what constitutes the region—rests upon a specific appreciation of Eurasian as well as Asia Pacific dimensions of Asian security. Asia Pacific is indeed an artificial construct but it is proving a very useful one. Beyond "Pacific chic," the "Pacific enthusiasts" and what I might label "Pacific hyperbole" is a more constructive argument which recognizes that the Asia Pacific concept has produced some very positive results which are not detrimental to European interests and which show few signs of developing in an inward looking direction. For the moment at least, an Asia Pacific setting is proving more conducive to frank and detailed discussion than an open multilateralism.

## Strengthening the Dialogue Process

Looking at the dialogue agenda for the remainder of the decade, one faces two temptations. The first is to declare the enterprise a success and sit back and let the invisible hand of market forces move the process forward. It has gathered a great deal of momentum and will no doubt continue to develop in productive, if unpredictable ways. The second temptation is to expect too much. The fact that a formal and inclusive dialogue channel along the lines of the ASEAN Regional Forum has been created so much faster than almost anyone predicted even two years ago can easily lead to the expectation that other institutional forums will readily and easily be created.

My own interpretation is that the first phase of dialogues and institution building is largely complete. The dialogue process has been constructed in such a way that it is seen as legitimate and valuable by almost all the governments of the region. There are now sufficient cohesion and lines of communication among a large number of key institutes around the Pacific to be able to provide a great deal of intellectual and research support for the concrete initiatives that will be forthcoming through the Senior Officials Meetings attached to the ARF and through specific "subregional" and conflict-specific initiatives. An incomplete but nevertheless workable framework has now been created.

There are two special challenges which will need to be faced in the second phase to come. The first is the ability to achieve some concrete results in the hard security areas of CSBMs and arms control. There will no doubt be multiple paths to this objective, some bilateral and some multilateral, some by direct means including specific proposals and some indirectly through an emphasis on transparency and registry measures. Whatever the path, it is clear that the more policy relevant track two channels face the difficult task of addressing areas of disagreement rather than areas of agreement. Not surprisingly, one of the reasons that a high level of comfort has been achieved is that controversial and difficult issues have been largely kept off the agenda. At some point soon this is bound to change.

The second special challenge is to move from cooperative research and dialogue programs to genuinely collaborative ones. The creation of research teams is expensive and complicated but necessary to raising the academic quality and policy relevance of the track two process.

Let me conclude with five specific measures to meet both of these challenges.

1. The financing of the nongovernmental and track two elements of the dialogue process has come largely from governments (the Canadian, Australian, Malaysian, Japanese, and American have probably been the largest sources) and private foundations in the United States and Japan. Although it may be sacrilege to say so, my reading is that there are sufficient funds available to support the conference and workshops which are part of the dialogue process.[10] Where new funds are needed is for collaborative research aimed at both specific policy problems and more basic research. Putting the teams together will be a complicated and expensive task. And it remains important to have the active involvement of younger scholars and researchers. One idea that should be considered is the creation of a series of regionwide postdoctoral fellowships in Asia Pacific security which could be tied to participation in an ongoing collaborative project.

2. It is very clear that there are more multilateral dialogues at the NGO and track two level than qualified researchers and thinkers to participate in them. And here arises the mater of graduate education and training. This is particularly the case in most Asian countries where there is the added burden of being able to work in English, the usual language for most of the dialogue activity. In addition to the problem of excessive exposure of "the usual suspects," to borrow the line from the film *Casablanca*, it is probable that the scholarly output of many of the leading figures in the field is slowed by the pressures of the conference circuit.[11] My own experience is that many of the channels have been successful in blending generations. There has been less success in bringing a significant number of women into the process and in moving the security dialogues outside the realm of specialists and into the realm of what Susan Berresford, the vice president of the Ford Foundation, has called "ordinary people."[12] This widening of participation will be difficult, though the difficulty will decline as the discussion of security broadens to include environmental issues, migration questions and the like.

3. Concerning exchange infrastructure, there does not seem to be a shortage of outlets for publications and findings through reputable journals and publishers. But there should be better instruments for consultation among the organizers of the main dialogue channels. CSCAP, or a CSCAP-like process, would be one way of doing this by convening an annual event which would review the activities of the numerous projects under way as well as reporting on the findings of the working groups formally sponsored by the council. Other steps should also be encouraged. The Australian calendar of regional security meetings is a valuable resource. It should be continued, perhaps in electronic bulletin board form as well as hard copy. There are very good communications networks by fax through the PacNet of the Pacific Forum/CSIS and e-mail through the Asia Pacific Foundation in Vancouver. What is missing is a central and accessible repository for commissioned

papers and conference reports which would assist the overall effort to be more cumulative. In other words, it would be helpful to have a modest project to "track" the various dialogue channels through a kind of "Dialogue Watch" to chronicle agenda items, participants, and main conclusions. At the moment, foreign ministries appear to be doing this more systematically than academic research institutes. The results of the tracking could easily be communicated through one of the existing communication vehicles.

4. Though at the moment the dialogue process is dynamic, flexible and creatively chaotic, it will be a challenge to maintain these virtues even in the medium term. The expenditure of energy and money has been considerable. And there is little question that there is a considerable duplication of effort and redundancy in the topics of discussion. CSCAP has the potential to play a coordinating role through its secretariat and annual meeting. At the same time, CSCAP should not aspire to becoming *the* dialogue channel. This would jeopardize the healthy pluralism of the current situation and potentially reduce the autonomy and independence of exchange activities. Over-centralization is potentially more dangerous to the dialogues than redundancy or inefficiency. It is also important that there be room for new institutes and individuals, from within Asia Pacific as now conceived and from outside it, to establish additional layers of dialogue activities.

   Yet there are reasons to be sceptical about the current utility of what Gerald Segal identifies as an "Asia/Pacific version of the International Institute for Strategic Studies," something along the lines of a "Pacific Security Institute." Beyond the issues of funding, location and management, is the more fundamental matter of regional resistance to establishing any independent, geographically fixed institution. An alternative conception is to continue developing national-based institutes and expand cooperation among them. CSCAP is envisioned to be one of the principal instruments for expanding this cooperation. Any serious discussion of a regional security institute will thus likely be postponed until after CSCAP demonstrates whether it can achieve the objectives it has set for itself.

5. Despite the fact that many of the current dialogues include participants from countries across the ideological spectrum, the vast majority of the funding, direction and energy is coming from a comparatively small number of locations, primarily ASEAN, Japan, Australia, the United States, Canada, and South Korea. The socialist countries regularly attend the track two dialogues but rarely initiate them. North Korea is a special case and no early progress can be expected. The real focus should be finding ways to engage Vietnam and China more fully in the regional process. The obstacles to this engagement need careful consideration and some creative solutions.

## Notes

1. Portions of this essay have appeared elsewhere, including a paper presented to the conference on "ASEAN Internal and External Cooperation in the 1990s and Beyond," Manila, January 13–15, 1993; and "The Council for Security Cooperation in Asia Pacific: Context and Prospects," first presented in Canberra at the Conference on "Economic and Security Cooperation in the Asia-Pacific: Agendas for the

1990s," July 28–30, 1993, and to appear in revised form in *The Pacific Review* in the summer of 1994. I very much appreciate the assistance provided by Herman Kraft, Peggy Mason, Charles Morrison, the Japan Center of International Exchange, AccessAsia administered by the National Bureau of Asian Research in Seattle and several other foundations and research institutes for generously providing information for the inventory presented in the Appendix to this chapter.

2. There was then, and later, considerable debate about whether the IPR's role extended beyond cross-cultural contact and exchange of individual views in a private framework to include more overtly diplomatic functions. See Lawrence T. Woods, *Asia-Pacific Diplomacy: Non-Governmental Organizations and International Relations* (Vancouver: University of British Columbia Press, 1993), esp. Ch. 3.

3. The clearest statement is by Yukio Satoh. In 1991, he chose the word "multiplex." See his "Asian-Pacific Process for Stability and Security," prepared for the conference on "ASEAN and the Asia-Pacific Region: Prospect for Security Cooperation in the 1990s," Manila, June 6–7, 1991. In 1993 he chose the word "multifaceted." See his "The United States and Japan in the Asia-Pacific Region: Points for Consideration," prepared for the 84th American Assembly, Arden House, New York, November 11–14, 1993. My categorization of the "facets" is slightly different than his.

4. Gerald Segal, "Asia/Pacific Security Studies in Europe" (see chapter 5 of this volume).

5. These are chronicled in Paul M. Evans, "Emerging Patterns in Asia-Pacific Security: The Search for a Regional Framework" in Jawhar Hassan and Rohanna Mahmood, eds., *Towards A New Pacific Order: Proceedings of the Fifth Asia-Pacific Roundtable* (Kuala Lumpur: ISIS Malaysia, 1991), pp. 55–61; Stewart Henderson, "Canada and Asia Pacific Security: The North Pacific Cooperative Security Dialogue," NPCSD Working Paper Number 1 (Toronto: York Centre for International and Strategic Studies), January 1992; and Gary Klintworth, "Asia-Pacific: More Security, Less Uncertainty, New Opportunities," *Pacific Review*, vol. 5, no. 3 (1992). A recent addition was offered by the Korean Foreign Minister Han Sung-Joo, when in October 1993 he called for the creation of a "Northeast Asia multilateral security framework." See his speech on "Korea and China in the Asia-Pacific" to the Asia Society, Hong Kong Center, October 27, 1993.

6. In addition to the lively essay by Hanns Maull, "Call-Girls in the Old World: Of Multilateral Think Tanks, Dialogue Programs and Other Promiscuous Activities in and Around Europe," prepared for this conference, see "The Role of Private Institutions in International Relations: Lessons from Trans-Atlantic Relations and Challenges for Japan," commissioned by NIRA and prepared by the JCIE, February 1991.

7. On CSCAP see Desmond Ball, "The Council for Security Cooperation in Asia Pacific," unpublished paper, Strategic and Defence Studies Centre, Australian National University; and Paul M. Evans, "The Council for Security Cooperation in Asia Pacific: Context and Prospects," *Pacific Review*, Summer 1994 (forthcoming).

8. The case for genuinely collaborative social science research is forcefully argued by David Featherman in his essay "Internationalization of the Social Sciences and Joint Endeavour," in *Challenges and Opportunities for U.S.-Japan Exchange in the New Era*, published by the Center for Global Partnership in August 1991.

9. A useful starting point is Lawrence T. Woods, "Non-governmental Organizations and Pacific Cooperation: Back to the Future," *Pacific Review*, vol. IV, no. 1 (1991), pp. 312–21 and his *Asia-Pacific Diplomacy* (see note 2).

10. I am informed by colleagues from government in several countries that funds for travel and conference expenses are more readily available to academics than government officials. This claim has not to my knowledge been independently verified.

11. The ideal conference participant/organizer: background in international relations; technical knowledge of various issues in international security; detailed knowledge of at least six countries in the region; comprehension of key regional trends in the areas of economics, politics, and society; ability to work in several languages including English; capacity for air travel and working at peak performance twelve time zones away from home base at least six times per year.

12. Susan B. Berresford, "Independent Institutions in the United States as Models," in *Challenges and Opportunities for U.S.-Japan Exchange in the New Era* (Tokyo: The Center for Global Partnership, 1991), p. 46.

# APPENDIX
## Inventory of Dialogue Channels

The following list identifies some of the various programs channels which are multicountry, ongoing, rather than single meetings, and which have as a general focus some element of Asia Pacific security matters.

Three sets of important activities have *not* been included. The first is the host of bilateral exchanges that exist between specific institutes or countries. My impression is that there are in fact more of these bilateral programs than multilateral, even though it is the multilateral that have grown dramatically in the past few years. Most major institutes around the Pacific have a regular bilateral series with one or more partners. The second is the non–Cold War dialogues of the late 1970s and early 1980s which are now completed. One example was the "Asia Dialogue," a regular program of meetings and publications sponsored by the Japan Center for International Exchange, the National Institute for Research Advancement, and the Institute for Southeast Asian Studies in the 1980s. The third is the dialogue and exchange activities associated with European, Atlantic and global processes such as the Non-Aligned Movement, the Pugwash Conference, the Williamsburg meetings, the Atlantic Council and the Trilateral Commission. The one exception to this rule is the inclusion of some of the UN activities that have a special focus on the Asia Pacific region rather than situating Asia Pacific concerns in a broader setting.

For purposes of convenience, the list can be divided into the larger annual or biannual events and the smaller, more focused workshops and conferences. I have added brief sections on (*a*) activities recently completed, though of some lasting significance if only through successor phases; and (*b*) projects currently at the planning (prefunding) stage. It is based on information available as of January 1994.

## I.   Annual and Biannual Meetings

1. The ISIS Malaysia/ASEAN ISIS **Asia-Pacific Roundtable**. It originated in 1987, has been held annually in Kuala Lumpur, and has developed into the largest annual event in Asia, with more than three hundred and fifty attending the roundtable in June 1993. Area coverage includes the broader Asia Pacific region, with attention to both Northeast and Southeast Asia, the latter predominating. Invitations are relatively open, though South Asia is not included as part of the region. Participants include academics, researchers, journalists and diplomats. After the 1993 roundtable there occurred a separate, by invitation only, meeting of military officials and diplomats from a selection of Asia-Pacific countries as arranged by the Malaysian Ministry of Defense. It is probable that this military gathering will convene on an annual basis in future.

2. The **Pacific Symposium** hosted by the US National Defense University. Annual meeting with a combination of academic and governmental (civilian and military) participants. It alternates between the NDU in Washington, DC and CINCPAC in Honolulu.

3. The **Asian Peace Research Association** meets on a regular basis and includes as participants academics, journalists, and government officials. The most recent meetings were held in Wellington, New Zealand in January 1992, attracting 170 people from twenty-three countries, and in Penang in November 1993. The meetings are open to all who wish to attend.

4. The **Western Pacific Naval Symposium**. A conference held in alternate years. The first was in Sydney in 1988; the second in Bangkok in 1990; the third took place in 1992 in the United States; Malaysia will host the fourth in 1994. Most of the participants are

naval officers at the CNO level from thirteen "like-minded" countries, though some academics attend.

5. The **Pacific Armies Management Seminar**. Annual meetings of senior officers (colonels to brigadier generals) from several countries in Asia with counterparts from Australia, New Zealand, the United States and Canada. No Communist or post-Communist countries are included (excepting Laos). The last was in January 1993 in Delhi, cohosted by India and the United States, with thirty-six nations invited.

6. The North Pacific Region Advanced Research Center in Sapporo, with support from the National Institute for Research Advancement, has organized an annual meeting since 1989. Participants have been nonofficials from the United States, South Korea, North Korea, the USSR/Russia, Canada and China. Now known as the **Hokkaido Conference on North Pacific Issues**, it hosts an annual conference which brings together by invitation about twenty academics and other researchers from seven North Pacific countries.

7. Since 1987 the Japanese Ministry of Foreign Affairs has sponsored an annual **International Security Forum** in Japan. The seventh was held in Tokyo in March 1994, with participants invited from universities and research institutes around the Pacific.

## II.   Multiple-Meeting Workshop and Conference Series

1. Created in 1977, the **ASEAN-Japan Dialogue** organized by the Japan Center for International Exchange (JCIE) in cooperation with the Institute of Southeast Asian Studies (ISEAS) and other institutions in ASEAN has progressed through five stages. Phases I and II looked at the broad dimensions of the relationship; Phase III (1983–84) examined trade and investment, mutual perceptions and security issues, and Phases IV and V have also included mention of security-related issues. Some of the discussions at the meetings in Phase VI (1991–93) also include security issues. Participants have principally been from universities and research institutes in Japan, ASEAN, with occasional participants from North America, Australia, South Korea, China and Hong Kong.

2. Since 1978 an international steering committee has organized eight conferences on **The Sea Lanes of Communication**. The most recent was hosted by the Center for Strategic and International Studies (CSIS) in Jakarta and the Indonesian Navy in January 1993. It is a nongovernmental forum but involves serving officials and officers in their private capacities. The participants initially included the United States, Japan, Korea and Indonesia. In the 1980s participation was widened to include the ASEAN countries, Australian and New Zealand. The Ninth conference is scheduled for Kuala Lumpur in 1994 as hosted by the Malaysian Institute of Maritime Affairs.

3. The regional security conferences organized by the United Nations. They began in 1989 with a series of annual meetings under the auspices of the **Katmandu Regional Center for Peace and Disarmament in Asia Pacific** together with related regional conferences sponsored by the UN and selected host countries, including bicentennial meetings in Kyoto beginning in 1991 and Shanghai in August of 1992. The next Katmandu meeting will take place in January 1994. Participants include in both series academics, journalists and diplomats, the latter in their personal capacity. The **UN Center for Disarmament Affairs** (prior to January 1992 titled the Department of Disarmament Affairs, then the Office of Disarmament Affairs) within the Department of Political Affairs has also sponsored a series of regional meetings of senior officials to promote the US Register of Conventional Arms. Representatives from seventeen Asia Pacific countries attended a meeting in January 1993 in Tokyo. The next meeting is scheduled for Hiroshima in May 1994.

4. **Yomiuri Shimbun** and the **Gaston Sigur Center for East Asian Studies** at George Washington University have organized a series of annual seminars, alternating between Tokyo and Washington. Participants have come from Japan, South Korea, North Korea, China, the United States and two Southeast Asian countries. The ninth meeting in the series was held in May 1993 in Tokyo and included participants from South Korea, Japan, China, Taiwan, Russia, Singapore and the United States. The Korean peninsula has been a principal theme with a focus on domestic politics, economics, foreign policy and security issues. George Washington University and Keio University, in cooperation with Mainichi Shimbun have organized two conference on the Korean peninsula, the first in Osaka in November 1992 and the second in Tokyo in August 1993.

5. The Institute for Global Security Studies in Seattle is organizing a series of meetings, **The Asia-Pacific Dialogues on Maritime Security**. The meetings are designed to bring together experts in the general area of maritime security to discuss informally the Asia-Pacific region. The first meeting was held in Vancouver in November 1991 in conjunction with Simon Fraser University and the second in Seattle in September 1992 in conjunction with the School of Marine Affairs at the University of Washington. The first meeting focused on naval arms control after the Cold War; and the second on maritime confidence building measures, the naval buildup in the region, and the possible contribution on regional naval cooperation. The third dialogue was held in Bandung, Indonesia, in June 1993 and hosted by the Center for Archipelago, Law and Development Studies. It dealt very broadly with broader security issues, including the Korean peninsula. Participants have been both officials and academic researchers from Australia, the United States, China, Canada, Indonesia, Japan, Korea, Malaysia, Singapore, Russia, Taiwan, Thailand, and Vietnam. A fourth dialogue is tentatively scheduled for the Institute of Security and International Studies in Bangkok in the summer of 1994 and a fifth for 1995, tentatively at the Malaysian Institute for Maritime Affairs in Kuala Lumpur.

6. The Australian National University through the Peace Research Centre and the Centre for Strategic and Defence Studies has hosted several meetings as part of a three-year project on **Regional Approaches to Defense and Security Building in Asia Pacific**. One example is the July 1991 workshop on "Naval Confidence and Security Building Measures in the Asia Pacific Region."

7. Since the mid-1970s **The Center for International Security and Arms Control (CISAC)** at Stanford University has hosted several dozen fellows from China, Russia and Korea and conducted arms control discussions with Chinese, Japanese and Korean experts. Recently CISAC has concentrated on questions related to US-China military ties and developing a dialogue among the navies of the North Pacific. In October 1991 it brought together a group of Japanese, Russian and US naval officers. In the summer of 1993 senior Chinese, Russian and US naval officers met in a series of closed workshops bringing together scholars and officials from the United States, North and South Korea, and Japan. The principal subject has been naval cooperation.

8. Since 1990, a series of meetings and workshops on **Managing Potential Conflicts in the South China Sea** have been held in Indonesia (and later in Manila) under the auspices of the Research and Development Agency of the Indonesian Department of Foreign Affairs. Workshops have been held in Bali in January 1990, in Bandung in June 1991, and in Yogjakarta in June 1992. Additional technical and focused working groups began work in May 1993, with the first workshop meeting in Manila in May 1993. The objective of the meetings is to explore methods for enhancing cooperation in the region. The meetings are technically nongovernmental, although government officials are in attendance and participate actively. Participation has been from across

maritime Southeast Asia and has also included Chinese officials and academics. A principal source of financial support has been the Canadian International Development Agency.

9. The **Asia Pacific Forum**. The first meeting was held in Karuziawa, Japan, in 1990 and was arranged by the ASEAN-ISIS with participation from the Japan Institute of International Affairs and Columbia University. At the second meeting in Manila, organized by Institute for Strategic and Development Studies, in January 1993, the list of participants was expanded to include Canadians and South Koreans. The conference in 1994 will also include Australians. Participants include academics, journalists and government officials present in their private capacities.

10. The Institute on Global Conflict and Cooperation at the University of California, San Diego, is organizing a series of meetings, **IGCC Northeast Asian Cooperation Dialogue**. The objective is to examine possibilities for building trust and cooperation among six countries in the region—Russia, China, North Korea (though its representatives did not attend the first meeting), South Korea, Japan and the United States. Participants include both policy officials (normally one from the military and one from the foreign ministry) plus two private individuals from each country. A planning session was held in July 1993 and the first meeting in San Diego on October 8–9, 1993. The second meeting is scheduled for Tokyo in April 1994 and will include one nongovernmental person, one diplomat and one military official from each country. Sponsorship is coming from both American and Japanese sources.

11. The Asia Society in New York and the Japan Institute of International Affairs are co-sponsoring a collaborative project, **Prospects for International Cooperation in Northeast Asia: A Multilateral Dialogue**, to explore current economic, political/security and transnational issues in Northeast Asia and to explore possible structures for managing future cooperation. Participants will come from Canada, China, Japan, Mongolia, North Korea, Russia, South Korea, Taiwan and the United States. The first meeting, focusing on economic issues, was held in New York in January, 1994. Subsequent conferences on political and security issues are scheduled for summer 1994 and spring 1995.

12. The National Bureau of Asian Research in Seattle has organized a series of meetings on **The New Russia in Asia** to create new channels for dialogue with Russian scholars, journalists, business leaders, legislators, and government leaders engaged in relations with Asia. Supported by the Rockefeller Brothers Fund, a planning meeting was held in Seattle in December 1992 and a first conference in Moscow in June 1993. Future conferences will be held in Alma Ata, Beijing, Seoul, Tokyo, and Washington. Participants are from Russia, the United States, China, Japan, Korea and the Central Asian republics.

13. The **International Institute of Strategic Studies** (IISS, London) has been organizing an occasional series of meetings on Asia Pacific security issues. It held its annual conference in Seoul in November 1992 and will hold its 1994 annual conference in Vancouver in September 1994. It is planning to sponsor at least one conference a year in Asia/Pacific. It has recently organized conferences in Hong Kong in June 1993 and Washington in October 1993 on the security and foreign policy dimensions of Chinese regionalism. It is planning an additional conference in Hong Kong in June 1994 on Chinese economic reforms and defense policy. Participants at IISS conferences include academics, researchers and officials present in their personal capacities.

14. The Ministry of Foreign Affairs in Thailand and the United Nations have taken the lead in organizing three **ASEAN-United Nations Workshops on Cooperation for Peace and Preventive Diplomacy**. The first workshop was held in Bangkok, March

22–23, 1993, and examined the role of multilateralism in Southeast Asia, the parameters of preventive diplomacy as a function of multilateralism in Southeast Asia, and issues for preventive diplomacy in Southeast Asia. The second in Singapore on July 6–7, 1993, examined Cambodia, natural resource competition, territorial and boundary disputes, the Treaty of Amity and Cooperation, the role of regional groupings and bodies in cooperation with the UN, and mechanisms for preventive diplomacy. The third was held in Bangkok, February 17–18, 1994, to examine forums and measures for preventive diplomacy, issues in preventive diplomacy and ASEAN-UN relations. The meetings involve academic and governmental participants from sixteen Asia Pacific countries, officials from the UN (including ESCAP) and the Ford Foundation.

15. The Research Institute for Peace and Security (RIPS) in Tokyo and the Korea Institute for Defense Analysis sponsor the **Five Countries Security Forum**. The focus is security cooperation in Northeast Asia with a focus on arms races, nuclear proliferation, arms sales and territorial disputes. Participants will come from the United States, Russia, China, South Korea and Japan. The first meeting was held in Seoul, November 3–5, 1993, and the second is scheduled for Tokyo in May 1995. RIPS also arranges regular bilateral dialogues with the China Institute for International Strategic Studies and the Institute for Strategic Studies (Mongolia).

16. The Japan Center for International Exchange (JCIE) in cooperation with the American Assembly of Columbia University has begun a four-part series on **The United States and Japan in Asia**. It is an extension of the Shimoda Conference which was a bilateral exchange involving principally American and Japanese participants. Beginning with the meeting at Arden House in New York on "Challenges for US Policy" in November 1993, the series also includes participants from several other Asia Pacific countries including Canada, Australia, Singapore, Malaysia, Indonesia, the Philippines, Taiwan, and China. Topics included political, security, economic, environmental and other issues. Three additional meetings were scheduled, the first in Japan in April 1994 on "Japan's International Identity"; the second in Singapore at the Institute of Southeast Asian Studies in September 1994; and the fourth, a smaller group discussion at the end of 1994 possibly in Hawaii. The first four meetings include both officials, present in their private capacities, academics, journalists and businesspeople.

17. The East-West Center and the Pacific Forum/CSIS have created the **Asia Pacific Senior Seminar** intended to discuss new ideas about East Asian security and to create new links among regional decision makers. Expected to be an annual event, the first seminar took place in Hawaii in December 1993. Participants included academics, civilian officials at the assistant or deputy assistant secretary level or above, and military officers with the rank of brigadier or colonel or above drawn from the United States, Canada, Australia, China, France, Japan, South Korea, Malaysia, New Zealand, the Philippines, Russia, Singapore, Taiwan, Thailand, and the United Kingdom.

18. Within ASEAN, there are several interconnected sets of meetings in which security issues are addressed, all of a track two nature, and all involving principally but not exclusively ASEAN participants:

   (a) The **ASEAN-ISIS Workshop on Enhancing Security Cooperation in ASEAN**. The first meeting was held in Kuala Lumpur in June 1993 and the second in Kuala Lumpur in October 1993.

   (b) The **Southeast Asia Forum**, an annual meeting begun in 1989. The most recent was held in Kuala Lumpur in October 1993.

   (c) The **ASEAN Colloquium on Human Rights**, hosted by the Institute for Strategic and Development Studies, held its first meeting in Manila in January 1994 and is expected to develop into a regular series.

(d)    Several administratively independent but thematically linked conferences include: **ASEAN into the 21st Century: Dealing with Unresolved Issues**, ISDS in Manila in January 1994 as part of the ASEAN ISIS program; **Workshop on the Spratly Islands—A Potential Regional Conflict**, ISEAS in Singapore in December 1993; the Institute for Security and International Studies (Bangkok) is planning a conference in Chiang Mai in November 1994 on **ASEAN-China Relations**; the Singapore Institute for International Affairs is organizing a meeting on **ASEAN-Korean Relations** to be held in Singapore in March 1994.

(e)    The **International Symposium on Interaction for Progress: ASEAN-Vietnam All Round Cooperation** held its third meeting in Manila in December 1993. The symposium series is hosted by institutions in Singapore, Vietnam, the Philippines, Malaysia and Canada.

(f)    The **Roundtable on Economic Development** organized by ISIS Malaysia and the ASEAN ISIS has held three meetings. The focus is normally economic issues, though security matters broadly conceived have been part of the discussion. The fourth roundtable was held in Kuala Lumpur in January 1994.

19.    The East-West Center in Honolulu has initiated a three-year project **Building Asia-Pacific Regional Institutions for the Post–Cold War Era**. It will examine the prospects and instruments for regional institution building in the areas of politicosecurity relations, management of economic interdependence, and regional values.

20.    The concept of **The Council for Security Cooperation in Asia Pacific (CSCAP)** was developed in late 1992 and formally announced in June 1993 by its ten founding institutes (the Strategic and Defence Studies Centre, ANU, Australia; the University of Toronto-York University, Joint Centre for Asia Pacific Studies, Canada; the Centre for Strategic and International Studies, Indonesia; the Japan Institute for International Affairs, Japan; The Seoul Forum for International Affairs, Korea; Institute of Strategic and International Studies, Malaysia; Institute for Strategic and Development Studies, Philippines; Singapore Institute of International Affairs, Singapore; Institute for Security and International Studies, Thailand; Pacific Forum/CSIS, US). It is the most ambitious proposal to date for a regularized, focused and inclusive nongovernmental process on Pacific security matters. Four subcommittees have been established—finance, bylaws, membership, and working groups—and reported to a formal meeting held in Lombok in December 1993. The main thrust of CSCAP is to create a more structured regional process through a new nongovernmental institution that is open to all countries and territories in the region. In its first stage it is being guided by a steering committee consisting of the founding institutes; co-chaired by the United States and Indonesia; and having the secretariat function performed by ISIS Malaysia. Participation is to be extended as quickly to all countries and territories of the Asia Pacific region. There is no final definition of the boundaries of "the Asia Pacific" though it is generally seen to be composed of the countries of Northeast Asia (including Russia and Mongolia), Southeast Asia, Australasia, and North America. It is expected that mainland China, Taiwan, Vietnam, and North Korea will be included in the organization as soon as feasible. Participating countries and territories will be required to create broad-based member committees composed of academics, government officials (acting in their private, unofficial capacities) and other relevant individuals. There will be one general meeting of CSCAP each year, probably arranged in the first two years in cooperation with the annual roundtable in Kuala Lumpur.

21.    The newly created **ASEAN Regional Forum** is a formal governmental process for ministerial-level discussion on regional security issues. Its membership includes the six members of ASEAN, the dialogue partners, Russia, China, Laos and Vietnam. It

builds upon the ASEAN PMC process and the attendant senior officials meetings held in advance of the PMC and held on an intersessional basis. The first SOM was held in Singapore, May 21–22, 1993, and the second will be held in May 1994 in Bangkok.

22. Also at the formal governmental level, though somewhat lower in profile, is the **Quintilaterals,** five-way consultations among policy planners from foreign ministries in the United States, Japan, Australia, Canada and the Republic of Korea. The most recent took place in Korea in October 1993. The next is scheduled for Vancouver in September 1994.

23. In the realm of speculation, it is possible that the **Asia-Pacific Leaders Conference** held in Seattle in November 1993 will develop into an annual meeting. Security matters might be a future topic of conversation.

## III. Recently Completed

1. **Security Cooperation in the Asia Pacific Region,** a four-way collaborative project involving the Pacific Forum/CSIS, ASEAN ISIS, the Japan Institute of International Affairs, and the Seoul Forum. It has sponsored three international meetings with participation from a broad range of Asia Pacific countries. The first conference was in Hawaii in 1991; the second in Bali in April 1992; and the third in Seoul in November 1992. The final meeting produced the Seoul Statement, signed by the directors of eleven institutes in the region.

2. **Pacific Security After the Cold War,** a four-part series organized by the Institute on Global Conflict and Cooperation, at the University of California at San Diego. It involved institutes in Moscow, Tokyo, Beijing and the United States, with additional participation from several other Asia Pacific countries. The final meeting in the series was held in La Jolla in May 1993. The IGCC is playing the leading role in a new program of track two discussions focusing on Northeast Asia with support from the Department of State.

3. **The North Pacific Cooperative Security Dialogue.** It arranged a major conference (Victoria, April 1991), four workshops ("Unconventional Security Issues in the North Pacific," Hawaii, December 1991, co-hosted by the East-West Institute; "Arms Control and CSBMs in the North Pacific," Ottawa, May 1992, co-hosted by the Canadian Institute for International Peace and Security; "History, Culture and the Prospects of Multilateralism," Beijing, June 1992, co-hosted by Peking University; "Changing National Military Security Perceptions," Yokohama, August 1992, co-hosted by the Research Institute for Peace and Security) and a final conference in Vancouver in March 1993. Participants came from universities, research institutes and government departments in Canada, China, Japan, North and South Korea, Russia, the United States, Mongolia, Southeast Asia, Australia, Hong Kong and the United Kingdom.

## IV. Currently Proposed

1. The Center for International Affairs at Harvard University is planning to create a three-year program bringing together leading intellectuals and institutes for purposes of an annual conference and working group meetings. Titled the **North Pacific Forum,** it is scheduled to hold its first meeting in the fall of 1994.

2. The Social Science Research Council in New York is developing a major council project on the broadly defined topic of **Asia-Pacific Security.** As currently conceived, it will involve a multiyear series of interrelated activities, coordinated by an international steering group and undertaken by collaborative working groups focusing on three themes: "Reconceptualizing Asia-Pacific Security"; "The Domestic Politics of National

Security Policy Making"; and "The Political Economy of Regional Security." The objective is to create a more systematic program of basic research that can support the policy process and informed public discussion in the United States and Asia.

# PART III

Foundations' Grant-Making Activities

# Foundation Funding for Asia Pacific Security Studies and Exchange Activities

## CHEN JIANG

## Foreword

The grant-making activities of foundations in the United States and other countries have both contributed to and reflected the burgeoning of interest in recent years in Asia Pacific security studies and exchanges. Foundation program officers like government planners and academic researchers have sought to respond to the needs and opportunities that have come in the wake of the collapse of the Soviet Union and the end of the Cold War.

The accompanying materials provide information on commitments made during the past three years by thirteen foundations for activities related to Asia Pacific security. Included for each foundation is a brief description of their security-related programs and a selected list of grants, by recipient, purpose and amount. The materials are based on the public reports and special submissions from the participating foundations. The grant lists are confined to activities most directly related to regional strategic, political and economic issues, and geographic area studies. They do not reflect the broader range of foundation activities, many of which relate to the newer agenda of security issues.

The thirteen foundations have in common an interest in issues of peace and security. They differ, however, in the scale of their grant making, the way they define their security interests, the geographic focus of their work and the types of activities they support. Some have focused specifically on efforts to halt the spread of nuclear weapons while others have sought to address a broader range of security issues. Some have supported projects which include, but are not limited to, Asia Pacific. Others have funded activities confined to security issues facing the region. Some have concentrated their support on research, some on conferences, meetings and other exchange activities, and some on public information and advocacy. Others have sought to strengthen individual and institutional capacities in and outside the region to address security issues.

Because of these differences, the figures in the Summary Table are not directly comparable. Nor are they necessarily indicative of trends in foundation support. They do suggest the magnitude of giving by the thirteen foundations during the past three years, the nature of which is best illustrated by the grant lists provided in the section for each of the foundations.

   We are indebted to Chen Jiang, Warren Weaver Fellow at the Rockefeller Foundation, for compiling the materials, and to the Rockefeller Foundation for making his services available. We are also indebted to each of the foundations which took the time to cull their records and provide relevant information.

New York                           Peter F. Geithner
December 1993                       Director, Asia Programs
                                   The Ford Foundation

# Foundation Grants for Asia Pacific Security Studies and Dialogues

**Table 16.1**
**Summary Table**

|  | 1991 | 1992 | 1993 |
|---|---|---|---|
| W. Alton Jones Foundation | $ 170,000 | $ 144,200 | N/A |
| The Asia Foundation[1] | 790,763 | 922,749 | N/A |
| Carnegie Corporation of New York | 225,760 | 316,700 | N/A |
| Center for Global Partnership | 2,465,565 | 1,035,152 | $ 205,000[2] |
| The Ford Foundation | 969,900 | 2,655,000 | 1,018,300 |
| The MacArthur Foundation | 1,293,175 | 590,000 | 1,183,565 |
| Ploughshares Fund | 25,000 | 20,000 | N/A |
| The Pew Charitable Trusts | 595,000 | 100,000 | 715,000 |
| Rockefeller Brothers Fund | 854,460 | 1,157,380 | 817,610 |
| The Rockefeller Foundation | N/A | N/A | 621,000[3] |
| The Sasakawa Peace Foundation | 2,308,063 | 1,847,478 | 3,904,462 |
| United States Japan Foundation | 277,393 | 473,382 | 668,941 |
| Winston Foundation for World Peace | N/A | 18,000 | N/A |

1. Includes South Asia.
2. Projects approved as of November 1993.
3. Includes South Asia.

# W. Alton Jones Foundation

Funding for Asia Pacific security comes under the foundation's Secure Society Program. The goal of the Secure Society Program is to eliminate the threat of nuclear war. This objective emerged from the foundation's overarching concern to protect the sustainability of life on earth. No human activity poses a threat to humankind and the environment as catastrophic as that of nuclear war. In 1990, W. Alton Jones started Common Security Initiative. The aim is to identify and, in some cases, solicit projects that promote Common Security in various ways: by defining and refining operating principles of military establishments that are consistent with Common Security; by working cooperatively with Soviet and other non-American researchers and activists to promote deep force reductions and strategic reforms; by developing popular support for solidifying the roles of multilateral institutions such as the Conference on Security and Cooperation in Europe; and by extrapolating East-West experiences with Common Security to new regions, such as Pacific Asia.

W. Alton Jones grants under the "Security Society Program" were in 1992 $4,700,000; in 1993 $5,300,000; and in 1994 are expected to be $5,600,000.

## Table 16.2
### Asia Pacific Security

|  | 1991 | 1992 | 1993 |
|---|---|---|---|
| The Australian National University: For development of a common security agenda in the Asia-Pacific region | $100,000 | | |
| Nevada, Pacific Campaign for Disarmament and Security: For development of a common security agenda in the Asia-Pacific region | 20,000 | | |
| Citizens' Coalition Against the Plutonium Fast-Breeder Program: For public education in Japan challenging the wisdom of Japan's use of plutonium in their fast-breeder reactor project and plutonium sea shipments projects | 50,000 | | |
| Seattle, Institute for Global Security Studies: A high level multinational dialogue on Asia-Pacific maritime security and related confidence building measures | | 25,000 | |
| Nautilus of America, Inc.: To provide the research required to stimulate international controls on long-range ballistic missile development | | $30,000 | |
| Citizens' Coalition Against the Plutonium Fast-Breeder Program | | 75,000 | |
| International Campaign for Tibet: To support the int'l campaign toward making Tibet nuclear-free | | 14,200 | |
| Totals: | $170,000 | $144,200 | N/A |

# The Asia Foundation

The Asia Foundation is a private American organization with headquarters in San Francisco, and fifteen field offices in the Asia-Pacific region. The foundation makes over fifteen hundred grants each year to government agencies and nongovernmental organizations in thirty-one Asian and Pacific Island nations. Since its creation in 1954, the foundation has promoted US-Asian understanding and cooperation and encouraged Asian-Pacific efforts to strengthen representative government, build effective legal systems, foster market economies, increase accountability in the public and private sectors, develop independent and responsible media, and encourage broad participation in public life. As part of its commitment to institutional development, the foundation also arranges project-related professional training and study tours to the United states and within Asia for hundreds of Asians each year. The foundation's Center for Asian Pacific Affairs facilitates US-Asian dialogue through its many seminars, conferences, research projects and publications. The foundation's grants in 1991 and 1992 in the fields of international relations and security are listed below.

**Table 16.3**
**International Relations and Security**

|  | FY1991 | FY1992 | FY1993 |
|---|---|---|---|
| **Afghanistan** | | | |
| Graduate Fellowship in int'l relations, law and diplomacy in the US | $15,287 | | |
| Graduate Fellowship in int'l relations, law and diplomacy in the US | | $33,859 | |
| **Bangladesh** | | | |
| Dhaka University, Department of Political Science: Participation in Asia Studies | 7,220 | | |
| **Cambodia** | | | |
| United Nations Interim Committee: For Co-ordination of Investigations of the Lower Mekong Basin (Mekong Secretariat): Workshop held in Phnom Penh, General Principles and Frameworks in International and Domestic Water Law as They Relate to Cambodia | | 6,418 | |
| **China** | | | |
| Beijing Foreign Studies University: Visiting scholar program in American studies in the US | 2,000 | | |
| Chinese Academy of Social Science, Institute of American Studies: Conference on American and Asia-Pacific Region in the Twentieth Century in Beijing | 16,000 | | |
| Shanghai Academy of Social Sciences: Visiting scholar program in Sino-American trade in the US | 6,125 | | |

**Table 16.3 (continued)**

| | FY1991 | FY1992 | FY1993 |
|---|---|---|---|
| Chinese Academy of Social Sciences: Visiting scholar program in international relations and attendance of Atlantic Council's Conference on Economics and Security Issues in Northeast Asia | 22,077 | | |
| Chinese Scholars of Political Science and International Studies, Inc.: Research project, China and the Asian-Pacific Region in the Year 2000 | 10,000 | | |
| Beijing University: Visiting scholars program in international relations in the US, a TV documentary on international relations in China, and participation in the second Pacific Rim university presidents conference in Thailand | 24,457 | | |
| Shanghai Academy of Social Sciences: Two visiting scholar programs in international relations in the US | 17,668 | | |
| Research on Sino-American relations in the US | 3,600 | | |
| Translation of the proceedings of a conference on strategic studies in Beijing | 1,000 | | |
| Research fellowship in the US on the American economic relationship with East Asia | | 1,279 | |
| Visiting scholar program in the US on economic reforms in the former Soviet Union and China | | 8,325 | |
| Chinese Academy of Social Sciences: Two visiting scholars programs in international relations in the US | | 21,615 | |
| Fudan University: In-country training program in international studies | | 3,000 | |
| Peking University: Observation program and two visiting scholars programs in international relations in the US and participation by an American professor at a symposium on Korean studies in China | | 10,520 | |
| Shanghai Institute of International Studies: Visiting scholar program in international relations in the US | | 9,225 | |
| Shanghai International Studies University: Research fellowship in political science in the US | | 9,000 | |
| State Science and Technology Commission: Master's degree program in international relations in the US | | 4,875 | |
| Translation of the proceedings of a conference on strategic studies held in China | | 1,000 | |
| Visiting scholar program in international relations in the US | | 8,325 | |

| Table 16.3 (continued) | FY1991 | FY1992 | FY1993 |
|---|---|---|---|

### *Indonesia*

| | FY1991 | FY1992 | FY1993 |
|---|---|---|---|
| Department of Foreign Affairs, Center for Education and Training: Two comparative tours of diplomatic training institutes in the US, Korea, Japan and ASEAN nations | 24,287 | | |
| Armed Forces of the Philippines; Center for Integrative and Development Studies Philippines; Institute for Security and International Studies, Thailand; Institute of Strategic and International Studies, Malaysia; Ministry of Foreign Affairs, Brunei; National Security Council, Philippines; Singapore Institute of International Affairs: Participation and organization in the third ASEAN Young Leaders Conference, Bali | 32,533 | | |
| Center for Strategic and International Studies: Participation in the Japan-US ASEAN conference in Japan | 2,167 | | |
| Indonesian National Committee of the Pacific Economic Cooperation Conference: Participation in the eighth General Meeting of the PECC | 1,721 | | |
| Center for Strategic and International Studies: Fourth US-Indonesia Bilateral Forum in the US | 9,106 | | |
| Department of Foreign Affairs: Participation in a conference on the relationship between Papua New Guinea, Indonesia, and the Southwest Pacific, held in PNG | 13,377 | | |
| Hasanuddin University, Center for Pacific Studies: Participation in a planning meeting in PNG for conference on Indonesian-Pacific relations, and participation in the Pacific Historians' Association conference in Guam | 3,929 | | |
| University of Indonesia, Faculty of Letters: Participation in an Indonesian conference on American studies; the second General Meeting of the Asian Federation of American Studies Associations in Malaysia; participation in a symposium on American studies in Japan, and an American studies newsletter and academic journal | 20,806 | | |
| University of Indonesia, Faculty of Letters: Participation in the Association of Asian Studies annual meeting in the US | 1,445 | | |
| Department of Foreign Affairs: Organization of the third Southwest Pacific Conference on Regional Peace, Stability, and Resilience, in Ujung Pandang, Sulawesi | | 20,000 | |
| Center for Strategic and International Studies: Organization and participant costs of the fourth ASEAN Young Leaders Conference in Bali | | 34,806 | |

## Table 16.3 (continued)

| | FY1991 | FY1992 | FY1993 |
|---|---|---|---|
| Bandung Institute of Technology: Master's degree program in American studies in the US | | 1,000 | |
| Department of Foreign Affairs and Hasanuddin University: Participation in The Asia Foundation's Berkeley Seminar on American Politics and Policy | | 13,320 | |
| Participation in the Association of Asian Studies Conference in Washington, DC | | 19,527 | |

### *Japan*

| | FY1991 | FY1992 | FY1993 |
|---|---|---|---|
| C. Itoh & Co.; Okamoto Associates: Participation in the Congressional Research Series workshop on US-Japan relations | 6,748 | | |
| Japan Broadcasting Corporation; Ministry of Foreign Affairs: Participation in the Young Professionals Conference in San Francisco | 5,703 | | |
| Japan Defense Agency: Fellowships in the US for Self-Defense Forces officers and Defense Agency career civilians | 49,556 | | |
| Ministry of Foreign Affairs: Participation in the Georgetown Leadership Seminar | 2,655 | | |
| Alaska Conservation Foundation and Aoyama Gakuin University: Participation in the 1992 Seoul symposium on the environment | | 4,802 | |
| Congressional Research Service, Library of Congress: Translation of a participation in the Symposium of US-Japan Relations, hosted by the New World Order and Japan/US Relations | | 19,872 | |
| Japan Defense Agency: Fellowships in the United States for Self-Defense Forces officers and Defense Agency career civilians | | 25,013 | |
| Research Institute for Peace and Security: Mongolian participation in a conference on Northeast Asia security issues | | 3,666 | |

### *Korea*

| | FY1991 | FY1992 | FY1993 |
|---|---|---|---|
| Korean Political Science Association: For publication of *Korean Politics and the Challenges of the World Order* | 9,979 | | |
| For participation in a US conference on recent changes in US-Korean trade and investment | 3,779 | | |
| Sisa Journal: Participation in a seminar on US foreign policy process | 4,500 | | |
| American Studies Association of Korea: For national workshop and an international seminar on American Studies in Korea; participation in Japanese symposium on US-Japan relations and their impact on Asia; and participation in four American studies conferences in Taiwan, Malaysia, and Japan | 19,279 | | |

| Table 16.3 (continued) | FY1991 | FY1992 | FY1993 |
|---|---|---|---|
| Hnyan University, Department of Political Science: Lectures on ocean pollution and foreign policy by visiting American scholar | 1,384 | | |
| Korea Institute for Defense Analyses: Participation in the annual meeting of the American Political Science Association in the US | 3,097 | | |
| Kyunhee University, Institute of International Peace Studies: Research and publication on arms control and disarmament on the Korean peninsula | 6,246 | | |
| Seoul National University, Institute of Russian and East European Studies: For an English language collection on Russian and East European Studies | 364 | | |
| Seoul National University, Institute of Social Sciences: For seminar, "The Post-Cold War World Order" | 5,590 | | |
| For tour of strategic studies institutes in the US and Canada | 4,263 | | |
| Inha University, Center for International Studies: Workshops on civil-military relations in a democratic setting | | 10,427 | |
| 1992 Seoul Symposium on Environmental Cooperation in the Northeast Asia Region | | 18,796 | |
| Korean Association of Southeast Asian Studies: Publication of *The Southeast Asian Studies Review Journal* | 6,424 | | |
| National YWCA of Korea: Asian regional conference on women and strategies for environmental protection | | 14,871 | |
| American Studies Association of Korea: Twenty-seventh International Seminar on American Studies | | 10,033 | |
| Center for American and Soviet Studies: International conference on the nuclear issue and arms control on the Korean peninsula | | 11,529 | |
| Korean Association of International Studies: Publication of *The New Trilateral Relationship of South Korea, North Korea, and the US* | | 7,027 | |
| Kyungnam University, Institute of Far Eastern Studies: Series of forums on US-Korean relations | | 11,363 | |
| National Assembly Secretariat: Participation in The Asia Foundation's Berkeley Seminar on American Politics and Policy | | 6,876 | |
| Yonsei University, Institute of East and West Studies: International Conference on Regional Maritime Cooperation in Northeast Asia | | 8,781 | |

**Table 16.3 (continued)**

| | FY1991 | FY1992 | FY1993 |
|---|---|---|---|
| Korea Military Academy: Tour of strategic studies institutes in the US and Canada | | 1,289 | |
| ***Laos*** | | | |
| Ministry of Foreign Affairs: English-language instruction in Malaysia | | 16,126 | |
| Ministry of Foreign Affairs: Thai-Lao dialogue on technical assistance between the Institute for Public Policy Studies and Lao MOFA | | 3,077 | |
| ***Malaysia*** | | | |
| Malaysian Association for American Studies: For the "International Conference on the US Legal System: Its Influence on Malaysia and Asia" and participation in the conference "America and the Asia-Pacific Region in the Twentieth Century" in Beijing | 13,462 | | |
| Association of Development Research and Training Institutes of Asia and the Pacific Participation in a conference in Macau, "The Changing World Community" | 2,672 | | |
| Institute for Strategic and International Studies: Meetings with officials at American strategic studies institutes | 371 | | |
| Malaysian Armed Forces Defense College; Malaysian Design Marking; University of Malaysia: Participation in Young Professionals Conference | 4,478 | | |
| Persatuan Malaysiana Muda: For the "International Malaysian Conference 1991: Malaysia and the World—an Overview" | 11,914 | | |
| University of Malaya: Participation in the 1991 Internationalization Forum at the East-West Center in Hawaii | 2,265 | | |
| Institute for Strategic and International Studies: Observation of the ninth Pacific Economic Cooperation Council general meeting in San Francisco in preparation for hosting the tenth meeting in Malaysia | | 7,582 | |
| Institute for Strategic and International Studies; the Malaysia Armed Forces, Armed Forces Headquarters; and the Malaysian Armed Forces Defense College: Participation in the first Asian-Pacific Defense Conference | | 5,872 | |
| Malaysian Armed Forces Defense College: Presentation at The Asia Foundation's Civil-Military Relations planning meeting in Washington, DC | | 2,226 | |

| Table 16.3 (continued) | FY1991 | FY1992 | FY1993 |
|---|---|---|---|
| Malaysian Association for American Studies: Participation in the twenty-sixth International American Studies Conference in Seoul | | 4,884 | |
| Ministry of Foreign Affairs: Participation in The Asia Foundation's Berkeley Seminar on American Politics and Policy and the Eighth Young Professionals Conference | | 18,448 | |
| Universiti Sains Malaysia, Student Affairs Department: National student forum, "Toward a Better Understanding of United Nations and Global Issues" | | 1,213 | |

### Maldives
| | | | |
|---|---|---|---|
| Ministry of Foreign Affairs: Participation in the International Law Institute seminars in the US | | 8,361 | |
| Ministry of Foreign Affairs: Deputy foreign minister's participation in the Georgetown Leadership Seminar in the US | | 5,639 | |

### Mongolia
| | | | |
|---|---|---|---|
| Association for the Conservation of Nature and the Environment: Participation in the Conference on Environmental Regulations in the Pacific Rim | 4,102 | | |
| Embassy of Mongolia; Institute of Oriental and International Studies; Ministry of Foreign Affairs: Participation in the Young Professionals Conference | 6,897 | | |
| Ministry of External Relations: Program in international relations at the Fletcher School of Law and Diplomacy | 13,005 | | |
| Ministry of Justice: One-year study program in international trade law at the University of Wisconsin Law School's East Asian Legal Study Center | | 11,295 | |
| Ministry of External Relations: Master's program at the Fletcher School of Law and Diplomacy | | 17,368 | |
| Ministry of External Relations: Participation in The Asia Foundation's Berkeley Seminar on American Politics and Policy | | 7,232 | |
| Baga Hurai: Study program in international relations at the Fletcher School of Law and Diplomacy | | 10,997 | |
| Center for Strategic Studies, Institute of International and Oriental Studies, and Market Research Institute: Study tour of Asian policy research institutions and attendance at the conference on security and cooperation in Asia and the Pacific held in Bali, Indonesia | | 22,810 | |

**Table 16.3 (continued)**

| | FY1991 | FY1992 | FY1993 |
|---|---|---|---|
| ***Nepal*** | | | |
| Ministry of Foreign Affairs: Participation in Georgetown Leadership Seminar | 6,716 | | |
| Attendance at an American studies and at the Japanese Association's annual meeting on American studies in Japan | | 1,476 | |
| Attendance at a conference on economic regional integration in the US | | 2,710 | |
| Georgetown Leadership Seminar in the United States and in The Asia Foundation's Berkeley Seminar on American Politics and Policy | | 13,674 | |
| ***Pacific Islands*** | | | |
| Ministry of Foreign Affairs, Fiji; Ministry of Planning and Economic Development, Cook Islands: Participation in the fifth Asia-Pacific Roundtable, Malaysia | 6,319 | | |
| Ministry of Health and Education, Tuvalu: Participation in the Conference on Environmental Regulations in Pacific Rim Nations in Hong Kong | 5,764 | | |
| University of Papua New Guinea, Faculty of Arts: Conference on Indonesian-Pacific Relations | 7,361 | | |
| Participation in the Berkeley Seminar on American Politics and Policy | | 14,269 | |
| Pacific Island Issues Seminar | | 14,030 | |
| The third Southwest Pacific Security Conference in Indonesia | | 10,072 | |
| ***Singapore*** | | | |
| Ministry of Foreign Affairs; National University of Singapore: Participation in the Young Professionals Conference in San Francisco | 4,008 | | |
| Singapore Institute of International Affairs: Program on current security issues | 11,344 | | |
| University of Malaya; University of the Philippines: Survey of Asian Studies Programs in ASEAN countries | 162 | | |
| Participation in the Berkeley Seminar on American Politics and Policy | | 5,156 | |
| ***Brunei*** | | | |
| Participation in the Berkeley Seminar on American Politics and Policy | | 7,086 | |
| ***Taiwan*** | | | |
| Academica Sinica; Ateneo de Manila University; Mahidol University; Thammasat University; University of Indonesia; University of Malaya; University of the Philippines: International workshops on labor flows in Asia | 9,327 | | |

| Table 16.3 (continued) | FY1991 | FY1992 | FY1993 |
|---|---|---|---|
| Twenty-first Century Foundation: Conference on the application of game theory to the analysis of strategic and diplomatic issues, and establishment of the Institute of Foreign Affairs | 18,462 | | |

### *Thailand*

| | FY1991 | FY1992 | FY1993 |
|---|---|---|---|
| Chulalongkorn University: Faculty of Political Science: Attendance at American studies symposia in Japan and Malaysia | 882 | | |
| Chulalongkorn University, Faculty of Political Science: Attending a conference on Southeast Asian studies in the US | 3,716 | | |
| Chulalongkorn University, Institute of Asian Studies: For research on the newly industrializing economies and a national workshop on Asian studies | 1,363 | | |
| Seminar on Burmese studies and participation in The Asia Foundation's Young Professional's Conference | | 8,659 | |

### *Vietnam*

| | FY1991 | FY1992 | FY1993 |
|---|---|---|---|
| Aspen Institute's American-Vietnamese Dialogue in Fiji | | 18,000 | |
| The Asia Foundation's Young Professionals Conference, Berkeley Seminar on American Politics and Policy, and participation in the Georgetown Leadership Seminar | | 20,260 | |

### *Other Countries*

| | FY1991 | FY1992 | FY1993 |
|---|---|---|---|
| The Asia Society: Participation at the US-Korea Bilateral Forum in Korea | 15,000 | | |
| Lingnan College, Hong Kong: Participation in a conference on the changing pattern of East Asian security | 5,000 | | |
| Leading Indian journalist to conduct research on US-India security relations | | 7,343 | |
| Partial support of the Japan America Society of Chicago's third Symposium on Security in the Pacific | | 20,000 | |
| Pacific Trade and Development Conference held in Washington, DC | | 20,000 | |

### *Center for Asian Pacific Affairs*

| | FY1991 | FY1992 | FY1993 |
|---|---|---|---|
| US National Committee for Pacific Economic Cooperation: Administrative support | 71,397 | | |
| Production and distribution of the Pacific Economic Outlook report on behalf of the Pacific Economic Cooperation Conference | 57,229 | | |

**Table 16.3 (continued)**

| | FY1991 | FY1992 | FY1993 |
|---|---|---|---|
| East Asian Institute, Columbia University, New York: For US participation in the America's Future Role in the Asia-Pacific Region and report publication | 23,000 | | |
| For Symposium, "East Asia Transformed," co-sponsored with National Bureau of Soviet and Asian Research | 25,438 | | |
| For the fourth US-Indonesia Bilateral Forum, co-sponsored with CSIS, Jakarta | 34,850 | | |
| For a conference and publication examining American interests in Asia | 14,026 | | |
| Management, production and distribution of the *Pacific Economic Outlook,* for the Pacific Economic Cooperation Council (PECC) | | 74,884 | |
| Series of working group meetings examining American interests in Asia | | 81,182 | |
| Berkeley Seminar on American Politics and Policy in collaboration with the Institute of Governmental Studies, University of California at Berkeley; and The Asia Foundation's State Legislative Fellows Project | | 74,426 | |

### Regional Program
| | FY1991 | FY1992 | FY1993 |
|---|---|---|---|
| For participation of Asian speakers in a conference on environmental regulation in Pacific Rim nations, held in Hong Kong | 28,655 | | |
| Institute for Social and Economic Research, Education and Information: Fourth ASEAN Muslim Social Scientists' Conference in Indonesia | 14,955 | | |
| Conference to bring together Asian, American and Canadian experts on environmental change and acute conflict | | 15,953 | |
| Conference on Northeast Asian security and cooperation to build regional confidence and linkages | | 10,000 | |

### Washington, DC
| | FY1991 | FY1992 | FY1993 |
|---|---|---|---|
| For the seventh annual Asian Embassies Seminar | 2,551 | | |
| Total | $790,763 | $922,749 | N/A |

# Carnegie Corporation of New York

The grant program on Cooperative Security has four primary areas of emphasis designed to encourage the application of cooperative security principles to the avoidance of catastrophic conflict. The first is concerned with helping the superpowers understand their interest in cooperating in the drastic reduction and restructuring of their nuclear forces, moving toward a situation in which there is acceptance of the principle that nuclear weapons can not be used and that the only reason to have them is to deter their use by others. The second concerns study of the applicability of cooperative security principles to restricting the supply of and reducing the demand for weapons of mass destruction and other modern weapons in regions of the world where there is now a high risk of war. The third involves support of efforts to help the Soviet Union and its former allies become more reliable and stable partners in cooperative security efforts by successfully negotiating their political and economic transitions to freer and more responsive systems. The program also has a continuing concern with helping policymakers and the attentive public understand these issues and have ample access to the information they need to make responsible decisions about them.

**Table 16.4**
**Asia Pacific Security**

|  | 1991 | 1992 | 1993 |
|---|---|---|---|
| The Brookings Institution, Foreign Policy Studies Program. The program will consider whether the principles of pan-European cooperative security arrangements can be extended to other regions of the world, such as the Middle East and Asia. (Total $1,200,000) | $ 60,000* | | |
| The Brookings Institution, Establishment of a Task Force on the Prevention of Proliferation. Separately funded working groups are weighing the relative merits of across-the-board global prohibitions and measures that are tailored to the Middle East, South Asia, and the Korean peninsula. (Total $331,520) | 165,760* | | |
| The Carnegie Endowment for Int'l Peace. This grant allowed Dr. Sandy Spector, Senior Associate at the endowment, to organize working groups on arms control and security in the Korean peninsula, while allowing Geoffrey Kemp to develop parallel groups on the Middle East and Southwest Asia. (Total $800,000) | | $48,000* | |

MIT, two study groups including a group
assessing the potential dangers of
nationalist ferment in the former Soviet
Empire, South Asia, and the Pacific rim.                           40,500*
(Total $1,350,000)

Stanford University Center for Int'l Security
and Arms Control, for research and training
in interactional security and arms control.
This grant is supporting the center's
conversion-privatization work as well as its
other projects developed with Soviet
specialists on reducing the nuclear danger
and on advancing cooperative security in Europe
and in the Asian-Pacific region.                                 228,200*
($1,141,000)

|  | | |
|---|---|---|
| Totals: | $ 225,760* | $ 316,700* | N/A |

* Author's estimate.

# Center for Global Partnership

The Center for Global Partnership (CGP) was established in 1991, and maintains offices in New York and Tokyo. Its primary objectives are to contribute to improvements in the world's welfare through intellectual collaboration among Japan, the United States, and other countries, and to enhance dialogue and interchange between Japanese and American citizens at the grassroots level, while emphasizing the multinational dimensions of the goal of global partnership.

CGP offers grants to nonprofit institutions and also initiates collaborative programs with those organizations. Broadly termed, its thematic interests are global issues, common domestic issues, and issues pertaining to Japan-US relations. Currently CGP's priority is on the general theme of "Japan and the US in the Asia-Pacific region."

Under the rubric of Intellectual Exchange, CGP has been supporting mainly collaborative "policy-relevant research" by research institutions in the United States and Japan, and "dialogue" projects facilitating conferences and symposia attended by scholars, policymakers and analysts, and by opinion leaders in such diverse fields as government, academia, business, media, education, labor, and philanthropy.

Peace and security issues form a substantial part of CGP's grants to date, and given the above-mentioned current thematic focus of Japan and United States in the Asia-Pacific region, a majority of the grants addressing that issue deal with the countries and subregions of the Asia Pacific region, including Russia, China, and the Korean peninsula, among others. A substantial number of grant projects are formed along the lines of Japanese-American bilateral collaboration, though also with strong third-country participation in many cases. CGP has also awarded several grants to projects dealing with the multilateral management of peace and security issues, such as collective security, peace enforcement and United Nations peacekeeping operations.

Thus far, Asia Pacific related grants provided by CGP have predominantly been for collaborative research or dialogue projects. One striking exception is the CGP's support for a two-year training program in international security issues for a younger generation of Japanese scholars and researchers. Also, most grants have been regional in orientation, though one issue-based project has dealt with the issue of arms transfer and nuclear proliferation.

The total grants awarded to security programs in 1991 were $2,215,565; FY1992: $1,035,152; and FY 1993: $205,000 (for projects approved as of November 1993).

### Table 16.5
### Asia Pacific Security

| | FY1991 | FY1992 | FY1993 |
|---|---|---|---|
| Asia Pacific Association of US-Japan Dialogue on Japan: Japan, the US, Regional Crisis Management and the UN | $230,769 | | |
| Center for Strategic and Int'l Studies US-Japan Global Forum: Leadership 2000. | 250,000 | | |
| CSIS, in cooperation with the Japan Forum on Int'l Relations, to form task forces on the environment, regional economic blocs, and Asian partnership. | 250,000 | | |
| City University of New York, The US and Japan in the Changing Environment of Multilateral Organization: Collective Security and Peace Enforcement | 193,050 | | |
| Claremont McKenna College, Keck Center for Int'l & Strategic Studies: US-Japan Partnership in Conflict Management | 43,000 | | |
| East-West Center Foundation, Building Asia-Pacific Regional Institutions for the Post–Cold War Era | 250,000 | | |
| Georgetown University, Japan's Future Global Role: Conference and Book | 61,800 | | |
| Int'l Cooperation Research Association, research and symposia on multilateralism | 38,462 | | |
| Japan America Society of Chicago, The Third Chicago Symposium: Security in the Pacific | 77,102 | | |
| Japan Economic Research Institute, Int'l Symposium "World Grand Design" | 27,538 | | |
| Japan Institute of Int'l Affairs: Enhancing Security in Southeast Asia | 158,896 | | |
| Japan Institute of Int'l Affairs: Japan-US Conference on Security in Asia | 63,468 | | |
| Japan Institute of Int'l Affairs: US-Japan Dialogue on China Policy | 276,923 | | |
| Japan Society, three-year policy forum: Structuring the US-Japan Relationship | 150,000 | | |
| Pacific Forum/CSIS, Korean Unification: Implications for US-Japan Relations | 200,000 | | |
| Research Institute for Peace and Security: Japan-US joint study on the former Soviet Union | 50,308 | | |
| University of Georgia, Center for East-West Trade Policy, Nonproliferation Export Controls: US-Japanese Interests and Initiatives | 44,249 | | |

| | | | |
|---|---|---|---|
| University of Illinois at Urbana-Champaign: Collective Research on Japan's Role in the Post–Cold War World | 100,000 | | |
| The Atlantic Council of the US, Young Leader's Seminar: "The Future of Prosperity in Northeast Asia" | | $24,750 | |
| Int'l Institute for Global Peace, IIGP/CSIA Conference on Cooperative Denuclearization | | 204,918 | |
| Int'l House of Japan: US-Japan Relations and Int'l Institutions After the Cold War | | 156,475 | |
| Int'l Institute for Global Peace, The New Russia in Asia: A project for research and int'l dialogue | | 88,524 | |
| Nixon Library and Birthplace, Fragile Friendship: US-Japan Relations and the Balance of Power in Post–Cold War Asia | | 30,000 | |
| Research Institute for Peace and Security: UN Peacekeeping Operation and US-Japan Relations | | 122,950 | |
| Research Institute for Peace and Security, US-Japan collaborative research on CIS/Russia | | 188,800 | |
| Research Institute for Peace and Security: Fellowship Program for Peace and Security | | 139,824 | |
| University of Georgia Research Foundation, Nonproliferation Export Controls: US-Japanese Interests and Initiatives | | 78,911 | |
| Center for Strategic and Int'l Studies: The Future of Asia Pacific Studies and Exchange Activities | | | $30,000 |
| Columbia University, the American Assembly, the US, Japan, and Asia: Challenges for US Policy | | | 175,000 |
| Totals: | $2,465,565 | $1,035,152 | $205,000[1] |

1. Projects approved as of November, 1993

# The Ford Foundation

The Ford Foundation supports research, advanced training, policy development, and public education to promote a more cooperative international security system involving the peaceful resolution of international problems. The foundation is also funding efforts to develop new ideas about peace and security at multilateral and regional levels and national defense policies relevant to the post–Cold War world. Emphasis is given to research and policy development in such areas as cooperative security, preventive diplomacy, peacekeeping, and peacemaking. The foundation's work in peace and security seeks to encourage projects in arms control and disarmament. The foundation also supports a wide range of intergovernmental international institutions working on conflict prevention and resolution.

Grants for international affairs initiatives in the United States and around the world in 1990 totaled $31.7 million; 1991: $ 26.7 million; and 1992 $ 35.6 million.

**Table 16.6**
**Asia Pacific Security**

|  | 1991 | 1992 | 1993 |
|---|---|---|---|
| Research Institute for Peace and Security: Support for a project on "Regional Approach to Confidence and Security Building in the Far East" | $10,000 | | |
| The Australian National University: Support for a project on "Arms Control in the Pacific: Problems and Prospects" | 10,000 | | |
| Institute for Eastwest Studies, Inc.: Interim support to encourage the involvement of Japan and China in the institute's activities | 25,000 | | |
| Institute of Southeast Asian Studies: Support for research, workshops and publications on arms and defense planning in Southeast Asia | 245,000 | | |
| Royal Government of Thailand: Support for reassessment of mechanisms for ASEAN regional security and economic cooperation | 49,200 | | |
| Japan Center for Int'l Exchange: Support for Japan-ASEAN Dialogue VI | 36,600 | | |
| Shanghai Institute for Int'l Studies: Support for staff development and int'l visits and exchanges | 98,000 | | |
| Jinan University: Support for joint activities by five Chinese institutes of Southeast Asian studies | 70,000 | | |

| Table 16.6 (continued) | 1991 | 1992 | 1993 |
|---|---|---|---|
| The China Institute of Contemporary International Relations: Support for the Institute's int'l exchange activities | 28,100 | | |
| National Committee on United States-China Relations: Support for the fifth meeting of regular symposium on Sino-American relations | 40,000 | | |
| Peking University: Partial support for a conference on int'l relations studies in China | 28,000 | | |
| Institute of Int'l Education, Inc.: Support for a new program of Int'l relations studies with the PRC | 330,000 | | |
| Institute for Eastwest Studies, Inc.: Support for the Institute's work on security, political culture, and economics and a one-time reserve fund | | $1,200,000 | |
| East-West Center Foundation: Support for a workshop on threat perceptions in the Asia Pacific Region | | 60,000 | |
| The Australian National University Support for two fellowships for Southeast Asians in the graduate program in strategic studies | | 38,000 | |
| Institute of Southeast Asian Studies Support for exchanges between ISEAS and El Collegio De Mexico | | 120,000 | |
| Institute of Southeast Asian Studies Support for an Indo-China Study Unit | | 300,000 | |
| Mennonite Central Committee: Support for the committee's Center for Educational Exchanges with Vietnam | | 32,500 | |
| Chulalongkorn University: Support for Southeast Asian participants in the second Southeast Asia-China Dialogue | | 18,000 | |
| The Johns Hopkins University: General support for the Johns Hopkins University-Nanjing University Center for Chinese and American Studies | | 250,000 | |
| The China Institute of Contemporary Int'l Relations: Support for the institute's int'l exchange activities | | 50,000 | |
| American Council of Learned Societies: Support for a program of training, research and scholarly exchanges with China in int'l affairs | | 300,000 | |

**Table 16.6 (continued)**

| | 1991 | 1992 | 1993 |
|---|---|---|---|
| Fudan University (Center for American Studies): Partial support for conference on China's search for modernization | | 28,500 | |
| China Center for Int'l Studies: Support for a conference on Asian-Pacific security and cooperation | | 50,000 | |
| Shanghai Institute for Int'l Studies: Partial support for a conference on Sino-US relations | | 10,000 | |
| National Committee on United States-China Relations: Support for the sixth meeting of a regular symposium on Sino-American relations | | 56,000 | |
| The Brookings Institution: Support for visit to the US by a group of int'l affairs specialists from China | | 32,000 | |
| Chinese Academy of Social Sciences: Partial support for conferences and research on the developing world and on the Northeast Asian region | | 46,000 | |
| Chinese Academy of Social Sciences: Partial support for a seminar and research on China's relations with Europe | | 22,000 | |
| National Committee on United States-China Relations: Support for the scholar orientation program for Chinese studies and scholars | | 42,000 | |
| Royal Government of Thailand: Support to strengthen ASEAN-United Nations cooperation in regional peace and security | | | $72,500 |
| President and Fellows of Harvard College: Support for exploration of a North Pacific forum | | | 3,500 |
| York University: Partial support to plan for an int'l conference on Asia-Pacific security studies | | | 35,250 |
| The Regents of the University of California: Research project on regional perspectives on evolving economic and political relations among China, Taiwan and Hong Kong-Macao | | | 75,000 |
| Institute of International Education, Inc.: Support for third South Asia regional dialogue and India-China exchange visit | | | 75,000 |
| Royal Government of Thailand: Support to strengthen ASEAN-United Nation cooperation in regional peace and security | | | 72,500 |

| **Table 16.6** (continued) | 1991 | 1992 | 1993 |
|---|---|---|---|
| Mennonite Central Committee: Support for the Committee's Center for Education Exchange Program with Vietnam | | | 28,200 |
| Socialist Republic of Vietnam: Support for research and training in int'l affairs | | | 180,000 |
| The Aspen Institute: Support for Vietnamese participation in the fourth Vietnamese-American Dialogue | | | 50,000 |
| Royal Government of Thailand: Support for a research study on the relationship between the PRC and the Khmer Rouge | | | 8,300 |
| Mennonite Central Committee: Support for Vietnamese study mission to Malaysia to investigate comparative political and economic institutions | | | 16,000 |
| New York University: Support for collaborative research on travel by Ho Chi Minh to the US in 1912 and 1913 | | | 14,450 |
| Nanjing University-The Johns Hopkins Univ. Center Fellowship: Support for Chinese students and visiting research fellows in int'l relations | | | 17,600 |
| Shanghai Institute of Int'l Studies: Support for the Institute's int'l exchange activities | | | 75,000 |
| The China Institute of Contemporary Int'l Relations: Support for the Institute's int'l exchange activities | | | 40,000 |
| Institute of Southeast Asian Studies, Zhongshan University: Support for joint activities of the five institutes of Southeast Asian Studies | | | 110,000 |
| Peking University: Partial support for a series of workshops on China's int'l relations from different regional perspectives | | | 25,000 |
| The China Society for Strategy and Management Research: Support for an int'l symposium on security and development in East Asia | | | 15,000 |
| Chinese Academy of Social Sciences: Support for fund to subsidize books on American studies at the academy's Institute of American Studies | | | 30,000 |

**Table 16.6 (continued)**

|  | 1991 | 1992 | 1993 |
|---|---|---|---|
| Chinese Academy of Social Sciences: Support for an int'l conference and research on China's relations with Europe |  |  | 50,000 |
| National Committee on US-China relations: Partial support for a program of visit to the US by Chinese scholars and officials |  |  | 25,000 |
| Total | $969,900 | $2,655,000 | $1,018,300 |

# The John D. and Catherine T. MacArthur Foundation

Funding for Asia Pacific security comes under the foundation's Program on Peace and International Cooperation. The program addresses the compelling need to develop better knowledge of the forces and mechanisms that contribute to cooperation, as well as conflict, among nations and peoples, and to provide for the wide dissemination of that knowledge to policymakers, scholars and citizens. The program fosters the development of fresh perspectives and the identification of new avenues for international cooperation by drawing new people, disciplines, and attention to issues of global security. It also seeks to increase public understanding so that citizens participate more directly in decisions about world affairs. The program has:

1. Supported graduate and postdoctoral training at universities and other research institutions and organizations through fellowships and program support in the United States and abroad.

2. Funded policy studies and public education efforts.

3. Encouraged individual scholars, and teams of scholars, to pursue cross-disciplinary research and writing projects to enhance understanding of international relations.

4. Attracted productive young scholars to the field and provided mature scholars with new opportunities to explore important issues from interdisciplinary and international perspectives.

5. Stimulated international networking and interactions that develop leadership, promote understanding of security issues, and identify new avenues for international cooperation.

6. Given organizations "seed money" to plan and develop new initiatives in peace and security studies.

The foundation will continue to explore new initiatives that contribute to progress toward a more open and cooperative international community and that strengthen the capacity of individuals and societies to address global problems.

## Table 16.7
### Asia Pacific Security

|  | 1991 | 1992 | 1993 |
|---|---|---|---|
| Beijing Institute of Applied Physics and Mathematics: In partial support of international networking and exchanges of information between Chinese and American Scientists on the technical problems of disarmament | $50,000 | | |
| Asian Peace Research Association: For the conference on "Peace and Security in the Asia-Pacific Region, Post–Cold War projects." | 50,000 | | |

**Table 16.7  (continued)**

| | 1991 | 1992 | 1993 |
|---|---|---|---|
| Consortium for Global Development: Wasting grant for three nonprofits whose work focuses on Asia. | 50,000 | | |
| Foster, Anne L.: *Experiencing Revolt in Colonial South East Asian: The European, South East Asian, and American Perspectives.* | 14,050 | | |
| Institute for Research on Public Policy: A seed grant for the research project, "Environment, Conflict and Security in the Pacific Basin." | 29,350 | | |
| Institute of Southeast Asian Studies: In partial support of an Indo-China Unit | 150,000 | | |
| Institute of Southeast Asian Studies: For workshop on development issues in Vietnam, Laos, Cambodia, Myanmar | 25,000 | | |
| International Development Law Institute: For the October 1991 training workshop held in Vietnam on the negotiation and arbitration of int'l contracts | 15,000 | | |
| Lin, Jing: *From Violence to Peaceful Revolution: A Study of Two Student Movements in Contemporary China* | 45,000 | | |
| Lintner, Berlil and Llintner: *Hseng Noung, War and Narcotics in Southeast Asia's Golden Triangle* | 50,000 | | |
| National Academy of Sciences: General support | 150,000 | | |
| Pacifica Foundation: In partial support of radio documentary on East Timor | 5,000 | | |
| Robinson, Court: *Closing the Circle: The Repatriation of Indochinese Refugees in Thailand* | 59,775 | | |
| University of California, Berkeley: In partial support of a conference entitled "China's Quest for Modernization: A Historical Perspective" | 25,000 | | |
| University of California, Irvine: In partial support of the April 1991 Soviet-American-Chinese workshop on environmental consequences of nuclear weapons development | 25,000 | | |

| Table 16.7 (continued) | 1991 | 1992 | 1993 |
|---|---|---|---|
| Chinese Academy of Sciences: For international symposium on "The Challenges Facing the Third World in the 1990s" | 50,000 | | |
| Princeton University, School of Engineering and Applied Science: Program on Nuclear Policy Alternatives project for research and training activities for nuclear arms reductions and nonproliferation. | 500,000 | | |
| Azzam, Maha: *Islam as an Ideology in the Middle East, the Central Asian Republics and South-East Asia in the 1990s* | | $60,000 | |
| Center on Budget and Policy Priorities: In partial support of the working group on the globalization of the international arms industry | | 50,000 | |
| Chang, Iris: *Tsien Hsue-Shen: Father of the Chinese Missile* | | 15,000 | |
| Institute for Research on Public Policy: For the participation of Asian scientists in the planning stages of the project "Environment, Conflict and Security in the Pacific Basin" | | 10,000 | |
| University of Maryland: In partial support of the student conference "Leadership in the New World Order: The Pacific Rim" | | 5,000 | |
| American Council of Learned Societies: In partial support of its activities to strengthen and broaden international studies in China | | 300,000 | |
| Parliamentarians for Global Action: In partial support of the Nuclear Test Ban and Non-Proliferation Program and the Peacekeeping and Collective Security Program (Total $200,000) | | 50,000* | |
| Pugwash Conferences on Science and World Affairs: In partial support of the international secretariat and the US Pugwash Committee (Total $500,000) | | 100,000* | |
| Stanford University: To plan a joint research project on cooperative security in Northeast Asia | | | $49,565 |

**Table 16.7 (continued)**

| | 1991 | 1992 | 1993 |
|---|---|---|---|
| National Public Radio: In support of its international news coverage and the establishment of a news bureau in Tokyo, Japan | | | 1,000,000 |
| Nautilus Pacific Research: In support of the bilateral nuclear inspectorate project in North and South Korea | | | 30,000 |
| Center for Strategic and Int'l Studies Jakarta, Indonesia: In support of the Bali Conference. | | | 20,000 |
| Institute of Applied Physics and Computational Mathematics: In partial support of international networking and exchanges of information between Chinese and American scientists on the technical problems of disarmament | | | 74,000 |
| Institute of Applied Physics and Computational Mathematics: For increased support for the Beijing arms control  conference of April 1994 | | | 10,000 |
| Total | $1,293,175 | $590,000 | $1,183,565 |

* Author's estimate.

# Ploughshares Fund

Ploughshares encourages international dialogue and a foreign policy based on multilateral global cooperation. It is increasing its attention to multinational participation in the global security debate, as well as to efforts to stop the spread of nuclear weapons and materials to nonnuclear nations.

**Table 16.8**
**Asia Pacific Security**

|  | FY1991 | FY1992 | FY1993 |
|---|---|---|---|
| Nautilus Pacific Action Research Ballistic Missiles | $15,000 | | |
| Pacific Campaign to Disarm the Seas | 10,000 | | |
| Nautilus Pacific Research Ballistic Missiles | | $20,000 | |
| Total: | $25,000 | $20,000 | N/A |

# The Pew Charitable Trusts

Funding related to Asia Pacific security comes under the Global Security Program. The goal of the Global Security Program is to promote effective interdisciplinary approaches to understanding and responding to emerging threats to global peace and security. The objectives are:

1. To advance interdisciplinary, policy-oriented research that can provide new insights about global security problems.

2. To develop a cohort of new specialists capable of understanding and responding to global security threats.

3. To support innovative approaches to solving global security problems.

4. To assess the impact of emerging global security threats on the evolution of the nation-state and the international system in a rapidly changing world.

The program will concentrate initially on issues of ethnic and sectarian conflict, and economic stress. Global Security commitments were in 1992 $3,300,000 and in 1993 $2,465,000.

**Table 16.9**
**Asia Pacific Security**

|  | 1991 | 1992 | 1993 |
|---|---|---|---|
| Pacific Forum, Center for Strategic and International Studies: In support of a research project on Asia-Pacific Security Cooperation and of an institution-building initiative in the Asia Pacific region | $395,000 | | |
| The George Washington University, Elliot School of International Relations: In support of the US-Japan Economic Agenda's program on "US-Japan High Technology Policy," and of the Institute for Sino-Soviet Studies program on "Peace, Security, and Economic Cooperation in East Asia" | 100,000 | | |
| The Asia Society: In support of an integrated program of policy research, international dialogue, and public education focused on the future of Southeast Asia | 100,000 | | |
| Foundation for American Economic Competitiveness: In support of the development and dissemination of eight case studies (several related to Asia) on the interrelationship between technology, and trade and investment policy | | $100,000 | |

| | | | |
|---|---|---|---|
| Pacific Forum, Center for Strategic and International Studies: In support of an integrated program of research, workshops and publications on Economic Interdependence and Challenges to the Nation-States | $265,000 | | |
| The Asia Foundation: In support of an integrated project involving research, workshops, fellowships and publications examining the economic and political dynamics underlying the emergence of market economies in Asia and Eastern Europe | 250,000 | | |
| Tulane University, School of Public Health, International Centre for Ethnic Studies, (Sri Lanka), Lazlo Teleki Foundation, (Hungary): To support a comparative study of ethnic conflict and political and economic transition in South and Southeast Asia, and Eastern and Central Europe | | | 200,000 |
| Total: | $595,000 | $100,000 | $715,000 |

# Rockefeller Brothers Fund

Funding for Asia Pacific security comes under the fund's "One World: World Security" program. Over the past several years, the focus of the RBF's world security program at the global level has been on restraining horizontal nuclear proliferation. Against a background of the rapidly changing international situation and increased public and governmental attention to the threat of horizontal proliferation following the end of the Cold War, the fund assisted several projects that are exploring new roles that existing organizations or entities might play in encouraging nuclear nonproliferation.

In East Asia, the RBF's world security program maintained an emphasis on support for multilateral projects, especially those that seek to expand international networks, both official and unofficial, to include countries that have not previously taken part in such efforts.

Payments under the "One World: World Security" in 1991 were $3,426,460; in 1992, $3,612,380; and in 1993, $2,328,325.

### Table 16.10
### Asia Pacific Security

|  | 1991 | 1992 | 1993 |
|---|---|---|---|
| The Academy of Political Science Publication: "China and East Asia: Implications for American Policy" | $12,000 | | |
| Asia Foundation: For the Democratization in Asian project | 60,000 | | |
| Asia Society, Inc.: For Pubic affairs project regarding the Korean peninsula | 100,000 | | |
| Brookings Institution: East Asia Studies program | 60,000 | | |
| Chinese Academy of Social Sciences: America and the Asia-Pacific Region in the Twentieth Century conference | 30,000 | | |
| Columbia University, East Asian Institute: Pacific Basin Studies program | 80,000 | | |
| Council on Foreign Relations: Study of foreign and economic relations of the US and Southeast Asia | 60,000 | | |
| Institute of Southeast Asian Studies: Scholarly exchange program | 70,000 | | |
| Institute for International Economics: Project on US-Japan economic relations | 80,000 | | |
| Japan Center for International Exchange: General support | 40,000 | | |

| Table 16.10 (continued) | 1991 | 1992 | 1993 |
|---|---|---|---|
| Lingnan College: Conference on economic and security concerns regarding the South China Sea | 22,000 | | |
| National Academy of Sciences: Managing the US-Japan relationship in science and technology project | 70,000 | | |
| Shanghai Institute for Int'l Studies: Chinese-Indonesian bilateral forum | 15,460 | | |
| United States National Committee for Pacific Economic Cooperation | 16,000 | | |
| Woodrow Wilson International Center: Programs on Northeast Asia | 40,000 | | |
| Yonsei University: Economic Reforms and Systems in East Asia and Eastern Europe | 49,000 | | |
| Pacific Institute for Studies in Development, Environment, and Security: For Sustainable Resource Management and Global Security project | 50,000 | | |
| United Nations Association of the United States of America: Program on Proliferation Norms and Asian Security | | $30,000 | |
| Asia Foundation: Democratization in Asia project | | 75,000 | |
| Asia Society: Study mission to North and South Korea | | 77,950 | |
| Atlantic Council of the United States: Study of US policy toward China | | 20,000 | |
| Australian National University: Pacific trade and development conferences | | 10,000 | |
| Brookings Institution: For East Asia Studies program | | 60,000 | |
| University of California, Berkeley: US-North Korean bilateral conferences | | 57,130 | |
| Graduate School of Int'l Relations and Pacific Studies (San Diego): Study of prospects for Korean reunification | | 44,000 | |
| Institute on Global Conflict and Cooperation (San Diego): Study of economic and political relations among China, Taiwan, and Hong Kong | | 40,000 | |

**Table 16.10  (continued)**

| | 1991 | 1992 | 1993 |
|---|---|---|---|
| Center for Strategic and International Studies, Honolulu: Integration the PRC into the Asia-Pacific Region project | | 35,000 | |
| Chicago Council on Foreign Relations: Asia and the Middle West project | | 150,000 | |
| Columbia University, East Asian Institute, Pacific Basin Studies program | | 80,000 | |
| East-West Center Foundation: South Korea-US Working Groups project | | 55,300 | |
| Institute for International Economics: Project on US-Japan economic relations | | 80,000 | |
| Japan Center for international Exchange: General support | | 40,000 | |
| Lingnan College: Conference on Hong Kong's role in the Asia-Pacific region | | 13,000 | |
| National Academy of Sciences: Managing the US-Japan relationship in science and technology project | | 75,000 | |
| National Bureau of Asian Research: The New Russia in Asia | | 50,000 | |
| Shanghai Institute for Interactional Studies: Conference on Northeast Asian Affairs | | 12,000 | |
| United Nations Association of the US, Japan, the United States: Regional Crisis Management and the UN project | | 50,000 | |
| United States National Committee for Pacific Economic Cooperation: For institutional development | | 14,000 | |
| Woodrow Wilson Center: Programs on Northeast Asia | | 40,000 | |
| Yonsei University: Economic Reforms and Systems in East Asia and Eastern Europe project | | 49,000 | |
| American Assembly: Conference on "the US, Japan, and Asia: Challenges to US policy" | | | $100,000 |
| The Asia Foundation: Democratization in Asia | | | 15,000 |

| Table 16.10 (continued) | 1991 | 1992 | 1993 |
|---|---|---|---|
| The Asia Society:<br>For the project, "Prospects for<br>Cooperation in Northeast Asia:<br>A Multilateral Dialogue" | | | 50,000 |
| The Australian National University:<br>For the next three meetings of the Pacific<br>Trade and Development Conference | | | 10,000 |
| The Brookings Institution:<br>Continued support for the East<br>Asia Studies program | | | 60,000 |
| Regents of the University of California,<br>Berkeley: Support for a series of bilateral<br>conferences over three years<br>involving Americans and North Koreans | | | 22,860 |
| Regents of the University of California,<br>San Diego: For a project to examine the regional<br>implications of the evolution of economic and<br>political relations | | | 40,100 |
| Chicago Council on Foreign Relations: For an<br>analysis of economic and political changes in<br>Northeast Asia from the perspective of their<br>impact on the Midwest of the US | | | 50,000 |
| Institute of Southeast Asian Studies:<br>For a program to identify and explore<br>the most effective ways of taking advantage<br>of the opportunities provided by the Asia-Pacific<br>Economic Cooperation conference | | | 50,000 |
| Japan Center for Int'l Exchange:<br>For its survey on Nongovernmental<br>Underpinnings of the Emerging Asia-<br>Pacific Region Community | | | 20,000 |
| Conference on US and Japan<br>Japan Center for Int'l Exchange:<br>General support | | | 40,000 |
| Japan Society:<br>Discussion of security and trade issues | | | 50,000 |
| Johns Hopkins University:<br>For a research and writing project<br>about the conflict on the Korean peninsula | | | 20,000 |
| National Academy of Sciences:<br>Managing the US-Japan relationship<br>in science and technology | | | 50,000 |
| National Bureau of Asian Research:<br>For a multinational project to study Russia's<br>new role in Asia, especially as it affects the<br>nations of Inner and Northeast Asia | | | 50,000 |

**Table 16.10 (continued)**

| | 1991 | 1992 | 1993 |
|---|---|---|---|
| United Nations Assoc. of the US: For a project to identify ways to strengthen the cooperative action of the US and Japan on multilateral security and related issues | | | 50,000 |
| United States National Committee for Pacific Economic Cooperation: Toward support of a development office for the US National Committee, the American organization of the Pacific Economic Cooperation Conference | | | 12,000 |
| University of Maryland Foundation: For project to examine the domestic interests and values contributing to difficulties in the US-Japan bilateral relationship and to suggest how their impact might be mitigated | | | 22,000 |
| Yonsei University: Symposium on the development of private organized philanthropy for East Asia | | | 47,150 |
| Yonsei University: For a project on structural transition and industrial cooperation in Northeast Asia | | | 33,500 |
| York University: Asia-Pacific Security Assessment | | | 25,000 |
| Total | $854,460 | $1,157,380 | $817,610 |

# The Rockefeller Foundation

The International Security Program of the Rockefeller Foundation has an average annual budget of $1.2 million (exclusive of the arms project). The program focuses exclusively on abolishing weapons of mass destruction, including chemical, biological, as well as nuclear weapons. In 1990, 1991 and 1992, it did not fund projects related to the Asia-Pacific region.

From 1993 on, it developed several Asian programs. Six grants related to Asia Pacific security; eight grants related to South Asian security.

**Table 16.11**
**Asia Pacific Security**

|  | 1991 | 1992 | 1993 |
|---|---|---|---|
| Nautilus of America/Peter Hayes, N. Korea NPT |  |  | $40,000 |
| PGA, Test Ban/3rd World Players (Total $39,000) |  |  | 8,000 |
| T.V. Paul/McGill Univ. Why Nations Renounce Nuclear Weapons (Total $25,000) |  |  | 8,000 |
| Arms Control Association (Total $50,000) |  |  | 10,000 |
| Nautilus of America/Peter Hayes Northeast Asia Peace and Security Network |  |  | 100,000 |
| Asia Society, North Korea Incentive Package |  |  | 25,000 |
|  |  |  | $191,000 |

*South Asian Security*

|  | 1993 |
|---|---|
| Stimson Center Confidence Building | $100,000 |
| S. Tahir-Kheli Pakistan/Gates Mission study | 25,000 |
| Carnegie Endowment | 12,000 |
| Jim Blight NP Lessons from Cuban Missile Crisis | 25,000 |
| National Institute of Advanced Studies (Bangalore, India) Carnegie Mellon | 100,000 |
| Center for Policy Research (New Deli) India NGO for NP | 100,000 |

| | | | |
|---|---|---|---|
| Regional Center for Strategic Studies, Regional NP network | | | 50,000 |
| Zia Mian, Peace and Arms Control | | | 18,000 |
| Total | N/A | N/A | $ 430,000 |

# The Sasakawa Peace Foundation (SPF)

The Sasakawa Peace Foundation (SPF), after its establishment in 1986, embarked upon a three-year development plan centered on researching program concepts and developing trial projects. Having completed this experimental period, the SPF has now initiated a five-year medium-term program.

Looking at global change from a Japanese as well as worldwide perspective, the SPF will address major issues in the development of an interdependent world. Despite a volatile world situation, foresight should result in a clearer view of the future, and allow the SPF to make more meaningful contributions to the international community.

The SPF will carefully examine the changing structure of the interdependent world community in order to determine its role and specific activities. Through its various policy-oriented programs, the SPF hopes to discharge its global responsibility by contributing its point of view to debates on the readjustment of global systems in a rapidly changing world.

The SPF will take up as its principal medium-term themes the interface between economic and security issues, development policies (both the development strategies of developing countries and the development cooperation policies of donor countries), and environmental issues.

**Table 16.12**
**Asia Pacific Security**

|  | FY1991 | FY1992 | 1993 |
|---|---|---|---|
| Center for Strategic and International Studies (US): Economics and Security in the Asia-Pacific region | Y 17,712,217 |  |  |
| The American Assembly (US): Rethinking America's Security | 13,238,744 |  |  |
| Institute of Strategic and Int'l Studies (Malaysia): The Fifth Asia-Pacific Roundtable | 10,169,475 |  |  |
| SPF: Association for Promotion of Interactional Cooperation: (Japan) Japan's Economy in an Interdependent World | 20,000,000 |  |  |
| SPF: Reconstruction of the Global Order—Beyond Crisis Management | 53,942,736 |  |  |
| SPF, The Royal Institute of Int'l Affairs (UK), The Woodrow Wilson Center (US): Trilateral Policy Dialogue | 45,800,278 |  |  |
| The Institute for East-West Security Studies: East-West Détente and Economic Security Interface | 13,157,375 |  |  |
| SPF: Survey of Czechoslovak-Japan Relations | 9,575,008 |  |  |

**Table 16.12  (continued)**

| | 1991 | 1992 | 1993 |
|---|---|---|---|
| The Institute of Southeast Asian Studies (Singapore): Forum for Development Strategies | 18,696,979 | | |
| The East-West Center (US): Conference on Northeast Asia Economic Cooperation | 21,069,657 | | |
| The Institute of Strategic and International Studies (Malaysia): Japan-Southeast Asia Conference | 10,561,495 | | |
| SPF: Vietnam, Laos and Cambodia in Transition: Reconstruction and Economic Development | 25,164,003 | | |
| Research (Japan) Institute for Regional Planning: Cross-Country Comparative Reviews of Informal Sector | 7,804,609 | | |
| Continuing Education Center of the Asian Institute of Tech, (Thailand): Human Resource Development for the People of Cambodia | 22,865,601 | | |
| The Club of Rome (France): Int'l Conference on Evolving Concepts of International Cooperation for Development | 14,906,211 | | |
| SPF and The French Institute of Int'l Relations: Reconstruction of the Global Order—Follow-up | | Y 18,948,867 | |
| East-West Détente and Economic Security Interface | | 13,159,553 | |
| Center for Strategic and Int'l Studies (US): Economics and Security in the Asia-Pacific Region | | 18,532,424 | |
| The Institute of Strategic and Int'l Studies (Malaysia): The Sixth Asia-Pacific Roundtable | | 11,917,433 | |
| The Asia-Pacific Association (Japan): Détente and Economic Cooperation in East Asia | | 2,751,248 | |
| Harvard University, JFK School, Japan-Russia-US Joint Research on the North Pacific Region | | 48,995,224 | |
| SPF, Emeritus Professor, Yoshio Gondoh of Kyushu University, Int'l Organization for Migration (Switzerland): Ethnic and Tribal Studies | | 2,082,041 | |

| Table 16.12  (continued) | 1991 | 1992 | 1993 |
|---|---|---|---|
| SPF, Continuing Education Center of the Asian Institute of Technology (Thailand): Human Resources Development for the People of Cambodia | | 22,851,712 | |
| SPF, The Institute of Strategic and Interactional Studies (Malaysia): Prospects for Asia | | 18,287,412 | |
| Research Institute for Regional Planning (Japan), Cross-Country Comparative Reviews of the Informal Sector | | 7,213,810 | |
| SPF, East-West Population Institute, of East-West Center (US) and Hawaii Asia-Pacific Institute (US): Conference on Northeast Asia Economic Cooperation | | 45,702,158 | |
| The Institute of Southeast Asian Studies (Singapore): Forum for Development Strategies | | 20,492,857 | |
| SPF, The French Institute of International Relations (France): Reconstruction of the Global Order—"Great Movements of People" | | | Y 32,000,000 |
| Center for Strategic and International Studies (US): Security and Economics in Asia | | | 195,000,000 |
| The Asia-Pacific Association (Japan): Détente and Economic Cooperation in East Asia | | | 9,000,000 |
| SPF, Institute of Strategic and International Studies (Malaysia): Commission for a New Asia | | | 30,000,000 |
| American Enterprise Institute for Public Policy Research (US): Trade and Technology in the Age of Global Competition | | | 19,900,000 |
| SPF, Hawaii Asia-Pacific Institute (US): Conference on Northeast Asia Economic Cooperation Phase III | | | 50,000,000 |
| SPF: Production of the Russian Far Eastern Yearbook—Phase III | | | 45,000,000 |
| SPF: Asian NGO Coalition for Agrarian Reform and Rural Development: NGO Networking | | | 29,860,000 |
| SPF, Research Institute for Regional Planning (Japan): International Network for Research and Training of the Problems | | | 27,000,000 |
| Japan Association for Preventing Mobile Accidents (Japan): Promotion of OSPAR Planning | | | 50,000,000 |

**Table 16.12 (continued)**

| | 1991 | 1992 | 1993 |
|---|---|---|---|
| International Society for Ecological Modelling (UK): Water for Peace in the Middle East | | | 16,670,000 |
| Conference on the Future of Asia-Pacific Security Studies and Exchange Activities | | | 3,150,000 |
| Total | Y 304,664,388 @132 $2,308,063 | Y 230,934,739 @125 $1,847,478 | Y 507,580,000 @130 $3,904,462 |

# United States Japan Foundation

The United States Japan Foundation (USJF) has been pursuing a long-term strategy, one which concentrates on fostering a broader and deeper understanding between the United States and Japan and which seeks to analyze both the problems between the two countries and opportunities for new cooperation. The foundation gives emphasis to precollege education programs in the US and in Japan and supports joint US-Japan study groups covering a wide range of public policy issues of importance to the future of the relationship between the two countries. In recent years, the foundation has supported study groups on such subjects as economic policy coordination, trade, and the problems of the global environment. Foundation-supported study groups have also focused on developments in Eastern Europe, Indo-China, China, and the future of the Korean peninsula. One of the principal objectives in this area of program activity is to create opportunities for Americans and Japanese to better understand one another's views on subjects which are important to the future of the relationship. At the same time, the foundation seeks to contribute to building closer links between research and public policy institutions in the two countries.

In 1991 the Foundation's grants payable amount was $2,513,306 and in 1992 $2,454,446.

**Table 16.13**
**Asia Pacific Security**

|  | 1991 | 1992 | 1993 |
|---|---|---|---|
| Columbia University: To support the third year of the US-Japan consultative group on Indo-China | $135,818 | | |
| Research Institute for Peace and Security (Japan): To support the third year of the US-Japan consultative group on Indo-China | 141,575 | | |
| Asia Society (NY): To support the second year of the US-Japan consultative group on policies toward the PRC | | $197,567 | |
| Center for Strategic and Int'l Studies: First year of the consultative group on the implications of Korean peninsula developments for US-Japan relations | | 150,000 | |
| Columbia University (NY): To support the fourth year of the US-Japan consultative group on Indo-China | | 15,815 | |

| | | | |
|---|---|---|---|
| Council on Foreign Relations: To support a study group on US policy toward East Asia. | | 10,000 | |
| American Assembly: US-Japan joint committee on policy in the Asia-Pacific region | | | $105,000 |
| Carnegie Endowment for Int'l Peace: First year of the consultative study group on nonproliferation and arms control after the Cold War | | | 173,980 |
| Center for Strategic and Int'l Studies: Second year of the consultative group on the implications of Korean peninsula developments for US-Japan relations | | | 151,000 |
| Columbia University: Fifth year of the US-Japan consultative group on Indo-China | | | 119,805 |
| George Washington University: Study group on options for liberalizing Asia-Pacific trade and investment | | | 119,156 |
| Totals: | $277,393 | $473,382 | $668,941 |

# Winston Foundation for World Peace

The general purpose of the Winston Foundation is to contribute to world peace, primarily through the permanent prevention of nuclear war. Because of the present situation within and among the nuclear powers, the foundation has chosen initially to direct its programs toward public policy. In the coming year, the foundation will concentrate its support in two areas: issues relating to preparation for nuclear war and to the domestic costs of national security doctrine. The foundation welcomes new ideas and approaches across the broad spectrum of peace activism.

**Table 16.14**
**Asia Pacific Security**

|  | 1991 | 1992 | 1993 |
|---|---|---|---|
| Nautilus Pacific Research: Ballistic missile test ban |  | $ 10,000 |  |
| Institute for Global Security Studies: Asia-Pacific dialogue on maritime CBMs |  | 8,000 |  |
| Total: | N/A | $ 18,000 | N/A |

# PART IV

Conference Summary

# Conference on
# The Future of Asia Pacific Security
# Studies and Exchange Activities

Hotel Sanur Beach, Bali
December 12–15, 1993

## AGENDA

### SUNDAY, DECEMBER 12

|  | Arrival of participants |
|---|---|
| 19:30 | Welcoming Reception and Dinner |

### MONDAY, DECEMBER 13

09:00 – 09:30 **Opening Session**
Remarks      Jusuf Wanandi
Peter F. Geithner

09:30 – 12:30 **Session One**
ASIA PACIFIC SECURITY TRENDS AND
IMPLICATIONS FOR SECURITY STUDIES
*Chair*        Susan L. Shirk
*Commentator*  Noordin Sopiee

10:00 – 10:30 Coffee Break

10:30 – 12:30 Discussion

12:30 – 14:00 Lunch

14:00 – 17:00 **Session Two**
REGIONAL SECURITY STUDIES AT THE NATIONAL LEVEL
*Chair*         Lau Teik Soon
*Commentators*  Charles Morrison
Chan Heng Chee
Michel Oksenberg

15:00 – 15:30 Coffee Break

15:30 – 17:00 Discussion

19:00          Dinner with keynote speech by General (ret.) L.B. Moerdani,
former Indonesian Minister of Defense and Security
Introduced by Carolina G. Hernandez, Chairperson, ASEAN-ISIS

## TUESDAY, DECEMBER 14

09:00 – 12:30  **Session Three**
MULTILATERAL RESEARCH AND DIALOGUE ACTIVITIES
*Chair*  Alexei Arbatov
*Commentators*  Tadashi Yamamoto
Desmond Ball

10:00 – 10:30  Coffee Break

10:30 – 12:30  Discussion

12:30 – 14:00  Lunch

14:00 – 15:45  **Session Four**
TRAINING AND EMERGING NEEDS
*Chair*  Le Mai
*Commentators*  John Bresnan
Masashi Nishihara

15:45 – 16:15  Coffee Break

16:15 – 17:45  **Session Five**
FOUNDATION PERSPECTIVE
*Chair*  Amos A. Jordan
*Panel*  Stephen Bosworth
Jun-etsu Komatsu
Kusuma Snitwongse

19:00  Dinner and Cultural Performance

## WEDNESDAY, DECEMBER 15

09:00 – 12:30  **Session Six**
THE FUTURE AGENDA
*Chair*  Hadi Soesastro
*Commentators*  Stuart Harris
Seizaburo Sato
Yuan Ming
Robert A. Scalapino

10:30 – 11:00  Coffee Break

11:00 – 12:30  Discussion

12:30 – 13:00  **Concluding Session**
Remarks  Jusuf Wanandi
Peter F. Geithner
Paul Evans

13:00 – 14:30  Lunch

# Summary of Discussion

## DAVID B. DEWITT[1]

## Session One: Asia Pacific Security Trends and Implications for Security Studies

After introductory remarks by the conference organizers on the objectives and structure of the conference, the lead commentator began by acknowledging the diversity of opinion on definitions of "the region" and of "security." He identified a consensus in the papers on two main points: first, all centered on a region which included Northeast Asia, Southeast Asia, Oceania, and North America with primacy of focus on Pacific Asia; second, all used a definition of security which was broad but focused on threats to peace and security at the level of the nation-state. He identified three trends in the region relevant to security concerns—a peace revolution, especially in the internal security of nations; an economic revolution; and advancements in human rights and democratization.

Further, he posited that Asia Pacific regional security studies should have not only an "intellectual function" (research, writing, teaching) but also an "action function." Four challenges were identified and discussed.

1. **Improving work in traditional areas.** It was noted that, as in much of the world, international relations research on Asia Pacific security has been dominated by a big-power, realist, Cold War paradigm predicated on active hostility between states. The commentator argued that more original thinking was now in order. We need to move beyond national perspectives, employing both regionalist perspectives and concepts such as public goods to reframe our questions; we have to engage in more objective and less nationalistic and propagandist studies; we must be more intellectually courageous; and we must be more creative in outlook and thinking.

2. **Responding creatively to new issues and priorities.** The list of "new" issues for the region includes: ideological conflicts over human rights, democratization, the role of Islamic fundamentalism, economic systems, environmental issues, etc., now arising in the wake of the demise of the Communist/anti-Communist conflict; arms procurement and proliferation; environmental degradation; AIDS; drugs; redrawing of national boundaries; implications of the transition to market systems; mass movements of people; an emerging Japan; the probable rise of the "new Chinese super state" and possible fragmentation of the nation; position and role of economics, trade, and technology; "new Russia"; the newly independent Central Asian repub-

lics; the position and role of the post–Cold War United States in the region; the implications of a newly integrated East Asia; the general effects of the emerging "natural economic territories" and growth triangles; the expansion of ASEAN. The commentator did not offer these in any order of priority.

3. **Responding to and participating in new intergovernmental institutions and processes**. While the last few years have seen substantial non-governmental and track two activity, there also have been expanded and new intergovernmental forums. It was suggested that the ASEAN Regional Forum and associated SOMs are an obvious focus for regional security activity, as well as ASEAN engaging in an expanded security dialogue with other Asian (possibly Northeast Asian) countries. The commentator believed that APEC should not deal with security matters because its agenda is already full. CSCAP also was mentioned as a new vehicle for undertaking joint or coordinated research which, as in PECC's relationship to APEC, could contribute to the ARF.

4. **Adopting new concepts and perspectives**. In the post–Cold War world, new concepts and understanding of security had to be engaged. The commentator paid specific attention to: the relationship between common, comprehensive, and cooperative security with the growing acceptance of the latter concept in Asia Pacific security discourse; the relationship between economic development and regional security; and the potential security threats arising from culturally determined differences in perception and understanding. The discussion which followed covered a number of broad themes.

*Definition of the Asia Pacific region*—There was some discussion about the geopolitical boundaries of the region. While one participant argued that the impact of disputes in South Asia made it important that India, Pakistan, and Sri Lanka be included in Asia Pacific security studies (Bangladesh was not mentioned), others suggested that this would pose a very real danger that South Asian problems would come to dominate the agenda. In general, it was acknowledged that although the primary focus of research should remain in the North Asia and Southeast Asia subregions, this should not be allowed to completely or arbitrarily limit the agenda. The growing relevance of subregional economic issues to Asia Pacific security dynamics also was noted.

*Definitions of security*—Discussion on the definition and range of security issues was wide and varied. Several participants noted that issues relating to the internal security of nations should be a central part of Asia Pacific security studies. A number emphasized that the traditional discussion of military threats, while necessary, was no longer sufficient when applied to the current situation. While new items were suggested (e.g., refugees, terrorism, civil-military relations), there was insufficient opportunity to investigate the criteria for ascertaining priorities for research and exchange given the contested nature of our understanding of security.

*Applicability of European experience and scholarship*—The similarities and differences between recent European security experiences and those in Asia

Pacific were raised by several participants. Security issues in Europe since 1989 have become more diffuse and uncertain. The ending of the Cold War removed the common and discrete threat of the bipolar security structure, the centrality of the ideological confrontation between capitalist democracies and Communism, and the domination of security discourse by the two superpowers. In this regard, the current European experience has moved from a singular external definition of threat to one in which both external factors and, particularly in central Europe, internal factors have come to define security challenges. Asia Pacific shares aspects of the European experience from which it might learn, but noticeably deviates from some of the core characteristics of Europe. In particular, it was noted that in Asia Pacific: there always has been a multiple of external threats to some countries often more complex than the previous East-West confrontation in Europe; there is now an overall reduction in the prominence of nationalist and internal security problems; there is an understanding of nationalism which is not seen as leading to excesses within or between states; and that private sector and economics are now leading the process of defining the priorities of politics and security. Processes and instruments which have emerged through the evolving European experiences—e.g., the CSCE, human rights, arms control, CSBMs, transparency, verification—occasionally were mentioned but did not receive focused attention.

*Other issues*—Participants raised several additional issues, including: the changing security logic of the region which has shifted from threat-based to risk-based; the need to balance research on the causes of conflict with the causes of peace; the relationship between democracy and peace, and between economics, pluralism, and comprehensive security; the role of the military in governance in the region; the place of the United Nations in security relations of the region; the continued vulnerability of some governments to insurgency; the question of political leadership; and the need to bring theory to the study of Asia Pacific security. One participant proposed a "layered" approach to security studies and dialogue, with the "real world" issue determining whether it is best to proceed from a subregional, regional, or global approach. Another noted that priorities in security studies should be "market driven" in order to ensure relevance. The importance of a strong interdisciplinary theoretical and conceptual base to regional security studies was raised by a number of participants. While acknowledging that this was difficult to achieve, one suggestion included a combination of cross-national training and establishing interdisciplinary teams for collaborative work.

## Session Two: Regional Security Studies at the National Level

The session aimed at comparative discussion of the fourteen country studies. The first commentator focused on Northeast Asia (including Russia, China, Korea, Japan); the second on Southeast Asia (including the countries in ASEAN, Indo-China and Burma), and China and Taiwan; and the third on the non-Asian contexts (including Australia, New Zealand, the United States, Canada, and Europe).

The opening presentation identified four primary factors affecting security relations in Northeast Asia: the new uncertainties arising from the changing commitments of the United States and the former Soviet Union; the reemergence of a multilateral system which invokes some deep-rooted historical suspicions; the rise of economic tensions no longer tempered by military security concerns; and new issues and concerns (e.g., internal stability of China; pressures on the DPRK; large population migrations) which could aggravate security relations. Further, it was argued that this region was not able to cope effectively as a security community with the rapidity and scope of change.

The commentator then focused on the specific country papers. At least three problems need to be addressed: the formal education and training of experts which is too narrow and based on a singular military definition of security; area or single country studies are rarely supplemented by an appreciation of the processes and significance of regionalization; insufficient exchange of knowledge, expertise, and ideas between the academic/research community and the governmental or policy-making centers. While there does seem to be some movement to alleviate these problems, a number remain unresolved. Indigenous education and training in security studies remain uneven. Training is too narrowly based with insufficient cross-fertilization or connections with the broader security community. Insufficient funding not only impedes research but also, when new young scholars emerge, constrains opportunities for professional employment. Further, it was noted that there is a general aging of the security studies communties. This is particularly acute in Russia where aging and other problems are (*a*) substantially reducing the number of trained and active security specialists and (*b*) destroying any kind of cohesive security studies community.

The second presentation noted that the papers were useful inventories of research but did not identify theoretical constructs or examples of innovation. Indeed, much of the work described even lacked the rigor of more classic strategic studies, resorting primarily to a descriptive empirical mode of presentation and analysis. The lack of any indigenous theory or conceptualization was notable, with most research focused on a single country (e.g., a state's foreign policy), with little effort to generalize or place findings in a comparative or regional context, and with constructs usually borrowed from Western scholarship generated in other regional settings. While all the papers indicated agreement that the definition of security had to include both internal and external factors, it was acknowledged that each country or subregion had its own particular set of priorities. For instance, China's security thinking turns less on external military threat than on threats from within, while most of the ASEAN states are turning from concerns over internal stability to the broader regional and international contexts of threats and risks. There was a sense that as scholars have improved opportunities to work with experts from outside their own countries, a convergence on concepts and approaches to security studies is likely to emerge. Finally, the commentator noted that while ASEAN-ISIS activities and the ASEAN Regional Forum together confirm the growing vitality and importance of track two multilateral dialogue as part of both the scholarly and policy communities, neither was a substitute for basic scholarship. There was concern that insufficient resources (time, personnel, funding) were being allocated to reflection and fundamental research in the security studies field in Asia. Until this happens, the security dialogue will be inherently unequal. The third and final presentation offered a synthesis and comparative assessment of the papers written on the non-Asian countries involved in Asia Pacific security studies. Security studies are deeply embeded in specific national contexts. Even within these "Western" countries, most notable was diversity—in the preferred definition of security and of what constitutes the Asia Pacific region; in the priorities for research; in the range of institutions which undertake Asia Pacific security studies and in their degree of connectedness with the policy communities and with each other; in the dominant paradigms or theoretical and conceptual underpinnings of the research; and in the purposes and emphasis of security studies. How can this diversity be explained? Again, the commentator offered a range of suggestions: whether one was working from the perspective of a nuclear or nonnuclear power, a liberal democracy or another form of government, or a large, medium, or small state; the different intellectual traditions, especially the role of the intelligentsia within civil society; the role of culture and the existence of a particular strategic or security culture; the preferred or dominant language of discourse; the intelligence and military capabilities; the objective internal and external security concerns; the relationship between government and universities; the importance given to the development of human resources; and the funding (private, public, sustained) of research institutions.

The commentator concluded by examining the aspects of Asia Pacific security studies which deserve particular attention. He argued that consensus was unlikely and that not only should diversity and pluralism be accepted but that they should be viewed as a strength. This is especially important as we move into a period of multilateralism in which new concepts and theories are required given the inadequacies of Cold War constructs. This led to the plea for some "unrealism" and "irrelevance" in research so as to reduce the risk that policymakers and governments will determine the research agenda. The field should not come together around a dominant paradigm or theoretical starting point too quickly. Finally, it was noted that while conferences had their place and were relatively easy to undertake, the emphasis must be put on research that is theoretically informed, conceptually sophisticated, and empirically rich.

The ensuing discussion focused on the role and place of intellectuals, universities, and scholarship on Asia Pacific security primarily in the countries of Northeast and Southeast Asia. Universities are usually but not always the principal locations for both teaching and research on international affairs generally and security studies in particular. A question was raised concerning the independence of scholars and institutions from governments. One participant asked, "Can intellectuals actually offer an alternative policy if this would disagree with the government's official position?" Another questioned the conditions under which it would be possible to undertake work which might be critical of the researcher's own government's preferences. It was noted that in East and Southeast Asian societies, change cannot be brought about by public displays or open opposition. Further, free research and discussion which had the potential of being critical of a specific regime would be easier to undertake if done collaboratively with an international group of colleagues rather than alone or within one country.

The content of education and training received special attention. One participant urged the conference not to ignore area studies, especially in the increasing number of circumstances in which the outlying, marginal, or border areas intersected with one or more other countries (e.g., Mekong river project; western provinces in China vis-à-vis the Central Asian republics). These highlight very specific and significant security problems which might otherwise be overlooked or ignored by focusing exclusively on the larger strategic issues. It was further argued that area studies expertise was more likely to ensure sensitivity to the specific influence of culture and language on theories, concepts, and discourse. The value of training outside one's own country was widely recognized. It was seen to improve levels of knowledge, understanding, and professionalism (e.g., being exposed to competing views, concepts, and approaches; to literature in another language) and to equip scholars to affect thinking at home.

Diverging somewhat from the expressed focus of the session, some of the discussion moved into various aspects of the nature of security in Asia Pacific. This ranged from exchanges on confidence building, deterrence, and reassurance to the uses and value of multilateral dialogue to revisiting the question of agenda items for study (e.g., What are the processes of mobilization and demobilization? What is the normal role and level of the military in the post–Cold War world or post-revolutionary period?). Some participants commented on the relationship between incentives and deterrence in creating alternative security processes and structures. Another approach was to inquire about the capacity for collective action. It was argued that cooperative strategies and reassurance, which is essentially multilateral, cannot simply replace deterrence, which is essentially bilateral. For example, concerning military force: where tensions can be resolved at the bilateral level, arms reductions are probable; in the context of multilateral conflict or where threats and/or risks objectively are present or in which there is heightened uncertainty, there remains an incentive to modernize and to expand one's military capabilities. Hence, there is a real need to promote multilateral dialogue (e.g., CSCAP at the nongovernmental and the ARF at the official level) and to develop a rich and sophisticated menu of incentives so that deterrence alone is not the principal means for security. There was a difference of opinion on whether ASEAN had become, or was destined to become, a "security community" as Karl Deutsch used the phrase, or if it would be better to use a phrase like "zone of peace," an idea indigenous to the region.

## Session Three: Multilateral Research and Dialogue Activities

The first commentator began by providing some personal experiences over many years which have confirmed support for multilateral dialogue, track two approaches, a focus on research and the substance of policy, and a recognition that Asia Pacific has intrinsic importance *as a region* and not simply as a disaggregated set of bilateral (e.g., Japan-USA) arrangements. Further, the European experience in regional security activities is important to the growth and understanding of the Asia Pacific region, not as a model for emulation but as a subject for comparative analysis. This led to several specific observations. First, joint studies and collaborative policy relevant research and dialogue have been vital in the trans-Atlantic and European community building experiences because they have assisted in avoiding or dampening conflicts within the community, allowing participants to unite against commonly perceived threats, containing internal threats, and enhancing a shared understanding and view of security. However, because the shared interests and challenges which face the emerging Asia Pacific community are less clear, it is important to search for shared objectives from the outset.

The commentator then listed several concerns. It is important that both the private *and* public sectors play a role in the future of the region. Pluralism and diversity are obvious characteristics of the region and these need to be understood and utilized as strengths. A balance between "product and process" is needed, emphasizing education, reorienting experts from bilateral to multilateral community thinking, and developing habits of dialogue and of working together. New modalities and institutions are required to better facilitate and sustain collaborative and cooperative undertakings—task forces, networking, institutional memberships, etc. On the question of the governance, management, and leadership of the multilateral processes, including dialogue and study, the commentator strongly favored a multilateral and shared approach rather than dominance by a single country. The pressures on human resources and infrastructure will increase concomitantly with the rise in the number of dialogue channels. Finally, funding remains a core issue, and the conference was reminded that enormous amounts of public and private money went into the creation and maintenance of the European and trans-Atlantic communities.

The second commentator opened with a provocative question: "Why is multilateralism—in structure, in process, in dialogue, and in security studies—now deemed essential when only three years ago a number of principal actors in the Asia Pacific were adamantly opposed and overtly hostile?" Four reasons were posited: the transformation from the Cold War bipolar system to a transition period which currently favors a somewhat ill-defined multilateral system; a mix of traditional with relatively new security issues which lend themselves to multilateral approaches; a recognition that security is determined by an increasingly broad range of factors, including economic and environmental, which often are best addressed through multilateral processes; and some new thinking about the concepts of security, including common, comprehensive, and cooperative security. Further, while multilateral dialogue at both the official and track two levels were both essential and well under way, more was now required to facilitate real progress.

The commentator noted that there was relatively little sustained, multilateral research activity to complement the dialogue process, and that while this needed to be promoted, so too did the development of concepts and intellectual constructs sensitive to the diversity of security cultures within the Asia Pacific and even indigenous to the region. As in the previous session, there was considerable concern about the potential risk of too readily importing theories and approaches which had developed at other times in other contexts. Turning to regional security forums and structures, CSCAP was identified as a worthwhile and ambitious project but a caution was added that the inclusion of the non-like-minded may mean (*a*) that specific, well-focused results are difficult to achieve, (*b*) that the China-Taiwan issue will be an impediment, and (*c*) that funding in support of sustained multilateral research projects will be a major concern. Linking nongovernmental programs to the official process was deemed to be invaluable, as were track two activities, but at the same time the nonofficial structures and activities, especially the research, had to retain intellectual independence. This could be particularly important concerning military or defense establishments, where the policy relevance of research would be enhanced through access to these establishments and in the process might also lead to confidence building measures and transparency so long as the research was undertaken multilaterally. But it was also noted that there is a real risk that such access might be inversely related to intellectual independence.

The discussion began with three questions relevant to the multilateral research and dialogue process. How far can we proceed with multilateralism as the defining security architecture of the region—merely as an extension of bilateral relations or as an evolving successor? Which are the most promising paths to pursue and how might they best be achieved? Which institutions can best contribute to moving these activities along?

One participant provided a cogent set of points then taken up by a number of others. There are "soft" and "hard" interstate issues, and confidence building is an important aspect of dialogue as it makes it less likely that a government will make a "hard" military response over a particular dispute; since it is virtually impossible to separate any multilateral discussion from existing bilateral relationshps, bilateralism should be built upon rather than replaced; over the past few years one can observe increased convergence between the network of bilateral military and defense arrangements and multilateral discussions on security issues; and while there is considerable ongoing dialogue, there is relatively little sustained research underway on security in the Asia Pacific region. Another commented that while research into multilateral security issues is not especially difficult, the real challenge will be to undertake *multilateral, fully collaborative* research into regional security. During the course of this discussion, participants also recommended what one called "open regionalism" which in this context had two meanings. The first is to understand the experiences in other regions, at other times, in other contexts, thereby introducing an explicitly comparative studies. The second is to include specialists from outside the "Asia Pacific" in discussion of "regional" security issues.

There was some discussion about the merits of multilateral dialogues and processes such as what is proposed by CSCAP. It was noted that research agendas, cooperative or even collaborative research, long-term "basic" research as well as shorter-term policy relevant research were all facilitated by a regular habit of inclusive dialogue. Dialogue thereby promotes confidence building, assists in developing the instruments of cooperation, and can contribute to public education. A further objective is the advancement of systematic social science research and knowledge about security challenges in the region, possibly thereby contributing to preventive diplomacy. However, all this requires the development of new forms of multilateral arrangements to promote professional social science research on regional security, and with this will come the ever-present challenge of funding in support of long-term research and training. There was no unanimity about the relative value of more basic and systematic long-term academic research as compared with explicitly policy relevant work, with one colleague noting rather starkly that most institutes within Pacific Asia eschewed academic research in favor of empirical research meant to explain and to present policy options. Another suggested that it was not an either/or issue, but rather that events of the day called for immediate engagement, so that the more academically focused research might have to wait.

One speaker noted that CSCAP requires a focused agenda concentrating on a number of issues relevant to ongoing official forums such as the ARF, and that the track two formula was essential for this to be effective. In this context, a number of subjects for research, in addition to those identified in previous sessions, were offered. These included: civil-military relations and roles the military play in each nation; the conventional arms buildup in the region from the perspective of both the vendors and the procurers; national security evolution as a result of democratization and the growth of the middle class in the region; the challenges to the interests of military and defense establishments and the implications for regional and subregional security; Japanese-Korean relations as a case study of historical legacies and their impact on subregional security relations; and the North Pacific subregion as an arena of unfulfilled shared interests and experiences, especially in comparison with the relative success of Southeast Asia in establishing ASEAN as an effective mechanism for regional security dialogue.

## Session Four: Training and Emerging Trends

This session focused primarily on exploring the capacity of institutions within the Asia Pacific region to train the younger generation of experts to have the capabilities to address the increasingly complex set of issues involved in security studies.

The two commentators stressed many of the same issues. There was broad agreement that the university is and should continue to be the principal institution in which to develop a new generation of experts. In addition to the obvious factors of the existing place of universities in most societies in spite of the growing funding difficulties most face, their role in attracting bright young students, and the presence of libraries and other intellectual resources including faculty, universities were seen to be the best place to ensure longer-term investment in "training the trainers." One of the commentators listed several requirements in developing security specialists: highly qualified trainers; highly promising trainees; good to excellent libraries, databases, and other institutional supports; attractive career opportunities; excellent publishing opportunities within the country and relevant region; regular opportunities to meet and to work with others, usually requiring high competence in the English language.

It was acknowledged that the number of universities which possess sufficient human and material resources to undertake advanced professional training are limited, and that most exist in the English speaking West (North America, United Kingdom, Australia). However, mention was made of significant advances in a number of Pacific Asian countries (e.g., Singapore, Malaysia, Phillipines, Korea) in both English language competence and the initial development of small communities of security studies experts. Further, it was pointed out that in some countries, the political culture militates against security studies and discourages the best and the brightest from building intellectual or policy-oriented careers dealing with issues of peace and war.

Another point of view was that while Asian students continue to go to non-Asian countries for postgraduate training, neither their programs of study nor their areas of specialization seem to conform adequately to the needs or the situations in their home countries. The graduate programs tend to concentrate on the discipline (e.g., political science) and on general phenomena (e.g., arms control, conflict resolution, causes of war) and theory without sufficient attention to the regional or subregional context or to focused policy relevant concerns. Finally, it was noted that while many of those interested in security studies would find employment either in government or in nonuniversity organizations (i.e., "think tanks"), generally the policy-oriented institutions in Pacific Asia, especially if they eschew basic research in favor of shorter-term empirical policy work, do not carry the same prestige or opportunities for professional advancement as do universities.

The ensuing discussion highlighted a number of different approaches. Some argued in favor of training at the postgraduate but nondoctoral level, focusing on developing a new professionally competent cohort of security specialists who could work within government as well as policy-oriented, nongovernmental institutions. Others were primarily concerned with balancing the realities of the current geographical location of educational expertise exists (i.e., outside of Pacific Asia) with the need to develop indigenous capacity at the most highly qualified levels. One participant asked, "What actually is the problem which needs to be addressed given that there have been four decades of Western social science education within Asia or accessible to many Asians?" Those states newly emerging from protracted warfare require substantial assistance in creating educational infrastructures and developing their own experts, while other countries which have traditional expertise need, for example, broadening or the development of a cohort of leading younger generation specialists. Another opined that there are enough scholars and researchers but not enough with real expertise in the increasingly complex area of security studies. This is increasingly acute given that more countries today are being called upon or are seeking to play new roles subregionally, regionally, and globally.

There seemed to be general agreement concerning current requirements: to retrain people already in positions of authority or influence but trained in traditional ways; to recognize that this is a new era demanding new thinking and, especially, the development of new theories, concepts, and constructs based on what is happening in the post–Cold War Asia Pacific arena and from the perspectives of the indigenous communities; to bring intellectuals and other security experts together in order to begin the process of building a community of common interests and understandings; to be informed about the changes in science and technology which may affect rather rapidly the security environment; and to break through Cold War animosities to embrace inclusively the Asia Pacific community in the development of security studies.

This "wish list" received a positive response but it also was recognized that the promotion of Asia Pacific security studies faced major impediments, not least being a very difficult financial climate coupled with complex regional politics, together mitigating any easy institutional or programmatic response. Nevertheless, some suggestions were offered, including: encouraging cooperation between public and private sectors; using think tanks and university-based "short courses" to facilitate retraining in security studies; providing adequate scholarships and fellowships to ensure continued movement of younger scholars throughout the region; creating student exchange programs and internships at various levels; maintaining an active conference and dialogue program to help create a security studies community; and a special focus on MA and PhD training. These suggestions were complemented by the observation that it was increasingly necessary to find ways to ensure cross-disciplinary education given that security challenges no longer could be assumed to be as straightforward as in past.

## Session Five: Foundation Perspectives

The chair of the session opened by noting that in the United States thirteen foundations provide almost all of the private funding available for security studies, and of these, six provide over 90 percent. While the support goes towards research, dialogue (conferences, workshops, etc.), and training, there seems to be no discernible pattern regarding themes, substance, or focus. Several areas were identified about which the research community seeks clarification from the foundations: How consciously do they prioritize the three functions noted above? How flexible are they in departing from these priorities in response to a proposal which doesn't fit the guidelines of the day? Are they proactive or reactive with regard to these priorities? Do they exchange information among foundation colleagues, either within or between foundations? Do they prefer to work with a potential grantee in developing a project or is the preference to receive only the formal submission? Do they favor or even prefer collaborative projects, and if so what are the operational parameters? How can foundation donors be drawn into the Asia Pacific arena when so much attention is being given to Europe and the former Soviet Union?

Representatives from The MacArthur Foundation, The US-Japan Foundation, The Japan Foundation Center for Global Partnership, The Asia Foundation, and the Chaiyong Foundation in Thailand each provided an overview of their respective foundation—the foundation history, the endowment, the range in the size of grants, their priorities, their style of work, and their interests in Asia Pacific and/or security studies. All of this information is readily available in the brochures provided by the foundations. Due to time constraints, the session ended without any discussion from the floor.

## Session Six: The Future Agenda

This final session was intended to address two related issues: first, how to push regional security within Asia Pacific beyond existing bilateral relations towards multilateral security arrangements; and second, how best to harness diverse national capabilities and perspectives to sustaining multilateral security processes in the region. Four commentators expressed their views on the issues covered in the preceeding sessions as well as the future agenda for Asia Pacific security studies.

The first commentator presented a number of questions requiring answers fundamental to the future regional security agenda. Working from the assumptions that policy is based on perceptions rather than some sense of "objective facts," and that part of the purpose of research is to bring those perceptions more closely into line with facts, the following issues need to be considered:

1. For whom and for what purposes is the research conducted? What are security studies? Does a focus on the causes of war and the use of force remain central?

2. What about theory? Greater conceptual clarity is required, especially in order to help put some structure on an area of research which has tended to be empirically rich but theoretically underdeveloped. However, theory must be relevant to ongoing policy needs, especially in order to help predict human behavior in such an important area as security.

3. What about research? Where does it fit with regional dialogue? In this regard, what is research and who does it? If it is to develop systematically new knowledge and understanding, including explanation and prediction which is additive and cumulative, then can this be accomplished so long as much of the work is conducted within government agencies and the military, is usually kept inaccessible by outside experts, and therefore does not actually engage the larger community nor raise the level of debate? What research needs to be done? While traditional areas will continue, out of necessity, this must become more sophisticated and, ultimately, be linked with research into the long list of nontraditonal security issues noted earlier. One also should expect that research priorities may vary with the characteristics of the country; e.g., small, middle, or large power, democracy and market economy compared with other political and economic systems.

4. How should research be done? Collaborative work is to be encouraged, but this can be very slow and costly. There obviously is a need to facilitate the development of indigenous research capabilities. How can emerging research needs be met? Security dialogues and forums, such as the ASEAN PMC, the ARF, and CSCAP, will stimulate research and will influence both the research and the policy agendas. Further, these cannot only help focus research and assist in the dissemination of data, of ideas, and of research findings, they can give visibility to and sustained interest in Asia Pacific security studies. However, there is no substitute for actual research.

The second commentator offered three main observations. First, organizations cannot produce new ideas; only individuals can do so. Therefore, it is important to promote and to facilitate serious research, the training of new experts, and the retraining of those already in positions of influence, making them aware of the implications of the rapidly changing and much more complex security environment. Second, dialogues should be encouraged and sustained, since they are vital to the creation and maintenance of a regional security community. While CSCAP could become an important vehicle in this regard in managing human resources, in networking among researchers, and in undertaking coordinated research, it should not be seen as monopolizing the regional security studies agenda. Further, the military and perhaps even the business community should be brought into such dialogue activities. Third, careful consideration should be given to determining which security issues are best handled at the regional level and which at the subregional level. Once this is accomplished, research working groups should endeavor to ensure inclusiveness of the relevant parties to the issues.

The third commentator focused on the question of training. There was general agreement that it was absolutely essential to establish a strong intellectual infrastructure for security studies throughout the Asia Pacific region. This included: exploring issues of institution building or institutional reinforcement; establishing courses and programs on regional security at both the undergraduate and graduate levels; facilitating cooperative and collaborative research as well as regular professional exchanges; ensuring that excellent young scholars get educated in a manner which will facilitate cross-cultural communications (i.e., knowledge and experience in multiple cultures and languages); and providing databases and libraries sufficient to maintain an active and competent research and teaching community in each country. A multilateral (and perhaps interdisciplinary) task force on security studies training was strongly recommended as an early step in this process. While the internationalization of security studies in itself posed major definitional and conceptual challenges, it also was suggested that the promotion of security studies experts needed to be undertaken within appropriate disciplinary contexts, thereby avoiding narrow overspecialization which could undermine the longer-term contextual value of this new resource. CSCAP was seen to have a potentially important role in this area.

The fourth and final commentator began by noting that we had to move beyond definitional issues, that for now we had to accept that Asia Pacific included at its core Northeast and Southeast Asia, with both North America and Australia and New Zealand as essential components; further, that security included both its traditional meaning of defense against any external attack, especially of a military nature, but extends to include challenges to core values, internal political process, and national economic system. In addition, under the security rubric one must now focus on the relatonship between stability and development, thereby also recognizing the enlarged set of issues which may be perceived as domestically destabilizing or aggravating relations between states. The traditional threats—borders, divided states, ethnic and religious cleavages— which historically have caused conflict between and within states are not gone, but today the conflicts are no longer between major states. Neither do they carry the potential of spillover into the global strategic environment as in the recent past. Rather, often in the context of nation-state building or consolidation, small and middle powers are now being challenged both internally and externally, while the great powers are preoccupied increasingly with internal issues of political cohesion and economic capacity. Today, there is no discernible regional or global order; hence, our paradigms are now open to challenge and require careful examination.

The commentator then turned to issues of dialogue and organizations which can promote and facilitate multilateral activities. Noting that an organization like CSCAP cannot itself create new ideas, it nevertheless can raise and identify issues and explore these by subjecting them to analysis from different cultural and national perspectives. In order to do this effectively, groups like CSCAP must accept the principles of multilateralism and must determine how to work simultaneously at bilateral, subregional, regional, and global levels. Working groups must call on experts from both within Asia Pacific and beyond it, although the precise role of such outside experts needs to be carefully considered (i.e., do they participate in plenary sessions of CSCAP?). Among the many possible topics for initial attention by CSCAP working groups, the following might be given priority: preventive diplomacy; early warning; weaponry, including nuclear, biological, and chemical proliferation as well as arms control and technology transfer; and dissemination of data, including comparative research (this might be done by a secretariat rather than a specific working group).

The general discussion concentrated on four issues: training and education; the value of comparative analysis; priorities for research and other activities, especially CSCAP; and the question of institution building. On the first issue, there was consensus around the central place of universities, the need to facilitate both degree (BA, MA, PhD) and nondegree (short courses, retraining) programs in security studies, and the requirement that more explicit attention must be given to linking knowledge relevant to the increasingly complex security agenda across disciplines. In addition to an infusion of new money, existing institutions must explore ways to address these new needs including cooperative programs both within and across countries while ensuring that specialization does not come at the cost of educating high quality experts having a broad and solid intellectual foundation. To the extent to which these issues were successfully approached, comparative analysis would be facilitated. It was argued, for instance, that experiences in Europe were relevant to Asia Pacfic security studies and policy development: Europe is involved in the Asia Pacific; security is indivisible and Europe will continue to have a central role globally; both the realist and interdependence paradigms have serious deficiencies as seen through the evolution of recent European security politics; technology change should be explored as an overarching paradigm of international politics; and the European experiences of imploding states, ethnonationalism as an emerging pattern of regional relations, and changes occuring simulatenously at multiple levels of operation.

The issue of the future agenda generated a range of opinion on the extent to which organizations such as CSCAP should be directive rather than merely facilitative. Some of the participants rejected the idea that CSCAP should play a central role in coordinating the broader dialogue process; others felt that this coordinating role was essential. There was overall agreement: that diversity of approaches and opinions should be encouraged and that achieving consensus not be a necessary goal; that annual meetings should include reports on working group activities; that WGs should be prepared to undertake topics not yet being addressed by others as of potential significance to Asia Pacific security; that the

ASEAN Regional Forum be viewed as both a principal guide to setting the priorities of the WG research agenda and be seen as a principal target for the dissemination of the results of WG analyses; and that database development, collation, and dissemination be seen as a primary CSCAP activity. In this context, there also was general approval of encouraging broad representation and participation; that is, ensuring that CSCAP not be the captive of a few, and that new and young scholars actively be sought out and brought into both the research and dialogue processes. Further, while conferences were viewed as important for community building and for the dissemination of research results as well as policy development, the priority should be research and publication. Among the ideas for immediate attention not previously mentioned, the following were noteworthy: establishing a track two process involving military officers and officials; integrating Asian specialists with international relations and security studies experts; and advancing CSCAP-type multilateral processes even when individual states in the region wish specific key security issues not to be multilateralized (e.g., Chinese views on the Taiwan Straits, Japan on the offshore islands).

The question of institution building was noted but not resolved. This was an issue addressed by a number of the country papers prepared for the conference as well as by some of the participants. Some indicated an interest in a broadening the ASEAN-ISIS type of arrangement; others in an independent, multilaterally managed new institution based in the region (possibly along the lines of a regional Institute for International and Strategic Studies); and still others questioned the value of any new institutions, preferring a more flexible, ad hoc networking among existing, evolving, and strengthened national-level institutions.

## Note

1. I wish to acknowledge the assistance of Kathryn Hitchings, Peta Irvine, and A. (Oky) Mochtan who served as rapporteurs throughout the conference. Because the conference proceedings were not taped, the rapporteurs' notes were a useful complement to my own.

# Contributors

**Alexei G. Arbatov**, Head of the Department on Arms Control and Security of the Institute for World Economy and International Relations (IMEMO) in the Russian Federation. He has published in the area of security, defense and arms control problems, both in Russia and in the West. His recent publications include "Nuclear Weapons Reductions and Limitations" in *Strategic Views from the Second Tier: The Nuclear Weapons Policies on France, Britain and China* (IGCC Studies in Conflict Cooperation, 1994) and "Russian Foreign Policy Priorities for 1993" in *Russian Security After the Cold War* (Brassey's, 1994).

**Tsedendambyn Batbayar**, Director of the Institute of Oriental and International Studies at the Mongolia Academy of Sciences, Mongolia. He serves as an adviser to the National Security Council in Ulan Bator. His most recent publications include year-end articles on Mongolia in *Asian Survey* and an article on Mongolia's foreign policy challenges in *Gaiko Forum* (February 1994).

**Young-Koo Cha**, Director of the Arms Control Research Center, Korea Institute for Defense Analyses. He has published several books and articles on international security and defense policy. He is the co-editor of *The Korean Peninsula: Prospect for Arms Reduction Under Global Détente*.

**Chen Jiang**, Warren Weaver Fellow at the Rockefeller Foundation in New York, is working in the Program of Internationl Security. In 1992, he received Ford Foundation support to do research at the Carnegie Endowment for International Peace in Washington, DC as a Resident Associate, focusing on nonproliferation issues. He has published articles in English and Chinese, including "The Gulf War: Causes and Impact," "Turkey's Strategy Toward Central Asia," "China's Policies Toward the Middle East," and others.

**Chen Qimao**, former President and now Chairman of the Academic Advisory Council of the Shanghai Institute for International Studies in China. He is also the President of the Shanghai Association for International Relations, and Deputy Executive Director of the Shanghai Center of International Studies. His major area is international strategic issues, and the political and economic development of the Asia Pacific region. Some of his more important papers from recent years include "New Approach of China's Foreign Policy in the Post–Cold War Era" in *Asian Survey* (March 1993) and "An Approach of the Establishment to New Political Order in the Asia Pacific Region" in *International Studies* (Spring 1992).

**Kevin Clements**, Head of the Peace Research Centre at the Australian National University and Secretary General of the Asia Pacific Peace Research Association. He is editor of *Peace and Security in the Asia Pacific Region* (1993), co-editor of

*Peace, Culture and Society: Trans National Perspectives* (1990) and has published widely on development, peace, and security issues. His current research interests are in the areas of preventive diplomacy, the reform of the United Nations, and regional peace and security concerns.

**David B. Dewitt**, Professor of Political Science and Director, Centre for International and Strategic Studies at York University, Canada. He was co-director of North Pacific Cooperative Security Dialogue Research Programme (1990–93) and is co-director of the newly formed Canadian Consortium on Asia Pacific Security (CANCAPS). His research interests focus on regional security and conflict management including evolving security in Asia Pacific and in the Middle East as well as Canadian foreign and security policy. He is contributing author and co-editor of *Building a New Global Order: Emerging Trends in International Security* (Oxford U.P., 1993), and of two forthcoming books, *Canada's International Security Policy* (Prentice-Hall, 1994) and *Confidence Building Measures in the Middle East* (Westview, 1994), as well as author of "Common, Comprehensive, and Cooperative Security in Asia-Pacific" in *The Pacific Review* (1994).

**Paul M. Evans**, Director of the University of Toronto - York University Joint Centre for Asia Pacific Studies and has been teaching international politics in the Department of Political Science at York University in Canada since 1982. He serves on the steering committees of several international research and dialogue programs, among them the Council for Security Cooperation in Asia Pacific (CSCAP), the Asia Pacific Forum, and the North Pacific Forum. He is co-directing the Canadian Consortium on Asia Pacific Security (CANCAPS) and co-chairing the CSCAP Canadian member committee. His recent essays include "Canada's Relations with China Emergent" in *Canadian Foreign Policy* (Summer 1993) and "The Council on Security Cooperation in Asia Pacific: Context and Prospects" in *The Pacific Review* (1994, forthcoming).

**Heng Hiang Khng**, Fellow at the Institute of Southeast Asian Studies, Singapore, is working on the subject of political structure in Vietnam. His recent publications include articles in *Contemporary Southeast Asia* such as "The 1992 Revised Constitution of Vietnam: Background and Scope of Changes" (1992), "Leadership in Vietnam: Pressures for Reforms and Their Limits" (1993) and "Vietnam 1992, Economic Growth and Political Caution" in *Southeast Asian Affairs* (1993).

**Brian L. Job**, Professor of Political Science and Director of the Institute of International Relations at the University of British Columbia in Canada. His current teaching and research focus is on international security relations, especially within the Asia Pacific region, the security dilemmas of developing states, the redefinition of Canadian foreign policy and security interests in the Post–Cold War era. Publications which reflect his current research interests include "Convergence and Divergence of Interests in the Changing Asia-Pacific Security Setting" (co-author) in *Pacific Partners: Canada and the United States* (Brassey's Inc., 1994) and "Canada and the Pacific" (co-author) in *Global Jeopardy: Canada Among Nations, 1993–94* (Carleton University Press, 1993).

**Pauline Kerr**, Editor of the *Australian Foreign Policy Papers* and a doctoral student in the Department of International Relations at the Australian National University in Canberra. She focuses on Asia Pacific security and her most recent publications include "Maritime Security in the 1990s: Achievement and Prospects" in *A Peaceful Ocean? Maritime Security in the Pacific in the Post–Cold War Era* (1993) and is co-author of "The Evolving Security Discourse in the Asia Pacific" in *Pacific Cooperation: Building Economic and Security Regimes in the Asia Pacific Region* (Allen & Unwin, 1994).

**Tsutomu Kikuchi**, Associate Professor of International Relations, Department of Law, Nanzan University in Japan. He is also the International Coordinator of the Pacific Islands Nations Task Force, Pacific Economic Cooperation Conference (PECC) and the Project Coordinator of the JIIA Research Committee on Japan and Emerging Regionalism in the Asia-Pacifc Region. He has published several articles on Australian Foreign Policy towards the Asia-Pacific region, US-Australia relations, Japan-Australia relations, regional cooperation in the Asia-Pacific region, Japan's role in the Asia-Pacific cooperation and others.

**Herman Joseph S. Kraft**, Research Fellow with the Institute for Strategic and Development Studies (ISDS) in the Philippines. His research interest is in strategic studies and he has written a monograph entitled "After the Bases are Gone: A Philippine Perspective on the Future of the Philippine-US Security Relations."

**Lee Lai To**, Acting Head of the Department of Political Science, National University of Singapore, is the second Vice Chairman of the Singapore Institute of International Affairs. His major research interests include contemporary Chinese politics and selected security issues in the Asia Pacific. Among his major publications are *The Reunification of China — PRC-Taiwan Relations in Flux* (Praeger Publishers, 1991), and *ASEAN and the European Community in the 1990s* (Singapore Institute of International Affairs, 1993) of which he is the co-editor.

**Andrew Mack**, Professor and Head of the Department of International Relations, the Australian National University, in Canberra. His current research interests focus on Asia Pacific security. His most recent publications include the edited volume *A Peaceful Ocean? Maritime Security in the Pacific in the Post–Cold War Era* (1993) and *Asian Flashpoint: Security and the Korean Peninsula* (1993). He also co-edited *Pacific Cooperation: Building Economic and Security Regimes in the Asia Pacific Region* (Allen & Unwin, 1994).

**Hanns W. Maull**, Professor of Foreign Policy and International Relations at the University of Trier, Germany. He is a member of the editorial board, *The Pacific Review*, the *Society's Yearbook of International Affairs* and its bi-weekly *Europa Archiv*. His recent publications include *Südafrika: Politik - Gesellschaft Wirtschaft am Ende der Apartheid* (Leske und Budrich, 1990) and *Japan and Europa: Getrennte Welten?* (Campus, 1993) of which he is the editor and contributor. He has published extensively in *Foregin Affairs, International Affairs* (London), *Politique Etrangère, Chuo Koron*. He also has extensive journalistic experience with op-ed contributions to, inter alia, the *International Herald Tribune* and is a regular columnist to *IL SOLE 24 ORE* in Milan.

**Charles E. Morrison**, Director of the Program on International Economics and Politics at the East-West Center in Hawaii, USA. He is also an affiliate research associate at the Japan Center for International Exchange in Tokyo. He has served as a research adviser to the Japan-United States Economic Relations ("Wisemen's") Group and the US-Japan Advisory Commission. Among his authored or edited books are *Japan, China, and the Newly Industrialized Economies of East Asia* (1989) and *The Pacific Islands — Politics, Economics and International Relations* (1991). He was the editor of the East-West Center's *Asia-Pacific Report* series.

**Satoshi Morimoto**, Senior Researcher at the Nomura Research Institute in Japan. Formerly he was the Director, Consular and Migration Policy Division of the Consular and Migration Affairs Department (MOFA), and Director of the Security Policy Division, Research and Planning Bureau of MOFA. He was the First Secretary of the Embassy of Japan in the United States and Counselor of the Embassy of Japan in Nigeria. He has published several articles on Japanese security policy and Asia-Pacific security questions.

**Gerald Segal**, Senior Fellow in Asian Studies at the International Institute for Strategic Studies in England, editor of *The Pacific Review* and Coordinator of the Economic and Social Research Council's Pacific-Asia Initiative. His publications include authored or edited books and monographs. Among his recent publications are *The World Affairs Companion* (Simon and Schuster, 1991 and 1993), *The Fate of Hong Kong* (Simon and Schuster, 1993), and *China Changes Shape* (IISS, March 1994).